Library of
Davidson College

LOGIC AND ARGUMENT

Logic and Argument

C. A. Kirwan

New York · New York University Press · 1978

© 1977 C. A. Kirwan
Library of Congress Catalog Card Number: 78-53099
ISBN 0-8147-4568-7

Printed in Great Britain

PREFACE

This book is about applied logic. Although logical concepts and techniques are expounded, and no knowledge of them is presupposed, my main aim has been to explain why, and under what conditions, a correct argument can be certified as correct by bringing the techniques to bear. So the emphasis is more philosophical than technical, and theoretical results are explored no further than is necessary for understanding this application.

Readers who do not seek, or already possess, technical competence up to the level of the predicate calculus may wish to skip much of chapters 3 to 8, where proof procedures in propositional, predicate, and modal logic are concurrently introduced and their soundness demonstrated. Chapters 9 and 10 examine problems of 'translation' from natural to logical languages. The load-bearing frame of the book surrounds these inner parts: chapter 1 explains what a calculus is, and how it comprises both a logical language and a proof procedure; chapter 2 deals with the idea of a deductively correct argument, showing what we need of a calculus if it is going to test correctness; and in chapter 11 the calculi set up in the middle chapters are put to work on examples.

I have profited much from the comments and criticism of Jonathan Barnes, Stephen Blamey, Robert Delahunty, Michael Lockwood, Christopher Peacocke, Mark Sainsbury and Paul Snowdon, all of whom read earlier drafts of the book or of some parts of it. I thank these friends warmly. I also thank Mrs. E. Hinkes and Mrs. D. Cuninghame for their careful typing.

Exeter College, Oxford Christopher Kirwan

CONTENTS

Preface   v

1. Constructing a Logical Calculus
   - 1.1 Introduction   1
   - 1.2 Schematic letters   3
   - 1.3 Variables   5
   - 1.4 Dummy letters   7
   - 1.5 Connectives   8
   - 1.6 Formulae   8
   - 1.7 Sequents   9
   - 1.8 The role of formation rules   10
   - 1.9 The role of interpretation rules   12
   - 1.10 The role of derivation rules   13
   - 1.11 Languages, systems, calculi   14
   - 1.12 Classification of calculi   16
   - 1.13 Metalogical notation   18
   - 1.14 Definitions   21
   - 1.15 Some properties of relations   23

2. Using a Logical Calculus
   - 2.1 Introduction   24
   - 2.2 Truth and correctness   25
   - 2.3 Deductive correctness   27
   - 2.4 Criterion of deductive correctness   28
   - 2.5 Form: Sentences versus schemata   32
   - 2.6 Form: Sentences versus propositions   34
   - 2.7 Validity: languages   41
   - 2.8 Validity: contexts   47
   - 2.9 Validity: domains   50
   - 2.10 Validity: worlds   55
   - 2.11 Definition of 'Valid Sequent'   58
   - 2.12 Proof   59
   - 2.13 Alternative route   63
   - 2.14 The powers of logic   65

3. Formation Rules and Definitions
   - 3.1 Syntax refined — 69
   - 3.2 Formulating the rules — 70
   - 3.3 Symbolic definitions — 74
   - 3.4 Scope — 77
   - 3.5 Indemnities — 78
   - 3.6 Other people's rules — 80

4. Interpretation Rules
   - 4.1 Formulating the rules for letters — 86
   - 4.2 Formulating the rules for connectives — 86
   - 4.3 Formulae into schemata — 92
   - 4.4 Truth-conditions and meaning — 95
   - 4.5 Pure semantics — 97
   - 4.6 Metatheorems on truth — 102
   - 4.7 Other people's rules — 106

5. Derivation Rules for Sequents
   - 5.1 Natural deduction — 112
   - 5.2 Formulating the rules — 116
   - 5.3 Sequent-derivations — 121
   - 5.4 Metatheorems on derivability — 126
   - 5.5 Abridged sequent-derivations — 135
   - 5.6 Other people's rules — 137

6. Derivation Rules for Formulae
   - 6.1 Axiomatic systems — 141
   - 6.2 Formulating the rules — 143
   - 6.3 Formula-derivations — 147
   - 6.4 Metatheorems on derivability — 148
   - 6.5 Abridged formula-derivations — 155
   - 6.6 Other people's rules — 156

7. Proving Validity
   - 7.1 Bivalence — 164
   - 7.2 Semantic methods — 169
   - 7.3 Logistic methods — 175
   - 7.4 Soundness of the formula systems — 179
   - 7.5 Soundness of the sequent systems — 183

Contents

8. Some More Metatheory
   - 8.1 Some more metalogical properties — 188
   - 8.2 Some more metalogical truths — 190

9. Formalising: PC and QC
   - 9.1 Introduction — 194
   - 9.2 Importing propositional letters — 196
   - 9.3 Importing subject letters — 198
   - 9.4 Importing variables and brackets — 202
   - 9.5 Importing propositional connectives — 204
   - 9.6 Importing the predicate-leading construction — 206
   - 9.7 Importing quantifiers — 213
   - 9.8 Existence and domains — 216
   - 9.9 Importing '=' — 220

10. Formalising: S5 and QS5
    - 10.1 Importing '□': preliminaries — 224
    - 10.2 An illusion of understanding — 225
    - 10.3 Some pitfalls — 226
    - 10.4 Necessity and accessible worlds — 228
    - 10.5 Necessity and reference — 230
    - 10.6 Necessity and identity — 233
    - 10.7 Necessity and domains — 235
    - 10.8 Essence — 238
    - 10.9 Necessity and 'if' — 240
    - 10.10 Importing '◇' — 241

11. Applications
    - 11.1 Proofs of correctness — 244
    - 11.2 Beyond the methods of this book — 261
    - 11.3 Fallacies — 269

Appendix One — 279

Bibliography — 281

Index — 289

Appendix Two — 298

CHAPTER ONE

Constructing a Logical Calculus

1.1 *Introduction*

The object of this book is to show how logic can be used for testing what is often called the 'validity', and I shall call the correctness, of arguments (on any subject matter). In Chapter 2 I shall examine a condition, whose fulfilment by any argument is enough to prove the argument correct, though its non-fulfilment is not enough to prove the argument incorrect. The four logical calculi described in Chapters 3 to 10 provide a basis for discovering, in many important cases, whether this condition is fulfilled, and Chapter 11 gives some examples of the calculi at work. The condition can be stated quite succinctly once we have adequate technical language at our disposal. It is: an argument is correct if it is an instance in some *logical language* of a *sequent* that is *derivable* in some *system* that is sound in that language. The task facing the reader in Chapters 1 and 2 is to gain understanding of the technical expressions in this statement and of the reasons for thinking that it is true. I have split that task into two parts: Chapter 1 will explain the words italicised above (and, naturally, some others by the way); Chapter 2 will argue for the truth of the statement as well as explaining the words 'correct', 'instance', 'sound' and some others, especially the key word 'valid'. The effect of this split is to make Chapter 1 an outline account of the nature of a logical calculus, without reference to its possible usefulness. Historically of course things were the other way round: logic grew and grows largely as an instrument for use—in testing arguments among other things. But there is no point in repeating the historical order in a survey, and it seems sensible to put 'What is it?' before 'What is it for?'

In the sense which I employ in this book 'logic' is synonymous with 'symbolic logic', 'formal logic' and 'mathematical logic'. It is called symbolic because it uses symbols, i.e. written marks that are not words; formal either because it can be studied in abstract (the sense used in 'formal semantics', p. 97, 'formal system', p. 15) or because it deals with forms or patterns of argument or because its operations are rule-bound; and mathematical either because it is commonly invoked in the quest for foundations of mathematics or because it is a part of mathematics. Logic has grown mightily since Kant rashly described it as 'to all appearance a closed and completed body of doctrine' (KANT *CPR* B viii, cf. KANT *L* pp. 10–1[1]), and the changes of the last hundred years or so have been in two directions. First, Aristotle's syllogistic, which was virtually all that Kant knew, has been shown to cover only a part of the subject, and that not the most fundamental. Among the ancients it was not Aristotle but the Stoic logicians, till recently unremembered and unhonoured, who first explored what the Kneales have rightly called 'primary logic' (W. & M. KNEALE pp. 175–6), now systematised in the *propositional calculus*. Syllogistic itself, though perfectly respectable, has turned out to be less useful in most ways than its modern counterpart the *predicate calculus*, which contains but goes beyond the propositional calculus. *Modal logic* was started by Aristotle but again owes most to modern development. So the first change brought about during the last century has been new foundations—almost a new subject, though partly anticipated by the Stoics. The second change is in the higher reaches where logic coalesces with parts of advanced mathematics. For the system which Kant knew was not only deficient but also elementary, a system of truths and rules which any intelligent person could understand and manipulate. Things are very different today, when work at the frontiers of the subject has become formidably complex and abstract.

This book is concerned only with elementary logic, with the new foundations laid by Frege, Peano, Russell, Lewis and others. There are many good treatments in print of this part of the subject, differing in various ways: in symbolism (unfortunately), in technical terminology, in arrangement and emphasis, and in doctrine. When the student has got past the stage of reliance on a single textbook—and in logic that ought to happen quite early—he faces the problem of assessing these differences in order to decide which of them, if any, matter: for divergent language may conceal the same opinions or different but compatible opinions, and it is only sometimes that

[1] References are expanded in the bibliography.

1.1 Introduction

real disagreement lurks. A part of my purpose is to bring some of these disagreements into the open and to take sides on them. In airing controversies I shall refer especially to five recent books which, though diverse in other ways, are like one another and the present book in being written from a fairly non-mathematical standpoint: they are QUINE *MofL*, HUGHES & LONDEY, MATES, LEMMON *BL*, and MASSEY. In my choice of terminology and notation I have tried to avoid gratuitous innovation, but I do introduce some technical words that are not used, or are not given the same sense, by any of these authors.

A logical calculus consists of a logical language plus derivation rules. I begin by considering the vocabulary of logical languages.

1.2 Schematic letters

The sentences 'John came' and 'John went' share a pattern, 'John___'; likewise the sentences 'John came' and 'Mary came' share the pattern '___came'. For reasons which will be explained in a moment, logicians write these patterns with letters rather than gaps: 'John f', 'a came'; and letter-filled sentence patterns are called sentence-schemata, or **schemata** for short (QUINE *MofL* p. 29, HUGHES & LONDEY pp. 1–2). A schema becomes a sentence when its gaps are filled, its letters replaced, by words ('substituted' for the letters, QUINE *MofL* ch. 26). Letters in this role are called **schematic letters**. Right from the beginning logicians have used schematic letters or a similar device, as in the following modern versions of ancient sets of schemata:

everything that f, g; everything that g, h; so everything that f, h.

if p then q; so if not q then not p.

The advantage of writing schemata with letters rather than gaps is twofold. First, it allows the convention to be adopted that repetition of the same letter, either in a single sentence-schema or, if the context so indicates, between one sentence-schema and another, demands replacement by the same word or phrase. This convention is familiar from algebra where, for example, the value of x can be calculated from $x + x = 2$ but not from $x + y = 2$; if gaps were left in place of the letters 'x' and 'y' these two equations could not even be distinguished. Replacement conforming to this convention is called **uniform**. It is important to notice that uniformity, while demanding the same replacement for the same letter, also permits, without demanding, the same replacement for different letters. For example either of the sentences 'John loves John' and 'John loves Mary' may replace the schema '*a* loves *b*' (or '*b* loves *a*'); only the former may replace the schema '*a* loves *a*' (or '*b* loves *b*').

The second advantage of letters over gaps is the possibility of restricting each letter to replacement by words or phrases of a single grammatical category. The logical languages to be studied in this book have an extremely simple grammar. For the purpose of classifying schematic letters they recognise only three categories: sentences, subjects, and predicates. I shall discuss the problems of recognising these categories in 9.2 and 9.3, but here is a preliminary outline. **Sentences** must be indicative, and the word will henceforward be short for 'indicative sentence' ('statement' QUINE *MofL* p. 1, 'declarative sentence' MATES p. 5). Subjects must be singular and definite, excluding phrases that begin with 'a', 'some', 'every', 'no' and the like (QUINE *MofL* p. 211 and MASSEY p. 225 call them 'singular terms', others 'referring expressions'). Grammatical objects can be subjects in this logical sense, as in 'Everyone loves Mary'. **Predicates** are what is left over when one or more subjects are removed from a sentence, and they are called one-place (unary, monadic), two-place (binary, dyadic) etc. according to the number of subjects, the same or different, needed to restore them into sentences. I shall write predicates with gaps to show the number and disposition of their places; so henceforward '___came', for example, will be a predicate, i.e. part of various sentences, not a schema, i.e. pattern of various sentences. (Other ways of writing predicates are as in '① came' or 'ξ came'.) Properly speaking the predicate in a sentence such as 'John is tall' is '___is tall', not '___tall'. But sometimes it makes for easier reading to treat 'is' in the manner of traditional logic as a copula between subject and predicate, not part of either (see p. 213). Notice that by the usage I adopt subjects and predicates are expressions rather than things or properties or relations indicated by expressions. Notice too that predicates can be extracted mechanically once the other two categories are recognised. But recognition of the other two is not mechanical, because they are defined by role, not form. For example 'belief that God is dead' and 'belief in God is

1.2 Schematic letters

dead' end with the same three words in the same order, but only in the former do those words function as a sentence (cf. GEACH *LM* p. 110). Or again the initial words in 'poison Napoleon', 'poison ivy' and 'poison kills' are the same, or at least have the same shape; yet only in the last does the initial word function as a subject.

I shall appropriate schematic letters to these three categories as follows. '*p*', '*q*', '*r*', supplemented as necessary (upper case in MATES and LEMMON) will be replaceable by sentences and will be called **propositional letters** ('sentential letters' MATES p. 45, 'sentence letters' QUINE *MofL* p. 121, 'propositional variables' HUGHES & LONDEY p. 2, LEMMON *BL* p. 7, 'sentential variables' MASSEY p. 12). '*a*', '*b*', '*c*', supplemented as necessary, will be replaceable by subjects and will be called **subject letters** ('individual constants' MATES p. 45). '*f*', '*g*', '*h*', supplemented as necessary (upper case except in HUGHES & LONDEY) will be replaceable by predicates and will be called **predicate letters** ('predicate variables' HUGHES & LONDEY p. 168, MASSEY p. 230). QUINE, HUGHES & LONDEY and MASSEY have no subject letters. LEMMON has them but uses different letters ('*m*', '*n*', '*o*') and a misleading title ('proper name', LEMMON *BL* p. 93); nothing in this book corresponds to Lemmon's 'arbitrary names' (LEMMON *BL* p. 107).

Let us say that a sentence or other string of words **fits** a schema when it results from the schema through uniform replacement of words or phrases by letters appropriate to their grammatical categories. The conventions about grammatical categories ensure that every sentence fits many schemata. For example 'John came' fits '*a* came', 'John *f*' and '*p*', and that is only a selection because we have a large, perhaps infinite, supply of subject, predicate, and propositional letters.

1.3 *Variables*

In the sentence

Charles praised Rex to his mother

'his' is used for backward linkage, but the linkage is ambiguous. One way of resolving the ambiguity in favour of 'Charles' is to repeat that name in place of 'his'. But in

(A)   Everyone praised Rex to his mother

linkage with 'everyone' cannot be elicited by repeating that word in place of 'his', because the meaning of

> Everyone praised Rex to everyone's mother

differs from both the possible meanings of (A). English idiom has many devices for resolving linkage-ambiguities of this general kind, e.g. the contrasts between 'him' and 'himself', or 'the former' and 'the latter' (see JESPERSEN pp. 220–1 QUINE *W & O* pp. 134–7). Logic adds another device, index-letters as in

> Everyone x praised Rex to x's mother
> Everyone x is such that x praised Rex to x's mother
> For everyone x, x praised Rex to x's mother.

The last two of these sentences are closest to the standard logical notation. They break up into two parts, a prefix 'everyone x is such that' or 'for everyone x', and what is called an **open sentence** 'x praised Rex to x's mother'. An open sentence is similar to a relative clause, completable into a full sentence by backward linkage to a suitable prefix. On their own open sentences are incomplete, and share that feature with schemata. But schemata are distinct from open sentences because their letters have different roles: in the one case as hooks for backward linkage, in the other marking gaps for filling by words. Linkage letters, or index-letters, are called **variables**. (It is best to ignore the etymology of this word, and its associations with mathematics; it is also best to ignore the fact that some authors, as we have seen, apply the word to schematic letters as well, blurring their difference of role.)

When an open sentence is fully linked up to prefixes, its variables are said to be **bound**; and any unlinked variable is said to be **free**. So the difference of role amounts to: schematic letters are replaceable, variables are bindable. Some logicians (e.g. QUINE *MofL* p. 121) use 'sentence' as a generic term, distinguishing complete sentences as 'closed'; but in my usage 'closed sentence' will be pleonastic, and open sentences will not count as sentences. An expression such as 'x loves a', containing both free variables and schematic letters, is an **open schema** (QUINE *MofL* p. 123); so in my usage 'closed schema' will likewise be pleonastic. An open sentence in which the variable 'x' and no other is free is an **open sentence in** 'x'; and similarly for other variables and groups of them. A sentence which results from linking an open sentence in any variables to prefixes, one in each of those variables, is called a **closure** of the open sentence. Kinds of closure are distinguished by the meanings of the prefixes: e.g. 'For every x, for every y, x loves y' is a **universal closure** of 'x loves y'; and 'For every x, for some y, x loves y' is a **mixed closure** of 'x loves y'.

The role of variables is conventionally assigned to the letters 'x', 'y', 'z', supplemented as necessary.

1.4 *Dummy letters*

Schematic letters have a role but no meanings. They are not like code-signs, which abbreviate or stand for words and phrases. Since a schema such as 'a is tall' is a pattern shared by 'John is tall', 'Mary is tall' and so on, its 'a' does not abbreviate 'John' or 'Mary' nor yet 'John or Mary or . . .' or 'John and Mary and . . .'. The letter is written not as proxy or substitute for some subject but to mark a gap open to any subject, and replacing it by a word is a contribution towards making a complete sentence where before was only a pattern, not towards recasting or translating an already complete sentence.

But not all logical calculi use schematic letters: an alternative is what I shall call **dummy letters**. Whereas the role of a schematic letter is to be capable of replacement by meaningful words or phrases, the role of a dummy letter is to be capable of having a meaning assigned to it, different on different occasions of use. So dummy letters are a kind of abbreviation, with the peculiarity that their meanings are left quite unfixed, except for restriction to a grammatical category. The logician might stipulate: 'You may use "F" to be synonymous with "is tall" or "loves Mary" or "loves" or any other predicate you choose'. In this role 'F' is a predicate, albeit with unfixed meaning; whereas 'f' in the schematic role, which I called predicate letter, is not a predicate. Likewise 'John f' is a schema, but 'John F', in the new role, would be a sentence, though of unfixed meaning.

These dummy letters are an alternative to schematic letters. No calculus needs both. So it is common to find the very same range of letters allotted the different roles by different authors; in MASSEY, for example, 'p', 'q', 'r', 'F', 'G', 'H' are all dummy, but in QUINE the same letters are all schematic. I shall choose the schematic interpretation, for reasons to be explained in 2.5, but I shall occasionally use upper case letters in the dummy role although these will not be part of the vocabulary of any of the calculi in the book. The word 'dummy' is from MASSEY p. 237; we must ignore the fact that QUINE once uses it to explain 'schematic' (*MofL* p. 29).

1.5 *Connectives*

Aristotle's logic already contained schematic letters. The major innovation of modern logic, as regards vocabulary, is to replace words like 'if', 'all', 'is the same as' by further symbols, usually not letters (FREGE *BS* p. 1) introduced on the analogy of '+' etc. in mathematics: e.g. '&' for 'and', '=' for 'is the same as'. These are **connectives**, otherwise called operators (HUGHES & LONDEY p. 9) or logical constants (MATES p. 45), constants because they are unlike the various kinds of letter so far described in having fixed meanings within each calculus (in fact their meanings are also fairly uniform between calculi, and between authors). If the meanings of the connectives are fixed by means of synonyms in English or some other language, as virtually happens in HUGHES & LONDEY (p. 20), the value of having them lies only in brevity. More commonly, translations into another language give only a rough and preliminary guide to their meaning (e.g. LEMMON *BL* p. 7), which is later fixed by other means. Then those other means are so chosen as to make it possible to devise systematic logical procedures—especially the procedures for proving validity to be discussed in Chapter 7—which would not be possible with words.

Connectives that attach to two expressions, as 'and' does to two sentences or 'is the same as' to two subjects, are called **binary**; those that attach to a single expression, as 'it is not the case that' does to a sentence, are called **unary**.

1.6 *Formulae*

My survey of the symbols used in logic is now complete. Aside from punctuation marks, which will be described in Chapter 3, the vocabulary of a logical calculus comprises: schematic letters (or dummy letters), connectives, and, for some calculi, variables.

1.6 Formulae

Symbols of these three kinds may be combined with words of English or any other language to make sentences such as 'John came & Mary came', schemata such as '*a* came & Mary came', open sentences such as 'John came & *x* came', and open schemata such as '*a* came & *x* came'. But the logician is particularly interested in expressions which, while like these examples in containing symbols from the logical vocabulary, are unlike them in containing nothing else; such purely symbolic expressions I shall call **formulae** (LEMMON *BL* p. 44). 1.2 already provided means of constructing formulae from the logical vocabulary sketched: e.g. '*p*' which is replaceable by any sentence and so functions on its own as a sentence-schema. Similarly the process of replacing subjects and predicates within a sentence might obviously be continued to the point at which no words remain: from 'John came' we would construct first 'John *f*' and then the purely symbolic expressions '*fa*' or '*fx*', which are formulae (in logic the predicate letters conventionally come first). Connectives extend the possibilities, allowing such schemata as '*p* and *q*' to be transformed into the purely symbolic schema '*p* & *q*', which is a formula.

1.7 Sequents

It is possible to develop logic just in terms of formulae—in this book they would be formulae interpreted as schemata fitted by sentences. But since we shall be concerned from Chapter 2 onwards with arguments, and arguments are expressed in sets of sentences, it is not surprising that a good deal of naturalness is gained by operating not with single formulae but with certain sets of formulae. We shall find that these are sets in which it matters which formula is last, although the non-last formulae, if there are any, may come in any order. Sets (or classes—I use the two words synonymously) in which order matters are called **ordered sets**, or *n*-tuples, or sequences. We can represent the jumble among non-last formulae by lumping them together into a set (possibly infinite, possibly empty) in which order does not matter, and then we can represent the special position of the last formulae by forming a two-membered ordered set (an ordered pair or couple) whose first member is the unordered set and whose second member is the last formula. Such a pair, consisting of a set (possibly infinite, possibly empty) of formulae followed by a formula,

I call a **sequent**. (This definition is in the spirit of LEMMON *BL* p. 12. Others would define a sequent as two sets of formulae in an order, or as itself a formula of a special kind—see p. 84. It is for the sake of conformity to MATES, and others, that I permit the initial set of formulae in a sequent to be infinite, though the methods of this book will apply, for simplicity, only to finite sequents.) One may be tempted to think of the members of a sequent as a premiss set and a conclusion, but the temptation ought to be resisted since, as we shall see in the next section, systematic logic characterises formulae and sequents in a purely abstract way.

The initial sets of formulae in two sequents sometimes need to be joined by the operation called 'union', i.e. pooled (QUINE *MofL* p. 108, LEMMON *BL* p. 11). The union of two sets is the set of things belonging to one or both of them; e.g. the union of the set 'p', 'q' with the set 'q', 'r' is the set 'p', 'q', 'r'.

1.8 The role of formation rules

A vocabulary does not make a language. We need also to know how the items in it may be combined into complex expressions (syntax) and what the items mean (semantics). Some of this work has been hinted at already, but we must now turn to a more systematic treatment, beginning with syntax. Syntax in logic has four peculiarities: it is laid down or stipulated, not discovered (for the logical language is being invented); the stipulation takes the form of explicit and exceptionless rules, called formation rules; only formulae and sequents are admitted, so that permissible complex expressions contain no words; and no reference is made at the syntactical stage to the roles of permitted formulae and sequents (e.g. as schemata). Instead they are abstractly described as **well-formed formulae** ('wffs' for short, LEMMON *BL* p. 44, HUGHES & LONDEY p. 47, MASSEY p. 13; MATES just uses 'formula', p. 45) and **well-formed sequents**.

Different formulae and sequents may be well-formed in different calculi; no formula or sequent can be so described absolutely. For example I shall use the expression 'QC-formula' as short for 'formula that is well-formed according to the formation rules of the calculus to be called QC'; and likewise 'QC-sequent'.

A preliminary example, for formulae, will help to show how sets

1.8 The role of formation rules

of formation rules are constructed and at the same time to bring out distinctions within them. In QC each propositional letter 'p', 'q' etc. will be a well-formed formula on its own, as will be the result of putting a finite number of subject letters 'a', 'b' etc., the same or different, after a single predicate letter 'f', 'g' etc. This admits as well-formed e.g. 'p', 'fa', '$hccbca$', but not (at least so far) 'a', 'Fa', 'af', 'pap', '$\&\&$', '$?$'. Notice three things. The method bypasses separate listing of a vocabulary: admissible symbols are just those that appear in the well-formed formulae. Secondly, predicate letters must precede subject letters (and variables); this convention could be relaxed by further formation rules, but will not be. Thirdly, the rules are abstract as forecast in the last section. They do not assert (or deny) that the letters admitted are to function as schematic letters, or the well-formed formulae as schemata. This is in spite of the fact that it is convenient to use expressions like 'propositional letter' as labels for particular groups of letters; when such labels appear in formation rules they should not, in this book, be taken to prejudge the question of role.

Continuing the example, the QC formation rules will next bring in certain connectives (as they may still be called, similarly without prejudice as to role). This leads to a complication. To take the typical case of '$\&$', we shall want to rule not only that '$\&$' makes a well-formed formula when inserted between two propositional letters, the same or different, as in '$p \& q$', but also that '$\&$' may join formulae that are themselves complex and, if necessary, bracketed, as in '$fb \& fa$', '$(hba \& r) \& r$'. Yet not every complex formula may enter into a combination, just as not every letter might: what is common to the two cases is that the combined items must themselves be well-formed formulae. So the formation rule for '$\&$' will be: '$\&$' between any two QC-formulae makes a QC-formula. Or putting it in an explicitly hypothetical way: if any two formulae, the same or different, are QC-formulae, so also is the result of inserting '$\&$' between them (strictly we should add 'and enclosing the whole in brackets', see 3.5).

Such hypothetical or conditional licences are a normal feature of formation rules. Characteristically a set of such rules licenses formulae in three stages: there are initial or **categorical** rules (basis clauses) laying down that formulae meeting certain specifications are licensed (these are called 'atomic' formulae); subsequent or hypothetical rules (induction clauses) laying down that if one or more formulae are licensed so also is a given related formula; and finally an **extremal** rule (LEMMON *BL* p. 46) laying down that no formula is licensed except under the preceding rules (and the definitions, see 3.3), i.e. that the set of licensed formulae is the smallest set satisfying the other rules—in technical language the set of well-formed formulae is the 'closure' of the set of atomic formulae under the relations of '&'-insertion etc. specified in the hypothetical rules. A set of rules of this type is said to give a **recursive** or inductive **definition** of well-formedness (HUGHES & LONDEY p. 49), 'definition' in the sense 'specification', 'recursive' because no formula can be licensed by its subsequent clauses unless some formula is licensed by its initial clauses: all the licences run back, as it were, to the categorical licences.

The formation rule for sequents will be: a sequent is well-formed in a calculus if and only if its component formulae are finite in number and all well-formed in that calculus.

1.9 *The role of interpretation rules*

Semantics follows syntax, and like that it is laid down, in logic, by means of explicit and exceptionless rules. The rules assign roles to all admitted symbols, but meanings to only some of them (the connectives). For that reason I prefer the broader title 'interpretation rules' in place of 'semantic rules'.

The role of variables is as in 1.3. The other letters may, as we have seen, be interpreted either as dummies or as schematic. If they are dummy letters, they are generally interpreted by means of truth-conditions for sentences, i.e. rules laying down the conditions under which an expression is a true or false sentence (see pp. 86–8). Roughly the rules are: any propositional letter is a true or false sentence; any predicate letter followed by a single subject letter is a true or false sentence according as the thing referred to by the subject letter has or lacks the property attributed by the predicate letter; and the same with complications for predicate letters followed by more than one subject letter. Such clauses stop short of assigning meanings to the letters, but indicate the limits within which we are free to assign them meanings on each occasion of use. If, on the other hand, the letters are to be interpreted schematically, as schemata or parts of schemata rather than of sentences, the interpretation cannot use truth-conditions, which are rules for constructing true or false sentences. Instead the rule for the propositional letters is simply that they are replaceable by sentences, and the truth-condition for the predicate-leading construction applies not to '*fa*' etc.—which are to be schemata—but to strings of ordinary words fitting '*fa*' etc., strings which the new construction artificially adds as sentences to natural languages, much as variables and open sentences were added in 1.3.

In the case of connectives assignment of role is simply assignment of meaning. This too is managed by means of truth-conditions, now hypothetical, e.g.: if two sentences are both true, so is the result of inserting '&' between them, and if not, not. Which sentences these hypothetical rules are to apply to will depend on the interpretation of the letters. If they are dummies, truth-conditions for connectives are generally made to apply only to symbolic sentences, i.e. to formulae such as '*P*', '*FA*' (so MATES, MASSEY). Then the truth-conditions as a whole give a recursive specification of true and false formulae, the letter-clauses being categorical, the connective-clauses hypothetical. This neat restriction of the connectives to formulae is not possible on the schematic view, by which if you want to put '&' into a sentence rather than a schema you must, in general, combine it with words. Schemata are not true or false; so if formulae are interpreted as schemata the truth-conditions for the connectives must apply to something other than formulae, viz. to sentences of a natural language enriched by those connectives.

1.10 *The role of derivation rules*

When rules of formation and interpretation are combined, the construction of a language is complete. A *calculus* adds further rules for passing from one formula or sequent to another. These can be presented in various ways, and are variously labelled derivation rules (LEMMON *BL* p. 8), transformation rules (HUGHES & LONDEY p. 96), or rules for deduction (QUINE *MofL* ch. 37) or inference (MATES ch. 7). My presentation will make them, like formation rules, entirely abstract: just as formation rules sort formulae and sequents into two lots, the well-formed and the rest, so derivation rules will sort them—or in practice those of them that are well-formed—into two lots, the **derivable** and the rest. Derivable formulae and sequents, like well-formed ones, are so only relative to a calculus; and e.g. 'QC-derivable' will mean 'derivable according to the derivation rules of the calculus QC'. Derivable formulae are often called theorems.

Derivation rules are always associated with methods of proving derivability; usually indeed, and in this book, they are presented as rules for constructing such proofs. I shall show in Chapters 2 and 7 how proofs of derivability form a part of one of the procedures that the book aims to provide: procedures for testing the correctness of arguments. But the procedures have other parts, as Chapter 2 will explain; logicians oversimplify when they describe derivation as deducing or inferring (see 5.1).

Most authors give derivation rules just for sequents or just for formulae. There is no need for both sorts in the same calculus. But I shall include both sorts, as alternative ways of developing each calculus.

1.11 *Languages, systems, calculi*

Formation rules plus interpretation rules make a **logical language** ('symbolic language' HUGHES & LONDEY pp. 47–8, 'formal language' LEMMON *BL* p. 42, 'artificial language' MATES p. 14, LEMMON *BL* p. 42, 'formalised language' FREGE *BS* p. 3). Logical languages differ from natural languages in being invented, and symbolic. Some have no further important difference (e.g. the language of set theory, see pp. 253–5); but most, including the four examined in this book, also contain symbols which are interpreted either as having unfixed meanings (dummy letters) or as having no meanings at all (schematic letters). These are languages only in an attenuated sense of the word, for few truths can be conveyed by them without supplementary explanation: even if the interpretation rules make provision for sentences as opposed to schemata, the meanings of the sentences are not in general fixed by the rules. For the same reason few sentences of a natural language can be translated into one of these logical languages, in any normal sense of 'translate'.

Words can however be translated into connectives. So it is possible to construct sentences with fixed meanings in which some words remain and others have been replaced by connectives, as in 'John came & Mary came'. Such mixed languages, e.g. English plus

1.11 Languages, systems, calculi

connectives interpreted as in QC, will be central in the devising of procedures for testing arguments. I shall say, for example, that any language enriched by the QC interpretation rules for connectives is a **QC-incorporating language**. A QC-incorporating language is not necessarily a logical language, in the sense of symbolic formation rules plus interpretation rules, for it may be a natural language to which connectives have been added with their QC meanings. If you like, the logical language of QC itself can be thought of as a schema for all QC-incorporating languages (cf. MASSEY p. 27).

Rules of interpretation and derivation need have no connection with one another. In particular it is possible to include the former without the latter, as in a logical language, or conversely. Derivation rules do, however, presuppose formation rules, specifying derivable formulae or sequents as a subset of well-formed ones. The combination of rules of formation and derivation without rules of interpretation is sometimes called a logic, otherwise a **logistic system** or formal system (HUGHES & LONDEY p. 93), names which I shall usually abbreviate to 'system' (having no need for wider uses of that word). Because of its lack of interpretation rules a system is wholly abstract: it assigns no meaning or role to any of its symbols. Quine has emphasised that the notion of truth is what ties logic to the world (QUINE *PofL* p. 35); in systems truth is not on the cast list.

Systems are of various kinds. In some the derivation rules specify certain formulae as derivable *from* certain sets of formulae, and these are called natural deduction systems. Others, called axiomatic, specify certain formulae, instead or additionally, as derivable absolutely, i.e. as theorems. Others again deal with derivable sequents. The systems in this book will be of two kinds: **sequent systems**, in which sequents alone are derivable (these are at least very similar to natural deduction systems), and **formula systems**, in which formulae alone are derivable (absolutely).

Any system can be put together with any logical language which shares the same formation rules. The result is a **calculus**. Thus a calculus turns out to be no more and no less than the combination of three sets of rules, one from each of the three types discussed in the previous three sections. A useful calculus is another matter: to be useful its formation rules must be appropriate to the other two sets, and those sets must be related at least by the relation of soundness, which I shall introduce in 2.12.

Interpretation rules are often, not quite aptly, called 'semantic'. This usage is probably responsible for a tendency to contrast logical languages as 'semantic' with systems as 'syntactic'. But the contrast is unfortunate too, since syntax is part of the study of language and systems are not languages by any stretch. The general study and comparison of systems is sometimes called proof theory, of logical languages model theory.

1.12 *Classification of calculi*

Calculi are classified by the connectives they contain. Here are the connectives used in this book, together with suggested ways of 'pronouncing' them (falling back, in many cases, on the name of the symbol) and a rough indication of the meanings they will be given by the interpretation rules.

Symbol	*Suggested pronunciation*	*Approximate meaning*
$\sim$	'tilde' or 'not'	not
&	'ampersand' or 'and'	and
$\vee$	'wedge' or 'vel'	or
$\supset$	'horseshoe' or 'hook'	if
$\equiv$	'if and only if'	if and only if
$\forall$	'ay'	for everything
$\exists$	'ee'	for something
$=$	'equals'	is the same as
$\Box$	'box' or 'necessarily'	necessarily
$\Diamond$	'diamond' or 'possibly'	possibly

The first five connectives in the list are truth-functional (see p. 104) and any calculus whose connectives are confined to this group is a version of the propositional or sentential calculus, or calculus of truth-functions. The next two, '$\forall$' and '$\exists$', are called **quantifiers**; when joined to variables they form examples of the prefixes discussed in 1.3. A calculus containing truth-functional connectives plus these quantifiers is a version of the predicate or functional calculus, and when, as in 1.3, the variables bound by quantifiers must occupy places suitable for subject letters the calculus is a first order, or lower, predicate calculus. By adding '$=$' we get a version

1.12 Classification of calculi

of the lower predicate calculus with identity. The last two connectives in the list are called modal. They may be added to any of the preceding groups to give, respectively, modal propositional calculi, modal predicate calculi, and modal predicate calculi with identity. Some authors reserve the word 'connective' for the first and last groups, excluding quantifiers and '='.

In this book four calculi will be treated: **PC** is a propositional calculus and **QC** a lower predicate calculus with identity ('Q' for 'quantifier'), **S5** is a modal propositional calculus (so called because it is the fifth in a series constructed by LEWIS & LANGFORD p. 501), and **QS5** is a modal lower predicate calculus with identity. Since these four are not the only specimens of their kinds the question arises how to tell when some calculus, e.g. in another book, is identical with one of them. What criteria of identity are we to adopt for calculi? I propose the following. (i) The rules of two versions may differ and yet have the same effect. That is, one may find two sets of rules, each comprising rules of formation, derivation and interpretation, according to which the same formulae are well-formed, the same formulae and sequents are derivable, and the symbols have the same interpretations. These will count as versions of the same calculus. (ii) It may be that the well-formed formulae of one version, though differing from those of another, 'match' them in the sense that each set results from the other by uniform substitutions of one symbol for another, e.g. 'P' for 'p' and '$-$' for '$\sim$', or by similar operations. If such matching runs right through the versions, applying also to interpretations and to the sets of derivable formulae or sequents, it is reasonable to treat the differences as merely notational. Versions so related will count as versions of the same calculus. (When there is partial but not exact matching it is a good deal harder to decide whether the differences between calculi are *partly* notational; but this book ignores the many cases where that problem arises, for which see HAACK ch. 1.) (iii) Two versions may differ in that one interprets letters as schematic, the other as dummy. This difference is unimportant in practice and I shall not allow it to count against identity. (iv) One version may give derivation rules for formulae, another for sequents. Two such versions will be counted the same calculus when (given that their formation and interpretation rules have the same effect) a formula is derivable in one of them if and only if the sequent

containing just that formula, once, is derivable in the other (see 8.2).
(v) Two versions of the same predicate calculus may have different policies over free variables (p. 83) or over vacuous quantification (p. 72).

1.13 *Metalogical notation*

Logic studies arguments and to that end studies sentences, formulae, sequents, symbols. These are its subject matter. It also *uses* arguments in order to prove results about the subject matter. Chapter 2 will be an example of such an argument, leading to the conclusion stated at the beginning of 1.1; and 7.4 will argue to the conclusion that any formula derivable in one of the four calculi is valid in that calculus. Such conclusions about the subject matter are often called metatheorems, to distinguish them from 'theorems' in the sense of derivable formulae; metatheorems are not formulae but statements about formulae (or about sentences, sequents etc.). Theorems and other formulae are expressed in a logical language; but metatheorems are expressed, partly or wholly, in a natural language such as English. The logical languages referred to in metatheorems are called **object languages** (objects of study) and the language such as English in which the metatheorems are expressed is called the **metalanguage** of the study.

Even at an elementary level a metalanguage is going to need technical terms. If it is English, it will be a use of English in which words like 'formula', 'instance', 'definition' are given special senses. This chapter has begun the task of elucidating such senses. The technical words might be said to constitute a metalogical vocabulary, vocabulary used not in the logical language but in talk about it. As a logician advances to more abstruse questions about his calculi, so he needs more such vocabulary. Quite soon, also, he will find that even technical English is excessively cumbersome. He will feel the need to abbreviate, and to write schematically: in other words he will feel the need for metalogical symbols. There is a danger, clearly, that the introduction of such symbols may deceive a reader (and writer) into thinking that they are part of the logical subject matter, so confusing logical with metalogical symbolism. In an elementary book such as this it might be possible to avoid the danger by doing without metalogical symbols altogether. But even at the level of this book a total

1.13 Metalogical notation

ban on them would be awkward, and perhaps ridiculous. I shall not attempt it. The rest of this section accordingly introduces the metalogical notation I shall use.

First, metalogical abbreviations. (i) 'PC', 'QC', 'S5' and 'QS5' will be names of different calculi. (ii) '$=_{\text{def}}$' will be short for 'is short for'. (iii) For referring to sequents it is useful to employ a small part of the symbolism of set theory. '{Romulus, Remus}' means 'the set whose only members are Romulus and Remus'. '⟨Romulus, Remus⟩' means 'the ordered set whose only members are Romulus and Remus in that order'. Since sequents are ordered sets whose second member is a formula and whose first member is a set of formulae, the sequent whose last formula is '$p \, \& \, q$' and whose other formulae are 'p' and 'q' will be referred to as

(B)   ⟨{'p', 'q'}, '$p \, \& \, q$'⟩

'Λ' is a symbol for the empty set; so the sequent whose last and only formula is '$p \, \& \, q$' will be referred to as '⟨Λ, '$p \, \& \, q$'⟩'. '∪' is the symbol for union; so '{'p', 'q'} ∪ {'r', 'p'}' means 'the union of {'p', 'q'} with {'r', 'p'} (this is the set {'p', 'q', 'r'}). For more on the symbolism of set theory see pp. 253–5. (iv) Lemmon's notation for (B) is '$p, q \vdash p \, \& \, q$', '⊢' interpretable as the conjunction 'therefore' (LEMMON *BL* pp. 11, 48). Although this is simpler, I reject it as much too easy to confuse with ' "p", "q" ⊢ "$p \, \& \, q$" ', whose standard meaning is

(C)   ⟨{'p', 'q'}, '$p \, \& \, q$'⟩ is derivable

so that '⊢' abbreviates the verb 'is derivable' (LEBLANC p. 31). In this book '⊢' will have the latter, metalogical, meaning, but to avoid confusion with Lemmon's usage I shall write the symbolic version of (C) as

⊢⟨{'p', 'q'}, '$p \, \& \, q$'⟩

Similarly '⊢ "$a = a$" ' will mean 'the formula "$a = a$" is derivable'. '⊢' is called the **turnstile**.

Secondly, metalogical variables. Rules, in this book, are universal statements, and rules about formulae or sequents state truths about all formulae or sequents of a certain class. The same goes for metatheorems, inferred from the rules. It is no good writing, for example, 'if "p" is a well-formed formula, so is "□ p" ' when one wishes to convey at the same time that if 'q' is a well-formed formulae, so is '$\Box q$', and that if '$=xC$' is a well-formed formula, so is '$\Box =xC$', and so on. The right formulation is obviously ' "$\Box$" followed by any well-formed formula is a well-formed formula'. Sometimes, though not in this simple case, such metalogical universality is most neatly conveyed by variables, as in 'Everything x is such that, if x is a well-formed formula, so is "$\Box$" followed by x'. But there are two reasons for not using the variables 'x', 'y', 'z' in formulating rules and metatheorems. First, those variables belong to the logical notation, so that it can be confusing to employ them metalogically as well. Secondly, it is convenient to have metalogical variables whose *range* is restricted to particular kinds of thing, one set for formulae, one for subject letters, one for sets of formulae, and so on. I shall use Greek and (mostly) boldface letters for this purpose, as follows:

'α', 'β', 'α_1', 'α_2' etc. for subject letters
'ν', 'μ', 'ν_1', 'ν_2' etc. for (logical) variables
    (LEMMON *BL* has 'v')
'π', '$\koppa$' (the obsolete Greek koppa), 'ρ', 'π_1', 'π_2' etc. for formulae (LEMMON *BL* and MASSEY have 'A', 'B', 'C', MATES 'ϕ', 'ψ', 'χ', HUGHES & LONDEY 'X', 'Y', 'Z')
'σ', 'τ'   for sentences
'ϕ', 'ψ'   for stencils (see p. 73)
'**l**'   for logical languages
'**n**'   for non-negative integers

Less commonly I shall use

'δ'   for predicate letters
'Γ', 'Δ', 'E'   for sets of formulae
'**d**'   for domains (see pp. 50–5)
'**v**', '**v**$_1$',   for valuations (see p. 98)
'**w**', '**w**$_1$'   for worlds (see p. 58).

It is unimportant whether these metalogical letters are thought of as variables or schematic letters. For example in the formulation 'If π is well-formed, so is "$\Box$" followed by π' it makes no difference whether we understand an elided prefix 'for all formulae π' or supply the gloss 'The following states a truth whatever formula is referred to by a subject put uniformly for "π" in it'. But notice that in the

1.13 Metalogical notation

latter case the subjects put for 'π' must be quoted formulae, as in 'if "p" is well-formed, so is "□" followed by "p"'.

Thirdly, quasi-quotation. It is tempting to abbreviate the specimen rule about '□' still further, into 'if π is well-formed, so is □π'. But strictly this is inaccurate. What we want is something that generalises 'If "p" is well-formed, so is "□p"', and so on; but because 'π' is for replacement by quoted formulae the suggested abbreviation generalises 'If "p" is well-formed, so is □"p"', and so on. So it is worth introducing a metalogical notation specially framed to abbreviate such phrases as ' "□" followed by π'. This is Quine's device of quasi-quotation or **corners**, according to which '⌜□π⌝' is short for ' "□" followed by π', '⌜(π & φ)⌝' is short for ' "(" followed by π followed by "&" followed by φ followed by ")"', and so on (see MASSEY pp. 16–7). The interpretation of an expression enclosed in corners depends on the reader's ability to recognise any metalogical variables it may contain: if there are none, the corners do the same work as ordinary quotation marks, and if the expression consists wholly of metalogical letters, the corners may be omitted without danger. Actually, many logicians omit corners altogether (so in effect MATES, and LEMMON *BL* and HUGHES & LONDEY tacitly). I shall give in to this temptation when no ambiguity results, sacrificing accuracy to simplicity.

1.14 *Definitions*

Three meanings of the word 'definition' often get confused in logicians' parlance. One is the sense in which you define a *class* by specifying conditions for membership of it. In this sense any adequate set of logical rules constitutes a definition, as we have seen that formation rules define recursively the class of well-formed formulae.

In a second sense a definition explains, or is intended to explain, the *meaning* of some word or phrase or symbol. I shall often use the word 'when' to introduce such definitions informally: e.g. 'a binary relation is reflexive . . . when . . .', p. 23. Formation and derivation rules can be regarded as definitions in this sense too, since they do in a way explain what is meant by the technical terms 'well-formed' and 'derivable'; e.g. 'is a QC-formula' means 'is a member of the smallest set such that . . .' with suitable completion (see

p. 12), and any preexisting associations between well-formedness and intelligibility, or between derivation and inference, can be ignored once the rules have been stated, and need to be ignored if the rules comprise an abstract system. But interpretation rules, although their semantic component helps to define in the first sense the class of truths-in-a-language, by no means define the *word* 'true' in the second sense. Their purpose being to contribute towards defining, explaining the meaning of, certain logical symbols such as '&', they require that the word 'true', which they call in aid, should already be understood. They cannot work the other way round, defining a special meaning of 'true' in terms of the connectives, because the connectives are so far unintelligible (DUMMETT p. 460). In this second sense, then, the interpretation rules define not 'true' but the connectives.

Thirdly, a definition may introduce one expression as an alternative, usually a shorter alternative, for another. This is the sense in which definitions are a way of eliminating redundant terminology, of extracting from a notation a primitive part which alone is theoretically necessary and for which the rest is no more than convenient shorthand. For example the following rules will be *eliminative* definitions of the connectives '$\Diamond$' and '$\supset$':

'$\Diamond$' $=_{\text{def}}$ '$\sim \Box \sim$'

for all well-formed formulae π and φ, $\ulcorner(\pi \supset \varphi)\urcorner$
$=_{\text{def}} \ulcorner \sim (\pi \mathbin{\&} \sim \varphi) \urcorner$.

The former of these examples is an 'explicit' definition, licensing replacement of '$\Diamond$' by other symbols, or conversely; the latter is a 'contextual' definition ('definition in use') licensing replacement of a type of expression ('context') containing '$\supset$' by a type of expression not containing it, and conversely. Definitions eliminating some type of symbol-containing expression will not do their work of eliminating the symbol completely unless all permitted expressions containing the symbol either are or can be rewritten as expressions of that type. Eliminative definitions may be definitions in the second sense too, for they may explain the meanings of the eliminated expressions. But plainly this requires a further condition: in the above examples we must already know the meanings of '$\sim$', '$\Box$' and '&'. Perhaps it is misleading to call eliminative definitions by that name unless the further condition is met; but logicians do use the name even in uninterpreted systems when it is not met, and their usage will be followed in this book. I shall call such eliminative rules as the above **symbolic definitions,** and I shall make them an adjunct to formation rules. That part of the vocabulary of a calculus which is not introduced by symbolic definition is called **primitive**.

1.15 *Some properties of relations*

Here are some definitions for future use. A **binary relation** holds or fails to hold from something x to something y (x and y need not be distinct): e.g. the relation expressed in the two-place predicate '—is taller than . . .'. A **ternary relation** similarly holds or fails to hold between three things, again not necessarily distinct: e.g. the relation expressed in the three-place predicate '—loves . . . more than , , , does'. A binary relation is **reflexive**, or 'totally reflexive', when for all x it holds from x to x; **irreflexive** when for *no* x does it hold from x to x; **transitive** when for all x, y and z, if it holds from x to y and from y to z, it holds from x to z; **intransitive** when for all x, y and z, if it holds from x to y and from y to z, it does *not* hold from x to z; **symmetrical** when for all x and y, if it holds from x to y, it holds from y to x; and **asymmetrical** when for all x and y, if it holds from x to y, it does *not* hold from y to x. A binary relation such as hating, which holds from some but not all things to themselves, is neither reflexive nor irreflexive. Likewise many binary relations are neither transitive nor intransitive, and many are neither symmetrical nor asymmetrical. See LEMMON *BL* pp. 179–87, QUINE *MofL* p. 159, HUGHES & LONDEY pp. 272–4, MASSEY pp. 37–8.

CHAPTER TWO

Using a Logical Calculus

2.1 Introduction

There are many possible reasons for studying logic. Russell, for example, was struck by "the importance of logical reform for the philosophy of mathematics" (RUSSELL *MPD* p. 65); his 'logicist' programme aimed at reducing "the primitive apparatus of the mathematician . . . to such purely logical terms as *or*, *not*, *all* and *some*" (ib. p. 71). Electrical circuits, as in computers, have structural analogies with the propositional calculus. Linguists increasingly look to logical languages for illumination of the far greater complexities in natural languages. And logic can, like any other subject, be studied and advanced purely for its own sake. Finally, and perhaps most obviously, modern developments make it profitable to revive the ancient and mediaeval ambition of using logic to test and display the correctness and incorrectness of arguments.

I am concerned in this book only with the last of these uses. It is of special, and growing, interest to philosophers, partly because the study of argument is one of the departments of philosophy and partly because even in other departments philosophers find that their arguments are often so subtle and abstruse as to need all the technical help that can be got towards elucidation and criticism. But there are two reasons why it would be a mistake to think that the application of logical techniques to the criticism of arguments should be of interest to professional philosophers alone. First, in this application logic seems to bring diminishing returns; it is the elementary parts of the subject that most conspicuously increase one's mastery of philosophical material. So even the novice or amateur student of philosophy ought to be introduced to the subject. Secondly, it is reasonable to expect that these elementary parts will help anyone who wants to think clearly on any topic: logic is a universal tool, and not very hard to apply profitably.

2.1 Introduction

Arguments, then, are the subject matter. But logic deals with only one of the desirable features of an argument, correctness, and with only one kind of correctness, the deductive kind. The next two sections will isolate these features.

2.2 Truth and correctness

An **argument** consists of a conclusion drawn from one or more premises (later I shall, for technical convenience, change 'one or more' to 'none or one or more'). If the conclusion comes last it is characteristically introduced by a 'so' or a 'therefore'; if first, the premisses may be introduced by a 'because' or a 'for'; and if in the middle, both kinds of particle may be used. In some arguments there are also intermediate conclusions, drawn from certain of the premisses and themselves used as premisses for drawing further conclusions. But when we find more than one final conclusion, not so used, then I shall say that we have more than one argument, perhaps sharing premisses. The words **'premiss'** and **'conclusion'** (unqualified) will henceforward exclude intermediate conclusions. Arguments with an infinite number of premisses are possible, but not important outside mathematics and not considered in this book. Nor is it going to be possible by the methods of this book to test arguments containing a premiss or conclusion that is neither true nor false (see 7.1).

Arguments are appraised as correct or incorrect. In place of 'correct' (MASSEY p. 42) many other words are in fairly common use, especially 'valid' and 'sound'. But these latter alternatives are dangerously ambiguous. 'Valid' often has the more restricted sense I shall give to 'deductively correct'; 'sound' sometimes means 'correct and having true premisses' (MASSEY p. 42). More important, the words 'valid' and 'sound' are often assigned technical meanings within logic itself, the one for a property of sequents and formulae and the other for a property of systems and calculi. Many students get deeply confused in the initial stages if the technical meanings are allowed to coexist with the non-technical, and especially if validity is allowed to be a property of both arguments and sequents. I shall reserve 'valid' and 'sound' for the technical meanings, which will be introduced in 2.7 and 2.12.

Although arguments are not themselves true or false, their

premisses and conclusions may be, and for our purposes must be. Yet the correctness of an argument does not consist in its having true premisses, or a true conclusion, or both. Many incorrect arguments have true premisses and a true conclusion, e.g. this from LEMMON BL p. 2:

(A)   Napoleon was French; all Frenchmen are Europeans; so Hitler was Austrian.

Conversely, many correct arguments have some or all false premisses, with or without falsity in the conclusion, e.g. this from the same page of LEMMON BL:

(B)   Napoleon was German; all Germans are Europeans; so Napoleon was European.

The correctness of an argument is thus independent of its having true premisses. However, there is some connection between correctness and truth: no correct argument combines all true premisses with an untrue conclusion—in Lemmon's words "from truths only truths follow" (BL p. 2). Let us speak of this combination of all true premisses with an untrue conclusion as the **offending combination**. Then avoidance of the offending combination is necessary for correctness. But it is not sufficient. The ways of avoiding the offending combination might be classified into these three: all true premisses with a true conclusion, some or all untrue premisses with a true conclusion, and some or all untrue premisses with an untrue conclusion. Though each of these three ways is exemplified by many correct arguments, each is also exemplified by many incorrect ones. Example (A) combines true premisses with a true conclusion and yet is incorrect; and it is easy to construct other examples on that model which are likewise incorrect while combining truth and untruth in one of the two remaining ways. The reason why this is easy is that the various combinations make no demand on the *relevance* of conclusion to premisses. In (A) itself the conclusion, though true, is irrelevant to the premisses; and so it might be with the other two non-offending combinations. In fact anyone who held that avoidance of the offending combination suffices to make an argument correct would be committed to the absurd view that every argument with at least some untrue premisses is correct, whatever its conclusion, and to the equally absurd view that every argument with a true conclusion is correct, whatever its premisses.

Correctness, therefore, is not just a matter of combining truth with untruth in certain ways. In 2.4 I shall try to show that for one kind of correctness the right account does involve the concept of truth, afforded by that of necessity. But this requires that we first isolate the intended kind of correctness from other kinds.

2.3 *Deductive correctness*

Aristotle, in introducing his syllogistic logic, defined a syllogism as an argument "in which, certain things being premissed, something else follows of necessity from their being so" (ARISTOTLE *An. Pr.* I 1.24^{b}18–20). If we allow 'things' to cover the singular case, and ignore 'else', this will nearly serve as a definition of 'correct argument': but not quite, because of the words 'of necessity'. Many, perhaps most, of the arguments we employ lack the feature that their conclusions follow of necessity from their premisses. Yet we rarely count that lack as a bar to correctness. For example I argue correctly if from the premiss that your grandfather's great-uncle carried a standard at the battle of Waterloo I conclude that he is not alive today, even though the conclusion does not follow of necessity from that premiss alone. Following of necessity defines, then, one kind of correctness which is not the only kind.

This special kind has many names. When it is present in an argument one may say that the conclusion of the argument 'follows logically from' (QUINE *MofL* p. 39, HUGHES & LONDEY p. 4), or 'is deducible from', or 'is a consequence of' (MATES p. 2) the premisses, or that the premisses '**entail**' the conclusion (LEMMON *BL* p. 1), or that the argument is 'deductive', or '**deductively correct**'. Accordingly it is a metalogical principle that

2.3 (1) An argument is correct if (but not only if) it is deductively correct, i.e. its premisses entail its conclusion.

The next task is to examine the standards, or criteria, of deductive correctness. Other standards, e.g. inductive, do not come within the purview of logic as understood in this book.

2.4 *Criterion of deductive correctness*

What are the conditions under which premisses entail conclusions? What makes an argument deductively correct? Consider this specimen argument:

(C)   Today is Monday; so tomorrow will be Tuesday.

(C) is, I shall contend, deductively correct just on condition that, i.e. if and only if, it could not have been Monday today without being Tuesday tomorrow. Before explaining and defending this contention it will be useful to generalise it over all arguments. There are broadly two ways of doing so, one bringing out the requirement of a necessary *connection* or relation between the premisses and conclusion of any deductively correct argument, the other pointing to a necessary *truth* which must lie behind the argument as what is sometimes called its 'principle'. Corresponding to these two ways of stating, in general terms, the conditions under which any argument is deductively correct—the criterion of deductive correctness, as I shall henceforth call it—there have grown up in logic two methods of testing arguments, one of which, using sequents, seeks to discover whether the argument has a valid form, while the other, using formulae, seeks to discover whether the principle of the argument is a formal, otherwise called logical, truth. In this and the next eight sections I shall confine attention to the first method, deferring the other to 2.13.

Generalising then in terms of the connection between premisses and conclusion we get: an argument is deductively correct if and only if its premisses could not all have been true without its conclusion being true. Two things are worth remarking in the language of this formulation. First, it imports the words 'premiss', 'conclusion', and 'true' which were not used in stating the conditions for the deductive correctness of (C) itself. The importation of such words, dubbed 'semantic ascent' by Quine (QUINE *PofL* pp. 10–3), is a method of obtaining the generality we are looking for. Secondly the words 'could not' are carried over from the statement about (C).

I use 'could not' as short for 'could not logically', invoking the notion of logical impossibility. This must be explained, if it can satisfactorily be explained at all, either (a) by contrast with other kinds of impossibility or (b) in terms of self-contradiction. (a)

2.4 Criterion of deductive correctness

Logical impossibility contrasts both with human incapacity or lack of opportunity (it is logically though not humanly possible for me to swim the Atlantic, or dine nightly with the Queen) and with physical impossibility (it is logically though not physically possible for a cobweb to cut cheese). These latter impossibilities are, we may say, relative to or contingent on things being as they are—contingent on the desires, wit and strength of men, the constitution of material bodies, and so on. By contrast logical impossibilities are impossible absolutely, no matter what. (b) It is also frequently and plausibly held that it is logically impossible for something to be the case if and only if anyone who says that it is the case contradicts himself, and hence that it is logically impossible for certain premisses to be true and a certain conclusion not true if and only if anyone who says that the former are true and the latter not true contradicts himself. There is some difficulty however in saving this account from being at once too wide and too narrow. On the one hand a certain kind of contradiction, sometimes called pragmatic inconsistency or logical oddity, infects sayings like 'I believe that it is raining, but it isn't'; yet there is nothing impossible about my believing that it is raining when it isn't, and there is likely to be no correctness at all, let alone deductive correctness, in the argument 'I believe that it is raining; so it is raining'. The logician needs to understand self-contradiction so as to exclude these cases. On the other hand there are logical impossibilities, such as the impossibility that root two is rational and in general the impossibility of the denials of mathematical truths, which are not very obviously self-contradictory. The weaker suggestion that the denial of a mathematical truth entails a self-contradiction without itself being one will not suffice to explain logical impossibility if the latter is in turn being used, as here suggested, to explain entailment.

Necessity, like impossibility, is to be understood in this book as logical, i.e. absolute. What is so-and-so of necessity is so-and-so and could not have been otherwise; it would have been so no matter what, whatever the facts; to anticipate language which will be introduced in 2.10, it is so in all 'worlds'. Anything true of necessity is called a **necessary truth**.

The suggested criterion of deductive correctness fastens on the combination mentioned on p. 26, the offending combination of true premisses with an untrue conclusion. But instead of claiming, absurdly, that a correct argument is any argument in which that combination is not present, the criterion claims that a deductively correct argument is any argument in which that combination could not have been present, i.e. in which *the offending combination is avoided of necessity*. So the 'could not have been' is vital. Were it replaced by 'are not' the criterion would collapse into what was rejected in 2.2; we should have the absurd consequences that every argument with some or all untrue premisses, and every argument with a true conclusion, is deductively correct.

As it is, the criterion faces a challenge. Just as the premisses of some arguments are not all true, i.e. are jointly untrue, so the premisses of some arguments could not all have been true, i.e. are jointly impossible. But if they could not all have been true, then *a fortiori* they could not all have been true without the conclusion being true, and so, by the criterion, the argument is deductively correct. That is to say, it is a consequence of the criterion that any argument with jointly impossible premisses is deductively correct no matter what its conclusion may be: every conclusion will be entailed by jointly impossible premisses. Furthermore any premisses are jointly impossible if one or more of their number is impossible on its own. So since, for example, 'Root two is rational' is not merely false but impossible, it will entail 'The Rhine is longer than the Rhone', 'The Rhone is longer than the Rhine', 'Root two is irrational', and so on indefinitely. There is a parallel consequence for conclusions. If the conclusion of an argument is a necessary truth, then it could not have been untrue. So *a fortiori* the premisses could not all have been true without the conclusion being true. So, by the criterion, the argument will be deductively correct. That is to say, it is a consequence of the criterion that any argument whose conclusion is a necessary truth is deductively correct no matter what its premisses may be: any premisses will entail a necessary truth. Since, for example, 'Root two is irrational' is not merely true but a necessary truth, it will be entailed by 'The Rhine is longer than the Rhone', 'The Rhone is longer than the Rhine', 'Root two is rational', and so on indefinitely.

These two consequences of the criterion are paradoxical, in the original sense of going against unreflecting opinion. They are paradoxical especially because they yield examples—not so readily as in 2.2, but readily enough—of deductively correct arguments in which

2.4 Criterion of deductive correctness

premisses and conclusion are irrelevant to one another. But are the paradoxes false? This question divides logicians. Most agree that the condition 'avoids the offending combination of necessity', like the weaker 'avoids the offending combination', is required for deductive correctness. But some insist that it is still not strong enough; for it lets in such arguments as 'The Rhine is longer than the Rhone, therefore root two is irrational', which they wish to exclude. Although various attempts have been made to devise other conditions which exclude these cases, the price of excluding them is surprisingly high. Here is a specimen argument from a pair of jointly impossible premisses to an irrelevant and arbitrarily chosen conclusion. The premisses are at the top, the conclusion at the bottom, and the horizontal lines represent 'therefore':

(D)
$$\frac{\dfrac{\text{Eugene is married}}{\text{Eugene is married or grass is pink}} \quad \dfrac{\text{Eugene is a bachelor}}{\text{Eugene is not married}}}{\text{grass is pink}}$$

If this argument is deductively correct, then so, surely, will be any argument from a set of jointly impossible premisses to any conclusion whatever. Yet how can this one fail to be deductively correct? It resolves into the simple arguments (let us call them inferences) 'Eugene is married; so Eugene is married or grass is pink', 'Eugene is a bachelor; so Eugene is not married', and 'Eugene is married or grass is pink; Eugene is not married; so grass is pink'. Anyone who challenges the argument must either reject one of these inferences as deductively incorrect or reject the principle that an argument which resolves into deductively correct inferences is itself deductively correct (technically that the set of things entailed by a given set is 'closed under entailment', i.e. entails only its own members, i.e. entails only things entailed by the given set). Inferences of these types have in fact been challenged, as has the principle of resolution (or transitivity of entailment as it is sometimes loosely called) but it seems to me as it has seemed to others that they are acceptable and consequently that we have to admit the deductive correctness of (D). Similar reasoning will confirm that a necessary truth is entailed by any premisses whatever. I conclude that the criterion of deductive correctness is, although paradoxical, acceptable as stated. (In agreement with this is e.g. BENNETT; in dissent e.g. ANDERSON.)

Notice that the paradoxes concern entailment, not proof. A conclusion entailed by jointly impossible premisses cannot be proved from them, because the premisses of a proof must be true. A set of premisses entailing a necessary truth as conclusion may, even if true, fail to prove that conclusion, because proofs must avoid begging the question. See p. 60.

The criterion of deductive correctness can be reformulated in various ways. In place of 'The premisses and conclusion avoid the offending combination of necessity' we may say 'The premisses **materially imply** the conclusion of necessity', where material implication is the relation which holds between premisses and conclusion when it is not the case that all the former are true and the latter untrue. In place of 'materially imply of necessity' we may say **'strictly imply'**, so that the criterion asserts that entailment is strict implication. For this reason the paradoxical consequences of the criterion are often known as the paradoxes of strict implication.

The criterion can now be set down as another metalogical principle:

2.4 (1) An argument is deductively correct if and only if its premisses strictly imply its conclusion, i.e. of necessity it is not the case that its premisses are all true and its conclusion untrue.

2.5 Form: Sentences versus schemata

The criterion of deductive correctness does not yet bring us to the point at which logical techniques can be applied to the testing of arguments. In order to apply them we need a new property which is technical not only in the sense of being explained in technical language (such as 'strictly implies') but also in the sense that it introduces the special concepts of symbolic logic, e.g. schemata, formulae, sequents: and this is the property of having a valid form. I shall explicate the property in the next seven sections: form in this one, having a form in 2.6, and validity in 2.7–11. The aim is to provide an explication under which it will be true to say that every argument having a valid form is deductively correct, but this will not be achieved until 2.11. Many logic books give little space to these matters, sometimes only a few lines.

2.5 Form: Sentences versus schemata

Suppose we take it that the following argument (E)—a trivial specimen for the sake of brevity—has (Es) for its form, or rather for one of its forms:

(E)   John is tall and John is handsome; so John is tall

(Es) p and q; so p.

How are the letters in (Es) to be interpreted? We could rewrite them upper case as dummy letters, so that (Es) would simply restate (E) in a partly symbolic language; or we can take them as schematic letters, so that (Es) gives the pattern of (E). On the former interpretation the two components of (Es) would be sentences which the sentences of (E) translate; on the latter they are sentence-schemata which the sentences of (E) fit. It is clear how the schematic interpretation elucidates the idea of form: not only (E) but infinitely many other arguments can be arranged into sentences which fit the schemata of (Es) according to the conventions for fitting explained in 1.2, and what those arguments have in common is a form or pattern. However if we are to exhibit this relationship among arguments through the other interpretation it is not enough to say that (Es) recasts (E) in symbolic language; we must add that (Es) is available for recasting the other arguments too. (E) has (Es) for its form, on the dummy interpretation, because the meaning of each of its component English sentences is the same as one among *many* admissible meanings of the dummy letters 'P' and 'Q'.

It can now be made explicit what a form (argument form) is according to each interpretation. In the one case it is a set of sentences in which at least one word or phrase is replaced by a schematic letter (I shall call such a set an **inference-schema**, HUGHES & LONDEY p. 3); having it will then be something like fitting it. In the other case it is a set of sentences in which at least one word or phrase is replaced by a dummy letter, i.e. a letter with unfixed meaning; having it will then be something like being synonymous with one of its admissible meanings. Forms are to contain nothing corresponding to intermediate conclusions.

Both these explications of 'form' need to be backed up by interpretation rules for symbols, in the one case rules about grammatical categories and uniformity of replacement determining which sentences fit a given schema, in the other by rules determining the admissible meanings of dummy letters and hence the admissible translations of sentences containing them into English and other natural languages. But it is probable that the rules could be framed so as to achieve an exact match between the two interpretations, and once a match is obtained there is no longer any practical difference between them, so that forms can be understood indifferently as sets of schemata or sets of semi-symbolic sentences. I follow the former course (with QUINE *MofL* p. 29 and HUGHES & LONDEY pp. 1–2, against MATES p. 69ff. and MASSEY p. 25), because the prescription to interpret symbols as open to various interpretations (meanings) seems mildly more confusing than the prescription to interpret them as schematic, and also mildly less natural as a way of explicating the concept of form.

Corresponding to this ambiguity in the meaning of 'form' is an ambiguity in the meaning of the verb 'formalise'. When a student of logic is asked to formalise an argument in a symbolism, it may be unclear whether he is meant to understand what he is doing as translating into a set of symbolic sentences or as exhibiting a pattern in a set of sentence-schemata.

2.6 *Form: Sentences versus propositions*

The elucidation of 'having a form' depends not only on the question examined in the last section, whether forms are to be construed as containing schematic letters or dummy letters, but also on the question to which I now turn, whether the arguments that have them are to be construed as sets of sentences or sets of propositions expressed in sentences. If a form consisted of semi-symbolic sentences, to have it might be either to be a set of sentences, e.g. in English, which translate it (so MATES and MASSEY) or to be expressible in such a set: here the difference amounts to that between (a) being synonymous with, and (b) being expressible in, a form. But if a form is, as I take it to be, an inference-schema, to have it may be either to be a set of sentences which fit it (so QUINE) or to be expressible in such a set (so HUGHES & LONDEY). I propose to use the words '**instantiates**' and 'is an **instance** of' as short for 'is expressible in a set of sentences fitting the successive schemata of' an inference-schema. So the second difference amounts to that between (c) fitting and (d) instantiating a form. The question for this section

2.6 Form: Sentences versus propositions

therefore, given the identification of forms with inference-schemata, becomes the question whether to identify having (a form) with fitting or instantiating.

It will turn out that this question depends on another which is the main subject of the section; namely what is the arithmetic, or criterion of identity, of arguments, i.e. under what conditions should we say that one and the same argument recurs and on what conditions that there occur two different arguments? It is uncontentious that the same argument recurs just when the same conclusion is drawn from the same premisses (hence adding or subtracting premisses produces a different argument). But this at once raises the further question 'When do we have the same premiss or conclusion?'. One suggestion can be discarded right away: that the identity of a premiss or conclusion depends on its authorship and time of utterance. A reason why this won't do is that we want to be able to say such things as that the same argument was used by Descartes and Locke, or that one of Locke's conclusions was a premiss in an argument of Hume's. To secure communication at all it must be possible for one person to say the very same thing as another; for if people could not in that way express agreement, they could not express disagreement either. Admittedly it is possible with things said, as in general with the products of action, to define a kind whose identity does depend on authorship and time of utterance: these are technically called sentence-tokens. But for the purpose of logical appraisal it is essential that we should be able to abstract from such tokens and collect them into groups. It is such abstractions that are counted when two utterances are counted as, for example, utterances of the same premiss.

But what should be the principle of collection or abstraction? There is no end to the variety of answers that could be given to this question, but if we have regard both to the logician's convenience and to the layman's predispositions two possibilities stand out as most attractive: we could rule that utterances are utterances of the same premiss (and similarly for conclusions and mixed cases) (a) if and only if they consist of the same words in the same order, or (b) if and only if they say the same things about the same things. To convey 'same words in the same order' we can conveniently appropriate the grammarian's word 'sentence', since it will be near enough true that every utterance of a premiss or conclusion is expressed in what is grammatically a sentence. Of course there remains the sense in which different utterances require different sentences, for they require different sentence-tokens; but these may still be tokens of the same sentence-type, and it is in the sense 'sentence-type' that I shall henceforward speak of sentences. Accordingly, we can formulate the first of the two proposed principles of collection as:

> The same premiss or conclusion recurs if and only if the same sentence is reused.

For the second principle I shall employ the word 'proposition', ruling that two utterances are utterances of the same proposition if and only if each is used to say the same thing about the same things. Some authors prefer 'statement' to 'proposition' in this role (LEMMON *SSP*), on the grounds that there are logicians who give the arithmetic of propositions in terms of meaning-the-same rather than saying-the-same (I shall come back to this) and other logicians who mysteriously hold that propositions *are* meanings (MATES p. 11); but even though philosophical usage of 'proposition' has been, as one might expect, very diverse over the centuries, it is the word most favoured in current logical writing for expressing the second principle of collection. (The usage of 'statement' is hardly less diverse; in QUINE *MofL* it means 'indicative sentence'). Given this terminology the second principle of collection can be formulated as:

> The same premiss or conclusion recurs if and only if the same proposition is re-expressed.

Before adjudicating between these principles of collection it is necessary to elucidate 'saying the same thing about the same things', the proposed criterion of identity for propositions. I do not attempt a full account of the nature of propositions, but confine myself mainly to negative points. (i) In the case of singular propositions the criterion amounts to 'attributing the same property to the same thing, or attributing the same relation to the same set of things in the same order'. (ii) The criterion is intended, of course, to have the consequence that sameness of proposition and sameness of sentence do not coincide. For example the single sentence 'Hamlet is sad' will express different propositions according to the reference (play or character) of its subject and the meaning ('saddening' or 'saddened') of its predicate; and the different sentences 'I am sad' and 'You are

2.6 Form: Sentences versus propositions

sad' will express the same proposition if 'sad' is univocal and the second is addressed to the current author of the first. (iii) Propositions are to be taken as true or false absolutely, and so in particular eternally. If someone says 'I am unmarried' on Monday and Wednesday, and gets married on the intervening Tuesday, he is not to count as having attributed the same property to himself on the two occasions of utterance, nor therefore as having expressed the same proposition twice. Rather the first utterance truly attributed, say, the property of being unmarried at 2.0 p.m. on 2nd June A.D. 1975 and the second falsely attributed the different property of being unmarried at 10.15 a.m. on 4th June A.D. 1975. So sameness of propositions entails sameness as regards truth or falsity. (iv) But obviously the converse entailment does not hold. (v) Similarly sameness of proposition entails but is not entailed by sameness of truth-conditions. Every necessarily true or necessarily false proposition is true or false on the same conditions, namely on all conditions, and yet there are different necessarily true propositions, and different necessarily false ones. In this respect my criterion differs from that in LEWIS p. 46. (vi) Sameness of proposition neither entails nor is entailed by sameness of meaning. Two sentences may have the same meaning and yet express different propositions, e.g. because they are used with different references ('I am sad' and 'Je suis triste' said by different people), and two sentences may differ in meaning and yet express the same proposition ('I am sad' and 'You are sad' said about the same person). In this respect my criterion differs from that in LEMMON *SSP*. (vii) Sameness of proposition neither entails nor is entailed by sameness of cognitive value (informative potential). There is perhaps no end to the information that a sentence could convey, so that all sentences have, in a way, the same cognitive value. But if we discount special circumstances (tone of voice, prearranged codes, and so on) we can still find sentences with the same informative potential which express different propositions, e.g. 'A puppy is a young dog' and ' "Puppy" means "young dog" '. The former sentence cannot tell a hearer anything, special circumstances aside, if he already understands it. But it can tell him something if he doesn't, namely what 'puppy' means (cf. CARNAP p. 63); and that is just what the latter sentence serves to tell him explicitly. On the other hand the propositions expressed by these sentences are different—in the one case a necessary truth about puppies, in the other a contingent truth about the English word 'puppy'. Conversely, two sentences may express the same proposition and yet convey information on different conditions. For example 'The Lord Protector had warts' will need recasting into other words if it is to get its message across to someone who does not know who the Lord Protector was, or does not understand English; and I shall argue in 10.6 that 'The morning star is the evening star' and 'The morning star is the morning star' can express the same proposition even though the latter entirely lacks informative potential. In this respect my criterion differs from that suggested in QUINE *PofL* p. 3. (viii) Some, e.g. CHISHOLM, identify propositions with objects of belief. This raises a problem. A man might, for example, (a) believe that 'sHertogenbosch is near the Maas while at the same time believing that Bois le Duc is not near the Meuse, through ignorance of the identities concerned. Does he believe and disbelieve (believe false) the same proposition? There is nothing contradictory about that supposition, but a contradiction would follow if we supposed, slightly differently, that a man might (b) believe that 'sHertogenbosch is near the Maas while at the same time *not* believing that Bois le Duc is near the Meuse, and if we treated this as a case of believing and not believing the same proposition. There are three ways out. We might conclude that case (b) cannot occur, but only case (a); or that case (b) can occur, but the propositions expressed by ' 'sHertogenbosch is near the Maas' and 'Bois le Duc is near the Meuse' are different, even when those sentences are used to attribute the same relation to the same two things; or that case (b) can occur, and the two sentences do express the same proposition, but believing that 'sHertogenbosch is near the Maas is not a matter of believing that proposition, or any proposition. I reject the second solution, leaving a choice between the other two (see also pp. 209–12).

We may now seek to adjudicate between the two principles of collection. A layman would, I submit, be likely to favour the second one. He would be likely to say, for example, that the same argument is presented twice in

(E) John is tall and John is handsome; so John is tall

(F) John is tall and handsome; so John is tall

and therefore that the same premiss recurs in (E) and (F), though in partially different words. This suggests that we should identify

2.6 Form: Sentences versus propositions

premisses and conclusions as propositions. Yet the layman's predispositions, even if I am right about them, ought not to weigh with a logician if he finds that they do not serve his theoretical purposes. Here a certain tension becomes apparent. The logician needs the premisses and conclusions he discusses to be capable of truth and falsity (and that will be assumed in defining 'valid', as it was for the criterion of deductive correctness) but he also needs them, like the arguments they compose, to have forms. It is more natural to think of form as a property of sentences, but also more natural to think of truth and falsity as properties of propositions. I shall try to show that this tension can be relaxed in either direction: either we can treat premisses and conclusions as sentences which fit schemata, and accept slight complications in the concept of truth; or (the way I shall take) we can treat premisses and conclusions as propositions which are straightforwardly true or false, and link them to schemata by the slightly more complicated relation of instantiating.

First as to form. It is clear that the inference-schema (Es), which was 'p and q; so p', is fitted by the sentences used in (E) but not, given the conventions of 1.2, by those used in (F). But the logician is looking for system and economy. He cannot be content to say that (F) has no relevant connection with (Es) and to devise some other schema, e.g. 'a is f and g; so a is f', which is fitted by the sentences used in (F); on the contrary he will wish to say that (Es) has the same role to play in the logical appraisal of (F) as of (E) and that both (E) and (F) have (Es) among their forms. His means of achieving this result will depend on whether he agrees with our supposed layman that the same premiss recurs in (E) and (F). If he does agree, he can rule (as I shall) that an argument which has a certain form need not actually be expressed in sentences which fit the schema; it suffices that it should be possible, conformably with the rules of the language employed, to express it in words which fit the schema: that is, he will relax the requirement of fitting to one of instantiating. And since, as he will say, the very same argument as is expressed in the words of (F) could be expressed in the words of (E), and (E) does fit (Es), this relaxed requirement is satisfied by (F). Now suppose secondly that the logician regards premisses and conclusions as sentences, and hence does not agree that the same premiss recurs in (F) and (E), nor therefore that those are the same argument. He will achieve nothing by allowing that it suffices if (F) could be expressed in words fitting (Es), for on his view (F) could be expressed only in the words in which it is expressed, and they do not fit (Es). Instead he must say something to this effect: that it suffices if (F) is being used to say the same thing as could be said in some *other* argument which fits (Es). It may be that he will not use the words 'say the same thing as' (he may talk of recasting, paraphrasing or the like), but that is what he must mean if he is to achieve the desired economy in schemata by making as many arguments as possible—but not too many—have (Es) among their forms. In this way he, like the logician who favours the second principle of collection, can accommodate his predilection to the demands of logical theory.

As to truth, the logician requires that premisses and conclusions be in some cases true; so, if they are to be regarded as propositions, there must be true propositions, if as sentences, true sentences. Some people have asserted that no sentences are true (or false), usually on the ground that no sentences are constantly true (or false). Many kinds of circumstance can change a sentence from true to false or conversely. For example the sentence 'Pillarboxes are green' can become true by a change in language (if 'green' acquires the meaning now given to 'red') or by a change in the context of utterance (if uttered after they have been painted green) or by a change in the frame of reference (if one is talking about Eire). These are facts. But they are not a good ground for denying that sentences are true or false (one might as well argue that chameleons are colourless); all they show is that the truth and falsity of sentences is relative. The relativity is admittedly a nuisance, and a reason for preferring to do logic in terms of propositions, which are true or false absolutely. Nevertheless it is not a decisive nuisance, and we shall find that it is unavoidable anyhow in the definition of validity.

In reference to truth, therefore, as in reference to form, both of the two principles for collecting utterances allow logical appraisal to proceed. How then are we to adjudicate between them? In favour of propositions some, as we have seen, assert that sentences are not capable of truth or falsity; but that is a mistake. In favour of sentences some urge that because propositions are abstract (MATES p. 11, they 'reflect no light') their existence is doubtful; but again we have seen that sentences, by which is meant sentence-types, involve exactly parallel abstraction from sentence-tokens (see

2.6 *Form: Sentences versus propositions*

COHEN, p. 162). Nor can there be any force in the objection against propositions that the idea of saying the same thing about the same things, on which their arithmetic rests, is an unclear one. For I have shown that the application of logical techniques to testing the correctness of arguments must use that idea in any case, though not necessarily those words, on pain of an unmanageable proliferation of schemata. Faced with this indifference from the point of view of logical theory it seems reasonable if after all we allow weight to the layman's feeling that the identity of arguments, and hence of their premisses and conclusions, depends not on the words in which they are expressed but on what is expressed in them. I therefore propose to treat premisses and conclusions as propositions and not sentences, and to develop the apparatus of logic in terms of propositions (following LEMMON *BL* and HUGHES & LONDEY). The other way (favoured by QUINE *MofL*, MATES and MASSEY) is equally respectable, and would involve only fairly minor adjustments.

We are now in a position to answer the question with which this section began. Since arguments are not to be treated as sets of sentences they cannot be said to fit any inference-schema; since they are to be treated as sets of propositions expressible in sentences they can be said to instantiate inference-schemata, i.e. to be expressible in sentences fitting them.

I shall henceforward use the words '**truth**' and '**falsehood**' for 'true proposition' and 'false proposition' respectively. This makes the word 'truth' ambiguous, because it will continue to be used also as the name of the property of being true; for the property of being false I shall use 'falsity'. These properties are called **truth-values**.

2.7 *Validity: languages*

The technical sense of 'valid' now to be introduced brings together the key logical concepts of form and truth. Our overall aim is to define validity in such a way that having a valid form ensures deductive correctness.

A first shot at the definition is this: an inference-schema is valid when all its instances avoid the offending combination of true premisses with an untrue conclusion. In the present section and the three which follow it this definition will need to be refined, in various ways and for broadly three reasons. One reason is that validity so defined is *shared* avoidance of the offending combination, whereas deductive correctness was found in 2.4 to require *necessary* avoidance. We shall need to investigate whether an argument whose avoidance of the offending combination is shared with all others of the same form is thereby certified as avoiding that combination of necessity; this will be the subject of 2.10. Another reason for refining the definition is to ensure that we can find valid forms; for it is practically useless to know that all instances of a valid form are correct if we cannot establish the validity of any forms. This will be the subject of the present section and 2.8. Thirdly, 2.9 will introduce reasons for a further refinement.

None of the refinements will relax the condition that *all* instances of a valid form avoid the offending combination. Because of this condition validity-claims can be destroyed—forms invalidated—by a single instance which has that combination. Such counterexamples are surprisingly easy to find. Their pervasiveness will provide a motive in this section for making validity relative to logical languages and applying it to sequents rather than inference-schemata containing words.

Consider the following arguments:

(G) Eugene is unmarried; so Eugene is not married.

(H) There are old men in London; so some men in London are old.

(I) All bishops are clergymen; so all redheaded bishops are redheaded clergymen.

(J) Homo est animal; Socrates est homo; ergo Socrates est animal.

These arguments are correct, and moreover each appears to have a valid form. For each is expressed and therefore expressible in sentences fitting, i.e. is an instance of, one of the following apparently valid inference-schemata:

(Gs) a is un-f; so a is not f.

(Hs) There are g fs in a; so some fs in a are g.

(Is) All fs are gs; so all h fs are h gs.

(Js) f est g; a est f; ergo a est g.

2.7   Validity: languages   43

But none of the inference-schemata is in fact valid, for they are also instantiated (for example) by the following arguments with the offending combination of true premisses and an untrue conclusion. 'Paolo is unAmerican; so Paolo is not American', 'There are many men in London; so some men in London are many', 'All bishops are clergymen; so all retired bishops are retired clergymen', 'Homo est species; Socrates est homo; ergo Socrates est species'. Now admittedly the failure of the inference-schemata (Gs)–(Js) to be valid is not enough to show that (G)–(J) have no valid forms, since there might be other inference-schemata instantiated by (G)–(J) which are valid. The possibility of other schemata arises in two ways: first, for each sentence that can correctly be used to express a proposition, there is always more than one schema fitted by that sentence (e.g. all indicative sentences fit 'p'); and secondly each proposition is expressible in more than one sentence (e.g. by translation into another language). The second possibility offers promise of vindicating the claim that (G)–(J) have some valid form. We might notice for example that (J) can also be expressed in the sentences (sticking to Latin) '*omnis* homo est animal; Socrates est homo; ergo Socrates est animal', which fits the inference-schema '*omnis* f est g; a est f; ergo a est g'. The latter schema is not proved invalid by 'Omnis homo est species; Socrates est homo; ergo Socrates est species' because the premiss expressed in 'Omnis homo est species', unlike that expressed in 'Homo est species', is untrue and hence the latter argument does avoid the offending combination. Similarly the alternative schema 'There are fs in a each of which is g; so some fs in a are g' is also instantiated by (H), but is not invalidated by the new argument beginning 'there are men in London each of whom is many; so . . .', which again avoids the offending combination through the untruth of its premiss. In a parallel way alternative schemata might be devised for (G) and (I).

These and other such examples suggest a first step in refinement of the notion of a valid inference-schema. By bringing to our notice the fact that a single proposition, e.g. that man is an animal, can be expressed in sentences which fit different sentence-schemata constructed around 'f' and 'g', e.g. 'f est g' and 'omnis f est g', they prompt us, as did (E) and (F) in 2.6, to try to reduce the variety of schemata treated by logic; and by setting the invalidity of (Js) which contains 'f est g' against the apparent validity of the variant with 'omnis *f* est *g*' they give us a reason for preferring the latter. In this way the failure of (Gs)–(Js) to be valid brings a dividend. Yet it also points to a problem, for it reminds us that even a picked list of inference-schemata such as 'Omnis *f* est *g*; . . .' *might* turn out to have instances with true premisses and untrue conclusions, and so not to be valid. Schemata (Gs)–(Js) were faulted by sets of sentences which, though capable of expressing arguments with true premisses and untrue conclusions, go against our initially simple expectations of the workings of adjectival phrases and of linguistic devices like 'un-'; sentences which exploit the unruliness—perhaps more strictly the idiomatic subtlety—of ordinary language. Such sentences shake our confidence, and make us wonder whether any ordinary-language schema can be trusted to be valid under the provisional definition and therefore whether any argument can be trusted to have a valid form.

Fear of such unruliness seems to have been felt from the beginning of logic. At any rate the modern response to it, substitution of formulae and sequents for ordinary-language schemata, is already adumbrated in Aristotle. Aristotle's logic covers propositions instantiating 'Omnis *f* est *g*', but in giving the schema for such propositions he used not the ordinary Greek corresponding to 'Omnis *f* est *g*', nor of course to the more obviously vulnerable '*f* est *g*', but an overtly unordinary and unidiomatic formulation which may be translated 'The *g* belongs to all the *f*'. It is reasonable to guess that he chose such formulations because he judged that the unruliness of ordinary language is due to constant use, especially use by the stupid, the careless and the imaginative; abstruse and technical idioms are more likely to behave soberly. The same response can be found in modern logic. Instead of distinguishing 'Man is an animal' from 'Man is a species' by pointing out that the former but not the latter instantiates 'Every *f* is a *g*', logicians sometimes label the former an example of a class-inclusion proposition, the latter of a class-membership proposition. The labels permit the invalid (Js) to be replaced by the valid

(Jt) the class of *f*s is included in the class of *g*s; *a* is a member of the class of *f*s; so *a* is a member of the class of *g*s.

The incorrect argument beginning 'Man is a species' is an instance not of this valid schema but of the invalid schema beginning 'The class of *f*s is a member of the class of *g*s'.

2.7 Validity: languages

Before showing how technical-language schemata like (Jt) go part of the way from being inference-schemata towards being sequents I should mention another response to the uneasiness produced by arguments like 'Paolo is unAmerican; so Paolo is not American' and the others mentioned. This is to protest that the arguments do not *really* invalidate schemata (Gs)–(Js) because their premisses and conclusions, although expressible in sentences fitting those schemata, are not *really* instances of those schemata. The relation between, for example, the sentence 'Paolo is unAmerican' and the schema 'a is un-f' is said to be purely grammatical, not logical; the latter gives the grammatical form of the former, but not the real or logical form of the proposition expressed by it. Thus instead of casting round for an alternative inference-schema immune against 'Paolo is unAmerican; so Paolo is not American', e.g. the repetitious ordinary-language schema 'a is not f; so a is not f' or the repetitious technical-language schema 'a is not a member of the class of fs; so a is not a member of the class of fs', the logician may stipulate that the original schema 'a is un-f; so a is not f' should itself be understood in a restricted sense—the sense, presumably, of one of these repetitious alternatives. No doubt the proposition intended by the sentence 'Paolo is unAmerican' is genuinely expressible in that sentence; but it is stipulated that the sentence fits the original schema 'a is un-f' only in a mechanical, 'grammatical', way, ignoring the proposition it is intended to express. Hence the sentences used in 'Paolo is unAmerican; so Paolo is not American', and similarly in the other allegedly invalidating arguments, are seen as misleading, though grammatically proper, expressions of the propositions intended in those arguments, for they wrongly suggest that the arguments have schemata (Gs)–(Js) for their logical forms.

This second response to the unruliness of ordinary language, which may be associated with the name of RYLE, brings into the open a difficulty already implicit in the first response. If we are to say that (Gs) fails to exhibit the real, logical, form of the argument expressed in 'Paolo is unAmerican; so Paolo is not American' we must have some independent idea of the meaning we wish to stipulate as logicians for the construction in (Gs), i.e. for the prefix 'un-'. We are asked to use ordinary language in an admittedly restricted, even if still ordinary, way; so the restrictions ought to be indicated. It is no good simply saying that the meaning of 'un-' in logic is to be such as to exclude the 'unAmerican' example as an instance of (Gs), for that may not be enough to immunise (Gs) against other incorrect instances; nor can we make a complete inventory of excluded arguments, for they may be infinite. It becomes important therefore, if we are going to treat schemata as immune against certain types of apparent, 'grammatical', counterexample, to have in view an *interpretation* of the words and constructions in the inference-schemata which supplements—or in this case constricts—ordinary usage. But if so, candour requires us to amend the definition of 'instance', and hence of 'valid', so as to make room for a reference to rules of interpretation.

I shall return to this point, but not before describing a third and final response to the unruliness of ordinary language, which goes one step further. The need to have rules of interpretation in view, revealed by the Rylean response, is as I have said already implicit in the first, Aristotelian, response. For a logician's use of technical expressions like 'belongs to all the' and 'is a member of the class of', though a use of special terminology rather than a special use of ordinary terminology, still may be ambiguous and may be obscure; it too ought to be backed by rules. One way of drawing attention to this requirement, and at the same time avoiding the often cumbersome language of technical schemata like (Jt), is to replace the technical terminology by symbols—connectives. Carried to its limit such replacement will leave schemata like (Jt) with nothing in them but connectives and schematic (or dummy) letters, plus punctuation and, if there are quantifiers, variables; that is to say, it will turn them into sets of formulae. So for example we might progress from the vulnerable (Js) via the 'Aristotelian' (Jt) and the restricted 'Rylean' interpretation of (Js) to the set of formulae

(Jf) $\{`\forall x\,(fx \supset gx)', `fa', `ga'\}$

But now we have gone too far, for we have dropped the word 'so' which indicated in the inference-schemata which component was to be matched to the conclusions of its instances. The method of logic is to replace this indicator by a requirement of order. In an argument the premisses and conclusion can come in any order whatever, although when the conclusion is marked with a 'so' or 'therefore' it is more perspicuous to put it at the end, and that convention has been adopted in the examples. We shall exploit the convention. A sequent, as was explained in 1.7, is an ordered pair whose first member is a set of formulae and whose second member is a formula; so we can change (Jf) from an unordered set of formulae to the sequent:

(Jq) $\langle \{`\forall x(fx \supset gx)\textrm{'}, `fa\textrm{'}\}, `ga\textrm{'}\rangle$

and rule that an argument instantiates that sequent when it is expressible in a set of sentences which, when ordered with the conclusion-sentence *last*, fit the successive formulae in the sequent.

When sequents, rather than (other) inference-schemata, become the things instantiated by arguments, validity becomes a property of sequents. Moreover the definition of 'instance', and so of 'valid', must now be made relative to interpretation, because sequents consist of formulae, formulae may contain connectives, and the meanings of connectives need to be specified through rules of interpretation, as in a logical language. Using 'l' as a metalogical variable ranging over logical languages, we can say that for any l a sequent is valid in l, l-valid for short, when all its instances in l avoid the offending combination; where an instance in l, l-instance for short, of a sequent is an argument expressible *in some l-incorporating language* in a set of sentences which, when ordered with the conclusion sentence last, fit the successive formulae of the sequent. Because a logical language combines meaning-rules for connectives with conventions for fitting words to schematic letters, the new metalogical notation has the extra advantage of making room for a reference to those conventions too: we replace 'fit' in the definition by 'l-fit', i.e. 'fit *according to the conventions of* l'.

2.8 *Validity: contexts*

By making validity relative to a logical language we protect validity claims against certain sorts of counterexample. But other sorts remain which are pervasive enough to call for further refinement of the technical apparatus. These further counterexamples are generated by wrong usage and by equivocation.

An instance of an inference-schema is an argument expressible in a set of sentences fitting that schema, and an l-instance of a sequent is an argument expressible in some l-incorporating language in a suitably ordered set of sentences l-fitting that sequent. But expressibility is vague. When we come to pin it down it seems natural to say, first, that what is expressible in a given sentence, or set of sentences, varies with the occasion of the sentences' use, and secondly that for each occasion of use it depends partly on the speaker's intention and partly perhaps on the hearer's understanding. For example any argument is expressible in a single word, or a gesture, on an occasion when that method has been prearranged as a code, or even conceivably when it has not but the utterer merely intends his performance so to be understood. Restriction to an l-incorporating language limits the medium but not the uses that can be made of it; for an utterer can intend to express some argument (or proposition), and even be understood as expressing it, though he violates the conventional or explicit meaning-rules of the language he employs. Such violation is wrong usage, and if we are to avoid fatuous counterexamples to a sequent's validity we must stipulate, what has so far been tacitly assumed, that an l-instance is an argument expressible in an l-incorporating language *without wrong usage*.

Even right usage does not ban ambiguity. To be sure the logical languages themselves are unambiguous, but the languages they enrich, such as English, contain many ambiguous expressions and constructions. For example there is no wrong usage involved in employment of the sentences

(K) Jonathan is one of the team's pitchers; every pitcher is a jug; so Jonathan is one of the team's jugs

to express an argument with true premises and an untrue conclusion; for every pitcher is a jug in one accredited sense of 'pitcher'. Yet such examples had better not be allowed to invalidate sequents. An l-instance must therefore be an argument expressible in an l-incorporating language *without ambiguity*.

But this further restriction is still not enough, if ambiguity is just multiplicity of sense or meaning. Consider the sentences in

(L) It's well-formed and derivable; so it's well-formed.

In a use of (L) the 'it's might refer to different things (tone of voice, or pointing, could indicate this) and different supplementations could be intended for the occurrences of 'well-formed' (e.g. well-formed in the propositional calculus, well-formed in the predicate

2.8 Validity: contexts

calculus). The difference of reference is certainly not a difference of meaning, or 'it' would have as many meanings as there are things; and the difference of supplementation is not necessarily, nor I think rightly, regarded as a difference of meaning ('well-formed formula' has neither, not both, the meanings 'PC-formula' and 'QC-formula)'. Yet here again it would be ridiculous to count (L) as invalidating the sequent $\langle \{`p \& q'\}, `p' \rangle$. To cover this kind of case as well as straightforward ambiguity I introduce the word 'equivocal', stipulating that an l-instance is an argument expressible in an l-incorporating language without wrong *or equivocal* usage. It turns out to be adequate for logical purposes to define an **equivocal** use of a sentence or set of sentences as a use in which (a) two occurrences of the same subject have different references or (b) two occurrences of the same predicate have different meanings or implied supplementation or (c) two occurrences of the same sentence have different content, i.e. express different propositions.

Occasions of use I shall call **contexts**; and an **l-context** (for any l) will be a context of right and unequivocal usage of some l-incorporating language. I now change the definition of 'l-instance' and 'l-valid' so that an l-instance of a sequent becomes an argument expressible *in some* l-*context* in a suitably ordered set of sentences l-fitting the sequent, and an l-valid sequent becomes a sequent all of whose l-instances in this new sense avoid the offending combination. The same redefinition of 'l-valid' could have been reached by first introducing a kind of validity that is relative to context: a sequent would be (let us say) l-valid$_1$ in a context when all arguments expressible in *that* context in some l-incorporating language in a suitably ordered set of sentences l-fitting the sequent avoid the offending combination. A sequent is l-valid under the redefinition if and only if it is l-valid$_1$ in every context of right and unequivocal usage.

There is a method by which reference to contexts might have been avoided: restriction to 'eternal' sentences, and adoption of a narrow criterion of identity for 'languages'. The restriction would stipulate that in order for a set of sentences to fit a sequent they must be eternal in the sense 'not capable of expressing different propositions in different contexts of right usage': so they must contain no ambiguous words or constructions, no incomplete predicates like 'well-formed', and no expressions with variable reference like 'it', 'now', 'John'. The criterion of identity would stipulate that all contexts are contexts of right usage in the language employed: violation of a meaning-rule simply creates a new 'language'. Reference to contexts would then become otiose in the definition of validity, and of instance. If sequents were interpreted as themselves sets of sentences—the dummy interpretation—these two stipulations could easily be built in: logical languages, as opposed to the natural languages enriched by them, are identified anyhow by the meanings of their connectives, and symbolic sentences, as opposed to verbal sentences fitting formulae, will be eternal provided that the *ad hoc* meanings of their component letters are suitably limited. But the stipulations are more irksome under the schematic interpretation, and I shall not follow those authors, e.g. Quine, who adopt them.

2.9 *Validity: domains*

In the last two sections reference to languages and contexts has been introduced into the definitions of 'instance' and 'valid' in order to reduce the risk that no inference-schema or sequent would be valid and no argument have a valid form. Reference to domains has different motives. Partly, many logicians have argued that the interpretation rules of the predicate calculus cannot be precisely stated without it, and partly its purpose is to simplify proofs that an argument has a valid form.

The problem about interpretation starts from the logical paradoxes, of which Russell's will serve as a specimen. Russell reasoned like this. Some properties of men belong to them as a class, not individually: for example Cicero is not numerous, but the class of men is numerous. Conversely Cicero is a man, but the class of men is not; it is not among its own members. This latter is the commonest situation, but some classes, e.g. the class of classes with members, do seem to be members of themselves; certainly there *are* classes with members, and this seems to show that the class of *them* has members, and so itself satisfies the condition for membership of it. Suppose we set aside such self-membered classes and 'form' the class of all those classes that are not self-membered. This class will have among its members the class of men, which is not self-membered, and many others. Will it have itself among its members? The paradox is that the condition for its being a member of itself is precisely that it

2.9 Validity: domains

should not be: it is if and only if it isn't. Russell's reaction was to construct a set-theoretic language in which the predicate 'is not a member of itself' did not make sense. A more modest reaction is to say that the predicate does not always make sense: in particular when we 'form' a class whose condition of membership is given by that predicate—the class of non-self-membered classes—it does not make sense to apply the predicate to that class. And in general we cannot assume that a predicate makes sense whatever it is applied to; so that if we try to specify its sense in the usual logical way by means of truth-conditions, the truth-conditions are liable to leave some, admittedly recherché, cases in which the truth-value of a sentence applying the predicate is indeterminate, and cannot be assigned one way or the other without contradiction.

If this is right, it affects the interpretation rules of the predicate calculus in the following way. Those rules need to lay down truth-conditions for the predicate-leading construction schematised in such formulae as 'fa', 'gcb' etc. The construction is meant to be available for every predicate in every language, or, on the dummy letter account, for every *ad hoc* meaning of 'F', 'G', etc. But Russell's paradox seems to show that it is not possible to lay down truth-conditions for every predicate which will give a determinate answer to the question what things the predicate is true of, i.e. what things it can be applied to so as to yield a truth, unless the range of things under consideration is limited in some way—perhaps to all things that are not classes or to all classes of a certain kind. These limitations will also affect the interpretation rule for '$\forall$', the universal quantifier. We want to say, schematically, that '$\forall x fx$' is true on condition that 'f' is true of everything, but for some replacements (or translations) of 'f' it will be impossible to maintain consistently either that the condition is fulfilled or that it is not. A sentence such as 'Everything either is or is not self-membered' may fail to make sense even though its component predicate makes sense.

The standard response to this difficulty is to conclude that each piece of discourse in which all the propositions are of determinate truth-value must have an implicit subject matter, a class of things which the discourse is about. Classes in this role are called **domains** or universes of discourse (LEMMON *BL* p. 104, MATES p. 55, QUINE *MofL* p. 97, HUGHES & LONDEY pp. 191–2, MASSEY p. 232).

Nothing prevents a domain from being disparate, e.g. men-and-numbers; nothing I have said prevents it being, on some occasions of discourse, universal (though there are in fact difficulties in set theory, originally due to Cantor, about the existence of a class comprising everything, see pp. 252–3). Equipped with this notion we can rewrite the set of interpretation rules of the predicate calculus as a collection of sets of rules, one for each possible domain. Let us say that a property or relation is **defined over a domain** when it makes sense to attribute the property or relation to each member or ordered set of members of the domain. Then relative to a given domain a sentence fitting (translating) 'fa', for example, will be true or false only if the subject fitting (translating) 'a' in it has for its reference a member of the domain and the predicate fitting (translating) 'f' in it attributes a property defined over the domain; the sentence being true if that property holds of that member, false otherwise. And relative to a given domain a sentence fitting (translating) '$\forall x fx$' will be true or false if and only if similarly the predicate fitting (translating) 'f' in it is defined over the domain—true if the predicate attributes a property which holds of every member of the domain, false otherwise. In effect '$\forall$' is to be interpreted not as 'everything' but as 'everything under discussion'.

But Russell's paradox is not the only motive for framing truth-conditions with reference to domains. Actually it is a contentious motive, since one might avoid the contradiction threatened by 'the class of non-self-membered classes is a non-self-membered class', and by the parallel sentences which other paradoxes generate, if one concluded not that their predicates lack sense but that their subjects lack reference: there simply are no such things to be 'formed' as the class of non-self-membered classes, exactly as there is no barber to be found who shaves all and only those who do not shave themselves (see QUINE *Paradox* p. 4). Let us turn then to the other motive, simplification of proofs that an argument has a valid form.

To prove that an argument has a valid form one would begin, of course, with the argument and seek a valid sequent of which it is an instance. Let us for a moment reverse that procedure, starting from the following sequent which is valid in the predicate calculus (QC-valid):

(Mq) $\langle \{`\forall x(fx\ \&\ hx \supset gx)\text{'}, `fa\ \&\ ha\text{'}\}, `ga\text{'}\rangle$

2.9 Validity: domains

If we now try to construct a QC-instance of (Mq), the QC interpretation rules for '∀', '&', '⊃' and the predicate-leading construction will permit such cases as the following:

> For any x, if x is happy and x is a person, x is honest; John is happy and John is a person; so John is honest.

> For any x, if x is derivable and x is a formula, x is well-formed; '$p \supset p$' is derivable and '$p \supset p$' is a formula; so '$p \supset p$' is well-formed.

Since the identity of arguments does not depend on the words in which they are expressed, and since instances are arguments, it follows that any paraphrase of the above words into more elegant English will still express an instance of (Mq) provided that it still expresses the same argument. Here are paraphrases:

> If anyone is happy, he is honest; John is a happy person; so he is honest.

> If any formula is derivable, it is well-formed; '$p \supset p$' is a derivable formula; so it is well-formed.

So far it is certain that we still have QC-instances of (Mq). But what happens if 'person' and 'formula' are elided from the second premisses? The elisions are not entirely neutral, since happy things do not have to be persons nor derivable things formulae (they might be sequents). Nevertheless I think it is reasonable to understand what results as still expressing the same arguments (the same premisses and conclusions), and therefore as still expressing QC-instances of (Mq). But now that the components corresponding to 'ha' have disappeared from the specimen arguments, the question arises whether we cannot simplify the sequent they instantiate from (Mq) to (Jq), which was

(Jq) $\langle \{\text{'}\forall x(fx \supset gx)\text{'}, \text{'}fa\text{'}\}, \text{'}ga\text{'}\rangle$

There is no doubt that (Jq), like (Mq), is QC-valid. The question at issue is whether the arguments variously expressed above are QC-instances of it. It would be useful if we could count them so, since (Jq) is shorter than (Mq) and so easier to prove valid. The trouble is that (Jq) contains nothing answering to 'one' and 'formula' in 'anyone' and 'any formula', and it can hardly be right usage to express the specimen arguments in yet further truncated sentences which omit those indications of subject matter.

There are several ways in which to construct sequents at least approximating to the brevity of (Jq) and still instantiated by the specimen arguments. One way would be to replace 'person' and 'formula' by dummy or schematic letters, somehow attached to the quantifier as in '$\forall x P(fx \supset gx)$' or '$\forall x_h(fx \supset gx)$' or even '$\forall h(f \supset g)$'. Another device, called many-sorted logic, is to reserve different sets of variables for different sorts of things, as 'π' is reserved for formulae in the metalogical notation of this book; e.g. if 'π' were put into the logical language we could permit '$\forall \pi(f\pi \supset g\pi)$' for 'if any formula is f it is g'. These devices have the disadvantage of calling for parallel restrictions on the admissible replacements of subject letters. The regular method (HUGHES & LONDEY pp. 191–2, LAMBERT & VAN FRAASSEN p. 83) is to leave the logical notation as it stands and appeal once more to domains in defence of the claim that the specimen arguments are instances of (Jq) itself. First we perform the further truncation of 'anyone' and 'any formula' into 'anything'. Then we reason that although it does not absolutely accord with right usage to express the specimen arguments in these new words, nevertheless it does so accord relative to the assumption that the subject matter of discourse is, respectively, persons and formulae (this licence is restricted in modal contexts; see 10.7). This being so, the two arguments are each expressible relative to some domain in sentences QC-fitting the shorter sequent (Jq), and we can change the definition of 'l-instance' once more so that that fact is enough to make them l-instances of (Jq): an l-instance of a sequent, we shall now say, is an argument expressible in some l-context and *relative to some domain* in a suitably ordered set of sentences l-fitting the sequent. An l-valid sequent then becomes a sequent all of whose l-instances in this further revised sense avoid the offending combination. Again the redefinition of 'l-valid' could have been reached by another way: count a sequent l-valid$_2$ in a domain when all arguments expressible in an l-context relative to *that* domain in a suitably ordered set of sentences l-fitting the sequent avoid the offending combination. A sequent is l-valid under the further redefinition if and only if it is l-valid$_2$ in every domain.

One further point about domains needs to be made. They are classes, but they have to be classes with members; or alternatively,

2.9 Validity: domains

instead of writing 'relative to some domain' in the revised definition of 'l-instance', we must write 'relative to some non-empty domain'. In the view of many authors the reason for this is a technical one: without the qualification certain sequents that are otherwise QC-valid in the new sense would cease to be so, through not being QC-valid$_2$ in the empty domain (MASSEY pp. 259–61). But the technical difficulty does not arise for the interpretation rules of the present book, according to which every sequent containing subject letters or quantifiers is QC-valid$_2$, vacuously, in the empty domain. A better reason is that the restriction to non-empty domains "is really no restriction at all" (W. & M. KNEALE p. 707), since no one can assume that his discourse has no subject matter. It follows from this that a proposition or argument is expressible relative to some domain if and only if it is expressible relative to some non-empty domain. If we explicate 'domain', therefore, as meaning 'domain of *discourse*', in the manner of the previous paragraph, 'non-empty' becomes redundant; the explication ensures that domains are non-empty classes.

2.10 Validity: worlds

The first shot, on p. 41, at defining validity brought out 'has a valid form' as meaning 'is an instance of an inference-schema all of whose instances avoid the offending combination'. In the last three sections this has been relativised to logical languages, applied to sequents, and generalised over (non-empty) domains and contexts of right and unequivocal usage. It remains to be investigated whether the property of having a valid form, so refined, carries with it the property of deductive correctness.

We must not be lulled here by the word 'valid'. I have noted on p. 25 that in one customary sense 'valid' just means 'deductively correct'; but in the technical sense under examination in these sections it does not mean that, and cannot because it is applied to forms of argument (sequents or inference-schemata) rather than arguments themselves. Nor can we simply assume that valid forms validate (SMULLYAN p. 3), i.e. that what *has* a valid form in the technical sense *is* valid in the customary sense (students of logic need to be wary of other words with a similarly dual role, e.g. 'implies', 'logical truth', 'consequence'; see p. 190).

To be valid under the provisional definition is to be truth-preserving, i.e. to be had by no argument leading from true premises to an untrue conclusion. So if one sticks to arguments having a valid form under that definition one will 'never be led astray' (PRIOR *FL* p. 15) in the sense of passing from truths to untruths. But we are looking for a test of correctness, and 2.2 has shown that it is possible to meet the condition of never passing from truth to untruth without always—or ever—arguing correctly, since the condition is met by anyone who argues from jointly untrue premises, whatever his conclusions. It is even possible to meet the condition and also avoid untrue premises without arguing correctly, since it is met by anyone who argues to true conclusions, whatever his premises.

It might seem then that the property of having a valid form, thus defined, provides no more assurance of correctness than does the property of avoiding the offending combination. But this is not fair. An argument which has a valid form, thus defined, not only avoids the offending combination but also *shares* avoidance of it with all other arguments of the same form. Shared avoidance is still different from what I argued in 2.4 to be the criterion of deductive correctness, necessary avoidance. On the other hand some logicians prefer to substitute shared avoidance as a better criterion, and their case must now be examined.

Quine, a notable champion of this alternative, would object to the criterion of deductive correctness defended in 2.4 on the ground that the notion of necessity (strict implication) which it invokes is unclear and ought in large part "to be dispensed with in serious science" (QUINE *PofL* p. 10). The right procedure "from the point of view of logical theory" is to "analyse" the deductive correctness of an argument into two circumstances: the argument has a certain form, and no argument of that form combines true premises with an untrue conclusion (QUINE *MofL* p. 39). Thus the criterion becomes shared avoidance of the offending combination.

Two doubts may be raised about Quine's proposal: is the notion of necessity really so obscure as to be unfit for serious science and, even if it is, are we justified in substituting shared avoidance as the criterion of deductive correctness? As to the unclarity of necessity and the concepts related to it—analyticity, logical possibility, strict implication—I do not intend to contribute to the debate that has surrounded this topic since the publication of Quine's article

2 *Dogmas* in 1951, beyond merely sketching what seem to be the major arguments on each side and indicating my response to them. It is said on the one side that the boundaries between the necessary and the non-necessary are intolerably hazy, and that necessity can be explicated only in terms of a circle of related concepts with no way of breaking out of the circle. It is said on the other side that the haziness must not be exaggerated—most truths can be classified without dispute as necessary or not necessary—and that explanation in a circle can still be efficacious (MATES p. 9); moreover there is no difficulty about understanding the notion of self-contradiction or inconsistency and 'It is necessary that' might as we saw in 2.4 be glossed 'It is self-contradictory that not' (see STRAWSON *ILT* ch. 1). Secondly, as to the proposal that necessity and the other concepts in its family ought to be dispensed with in the criterion of deductive correctness, it is not obvious that they are dispensable even if unclear. A single argument which avoids the offending combination may still be incorrect: how is it protected against this risk by sharing that avoidance with other arguments of the same form? Where is the safety in numbers? It is as though someone, noticing that he cannot assure a catch of fish by buying a fishing rod, were to seek the assurance by joining a fishing club all of whose members have rods (cf. LEMMON *BL* p. 81 "this condition at least").

For these reasons we must keep the criterion of deductive correctness defended in 2.4. It might still be true that shared avoidance brings necessary avoidance in its train, and so satisfies that criterion —i.e. that there is, in this logical case, safety in numbers. So it might still be true that every argument having a valid form, under our provisional definition of 'valid', is deductively correct according to the criterion of 2.4. To some this seems 'intuitively acceptable' (HUGHES & CRESSWELL pp. 10, 28–9, SUPPES pp. 21–2), but to me it seems to need proof, which I am unable to supply.

The alternative is to set up a stronger definition of 'valid form', and in particular of '1-valid sequent'. I do so by means of the notion of possible facts, i.e. what might have been the case. A true proposition is true given the actual facts, but many true propositions would not have been true given other possible facts. Combinations of truth-value can likewise be made relative to possible facts. For example the argument 'Something is black; so something is white' combines a premiss which would (still) have been true had there currently been no white things, with a conclusion which would in that case have been untrue. So even though it avoids the offending combination given the actual facts, it would not have done so had things been appropriately otherwise. Sets of possible facts are conventionally distinguished as possible worlds, or just **worlds**. In these terms the new and stronger definition of 'valid' will stipulate that a form is valid (a sequent l-valid) only when all arguments having it (all its l-instances) avoid the offending combination in every world, i.e. would avoid it whatever the facts, i.e. avoid it of necessity (cf. p. 29). As before the definition could have been reached in a more roundabout way: count a sequent l-valid$_3$ in a world when all l-instances of it avoid the offending combination in *that* world. A sequent is l-valid under the stronger definition if and only if it is l-valid$_3$ in every world.

The difference between this and the provisional definition of 'valid form' is a difference between the strict and the material. In the one case a form is valid when the premisses of all arguments having it strictly imply their conclusions; in the other case it is valid when they materially imply their conclusions. Some logicians offer both definitions of 'valid' side by side (HUGHES & LONDEY pp. 4, 17, LAMBERT & VAN FRAASSEN pp. 8, 85) or both definitions of 'has a valid form' side by side (MATES p. 16). But this is unsatisfactory without a proof, which they do not supply, that the definitions in each pair come to the same thing, i.e. that shared material implication brings strict implication in its train.

2.11 *The definition of 'valid sequent'*

Here are the results of the last four sections.

2.11 (1)   An l-instance of a sequent (for any logical language l) is an argument expressible in some context of right and unequivocal usage of some l-incorporating language, relative to some domain, in a set of sentences which, when ordered with the conclusion-sentence last, fit by the conventions of l the successive formulae of the sequent.

More briefly: an l-instance of a sequent is an argument expressible in some l-context and domain in a set of sentences l-fitting the sequent. In 7.1 this will be tightened still further to 'argument whose premisses and conclusion are all true or false . . .'

2.11 The definition of 'valid sequent'

2.11 (2) An l-valid sequent (for any logical language l) is a sequent all of whose l-instances avoid the offending combination of necessity, i.e. are arguments whose premisses strictly imply their conclusions.

A clarification is needed at this point. 'Inference-schema' was defined on p. 33 with an eye only to arguments of the normal type having at least one premiss; hence inference-schemata were assumed to contain at least two sentence-schemata. But some sequents pair the empty set of formulae with a formula, so containing only one formula. To make sure that not all one-formula sequents are valid we have to provide them with instances, and therefore we have to admit the possibility of arguments without premisses. The simplest way is to identify such 'arguments' with their conclusions, thus treating all propositions as premissless arguments. Then a one-formula sequent will be valid, i.e. each of its l-instances will of necessity avoid combining true premisses with an untrue conclusion, if and only if each of its l-instances of necessity avoids being untrue, i.e. is a necessary truth (cf. LAMBERT & VAN FRAASSEN p. 28).

2.11 (3) 'has a valid form' is to be given the technical sense 'is, for some logical language l, an l-instance of an l-valid sequent'.

With these definitions we can establish a further metalogical principle, to add to 2.3 (1) and 2.4 (1). Take any argument which has a valid form. By 2.11 (3) it is an l-instance, for some l, of some l-valid sequent. By 2.11 (2) the premisses of every l-instance, for that l, of that sequent strictly imply the instance's conclusion. So the argument's premisses strictly imply its conclusion. So:

2.11 (4) The premisses of an argument strictly imply its conclusion if it has a valid form, i.e. if for at least one logical language l it is an l-instance of at least one l-valid sequent.

2.12 Proof

If we know that some argument is an l-instance, for some l, of an l-valid sequent, metalogical principle 2.11 (4) permits the inference that its premisses strictly imply its conclusion. Then metalogical principle 2.4 (1) permits the further inference that it is deductively correct. Finally by metalogical principle 2.3 (1) we can conclude that it is correct. The point of using this chain of inferences is that there exist logical techniques for proving, in some cases, that an argument is an l-instance for some l of an l-valid sequent. The proofs are of course metalogical, because they prove that an *argument* has a certain property.

Metalogical proofs ought to be as rigorous as possible, but they do not differ from other rigorous proofs except in being metalogical, i.e. having a logical subject matter. It will be as well at this stage, therefore, to say something general about the concept of proof. A proof is generally an argument, but it is more than a correct, even deductively correct, argument, for that might have a false conclusion. It is also more than a correct argument with true premisses, because then one could prove any true conclusion by deducing it, for example, from itself or from the conjunction of itself with any other true premisses: but clearly 'p; q ; so p' is not the schema of any proof, whether metalogical or otherwise (this faults HUGHES & LONDEY p. 44). The remaining necessary condition for proof by argument can be stated in Aristotle's way: the premisses of a probative argument, and the principles of inference by which its conclusion is drawn from them, must be more evident than the conclusion (*An. Post.* I 2.71^{b}21). The hearer must be 'carried along' from premisses which he is initially willing to accept as true (once he understands them), by inferences which he is willing to accept as correct, to a conclusion which he is not initially willing to accept as true. This shows that proving can be treated as a relative matter: what proves a conclusion to one audience may not do so to another. But the advancement of knowledge, and especially the writing of books, depends on the fact that the relation of being-more-evident-than is to some extent a natural one, so that some arguments are 'naturally probative' in a sense which rather uneasily straddles the difference between 'Everyone who understands them finds their conclusions relatively non-evident' and 'Everyone who understands them ought to find their conclusions relatively non-evident'. An argument which fails as a proof because it asserts its conclusion among its premisses is said to **beg the question**. This is not so clear a definition as it seems, because asserting shades into 'implying' and yet the premisses of a good proof must, of course, imply its conclusion in some sense, e.g. 'entail' (see MILL, II iii 2). So the

2.12 Proof

label 'begging the question' comes to be used in a general way to describe any argument which fails to meet the condition of relative evidentness. The concepts of proof, evidentness, and begging the question are epistemological, rather than logical. But though logic, as I understand the word, does not study proofs, it uses them.

Begging the question is often called a fallacy, but it is not a fallacy in the sense 'incorrect argument'. Indeed its clearest cases, instances if 'p; q; so p', are patently correct. This point was noticed by PETER OF SPAIN (7.54); see HAMBLIN p. 33.

Metalogical proofs have a recurrent pattern. Typically they seek to show that all entities of a certain class or classes—e.g. well-formed formulae, or sentences, or l-contexts—have a certain feature if certain conditions are met, or if and only if they are met. A proof which aims at such a result will start off by making assumptions of two kinds. First, it will 'take' or 'select' an arbitrary member of each of the classes concerned: 'Let π be a formula and σ a sentence fitting it' or some such. Secondly it will 'suppose' or 'hypothesise' that the conditions are met. Then it will proceed, using results previously arrived at, to deduce that the desired feature does hold of the chosen member. If the conclusion is to contain 'if and only if', this process must next be repeated in the reverse direction. Finally the conclusion is formed by putting each supposition into an 'if' clause and generalising over all members of the classes concerned. We shall see on p. 248 how this pattern is reproduced in some predicate calculus sequent-derivations.

If the metalogical principles 2.3 (1), 2.4 (1) and 2.11 (4) are to be used as I have suggested in proofs of correctness, then three conditions must be met. First, the correctness of the metalogical arguments from these principles to the conclusion that a given argument is correct must be relatively evident. It is important to notice this fact, which shows that although logic seeks to prove correctness it depends on prior acceptance that certain kinds of argument (in this case among the instances of predicate calculus sequents) are correct; cf. LAMBERT & VAN FRAASSEN p. 170. Secondly, the metalogical principles must themselves be proved; I have attempted to do so in the present chapter. Thirdly, there must exist ways of proving what was hypothesised in the first sentence of this section, that certain arguments are l-instances for certain ls of certain l-valid sequents. This last requirement in turn breaks down into two stages:

finding a sequent of which the argument is an l-instance for some l; and proving that the sequent is l-valid for that l.

The second stage, proof of validity, can be direct or indirect. In some logical languages, notably the propositional calculus, there are quite simple direct methods for proving a valid sequent valid—and in fact for proving an invalid sequent invalid. Two of these will be discussed and others mentioned in 7.2. Direct methods can be used in other calculi too, but it is generally more convenient to proceed indirectly through the notion of derivability. An indication of this is the name 'proof theory' for the study of logistic systems, which deal with derivability. Logistic systems include, indeed in this book will be constituted by, methods of proving the derivability of all their derivable sequents (and formulae).

Proof theory might be studied for its own sake, but it will not serve the purposes of this book unless some connection can be established between derivability and validity. A derivable sequent is derivable relative to rules of derivation; a valid sequent is valid relative to a language, i.e. rules of interpretation. What we need therefore is a further technical concept linking the two kinds of rules, and this is the concept of the soundness of a system in a language (see MATES p. 139, MASSEY p. 280). A sequent system is called sound with respect to a language l, **l-sound** for short, when every sequent derivable in it is l-valid. Given this definition it is easy to deduce a further metalogical principle:

2.12 (1) An argument has a valid form if for at least one logical language l it is an l-instance of at least one sequent which is derivable in at least one l-sound sequent system.

A proof of correctness which goes through 2.12 (1) as well as 2.3 (1), 2.4 (1) and 2.11 (4) needs three starting points instead of two. It must establish that the argument under scrutiny is an l-instance of some sequent, that the sequent is derivable in some sequent system, and that the system is l-sound, i.e. all its derivable sequents are l-valid. This last property cannot be assumed. Although a calculus is defined as a system sharing formation rules with a logical language, and so must contain sets of derivation and interpretation rules, these two latter sets are stated quite independently of one another and might fail to 'match'. Indeed given a derivable sequent it is always going to be possible, obviously, to invent some interpretation of its symbols under which it turns out not to be valid. A calculus is called 'argument sound' when the sequents derivable in it are all valid in it. So for each calculus we shall need a proof of argument soundness.

2.13 *Alternative route*

In 1.11 I noted the existence of formula systems, in which derivability is a property of formulae rather than sequents. If one were to use formula systems for proving the correctness of correct arguments, at least principle 2.12 (1) would have to be replaced. In practice it is normal to replace 2.4 (1) and 2.11 (4) also, proceeding by an alternative route which must now be briefly traced.

We need to go back to the criterion of deductive correctness, and to describe the second of the two ways I distinguished in 2.4 of generalising the assertion that the argument expressed in 'Today is Monday; so tomorrow will be Tuesday' is deductively correct if and only if it could not have been Monday today without being Tuesday tomorrow. The new generalisation yields: an argument is deductively correct if and only if the conjunction of its premisses with the negation (denial, contradictory) of its conclusion could not have been true, i.e. if and only if the negation of that conjunction is a necessary truth. Technical abbreviation now re-enters. The negation of the conjunction of an argument's premisses with the negation of its conclusion may be called the **material conditional corresponding to the argument**. Hence the criterion of deductive correctness can now be put in the form:

2.13 (1) An argument is deductively correct if and only if its corresponding material conditional is a necessary truth.

In this formulation there is no longer talk of one thing's materially implying another; just of a single material conditional's being true.

The status of negations and conjunctions, and hence of material conditionals, is as much in need of clarification as was that of premisses and conclusions. According to QUINE (*MofL* pp. 1, 5, 12) and MATES (p. 7 and, speaking of logical languages, p. 49) these things are sentences, and Quine and Mates make the extra stipulation that one sentence is to count as, for example, the negation of another only if it is formed from that other by the addition of some negative expression or connective (thus no two sentences are, in their usage, negations of each other). But since the reasons which favour doing logic in terms of propositions rather than sentences carry over from the sequent route to the formula route, I shall construe negations, conjunctions, and conditionals as propositions (so LEMMON *BL* pp. 7, 19, HUGHES & LONDEY p. 20).

As the word 'conditional' suggests, it is possible, and in the Quine–Mates usage necessary, to frame conditionals by means of some word or connective answering to 'if'. For example the material conditional expressed in 'It is not the case that both today is Monday and tomorrow will not be Tuesday' can be expressed less clumsily in 'If today is Monday, tomorrow will be Tuesday'. For this reason the conjunction of the premisses of an argument is known as the **antecedent** of the corresponding material conditional and its conclusion as the **consequent** (arguments, which may be correct or incorrect, have premisses and conclusions; conditionals, which as propositions may be true or false, have antecedents and consequents). But the 'if' idiom carries dangers familiar to students of logic, both because not all 'if' sentences express conditional propositions, e.g. 'If the song is set too high, transpose it', and because in the case of those that do express conditional propositions it is often unclear whether the conditional is 'material' or not (QUINE *MofL* pp. 19–23 and see 9.5).

I next define the notion of a formal truth, or, as it is more usually called, **logical truth**. This is analogous to 'argument having a valid form' and runs into analogous difficulties. Should a logical truth fit a schema or translate a symbolic sentence? Is it to be a sentence or a proposition? Is it to be an instance relative to some logical language and in some context and domain? In the end we emerge with these three definitions corresponding to 2.11 (1)–(3):

2.13 (2) An l-instance of a formula is a proposition expressible in some context of right and unequivocal usage of some l-incorporating language, relative to some domain, in a sentence which fits the formula by the l conventions.

In 7.1 this will be tightened to 'true or false proposition . . .'.

2.13 (3) An l-valid formula is a formula all of whose l-instances are necessary truths.

2.13 (4)   'is a logical truth' is to be given the technical sense 'is, for some logical language l, an l-instance of an l-valid formula'.

By reasoning parallel to p. 59 it follows that

2.13 (5)   The material conditional corresponding to an argument is a necessary truth if it is a logical truth, i.e. is for at least one logical language l an l-instance of at least one l-valid formula.

As with sequent systems, a formula system is sound with respect to a logical language l, l-sound for short, when all formulae derivable in it are l-valid. A calculus is called 'statement sound' when all formulae derivable in it are valid in it. Hence as in 2.12 (1)

2.13 (6)   The material conditional corresponding to an argument is a logical truth if for at least one logical language l it is an l-instance of at least one formula which is derivable in at least one l-sound formula system.

2.3 (1), 2.13 (1), 2.13 (5) and 2.13 (6) combine to provide the alternative route from proof of derivability in a formula system to proof of correctness.

2.14 The powers of logic

How much help can logic give in the enterprise of testing arguments? If the methods of this book are to apply, the premisses of a tested argument must be finite in number (p. 25) and, together with the conclusion, all true or false (7.1). But there are three more general and serious limitations.

(i) In order to be useful (e.g. in a proof) an argument must normally have true premisses as well as being correct. We have seen in 2.2 that these properties are independent of one another. But the truth of premisses cannot be tested by logical means, save in the exceptional case where they are logical truths or logical falsehoods.

(ii) A test of correctness will be a metalogical proof, proving an argument correct or incorrect as the case may be. But proofs of incorrectness fall outside the main methods of this book, because they do not involve the concept of validity. The reason is that whereas every l-instance of an l-valid sequent is correct, not every l-instance of an l-invalid sequent is incorrect. On the contrary, *every* correct argument instantiates *some* invalid sequent: e.g. every one-premiss argument, correct or incorrect, **PC**-instantiates the **PC**-invalid sequent $\langle \{`p'\}, `q' \rangle$. Hence proofs of invalidity, though available, afford no more than a challenge, showing that a sequent which might have been thought to certify some argument as correct fails to do so because it is actually invalid in some calculus. There always remain the possibilities that the sequent is valid in some other calculus, or that the argument instantiates some other sequent which is valid in some calculus (LAMBERT & VAN FRAASSEN p. 51), or that the argument is deductively correct though not in virtue of its form, or correct though not deductively correct. Logic can indeed assist in proofs of incorrectness, by another method that will be described on pp. 270–1. But the main method, through validity, is only a method of proving correctness.

(iii) Even when confined to proofs of correctness the main method is not 'effective', in the sense of prescribing a step by step procedure which if duly applied is bound to lead in a finite number of stages to an affirmative answer to the question 'is such and such an argument correct?' whenever an affirmative answer is the right one. This may be surprising to those who are aware of logic's reputation as a mechanical science, in which insight and ingenuity are thought to be supplanted by mere (even if complex) computation. But the fact is that computations take us only part of the way. Logic breaks up proofs of correctness into two main stages (see QUINE *W&O* p. 159 on this "division of labor"): finding, for a given argument, some sequent of which it is an l-instance in some l; and proving that the sequent is l-valid. The proving can sometimes be managed by computation—though the indirect methods that I shall stress in this book, of proving validity through derivability in some sound system, call for ingenuity as well. But the finding is not at present reducible to rule. Arguments are normally presented in a set of sentences of some natural language. Transformation from these sentences into an instantiated sequent or formula, which I shall call formalising, involves replacing some words by schematic letters and translating others into connectives. Linguists aspire to mechanise translation; but translation between English and the logical languages of this book is not mechanical (MATES p. 69).

2.14 The powers of logic

Even if it could be made so—perhaps for other logical languages —it is doubtful whether the remaining tasks of the formaliser, notably certifying right and unequivocal usage, could ever be mechanised.

The range of arguments that can be proved correct by the methods of logic depends, of course, on the richness of the logical calculi available. The four calculi covered in this book, and particularly the first two of them which almost *are* logic in the eyes of many contemporary philosophers, constitute a powerful tool for proving correctness. On the other hand it is easy to devise arguments which are at least apparently correct, and apparently correct in virtue of their form, but which probably do not instantiate valid sequents of any of the calculi in this book. Here are some examples:

(P) The man in the brown hat is a spy; so some spy wears a brown hat.

(Q) You are required to reserve a seat if you travel on the 10.50; so you are permitted to travel on the 10.50 only if you reserve a seat.

(R) What is past is inevitable; so whatever is possible will come to be (the Master Argument of Diodorus; see PRIOR *PPF* pp. 32–3).

(S) John believes that Napoleon won the battle of Waterloo; so if he believes that Napoleon was an Englishman, he believes that an Englishman won the battle of Waterloo.

Work has been done or is in progress on calculi which comprehend these arguments. (P) belongs to the theory of definite descriptions (see QUINE *MofL* pp. 227–30, LEMMON *BL* pp. 166–7), (Q) to deontic logic, (R) to tense logic, (S) to intentional logic, the logic of 'propositional attitude' verbs like 'believe'. But such developments are outside the scope of this book.

Finally, a word of perhaps needless caution. In approaching the question 'Is such and such an argument correct?' through the question 'Does it (its corresponding material conditional) instantiate in such and such a language a sequent (formula) which is derivable in some system which is sound in that language?' the logician increases the number of errors and confusions into which it is possible to fall. He also makes it easier, sometimes much easier, for thinkers to avoid error and confusion—once they have mastered the skills involved. Often, especially when an argument is known to be difficult or disputed, the benefits of symbolism are worth the price. But it cannot always be so. This is a matter for judgment in each particular case.

CHAPTER THREE

Formation Rules and Definitions

3.1 Syntax refined

In the grammar of a language the part called syntax deals with two sorts of question: what combinations of words are permitted (basically, how to construct a grammatical sentence) and how combination determines the meanings of phrases and sentences from the meanings of words. These questions overlap because of the still current practice of stating the former kind of rules, composition rules, in terms of parts of speech or grammatical categories, which classify words and phrases according to the way in which they contribute to the meanings of sentences. Hence instructions for testing whether some string of English words, e.g. 'Pigs fly', is a grammatical sentence will, when they are given in the currently standard manner, be useful only to someone who knows that 'pigs' is a noun and 'fly' can be a verb, which is just the knowledge that bridges the gap between understanding the meanings of those words, e.g. from a dictionary, and understanding the meaning of the sentence formed from them. On the other hand standard composition rules plus the information in a dictionary are not enough to reveal the meaning of every English sentence. For example the meaning of 'People eat frogs' depends on which noun is subject, which object; and 'subject' and 'object', unlike 'noun' and 'verb', do not figure in composition rules because they do not name parts of speech. Here the two aspects of syntax, rules for telling whether a sentence is grammatical and rules for inferring sentence-meaning from word-meaning, fail to coincide.

In current linguistic theory it is customary to label questions about meaning as falling under 'semantics', and to contrast semantics with syntax. In view of what has just been said the contrast is a blurred one, but it could be sharpened by restricting the application of the label 'syntax' in two ways: questions about the dependence of sentence-meaning on word-meaning would have to be banished from syntax into the 'semantics of constructions', and composition rules would have to be stated in a meaning-neutral way, i.e. in terms of a description and classification of elementary expressions which makes no reference to their shared or different roles in contributing to the meanings of sentences. The kind of syntax which emerges from this refining process is what logicians call a system of formation rules. Logical formation rules take, or specify, a set of elementary expressions, divide them in some meaning-neutral way into classes, and state in terms of this classification how to make compounds (strings) out of the elements.

It may be asked why logic insists on such a refined notion of syntax, especially since the refinement is ignored in the syntax of natural languages on which logical formation rules are often assumed to be modelled. The reason is that logic is tied as closely to mathematics as to linguistics. From an initial interest in patterns common to different inferences, i.e. in inference-schemata, the logician has come to discern patterns common to different inference-schemata and patterns shared with things which are not inference-schemata at all. As in mathematics, this leads to independent study of the secondary patterns without regard to what they are patterns of—to the study, for example, of relations among formulae without regard to the fact that they are relations among elements of inference-schemata. An expression representing a pattern which is shared by inference-schemata among other things is an expression which can be interpreted as an inference-schema. Hence any decision to leave open the question what some pattern is a pattern of carries with it the decision to leave such representative expressions uninterpreted. If formation rules are to come at this abstract, uninterpreted, stage, they must either avoid words like 'word', 'noun', 'sentence', 'schematic letter', 'subject letter', 'sentence-schema', or, if they use any of them (as I shall), they must use them without prejudice to interpretation.

3.2 Formulating the rules

The rules I adopt are set out in Appendix Two.

The formation rules of the propositional calculus can be stated like this: [FL] every propositional letter is a well-formed formula;

3.2 Formulating the rules

[F∼] the result of writing '∼' followed by a well-formed formula is a well-formed formula; and [F&] the result of writing '(' followed by a well-formed formula followed by '&' followed by a well-formed formula followed by ')' is a well-formed formula. This set of rules constitutes a recursive definition of well-formedness in the sense explained in 1.8, except that it contains so far no extremal clause. The first rule in the set is categorical; if stated as above it must be accompanied by a specification of what are to count as propositional letters, viz. the infinite series beginning 'p', 'q', 'r', 'p_1', 'q_1', 'r_1', 'p_2'. The other two rules are hypothetical and could be put in the form 'If such-and-such is (are) well-formed, so also is such-and-such'. Already in this simple case it is going to be convenient to introduce metalogical symbolism, as forecast in 1.13. If we use 'PC-formula' as short for 'formula that is well-formed in the propositional calculus' and 'π', 'φ' as metalogical variables ranging over formulae, the hypothetical rules can be reformulated as: for any π and φ, if π and φ are PC-formulae, so also are $\sim\pi$ and $(\pi\,\&\,\varphi)$. Here '$\sim\pi$' and '$(\pi\,\&\,\varphi)$' are lazy shorthand for '⌜$\sim\pi$⌝' and '⌜$(\pi\,\&\,\varphi)$⌝', which in turn mean 'the result of writing "∼" followed by π' and 'the result of writing "(", then π, then "&", then φ, then ")" '. So we are not to suppose that '$\sim\pi$' *is* a PC-formula: in fact it is not, since 'π' is not in the series of propositional letters. Rather the '∼'-rule licenses as PC-formulae such formulae as '$\sim p$', '$\sim q$', '$\sim\sim p$', '$\sim(p\,\&\,q)$', '$\sim(q\,\&\,p)$' '$\sim(\sim q\,\&\,p)$' and so on. This set is obviously infinite, and would be so even if there were not an infinite supply of propositional letters. Notice too that 'for any π and φ' means 'for any π and φ, not necessarily distinct': so we have also such PC-formulae as '$(p\,\&\,p)$', '$((\sim r\,\&\sim p)\,\&\,(\sim r\,\&\sim r))$'.

In the predicate calculus with identity all the foregoing kinds of formulae are well-formed, and more. We now need to add a list of predicate letters, viz. the infinite series beginning 'f', 'g', 'h', 'f_1', and a list of subject letters, viz. the infinite series beginning 'a', 'b', 'c', 'a_1'. Two new categorical rules state that: [FP] any predicate letter followed by one or more subject letters, the same or different, is a well-formed formula; and [F=] '=' between two subject letters, the same or different, is a well-formed formula. These rules license respectively such formulae as 'fa', '$gbbcb$', and '$b = b$', '$c = a$'. Notice that '=' thus becomes a logical symbol, unlike '$=_{\text{def}}$' which is metalogical. The predicate calculus also adds a list of variables, viz. the infinite series beginning 'x', 'y', 'z', 'x_1', and a hypothetical rule for '$\forall$'. The statement of this rule is more difficult because a well-formed formula starting, for example, with '$\forall y$' will need to be followed by formulae containing the variable 'y' (e.g. 'fy', '$(gay \& p)$') and nothing said so far licenses formulae containing variables as well-formed. In fact the rules I adopt do not permit free, i.e. unquantified, occurrences of a variable in any well-formed formula. So the construction of a well-formed formula beginning '$\forall$' has to proceed in two stages. First, taking a well-formed formula containing a subject letter, e.g. 'fc', '$(gaa \& p)$', we transform it into something that is not well-formed by substituting a variable for at least one occurrence of one of the subject letters in it, as in 'fy', '$(gay \& p)$'; secondly we prefix '$\forall$' followed by the chosen variable, as in '$\forall y fy$', '$\forall y(gay \& p)$'. The mutilation of one well-formed formula thus makes it suitable for grafting into another. This process involves at its first stage the operation of *substituting* some one variable for occurrences of some one subject letter. Although in the present case substitution is a simple affair, the correct statement of substitution rules can become very tricky elsewhere; I shall return to the subject in 6.6.

The rule for '$\forall$' sketched above would permit construction of such formulae as '$\forall x \forall x fxx$' and '$\forall z \sim (\forall z gzz \& p)$' in which it is not clear which of two quantifiers 'binds' which occurrences of a variable. There are two ways of dealing with this uncertainty. We could wait for the interpretation rules to indicate when a quantifier is forestalled by another in its attempt to bind a variable, and when in particular it is forestalled in all its attempts and so becomes 'vacuous' (HUGHES & LONDEY p. 295; this is the method of MASSEY p. 239, MATES p. 45). Or we could emend the formation rule so as to forbid all such uncertainties, and forbid vacuous quantification. I shall follow Lemmon in adopting the latter course, by ruling that the well-formed formula into which a variable is substituted for a subject letter may not already contain that variable (LEMMON *BL* p. 142). Although this emendation is effective in preventing such uncertainties, it is an underdiscriminating instrument for the purpose; it is not so sweeping as to ban '$(\forall x fx \& \forall x gx)$', for example, which is constructed by the '&'-rule from two perfectly well-formed formulae '$\forall x fx$' and '$\forall x gx$', but it does ban—or rather fail to license—such barely ambiguous groupings as '$\forall x(fx \& \forall x gx)$' which would have to be

3.2 Formulating the rules

constructed by substituting 'x' into a well-formed formula already containing 'x', such as '$(fa\ \&\ \forall xgx)$'.

We can think of the construction of '$\forall$'-formulae in another way which will be useful later on. Instead of starting from a well-formed formula, e.g. '$(gaa\ \&\ p)$', and deleting occurrences of a subject letter in it so as to substitute occurrences of a variable, we are to start from a formula in which there are already gaps. Such formulae with one or more gaps in I call **stencils** (MATES p. 178). In a peripheral passage of 6.6 it will be necessary to mark these gaps by numerals, which may be repeated, so yielding stencils such as '$(ga①\ \&\ p)$', '$(g②①\ \&\ p)$', '$g①①\ \&\ p)$'; but the rules in Appendix Two require only the numeral '①', or blanks as in '$(g\_a\ \&\ p)$', '$(g\_\_\ \&\ p)$'. (This definition of 'stencil' differs from Mates's in not stipulating any particular kind of filling for the gaps, nor that a filled up stencil necessarily becomes a well-formed formula. Quine's passing use of the word, *MofL* p. 146, is different, referring to mutilated sentences, not mutilated formulae; the stencils we are concerned with will get interpreted as what Quine calls predicate-schemata, *MofL* p. 150.)

The '$\forall$'-rule restated in terms of stencils will say that if a stencil becomes a well-formed formula by having its gaps filled uniformly by a subject letter, it also becomes a well-formed formula by having its gaps filled uniformly by a variable and then having '$\forall$' followed by the variable prefixed to the whole; i.e. [F$\forall$] if the result of inserting a subject letter once into each gap in a stencil is well-formed, so also is the result of inserting a variable (not already present) once into each gap in it and prefixing '$\forall$' followed by that variable.

As before, these predicate calculus rules can be shortened by metalogical notation. I use 'QC-formula' for 'formula that is well-formed in the predicate calculus with identity', 'α', 'β' as metalogical variables ranging over subject letters, 'ν' as a metalogical variable ranging over variables, and 'ϕ', 'ψ' as metalogical variables ranging over stencils. Once more '$\forall \nu$' is a lazy way of writing '⌜$\forall \nu$⌝', i.e. 'the result of writing '$\forall$' followed by ν'; and '$\alpha = \beta$' similarly. But '$\phi \alpha$' will have a special meaning, not 'the result of writing ϕ followed by α' but 'the result of inserting α once into each gap in ϕ'; similarly for '$\phi \nu$', '$\phi \beta$' etc. The formulation of F= and F$\forall$ now becomes: for any α and β, $\alpha = \beta$ is a QC-formula; and for any α, ν, and ϕ not already containing ν, if $\phi \alpha$ is a QC-formula, so also is $\forall \nu \phi \nu$.

Formation Rules and Definitions

The formation rules for the modal calculi S5 and QS5 are obtained by adding, to PC and QC respectively, a rule licensing as well-formed any well-formed formula preceded by '$\Box$'; for example '$\Box p$', '$\Box \sim q$', '$\Box\Box p$', '$\Box(\sim q \ \& \ \Box r)$' become well-formed in S5, and additionally such formulae as '$\Box \forall x f x$', '$\Box f a$' and thence '$\forall x \Box f x$' become well-formed in QS5. The symbolic formulation of the rule is: [F$\Box$] for any π, if π is an S5-(QS5-) formula so also is $\Box \pi$.

Although in an obvious sense (see p. 193) QS5 is an extension of both S5 and QC, which in turn are extensions of PC, it is worth noticing that the extensions to each class of well-formed formulae cannot be made by simply tacking on new formation rules to the old; or rather that only suffices if we reinterpret 'well-formed' in the old rules as now meaning well-formed according to the new ones. This is because we want to count, for example, '$(fa \ \& \ p)$' as a QC-formula and '$(\Box r \ \& \ p)$' as an S5-formula. Only an '&'-rule will license them as well-formed, but the original '&'-rule permitted '&' only between PC-formulae, so excluding both 'fa' and '$\Box r$' as components. A full statement of the QC formation rules must include adaptations of the PC rules, in which 'QC-formula' is written for 'PC-formula' throughout; and similarly in the other cases.

Formulae that are licensed as well-formed by one of the categorical rules of a calculus are called **atomic formulae** of that calculus. The atomic formulae of PC and S5 are the propositional letters; of QC and QS5 those plus formulae consisting of predicate letters followed by subject letters, and also formulae such as '$a = a$', '$b = c$'.

A sequent is well-formed in a calculus if and only if its component formulae are finite in number and all well-formed in that calculus. For example any finite sequent of S5-formulae is an S5-sequent.

3.3 Symbolic definitions

A recursive definition, i.e. specification, of well-formed formulae will need to end, as we saw in 1.8, with an extremal rule to the effect that the set of well-formed formulae is the smallest set satisfying the other rules, so that everything left unlicensed by those rules is denied a licence. But there are many formulae left unlicensed by the rules stated in 3.2 which nevertheless appear in most presentations of the four calculi distinguished there; and these are formulae

3.3 Symbolic definitions

containing other connectives than '∼', '&' '=', '∀', '□'. Any of three policies, apart from outright rejection, could be adopted for such connectives. We could supply them with their own formation rules; we could bring them in by eliminative definition; or we could keep them outside the logical notation itself but permit them as convenient shorthand in what are strictly ill-formed formulae.

The advantage of avoiding the first course is to reduce the number of interpretation and derivation rules that will be needed at a later stage. For the other courses have the effect of saying that the connectives '∼', '&', '=', '∀', '□' constitute, together with letters and variables and punctuation, the whole of the primitive vocabulary of the four calculi. Any further symbols introduced by eliminative definition or by informal convention are to be seen as merely shorthand for the primitive notation, a concession to men's obtuseness in detecting the structure of long formulae (machines wouldn't want them). We might, it is true, positively welcome the opportunity of stating independent formation rules for a wider vocabulary of connectives; and this will happen especially if we are interested in comparing variant sets of interpretation and derivation rules which agree over formulae containing '∼', '&', '=', '∀', '□' but diverge elsewhere. Intuitionist logic can be presented as such a variant. But for the purposes of this book the vocabulary of 3.2 will suffice as primitive.

Given, then, that further connectives are worth admitting but do not need independent formation rules because their role is to serve as dispensable shorthand, it makes no practical difference whether we license formulae containing them as well-formed, or tolerate them as unlicensed conveniences. I shall do the former, so inserting symbolic definitions among the logical rules. There are five main definitions, one each for the connectives '∨', '⊃', '≡', '∃', '◇'. The last, which comes into play only in S5 and QS5, is very simple: [Def◇] '◇' is short for '∼□∼'. The others are contextual definitions (p. 22) displaying not a primitive formula which abbreviates to the new symbol but a formula containing primitive connectives which abbreviates to a formula containing the new symbol. If we take '∨' as an example, '∼(∼p & ∼q)' is to abbreviate to '(p ∨ q)', and the corresponding abbreviation is to be permitted with any other well-formed formula (whether or not it is a propositional letter) in place of 'p' and 'q'. In metalogical notation this becomes: for any well-formed formulae π and ρ, [Def ∨] $(\pi \vee \rho)$ is short for $\sim(\sim\pi$ & $\sim\rho)$. Similarly the definitions of '⊃' and '≡' are: for any well-formed formulae π and ρ, [Def ⊃] $(\pi \supset \rho)$ is short for $\sim(\pi$ & $\sim\rho)$; and [Def ≡] $(\pi \equiv \rho)$ is short for $((\pi \supset \rho)$ & $(\rho \supset \pi))$. These belong to all four calculi. Finally in QC and QS5 we have: [Def ∃] for any variable v, $\exists v$ is short for $\sim\forall v\sim$.

The definitions are to be understood, of course, as two-way licences, to abbreviate and to expand. Their use does not have to involve the whole of any formula. For example the formulae '$(p$ & $\sim(\sim r$ & $\sim\forall x fx))$' and '$\sim\sim(\sim r$ & $\sim\forall x fx)$' both contain '$\sim(\sim r$ & $\sim\forall x fx)$' as an embedded part; so Def∨ licenses their abbreviation to '$(p$ & $(r \vee \forall x fx))$' and '$\sim(r \vee \forall x fx)$'. It is however required that the units which finish up attached to the new connective should be well-formed formulae (hence 'for any well-formed π and ρ' in the formulations); we may not shorten '$\sim(\sim(p$ & $\sim q)$ & $r)$' to '$((p \vee q)$ & $r)$' by taking the ill-formed '$(p$' as the first unit and the ill-formed '$q)$ & r' as the second. This requirement makes a difficulty in any version of the predicate calculus which excludes free variables from well-formed formulae, since the definitions cannot be applied as we should want in order to shorten, for example, '$\forall x \sim(\sim fx$ & $\sim p)$' into '$\forall x(fx \vee p)$': 'fx' is not well-formed. The way out of this difficulty that I shall take is to add a hypothetical definition rule: for any a, v, ϕ and ψ, if ϕa is short for ψa, $\forall v \phi v$ is short for $\forall v \psi v$ (and so $\exists v \phi v$ is short for $\exists v \psi v$). The extra convenience of having this hypothetical rule is not great; Lemmon manages without it.

How do the definitions ensure the well-formedness of formulae not in primitive notation? Had we proceeded by way of extra formation rules instead of definitions, such formulae would have turned out well-formed under the extra rules. Had we adopted the third alternative of treating the definitions as informal conventions, the formulae would have remained ill-formed, though tolerated. As it is we have the following kind of situation: '$\sim(\sim p$ & $\sim q)$' and '$\sim\sim\forall x \sim\sim \square \sim fx$' are well-formed by the original formation rules; and '$(p \vee q)$' and '$\sim \exists x \Diamond fx$' abbreviate them by the definitions. Is this enough to make the latter well-formed? The answer depends on whether we understand the definitions as producing new formulae or as rewriting the same formulae in different notation. If they rewrite the same formulae, no more needs to be said; for '$\sim(\sim p$

3.3 Symbolic definitions

& ~q)' is well-formed, '(p ∨ q)' is that same formula, and it therefore follows that '(p ∨ q)' is well-formed. But it is perhaps more natural to regard the criterion of identity for formulae as 'same symbols in the same order' (compare sentences), with the consequence that definitions produce different formulae. If so, there seems to be need of an extra formation rule after all, to the effect that the definitions preserve well-formedness, i.e. never lead from a well-formed to an ill-formed formula. Its formulation could be: for any π and ♀, if ♀ is short for π and π is well-formed, so also is ♀ (so MATES in the case of derivability, p. 98). My own procedure will be a sort of compromise between these two: I shall understand the role of symbolic definitions in such a way that the operation of shortening or lengthening a formula by means of them produces a different formula, but preserves the logical properties of well-formedness and derivability; and this will include the provision that a sequent which results by definition from a derivable sequent is itself derivable. The compromise can be sufficiently indicated by referring to the definitions in the extremal formation and derivation rules, so that the former becomes: nothing is a well-formed formula except in consequence of the preceding formation rules and the symbolic definitions.

The vocabulary of a calculus is the set of all those symbols which are introduced by the formation rules and definitions of the calculus, i.e. which appear in its well-formed formulae and sequents. So we can speak of 'f', for example, as a QC or QS5 letter, and '◇' as an S5 or QS5 connective.

3.4 Scope

The scope of an occurrence of a connective in a formula is the shortest unbroken part of the formula encompassing that occurrence which is itself well-formed or would be if subject letters were substituted for variables in it—the shortest 'well-formed' part in a loose and inaccurate sense which covers formulae like '$fx \supset fx$' that have been mutilated ready for grafting to quantifiers. Consider, for example, the formula '$\forall y(\square\square p \supset gy)$'. The occurrence of '$\forall$' in it occurs in various unbroken parts of it, '$\forall$', '$\forall y$', '$\forall y($', '$\forall y(\square$' and so on. None of these is well-formed except the whole formula (which is to count as a part of itself for the purpose of determining scope).

The first occurrence of '□' occurs in even more parts, some extending leftwards from it, as '□', '(□', '*y*(□' etc., some rightwards, as '□□', '□□*p*' etc., some in both directions. The shortest of these which is well-formed is '□□*p*'. Similarly the scope of the second occurrence of '□' is '□*p*', and the scope of '⊃' is '(□□*p* ⊃ *gy*)' which, although not itself well-formed, becomes so when a subject letter is substituted for '*y*' in it. In the case of an occurrence of a primitive connective the rule means that the scope of the occurrence in a well-formed formula is that part of the formula to emerge, in the process of formation, at the moment when the occurrence was introduced; and in the case of an occurrence of a non-primitive connective it is that part of the formula to emerge at the first moment at which the occurrence could have been introduced by the connective's definition.

Obviously connectives do not have a scope in every formula; for example '⊃' has no scope in '⊃(*p*'. But every occurrence of a connective in a well-formed formula does have a scope.

A connective which has for its scope the whole of some formula is called the **main connective** of that formula (LEMMON *BL* pp. 48, 66, QUINE *MofL* p. 50). Every well-formed formula or well-formed part of one that contains a connective at all must contain a main connective, and no such formula or part can contain more than one. In the following examples the main connectives are underlined: '∀̲*x*(*fx* ∨ (*p* ∨ *p*))', '(∀*x*(*fx* ∨ *p*) ∨̲ *p*)', '(∀*xfx* ∨̲ (*p* ∨ *p*))'.

3.5 *Indemnities*

The formation rules of a calculus are framed with an eye to the elimination of syntactical ambiguity. This is the sort of ambiguity which makes it impossible to solve the equation $2x = 2 - 1 - 1$ until we know whether to bracket the right-hand side as '(2 − 1) − 1' or as '2 − (1 − 1)', and which makes it impossible to tell what is the antecedent of 'she' in 'If you are kind to a girl's mother, she will be kind to you'. An ambiguity similar to the second of these cases is present in such formulae as '∀*x*∀*xfxx*', which F∀ was framed so as to avoid licensing. An ambiguity similar to the first is present in '(*p* ⊃ *q* ⊃ *r*)', which will be short for '∼(*p* & ∼∼(*q* & ∼*r*))' or '∼(∼(*p* & ∼*q*) & ∼*r*)' according as its first or second '⊃' is taken as main connective.

3.5 Indemnities

The ambiguity afflicting '$(p \supset q \supset r)$' is an ambiguity of scope. Such ambiguities are prevented in well-formed formulae by the requirement in the formation rule for '&' and the definitions of ' $\vee$ ', ' $\supset$ ', ' $\equiv$ ' that the formula produced be surrounded by outer brackets. Brackets will always be present to distinguish, for example, ' $\sim(p \vee q)$' or '$\forall x(fx \vee p)$', in which ' $\sim$ ' and '$\forall$' are the main connectives, from '$(\sim p \vee q)$' or '$(\forall x fx \vee p)$', in which ' $\vee$ ' is. But the formation rules and definitions go further than avoidance of such scope-ambiguity demands, resulting in a certain amount of needless bracket-clutter. Here, as with primitive connectives, it would be possible to secure economies by extra formation rules or definitions; but in this case the extra rules would be quite complicated to state and work with. The universal practice among logicians is to close the formation rules, by an extremal rule, at the point at which I have closed them or earlier, and to introduce bracket-economies informally, as indemnities against breaking the extremal rule. By means of them we produce what are strictly ill-formed formulae, but formulae that can readily be 'thought back' into a well-formed state, e.g. for the purpose of determining scope through the rules of the last section. Anyone who finds this process confusing does well to retain, for a time at least, all the brackets demanded by the formation rules and definitions.

I adopt four indemnities. (i) The pair of brackets enclosing the whole of any well-formed formula may be omitted (LEMMON *BL* p. 46, HUGHES & LONDEY p. 50, MATES p. 51, MASSEY p. 34). (ii) The binary connectives common to all four calculi are to have *dominance* in the order ' $\equiv$ ', ' $\supset$ ', ' $\vee$ ', '&', i.e. backwards through the order in which their definitions and formation rules were stated in 3.2 and 3.3 (cf. QUINE *MofL* p. 25, MASSEY pp. 35, 60). What this means is that, for example, '$p \equiv q \supset r$' should be construed as ' $\equiv$ ' joining 'p' to '$q \supset r$', so simplifying '$p \equiv (q \supset r)$', and the bracketed part of '$(p \& q \supset r) \vee r$' should be construed as ' $\supset$ ' joining '$p \& q$' to 'r', so that the whole simplifies '$((p \& q) \supset r) \vee r$'. Such formulae as '$((p \equiv q) \supset r)$' remain well-formed, of course, though not amenable to internal bracket-economy. Like Lemmon (*BL* p. 46) I shall not in practice exploit the dominance of ' $\vee$ ' over '&', which is not memorable. (iii) '$\sim a = b$' may be written '$a \neq b$', and similarly for other subject letters and variables (HUGHES & LONDEY p. 295); also brackets may be added around such formulae as '$a = b$', 'a ≠ b', where this makes for clarity. (iv) '((p & q) & r)' and '(p & (q & r))' may alike be written '(p & q & r)', and similarly in the case of '∨' (but not in mixed cases, nor in runs of '⊃' or '≡'). This convention can be applied and then re-applied, to produce runs of more than two '&'s or '∨'s; it can also be applied, of course, in cases where the component formulae are not just propositional letters (so an exact statement of it would use 'π' and '$\female$'). Examples of its use are 'r & ∃x(fx ∨ gx) & ~r', 'p ∨ p ∨ (q ⊃ p) ∨ □p'. Unlike the first three indemnities this one does import scope-ambiguity, but the ambiguity is 'tolerable' (MASSEY p. 38) because of the fact that in the calculi of this book '&' and '∨' are *associative* (like '+' and '×' in arithmetic). What that means is that (a) for any well-formed formulae, π, $\female$ and ρ, $((\pi \,\&\, \female) \,\&\, \rho)$ and $(\pi \,\&\, (\female \,\&\, \rho))$ can replace each other anywhere in a derivable or underivable formula or sequent without its ceasing to be derivable or underivable as the case may be, and so can $((\pi \vee \female) \vee \rho)$ and $(\pi \vee (\female \vee \rho))$; and (b) the same goes for valid and invalid formulae and sequents. Proofs of metatheorems (a) and (b) will be assumed; parts of them are contained in Chapters 5–7 and further parts in HUGHES & LONDEY chs. 16 and 10.

Given these four indemnities all but the last of the following are available as ways of simplifying the well-formed formula which comes first among them:

$(p \equiv ((\sim b = b \,\&\, (q \supset r)) \,\&\, r))$	QC-formula
$p \equiv ((\sim b = b \,\&\, (q \supset r)) \,\&\, r)$	omitting outer brackets
$p \equiv ((b \neq b \,\&\, (q \supset r)) \,\&\, r)$	abbreviating '$\sim b = b$'
$p \equiv (b \neq b \,\&\, (q \supset r)) \,\&\, r$	'$\equiv$' dominates '&'
$p \equiv b \neq b \,\&\, (q \supset r) \,\&\, r$	'&' associative
$p \equiv b \neq b \,\&\, q \supset r \,\&\, r$	wrong

The last formula is indemnified, but because '⊃' dominates '&' it simplifies the different QC-formula '$(p \equiv ((\sim b = b \,\&\, q) \supset (r \,\&\, r)))$'.

3.6 Other people's rules

There are eight main ways in which a set of formation rules covering the four calculi PC, QC, S5, QS5 may differ from those I adopt.

(1) It may use different symbols, e.g. '*P*' or '*A*' for '*p*', '→' for '⊃'. Some of these differences are listed in Appendix One.

3.6 Other people's rules

(2) It may add extra connectives. For example the modal connectives '$\Diamond$', '$\dashv$', '$\equiv$' (MASSEY pp. 190, 192) are definable as follows: for any well-formed π and φ, $\pi \Diamond \varphi$ is short for $\Diamond(\pi \& \varphi)$, $\pi \dashv \varphi$ is short for $\Box(\pi \supset \varphi)$, and $\pi \equiv \varphi$ is short for $\Box(\pi \equiv \varphi)$.

(3) It may use a different set of primitive connectives. We have already seen in 3.3 that it is possible, and for some purposes desirable, to enlarge the set of primitive connectives beyond '$\sim$', '&', '$\equiv$', '$\forall$', '$\Box$'. MASSEY adds '$\vee$' and '$\exists$', LEMMON BL '$\vee$', '$\supset$', '$\exists$', QUINE $MofL$ '$\vee$', '$\supset$', '$\equiv$', '$\exists$'. (None but MASSEY have modal connectives.) It is also possible to use an equally small but different set, replacing '$\sim$' and '&' by '$\sim$' and '$\vee$' (HUGHES & LONDEY pp. 51–2) or by '$\sim$' and '$\supset$' (MATES pp. 98, 166), '$\forall$' by '$\exists$' (MATES p. 166), or '$\Box$' by '$\Diamond$' (MASSEY p. 184). Each of these changes will of course affect the symbolic definitions. E.g. if '$\sim$' and '$\vee$' are primitive but '&' is not, $(\pi \& \varphi)$ is read, for any well-formed π and φ, as short for $\sim(\sim\pi \vee \sim\varphi)$; and if '$\sim$' and '$\supset$' are primitive but '&' is not, $(\pi \& \varphi)$ is read as short for $\sim(\pi \supset \sim\varphi)$. Rules of interpretation must obviously be different too, since they have to be given for each primitive connective; and it turns out to be necessary to change the rules of derivation if the same calculi are to be preserved. But all these changes can be so managed that the same calculi are preserved, i.e. the resulting rules have exactly the same effect as before, in the sense explained on pp. 17–18 (this fact would be very laborious to prove comprehensively). It can also be proved that if we stick to the connectives of the present book or notational variants for them, any choice of primitive connectives from among them must include '$\sim$' together with '&' or '$\vee$' or '$\supset$' (plus, of course, '$\forall$' or '$\exists$', and '$\Box$' or '$\Diamond$') if it is to be adequate for stating the four calculi. There are ways of economising still further in primitive notation (HUGHES & LONDEY pp. 54–5, LEMMON BL p. 74, QUINE $MofL$ p. 18, MASSEY pp. 49–51, 193–4), but they involve connectives with different interpretations from any that I use.

(4) Punctuation. Although brackets are currently the commonest punctuation marks in logic and are used as in 3.2 by LEMMON BL, HUGHES & LONDEY, MATES and MASSEY, two other devices are sometimes found: dots and order. One way of converting brackets into dots, which results in a system similar though not identical to

that of QUINE *MofL* pp. 25–6, is as follows. (a) Number brackets in pairs from the inside outwards, as in:

$$(\forall x(fx \lor ((q \supset fx) \equiv p)) \supset (q \supset p))$$
$$4321123114$$

(b) Excise end brackets, thus:

$$\forall x(fx \lor ((q \supset fx) \equiv p)) \supset (q \supset p$$
$$3211231$$

(c) If any two brackets adjoin, excise that with the lower number, thus:

$$\forall x(fx \lor (q \supset fx) \equiv p) \supset (q \supset p$$
$$32131$$

(d) Replace each remaining bracket by the same number of dots as its number, thus:

$$\forall x:.fx \lor :q \supset fx .\equiv p :. \supset .q \supset p$$

The alternative device of order makes punctuation superfluous by writing each binary connective in front of and not between the two formulae in its scope, thus:

$$\supset \forall x \lor fx \equiv \supset qfxp \supset qp$$

This is the method of the Polish notation given in Appendix One, in which the same formula would appear as:

$C\Pi x A\phi x E C q\phi x p C q p$

In Polish notation scope extends only to the right and the main connective always leads.

(5) There are quite important variations in the formation rule for atomic formulae with leading predicate letter. In QUINE *MofL*, HUGHES & LONDEY (p. 296) and MASSEY (p. 239) the predicate letter must be followed by one or more variables, and subject letters are absent from the logical vocabulary. The corresponding rule in MATES (p. 45) permits both subject letters and variables, separately or mixed. In LEMMON, whom I have followed in this respect, variables can occur in well-formed formulae only when quantified, i.e. bound. But Lemmon's rules differ from mine in another way,

3.6 Other people's rules

by admitting into atomic formulae not only 'a', 'b', 'c' etc. which he calls 'arbitrary names' but also 'm', 'n', 'o' etc. which he calls 'proper names' (LEMMON *BL* pp. 139–40). Hence of the formulae 'fx', '$\forall x fx$', 'fa', 'fm' only the middle two are well-formed in this book, only the first two (ignoring differences of notation) in QUINE *MofL*, HUGHES & LONDEY, and MASSEY, only the first three in MATES, and only the last three in LEMMON *BL*.

The basic difference here is over the question whether to add to the well-formed formulae of 3.2 (which Mates calls 'sentences', p. 45) a set of other well-formed formulae in which variables occur free. If we do admit formulae containing free variables as well-formed, the resulting calculi are likely (but not in MATES) to include derivable sequents such as $\langle\{`\forall x fx`\}, `fx`\rangle$ which have no instances in the calculi since some of their component formulae are fitted only by open sentences, in which no premisses or conclusions are expressible. Similarly the derivable formulae are likely to include formulae fitted only by open sentences. The presence of these drone sequents and formulae does not matter so long as they have working colleagues like $\langle\{`\forall x fx`\}, `fa`\rangle$; but it invites the speculation that we are intended to *identify* the role of free variables with that of subject letters; and in HUGHES & LONDEY and MASSEY, where subject letters are excluded and all admissible letters are described as kinds of variable (propositional, predicate, or 'individual'), it becomes clear that no distinction is intended between the role of schematic or dummy letters on the one hand and of free variables on the other. Massey, following the dummy interpretation, is explicit: "Individual variables may function in either of two quite disparate ways. They may play the role of referring singular terms or they may function as pronouns, that is, as devices for cross-reference" (MASSEY p. 237, cf. HUGHES & LONDEY pp. 290–1). The first function is to belong to free variables, the second to bound. This approach has the advantage of economy in notation, but it is arguably confusing in assigning more than one role to the same letters and certainly complicating at the stage of interpretation and derivation rules. That is why I follow MATES in distinguishing variables from subject letters and LEMMON *BL* in banning free variables from well-formed formulae. But I do not understand, and shall not employ, Lemmon's distinction between 'arbitrary names' and 'proper names'.

(6) It is a surprising and idiosyncratic feature of Hughes & Londey's book that even the most extensive of the many versions of the predicate calculus they discuss, the 'Full Lower Predicate Calculus', does not include among its well-formed formulae all the well-formed formulae of the propositional calculus, and so is not an extension of the propositional calculus in the sense to be explained on p. 193. In fact it includes no such formulae, because it includes no propositional letters (HUGHES & LONDEY pp. 294–6).

(7) A sequent is a set of formulae paired with a formula. It is therefore no more itself a formula than an argument, which could be regarded as a set of propositions paired with a proposition, is itself a proposition. Metalogical abbreviation permits the construction of (metalogical) formulae such as '⟨{'∀xfx'}, 'fa'⟩' to *refer* to sequents, but again the things so referred to are no more themselves formulae than the thing normally referred to by the word 'Napoleon' is itself a word. However it would be possible to conceive sequents quite differently, as themselves a special kind of formulae (what Lemmon calls 'sequent-expressions', *BL* p. 48). The following is a way of doing so: add '→' to the logical notation, and allow commas as an extra mark of logical punctuation; then add to the formation rules the further rule 'for any n and any well-formed formulae $\pi_1, \ldots \pi_n$, φ, $\ulcorner \pi_1, \ldots \pi_n \to \varphi \urcorner$ is a sequent; nothing else is a sequent.' Specimen sequents would be: 'p, $q \to r$', '$\exists xfx$, $\exists xfx$, $\exists xfx \to p$', '$\to \Box \Diamond (p \vee \sim p)$'. The earliest sequent systems, due to GENTZEN (cf. LEBLANC, pp. 10, 30–1), were presented as applying to sequents so conceived; but my method requires fewer derivation rules.

(8) We saw in 3.2 that F∀ can be stated either in terms of substituting into a formula or in terms of filling up a stencil. Just as the latter invites the introduction of metalogical stencil-variables, so the former invites the introduction of a metalogical notation for substituting, which usually looks like this (HUGHES & LONDEY, p. 85, cf. MATES p. 50): '$\pi(\nu/\alpha)$' is short for 'the result of substituting ν for α throughout π'. F∀ cannot be stated exactly in this notation, because of the word 'throughout' in the above definition; but its effect can be captured by 'for any α, ν, and π, if π is well-formed and contains α but not ν, $\forall \nu \pi(\nu/\alpha)$ is well-formed'.

As a further alternative we could adapt an idea of Lemmon's (*BL* p. 143) and define 'propositional function in $\nu_1, \ldots \nu_n$' as short

3.6 Other people's rules

for 'formula containing each of $v_1, \ldots v_n$ free but not bound, which becomes well-formed when subject letters are substituted for $v_1, \ldots v_n$ throughout'. Propositional functions are thus formulae such as '$(gax\ \&\ p)$', well-formed except for occurrences of free variables which do not occur bound elsewhere in them—formulae ready mutilated for grafting to a quantifier. F∀ then becomes: for any π and v, if π is a propositional function in v, $\forall v\pi$ is well-formed. (On the schematic interpretation propositional functions so defined get interpreted as open schemata; on the dummy interpretation as open sentences. For remarks on the history of the expression 'propositional function' see QUINE *MofL* pp. 123, 148).

CHAPTER 4

Interpretation Rules

4.1 Formulating the rules for letters

The rules I adopt are set out in Appendix Two.

Interpretation Rules for each calculus are in two parts, one interpreting the letters, one the connectives. In the propositional calculus the first part merely confirms the propositional (schematic) letters 'p', 'q', etc. in that title, which so far they have enjoyed only by courtesy, and adopts the conventions of 1.2 for fitting sentences to letters. I shall write '**PC**' etc. bold-face to indicate that we are now dealing with the 'semantic' side of the calculi. So the interpretation rules for the PC letters determine when an expression **PC**-fits one of them.

In the predicate calculus with identity the same rules carry over; and in addition the predicate letters, subject letters, and variables are confirmed in their titles and the conventions of 1.2 adopted for fitting expressions to them. So '**QC**-fit' replaces '**PC**-fit'.

S5 has the same rules, at this stage, as **PC**; and QS5 as **QC**.

4.2 Formulating the rules for connectives

The second part of the interpretation rules—covering the predicate-leading construction as well as connectives, and also set out in Appendix Two—introduces the idea of a truth-condition, which must now be explicated. Truth-conditions belong primarily to sentences, and sum up the conditions contributing to a sentence's truth. The contributing conditions are of four kinds. (i) A sentence's truth normally depends on its (conventional) meaning or range of meanings, i.e. on the language to which it belongs or in which it is used. (ii) Sentences also depend for their truth on the context of use, e.g. the speaker, the addressee, the time of utterance, and other such circumstances. For example 'You have read Chapter 1' might be

4.2 Formulating the rules for connectives

true of you but not of your father, in 1979 but not 1978, about Chapter 1 of this book but not of *Pride and Prejudice*. Among these circumstances are the speaker's intentions, especially whether to observe right usage and avoid equivocation. (iii) The truth of some sentences depends on the frame of reference, i.e. domain. As we saw on p. 40, 'All pillarboxes are green' would be true if used in talk about Eire rather than Britain. (iv) The truth of most sentences depends also on the facts—on which is actual among all the possible worlds. Sentences lacking this dependency, e.g. 'It's raining or not raining' in English, can be used to express necessary truths. Worlds, as I invoke them, are independent of languages, contexts and domains: 'is true in world w' will mean 'can be used to express a proposition which would be true given w', not 'could, given w, be used to express a truth'.

Plainly no sentence is true under all conditions (see p. 40) and when one says 'It is true' about some sentence without qualification one must assume certain elided conditions, which would naturally be: right and unequivocal usage, the actual facts, and the context and domain within which the commenting, metalinguistic, sentence 'It is true' is uttered. Or again one might specify some of the relativities, eliding the rest, as in 'It is true today', or 'It would be true if pigs could fly'. The latter will be my procedure in talking about the truth of sentences containing connectives.

We shall need eventually, in Chapter 7, to cross a bridge between the truth of sentences and the truth of propositions. The bridge is: a sentence is true in a language, context, domain and world if and only if it can be used, in that language and context and relative to that domain, to express a proposition which would be true given that world. This serves to explicate 'true sentence' in terms of 'true proposition' or, if you prefer, the other way round. 'Can be used' brings out the fact that sentences do not in general depend for their truth (at a time) on utterance (at that time), let alone on assertion; they can remain true, so to speak, throughout the night.

If we may assume that the first paragraph of this section covers the main conditions contributing to the truth of a sentence, then the conventional meaning of a sentence determines a fairly full specification of the way in which its truth depends on the other conditions. But if truth-conditions are to be used as rules of interpretation, i.e. for revealing meaning, the converse must be assumed also: that some fairly full specification of the way in which a sentence's truth depends on the other conditions determines its conventional meaning. Working to that assumption, which will be examined in 4.4, we shall need to state truth-conditions for sentences in the form 'In a language, context, domain and world of certain kinds, the sentence is true if and only if . . .' where the 'certain kinds' are not too restrictive. An example would be: in any context of right German usage and utterance by some person at some time, any domain including hats, and any world in which pigs could fly, "Mein Hut ist grün" is true if and only if that person's hat would be green at that time if pigs could fly.

None of the connectives will be interpreted as sentences. How then can they have truth-conditions? The answer is that the meaning of each connective will be given by stating truth-conditions not for a single sentence but for the set of all sentences which embed the connective in a certain standard way; and these truth-conditions for sets of sentences are called, in a secondary sense, truth-conditions for the connectives. So the form of rule for a connective will be: in a language, context, domain and world of certain kinds, the result of affixing the connective in a certain way to certain categories of expression is true if and only if . . .', where 'is true' still means 'is a true sentence'.

In the interpretation rules truth-conditions will be accompanied by falsity-conditions, which are not redundant because there might be conditions under which a sentence has both truth-values, or neither. Truth-conditions and falsity-conditions combine into rules of the form 'In a language, context, domain and world of certain kinds, the result of affixing the connective in a certain way to certain categories of expression is true or false according as . . . or—', where the last six words mean 'true if and only if . . ., false if and only if—'. Henceforward I shall speak of these bipartite rules simply as truth-conditions.

A final preliminary. Sets of truth-conditions may be recursive, i.e. may include hypothetical clauses determining the truth-values of sentences in terms of semantic features (including truth-value) of other expressions (including sentences). Only the categorical clauses need to specify truth-values in terms of non-semantic features—e.g. the greenness of a hat rather than the truth of another sentence. But since the connectives, and also the predicate-leading

4.2 Formulating the rules for connectives

construction, are to be introduced as enrichments of natural languages, these categorical clauses are not among the logical interpretation rules, all of which will be hypothetical.

We can now formulate the PC truth-conditions as follows: given (i) any language incorporating the logical language of the propositional calculus, (ii) any context of right and unequivocal usage, (iii) any domain, and (iv) any world, then [T∼] the result of prefixing '∼' to any sentence is true or false in that language, context, domain, and world, according as the sentence itself is false or true in them; and [T&] the result of inserting '&' between any two sentences, the same or different, and enclosing the whole in brackets is true or false in them according as both sentences are true in them or at least one is false, and the other true or false, in them. This rigmarole had better be abbreviated. I shall compress conditions (i) and (ii) into 'in any PC-context' (see p. 49). 'is T' and 'is F' will be short for 'is a true sentence' and 'is a false sentence' respectively. 'σ' and 'τ' will be metalogical variables ranging over sentences; and '∼σ' and '(σ & τ)' will be lazy abbreviations, as in 3.2, for '⌜∼σ⌝' and '⌜(σ & τ)⌝'. Then the rules become: for any σ and τ, in any PC-context, domain, and world, ∼σ is T or F according as σ is F or T; and (σ & τ) is T or F according as σ and τ are both T or one of them is F and the other F or T.

In the predicate calculus with identity T∼ and T& carry over with 'QC-context' in place of 'PC-context'. Three new truth-conditions are added, to interpret '=', '∀' and the predicate-leading construction. This last is intricate, mainly because it needs to be generalised over predicates with any number of places. For one-place predicates it runs: in any QC-context, domain and world, a predicate followed by a subject is T or F according as the subject refers in the context to a member of the domain and the predicate can be used in the context to attribute a property, defined over the domain (see p. 52), which would or would not hold of that member given that world. Notice that the first part of the condition applies to both T and F sentences of the construction; so that if a subject does not succeed, in some context of right and unequivocal usage of a QC-incorporating language, in referring to a member of some domain, or a predicate is not defined over the domain, any predicate-leading sentence containing one of them will be neither T nor F in that context and domain. This feature is to survive generalisation;

I shall comment on it in 9.6, as also on 'attributes a property which holds of'. For two-place predicates the rule is: in any QC-context, domain and world, a predicate followed by two subjects, the same or different, in an order is T or F according as the subjects refer to members of the domain (perhaps the same member) and the predicate can be used to attribute a binary relation, defined over the domain, which given that world would or would not hold between those members in that order. 'Two subjects which are the same' means 'two occurrences of the same subject'. 'Perhaps the same member' takes care of the point that in a context of unequivocal usage occurrences of the same subject must, and occurrences of different subjects may, refer to the same member of the domain. A predicate-leading sentence could well be T in such a co-referring context, because some binary relations hold between a thing and itself; for example being the same size as holds between Paris and itself, or as we may alternatively say, holds of the ordered pair ⟨Paris, Paris⟩. Before generalising it will be useful to introduce the abbreviation 'is true of' for 'can be used to attribute a property/ relation defined over the domain which holds of/between', and similarly 'is false of' for '... which does not hold of/between'. Notice that according to this abbreviation only predicates—linguistic expressions—are true or false of things, whereas properties and relations hold or fail to hold of or between things. Notice too that while one-place predicates are true or false of things simply, two-or-more place predicates are true or false of things in an order. For example in an English context and domain the predicate '... is a city' is true of Paris and false of St Tropez, and the predicate '... is north of—' is true of Paris and St Tropez in that order but not the reverse order. We can now generalise the rule with moderate succinctness over all predicates: [TP] for any positive n, in any QC-context, domain and world, an n-place predicate followed by n subjects, the same or different, in an order is T or F according as the subjects each refer to a member of the domain and the predicate is true or false in that world of those members in that order.

The truth-condition for '=' is: [T=] in any QC-context, domain and world, '=' between two subjects, the same or different, is T or F according as the subjects refer to members of the domain which are the same or different. Thus the truth of an '=' sentence in a context requires the identity of the things referred to in that context

4.2 Formulating the rules for connectives

by the subjects flanking '=', not the identity of those subjects (which are expressions). But where the subjects are identical, the sentence must be T on pain of equivocation.

The truth-condition for '∀' brings in open sentences in some variable v, i.e. expressions (whether predicate-leading or not) in which an n-place predicate is attached to n occurrences of v. The general idea is that ∀v followed by an open sentence in v is T if and only if the result of putting some subject uniformly in place of v in the open sentence is T *whatever* the subject unequivocally—even if wrongly—refers to; e.g. '∀x x is wise' is T if and only if 'Jim is wise' is T no matter which member of the domain 'Jim' refers to. In other words the truth of the resulting closed sentence must survive every uniform change in the referring part of the context, whether or not the change preserves right usage. But there is a proviso: the chosen subject must not already occur in the open sentence. This is because we want such a sentence as '∀x x is the same age as Charles' to share the truth-condition of 'Everything is the same age as Charles', and so to be F even though 'Charles is the same age as Charles' comes out T, in some domains, whatever 'Charles' unequivocally refers to. So the rule is: [T∀] for any variable v, in any QC-context, domain and world, ∀v followed by an open sentence in v is T or F according as the result of replacing v uniformly by some subject not already contained in the open sentence is T in every unequivocal context differing from the QC-context at most as to the reference within that domain of the subject, or F in some such context.

In the two modal calculi 'S5-context' replaces 'PC-context' and 'QS5-context' replaces 'QC-context'; with these changes the same rules carry over as in PC and QC respectively. The single extra rule is: [T□] for any σ in any S5-(QS5-)context, domain and world w, □σ is T or F in w according as σ is T in every world or F in some world. 'is T in every world' means 'can be used to express a proposition which would be true whatever the facts, i.e. to express a necessary truth'. But whether this rule succeeds in making '□' synonymous with the English 'necessarily' is a harder question than may appear; see Chapter 10.

The syntax of the connectives, in that unrefined sense in which syntax assigns expressions to parts of speech or categories, is easily deduced from the truth-conditions. '&', for example, always joins two sentences, one or both of which may be an open sentence when '&' falls within the scope of '∀', and it always makes a sentence out of them, open or closed. The important part of this syntactical information is that '&' between two sentences makes a sentence: it is, when it operates on (closed) sentences, a *binary sentence-forming operator*. Inspection of the other truth-conditions will show that all the connectives, and the predicate-leading construction, are sentence-forming in the following ways:

4.2 (1) Any *n*-place predicate followed by *n* subjects makes a sentence; '=' between two subjects makes a sentence; if σ and τ are sentences, so are ∼σ, (σ & τ), □σ; if *v* is a variable, ∀*v* followed by an open sentence in *v* makes a sentence.

4.3 *Formulae into schemata*

The notation introduced in Chapter 3 was uninterpreted. Interpretation seeks to convert it into an instrument for testing arguments. The rules of 4.1 and 4.2 effect this conversion by means of two consequences: they ensure that all well-formed formulae of PC, QC, S5 and QS5 are schemata or sentences, and they come near enough to fixing and revealing the meanings of the connectives. This section establishes the former consequence.

Let us start by considering those well-formed formulae which are in primitive notation and also contain a letter from one or more of the groups called, at first only by courtesy, 'propositional', 'predicate', and 'subject'. The schematic interpretation confirms the titles, and so demonstrates that such well-formed formulae will be interpreted as schematic in some way. But whether they are schemata, i.e. sentence-schemata, will clearly depend on the interpretation of the connectives. For example if '&' meant 'therefore', '*p* & *q*' would be an inference-schema. We can advance one step further by reflecting on the syntax of the connectives, given in 4.2 (1). Since '&' makes sentences out of sentences it will make (sentence-) schemata out of (sentence-) schemata, and in general it follows from 4.2 (1) that

4.3 (1) any predicate letter followed by one or more subject letters makes a schema; '=' between two subject letters makes a

4.3 Formulae into schemata

schema; if π and φ are schemata, so are $\sim\pi$, $(\pi \mathbin{\&} \varphi)$, $\Box\pi$; if ν is a variable, $\forall\nu$ followed by an open schema in ν makes a schema.

From 4.3 (1) we can tell straight away that '$(p \mathbin{\&} q)$' is a schema, since 4.1 has already interpreted 'p' and 'q' as schematic letters marking places for sentences, and such letters are schemata. But we cannot yet tell whether more complex formulae such as '$\forall x f x \mathbin{\&} (p \mathbin{\&} q)$' are schemata. In order to prove the generalisation over all well-formed formulae, in the majority group, I shall use an argument by what is known as strong mathematical induction, and I shall go through the argument carefully, because there will be several crucial proofs by strong induction later in the book (especially 7.4, 7.5). We start by ordering all well-formed formulae according to the number of symbols they contain (it matters that there are none of infinite length, but not that many share the same length). The principle of strong induction, which is used but not proved in the argument (see pp. 266–9), holds that the conclusion wanted will follow from an intermediate conclusion, namely: for any n, if all well-formed formulae of length less than n are sentence-schemata, so are all of length n (thus the thought behind the principle is that if wherever you start, even at the nil length, you always get a schema at the next step, then you always get a schema). Since this intermediate conclusion is general and hypothetical, its proof proceeds by *taking* a length of formula, *supposing* (the 'inductive supposition' or 'induction hypothesis') that all well-formed formulae of less than that length are schemata, and *showing* that it follows regardless of the length chosen that all well-formed formulae of that length are schemata.

The proof is carried out in stages, relying at each stage on what the formation rules tell us about well-formed formulae and what the interpretation rules tell us about symbols. The inductive supposition is only needed in the later stages. First, we must notice that by the extremal formation rules every well-formed formula in primitive notation either (a) is a propositional letter or (b) is an atomic formula containing a predicate letter or (c)–(e) has a primitive main connective. If any primitive well-formed formula of the chosen length falls under case (a), it is a schema by the interpretation of propositional letters. If any primitive well-formed formula of the chosen length falls under case (b), 4.3 (1) shows that it is a schema provided that its first component is a predicate letter and its others subject letters; and they are by the interpretation. As regards primitive well-formed formulae falling under the other cases we must consider each connective in turn. (c) If a well-formed formula of the chosen length has '=' for its main connective, 4.3 (1) shows that it is a schema provided that its component letters are subject letters; and they are by the interpretation. (d) If its main connective is '∀', 4.3 (1) shows that it is a schema provided that its first component is a variable and its second an open schema in that variable. Its first component is a variable by the interpretation. Its second component has two features: (i) it contains a schematic letter (for we are assuming still that the formula as a whole does); and (ii) it is a propositional function in the variable (pp. 84–5), i.e. it becomes well-formed when a subject letter is substituted for each occurrence of the variable. But the formula produced by such substitution is the same length as the propositional function and so shorter than the original formula, which prefixed '∀' and a variable. It is also well-formed. Hence by the inductive supposition, which here comes into play for the first time, it is a schema. Hence the propositional function (i) contains a schematic letter and (ii) results from a (closed) schema by substituting variables for subject letters; and this makes it an open schema. (e) Finally if a primitive well-formed formula of the chosen length has some other main connective, 4.3 (1) shows that it is a schema provided that its component formula or formulae are schemata; and they are by the inductive supposition, because they are well-formed and shorter than it. This completes the survey of cases and so proves the intermediate conclusion, whence it follows by the (assumed) principle of strong induction that all well-formed formulae which contain a schematic letter and are in primitive notation are schemata.

It remains to extend this result to well-formed formulae in primitive notation that contain no schematic letters, and to well-formed formulae not in primitive notation. The former can be formed in only one way, out of sub-formulae whose only connectives are '=' together with '∀'. As might be expected they come out as sentences not schemata under the interpretation rules. They cannot, therefore, be fitted by sentences in the sense introduced in 1.2. But it is useful to extend that sense in the following way. We count sen-

4.3 Formulae into schemata

tences as the limiting case of schemata, and say that every schema of the limiting kind is fitted just by itself. A consequence of this will be that the formula '$\forall x(x = x)$', for example, has as its sole QC-instance and QS5-instance, relative to a domain, the proposition that every member of the domain is identical with itself. This extension in the sense of 'schema' allows clause (d) of the induction to cover such cases.

Finally, each well-formed formula in non-primitive notation abbreviates a well-formed formula in primitive notation, and therefore, by the induction, abbreviates a schema; and what abbreviates a schema is a schema.

4.4 Truth-conditions and meaning

If truth-conditions are going to amount to interpretation rules, they must both fix and reveal meaning.

Certainly not all truth-conditions reveal meaning. For example the rule '⌜σ and τ⌝ is T if and only if σ is T and τ is T' cannot be informative in that formulation, since its right hand side uses, and so relies on prior understanding of, the very construction it seeks to interpret—'and' between sentences. But the rules of 4.2 avoid this defect, by keeping the language of interpretation, the metalanguage, free of symbols from the language to be interpreted, the object language.

Truth-conditions for sentences do not always fix meaning. For example the sentence 'If it's raining, it's raining' is T in unequivocal English under all conditions, F under none. Yet that fact does not distinguish it in meaning from any other sentence in which a necessary truth is expressible, e.g. 'Two plus two equals four', and so does not fix its meaning. Truth-conditions for connectives protect themselves to some extent from this defect by taking sentences in sets. But the protection is insufficient. For example the English expression 'and two plus two equals four and' shares the truth-condition of 'and' when put between sentences, viz. making a T sentence when flanked by two T sentences, an F sentence when flanked by T or F sentences at least one of which is F. Yet presumably the expression differs in meaning from 'and'. Admittedly this difference might be exposed by other truth-conditions, forming together a *theory* of truth. It has been suggested by Davidson that although truth-conditions do not all fix meaning individually, still "a theory of truth shows how we can go from truth to something like meaning" (DAVIDSON *DCT* p. 84, cf. *T&M* p. 9). Even so we do not get all the way. For example 'but' and 'and', between sentences, surely differ in English meaning; yet replacement of one by the other seems to affect appropriateness or felicity rather than truth, and it is hard to see how any truth-conditions could expose it. Such examples caused Frege to distinguish two aspects of meaning, sense ('Sinn') and tone ('Beleuchtung', 'Färbung', DUMMETT p. 2), only the former of which is fixed by truth-conditions.

Interpretation rules for the connectives can deal with tone in one of two ways: either by adding a rider that the connectives have no tone (cf. HUGHES & LONDEY p. 20 on '$\supset$': "We are not concerned with or attempting to represent anything but material implication"), or by leaving tone, and so meaning, unfixed. Both solutions acknowledge the quite serious limitations of expressive power in logical languages. For example '&' differs from 'but' and 'and' not only in its more restricted syntax (it must join open or closed sentences) but also in its inability to convey the adversative tone of the former or the suggestion of temporal succession sometimes present in the latter (STRAWSON *ILT* p. 80). Likewise '$\forall$' cannot express the suggestion of 'severally' present in 'the general addressed each of the soldiers' but absent from 'the general addressed all the soldiers'. These examples could be multiplied.

The latter of the two solutions, ignoring tone, weakens the claim of logical interpretation rules to interpret: they leave one aspect of meaning unfixed. In communication this would matter. But our purpose is the more limited one of testing arguments by translating into symbols (cf. FREGE *BS* p. 3: "in my formalised language ... only that part of judgments which affects the *possible inferences* is taken into consideration"), and for that purpose knowledge of truth-conditions suffices, as I shall now show through a representative example. Suppose that 'and' in English has the same truth-condition as '&' in some logical language l, and suppose that we construct a variant of l in which 'and' is substituted for '&', leaving this truth-condition constant (thus the variant logical language is permitted, for the nonce, to contain a word as well as symbols). Then take two sequents, one containing '&', the other resulting from it by substitution of 'and'. The crucial fact, which will become

4.4 Truth-conditions and meaning

obvious in Chapter 7, is that *validity* turns only on truth-conditions. Because of that fact the '&'-sequent will be l-valid if and only if the 'and'-sequent is valid in l's variant; that is, all l-instances of the one will have premisses which strictly imply their conclusions if and only if all l-variant-instances of the other do. Now although this does not entail that every l-variant-instance of the 'and'-sequent is an l-instance of the '&'-sequent, it does nevertheless show that acceptance of that conclusion will *not lead us astray* in a test of correctness: treating some argument as an instance of the one sequent will certify it as correct if and only if treating it as an instance of the other would also so certify it. Hence we can safely say of any argument that it is an instance of, i.e. expressible in sentences fitting, the '&'-sequent if it is an instance of, i.e. expressible in sentences fitting, the 'and'-sequent; and therefore that it is expressible with '&' if expressible with 'and', provided only that '&' and 'and' have the same truth-condition. Other purposes call for other standards of accuracy in translation, and sameness of meaning is normally a part of the ideal. But in logic sameness of truth-condition suffices. It therefore does not matter if we are left ignorant of the tone of logical connectives, or if, as might happen under the first solution, we know that their tone differs from that of the English words they supplant.

4.5 Pure semantics

Logical interpretation rules are often presented in terms which stick more closely than 4.1 and 4.2 to the language of mathematics, and such presentation is called formal or pure semantics, or model theory. Although the important thing for the purposes of this book is to get the logical symbols interpreted, not to dress the interpretation in mathematical clothes, there are two reasons for introducing pure semantics in the present section: many other elementary text-books, e.g. MASSEY and MATES, make at least a bow in its direction, and an extension of its concepts will provide the easiest, though a roundabout, way of proving soundness in Chapter 7.

In two respects pure semantics differs strikingly from the formulations of 4.1 and 4.2: it deals with well-formed formulae not sentences, and it introduces the notion of a 'valuation' which itself stands in need of explication. Because of this latter feature the initial statement of formal semantics for a calculus is quite abstract, and does not reveal the functions of the symbols at all.

We are to consider structures consisting of three items, a domain (only needed for QC and QS5), a set of worlds (only needed for S5 and QS5) and a valuation. Such a structure is sometimes called a model (HUGHES & CRESSWELL pp. 72, 146) but that word is used in a different sense by MASSEY (p. 248) and MATES (p. 60). A **valuation,** or value-assignment, in each model is a set of elements, and each element must be of one of the following kinds: (i) an ordered pair pairing a subject letter with a member of the model's domain, (ii) an ordered pair pairing a predicate letter with a set of ordered sets, each consisting of members of the domain followed by one world from the model's set of worlds, or (iii) an ordered triple grouping a well-formed formula, a truth-value, and a world from the set of worlds. In PC and S5 we need only elements of the last kind, since there are no subject letters or predicate letters, and in PC and QC the elements are simplified by the excision of worlds. The effect of these general requirements is that a valuation consists of elements each of which pairs a subject letter with a member of the domain, or a predicate letter with a property or relation conceived as a set of ordered sets of members of the domain (perhaps relative to a world), or a well-formed formula with a truth value (perhaps relative to a world). The items so paired with letters and formulae are called **values** of the letters and formulae under the valuation.

Valuations must meet three other conditions, two general and one special to each calculus. The first general condition is that in each valuation no two values may compete for the same letter or formula: for example a valuation may contain the elements $\langle \text{`}a\text{'}, \text{Napoleon}\rangle$ and $\langle \text{`}b\text{'}, \text{Wellington}\rangle$, or $\langle \text{`}a\text{'}, \text{Napoleon}\rangle$ and $\langle \text{`}b\text{'}, \text{Napoleon}\rangle$ but not $\langle \text{`}a\text{'}, \text{Napoleon}\rangle$ and $\langle \text{`}a\text{'}, \text{Wellington}\rangle$. Without this requirement a valuation would already be, in set-theoretic terms, a relation (set of ordered sets); with it, it becomes that kind of relation which is called a function. Because valuations are functions the usual metalogical symbolism for stating that $\langle \text{`}a\text{'}, \text{Napoleon}\rangle$ or $\langle \text{`}p\text{'},$ truth, this world$\rangle$ is an element of some valuation v is 'v(`$a$') = Napoleon' or 'v(`p', this world) = truth'; notice that ' = ' is here a metalogical symbol. The second general condition is that valuations in a model must be complete, in the sense that they pair values with every well-formed formula and letter, except variables, in the

4.5 Pure semantics

logical language and if necessary relative to every world in the model's set of worlds; so they are infinite functions which, in set-theoretic language, map the set of well-formed formulae and letters (sometimes formula-world pairs and letter-world pairs) onto a set of values. Thirdly, a valuation belongs to a particular calculus (is a PC-valuation etc.) by conforming to the value rules of the calculus. The value rules, which correspond to the truth-conditions of 4.2, are as follows (I use 'v' and 'v_1', 'w' and 'w_1' and 'δ' as metalogical variables ranging over valuations, worlds and predicate letters respectively, '1' and '0' as metalogical abbreviations for 'truth' and 'falsity', and 'iff' for 'if and only if'):

PC For any PC-formulae π and φ and PC-valuation v, $v(\pi) = 1$ or 0 and

V∼ $v(\sim\pi) = 1$ iff $v(\pi) = 0$
V& $v((\pi\ \&\ \varphi)) = 1$ iff $v(\pi) = v(\varphi) = 1$

QC For any $a, a_1, \ldots a_n, \beta, v, \delta, \phi$ containing no a or v, QC-formulae π, φ, QC-valuation v and domain, $v(\pi) = 1$ or 0, $v(a)$ is a member of the domain, for some positive n $v(\delta)$ is a set of ordered sets each containing n members of the domain (the same or different), and

V∼ and V& as in PC
VP $v(\delta a_1, \ldots a_n) = 1$ iff $\langle v(a_1), \ldots v(a_n)\rangle$ is a member of $v(\delta)$
V= $v(a = \beta) = 1$ iff $v(a) = v(\beta)$
V∀ $v(\forall v \phi v) = 1$ iff $v_1(\phi a) = 1$ for all v_1 which differ from v at most in pairing some other member of the domain with a.

S5 For any S5-formulae π and φ, world w in a set of worlds, and S5-valuation v, $v(\pi, w) = 1$ or 0 and

V∼ $v(\sim\pi, w) = 1$ iff $v(\pi, w) = 0$
V& $v((\pi\ \&\ \varphi), w) = 1$ iff $v(\pi, w) = v(\varphi, w) = 1$
V□ $v(\Box\pi, w) = 1$ iff $v(\pi, w_1) = 1$ for all worlds w_1 in the set.

QS5 For any $a, a_1, \ldots a_n, \beta, v, \delta, \phi$ containing no a or v, QS5-formulae π, φ, world w in a set of worlds, QS5-valuation v and domain, $v(\pi, w) = 1$ or 0, $v(a)$ is a member of the domain, for some positive n $v(\delta)$ is a set of ordered sets each containing n members of the domain (the same or different) followed by one world from the set of worlds, and

$V\sim$, $V\&$ and $V\square$ as in $S5$
VP $v(\delta a_1, \ldots a_n, w) = 1$ iff $\langle v(a_1), \ldots v(a_n), w\rangle$ is a member of $v(\delta)$
$V=$ $v(\alpha = \beta, w) = 1$ iff $v(\alpha) = v(\beta)$
$V\forall$ $v(\forall\nu\phi\nu, w) = 1$ iff $v_1(\phi a, w) = 1$ for all v_1 which differ from v at most in pairing some other member of the domain with a.

'Differs from v' is shorthand for 'differs from v in its pairings with letters'. Notice that in QS5 $V=$ alone makes no provision for pairing different values with a formula relative to different worlds in a single valuation; see HUGHES & CRESSWELL pp. 192–6.

Each valuation can be thought of as constructed in two stages. It starts with an *initial* assignment pairing every letter (except variables) with a truth value or member of the domain or set of ordered sets of members of the domain as appropriate, perhaps relative to every world in the set of worlds; and then it *extends* the initial assignment to all well-formed formulae by the rules $V\sim$ etc.

How do these value rules tie in with the truth-conditions of 4.2? One notable difference is that even if the pure semantics tells us that '1' means 'truth' and '0' means 'falsity', it explains 'valuation' only through truth-conditions of the metalogical sentences that result from '$v(\pi)$ = truth' and '$v(\pi)$ = falsity' by putting designations of a well-formed formula for 'π' and a valuation for 'v'. We saw in 1.14 that, although truth-conditions can in principle reveal meaning, these ones cannot reveal both the meaning of 'valuation' and the meanings of the connectives at one and the same time. Hence the value rules cannot interpret the connectives until '1', '0' and 'valuation' (and also, if necessary, 'domain' and 'world') are independently explicated—until, that is, the pure semantics is converted into applied semantics. The simplest satisfactory conversion for PC explicates a pairing of 1 (or 0) to a formula π as a declaration that π is synonymous with some T (or F) sentence (MASSEY p. 25). So construed the value rules would presuppose that formulae had been interpreted as sentences, not formulae.

4.5 *Pure semantics*

To fit in with a schematic interpretation of the logical letters, and also to accommodate contexts and domains and worlds, a pairing of 1 (or 0) to a formula must be a replacement of the formula by a T (or F) sentence, that accords with the PC fitting conventions, in a PC-context and domain and world. Then V$\sim$, for example, cashes out as follows: in any replacement that accords with the PC fitting conventions, of PC-formulae by T or F sentences in a PC-context and domain and world, $\sim\pi$ is replaced by a T sentence if and only if π is replaced by an F sentence.

V$\sim$ so explicated still differs from T$\sim$ because it applies to formulae not sentences. But the effect is the same. By the PC fitting conventions every sentence PC-fits a PC-formula, and by the value rules so explicated every PC-formula is PC-fitted by a sentence. Hence for every sentence σ there is a replacement in accord with the PC fitting conventions which replaces $\sim\pi$ by $\sim\sigma$ and π by σ, for some PC-formula π; and conversely for any PC-formula π there is some such replacement and sentence σ. This sameness of effect has a more general application. A simpler way of stating the explicated version of V$\sim$ is as follows: in any PC-context and domain and world, any sentence PC-fitting $\sim\pi$ is T or F according as the *corresponding* sentence PC-fitting π is F or T, where the sentence corresponding to the first is the result of lopping '$\sim$' off the first, i.e. the one which stands to the first as π stands to $\sim\pi$. In general therefore the device of using the word 'corresponding' enables us, if we wish, to state truth-conditions in terms of schemata rather than sentences. The device could even be extended to propositions: we might have stated T$\sim$ without preliminaries as to context and domain in the form 'a PC-instance of $\sim\pi$ would be true or false given any world according as the corresponding PC-instance of π would be false or true given that world', where 'corresponding PC-instance of π' means 'proposition expressible in the same PC-context and domain in the corresponding sentence PC-fitting π' (cf. STRAWSON *ILT* p. 30 footnote, p. 67).

In QC the pairing relation in a valuation becomes more variegated because it can also hold between subject letters and things, and between predicate letters and sets of ordered sets of things. If we were aiming, like MASSEY and MATES, at an interpretation of letters as dummies, we could explicate 'v(α) = Napoleon' as 'in v α is declared synonymous with some subject which can be used to refer to Napoleon' and 'v(δ) = the set in which each mother is paired once with each of her children' as 'in v δ is declared synonymous with some predicate true just of mother-child pairs in that order'. It is important to notice that the explications of the pairing relation are not the same in these cases, and not the same as for the propositional case. There the explication brought in sentences, here subjects and predicates. It seems reasonable to say that in this applied semantics the metalogical word 'valuation' gets interpreted as ambiguous. So it does in the explication which goes with schematic letters: 'is declared synonymous with' gives way to 'is replaced by', and a QC-valuation (in a domain) is a replacement that accords with the QC fitting conventions, in a QC-context and world (and that domain). Then the QC truth-conditions of 4.2 result, but adapted to QC-formulae and letters.

Similarly an S5-valuation (in a world) is a replacement that accords with the S5 fitting conventions, in an S5-context and domain (and that world); and a QS5-valuation (in a domain and world) is a replacement that accords with the QS5 fitting conventions in a QS5-context (and that domain and world).

4.6 Metatheorems on truth

We saw in 3.3 that it is not quite obvious whether the definitions of non-primitive connectives serve to make formulae containing them well-formed. But indubitably they do serve to interpret the non-primitive connectives. The process is familiar from ordinary language-learning: by explaining that one word or construction is short for others we teach the meaning of the former to anyone who already understands the latter. Without definitions the symbols '$\vee$', '$\supset$', '$\equiv$', '$\exists$' '$\Diamond$' could be assigned any truth-conditions we pleased, but given the definitions their truth-conditions are fixed by those of the primitive connectives defining them. How they are fixed will now be shown by proving them as metatheorems, starting with '$\vee$'.

Take a PC-context, domain and world, and sentences σ and τ, and suppose that σ and τ are each T or F in that context, domain and world. There are four permutations of truth and falsity between σ and τ. Case (i): σ and τ are both T. Then by T$\sim$ $\sim\sigma$ and $\sim\tau$ are both F; so by T& ($\sim\sigma$ & $\sim\tau$) is F; so by T$\sim$ $\sim(\sim\sigma$ & $\sim\tau$) is T.

4.6 *Metatheorems on truth*

But the formula '$\sim(\sim p\ \&\ \sim q)$' shortens to '$(p \lor q)$', and since these formulae are schemata for sentences it follows that any sentence $\sim(\sim\sigma\ \&\ \sim\tau)$ shortens to $(\sigma \lor \tau)$; so $\sigma \lor \tau$ is T. Case (ii): σ is T and τ is F. Then by T$\sim$ $\sim\sigma$ is F and $\sim\tau$ is T; so by T& $(\sim\sigma\ \&\ \sim\tau)$ is F; so by T$\sim$ $\sim(\sim\sigma\ \&\ \sim\tau)$ is T; so again $\sigma \lor \tau$ is T. Case (iii): σ is F and τ is T. This works out just like the previous case; again $\sigma \lor \tau$ is T. Case (iv): σ and τ are both F. Then by T$\sim$ $\sim\sigma$ and $\sim\tau$ are both T; so by T& $(\sim\sigma\ \&\ \sim\tau)$ is T; so by T$\sim$ $\sim(\sim\sigma\ \&\ \sim\tau)$ is F; so $\sigma \lor \tau$ is F. Putting the four cases together we come out with the following truth-condition: [T$\lor$] for any σ and τ, in any PC-context, domain and world, $\sigma \lor \tau$ is T or F according as at least one of σ and τ is T (and the other T or F) or both are F.

It is helpful to represent the above argument in a diagram called a (generalised) **truth-table**. Start by supposing, tacitly, some PC-context, domain and world. List in rows the four permutations of truth and falsity between sentences σ and τ (or it could be done through formulae, following the suggestion in 4.5). Then use the truth-conditions for '$\sim$' and '&' to compute in successive columns the T-or-F ratings, in the supposed context, of the complex parts of $\sim(\sim\sigma\ \&\ \sim\tau)$. Finally transfer those ratings to the abbreviation $\sigma \lor \tau$. Thus:

σ	τ	$\sim\sigma$	$\sim\tau$	$(\sim\sigma\ \&\ \sim\tau)$	$\sim(\sim\sigma\ \&\ \sim\tau)$	$\sigma \lor \tau$
T	T	F	F	F	T	T
T	F	F	T	F	T	T
F	T	T	F	F	T	T
F	F	T	T	T	F	F

The above truth-table displays a metalogical argument whose conclusion, a metatheorem, can be recorded on its own in a diagram taking either of the following forms:

σ	τ	$\sigma \lor \tau$
T	T	T
T	F	T
F	T	T
F	F	F

	$\sigma \lor \tau$	τ T F
σ	T	T T
	F	T F

Such a diagrammatic representation of a truth-condition is called a **matrix** (LEMMON *BL* p. 65, 'basic truth table' HUGHES & LONDEY p. 33): obviously it is available for recording primitive and non-primitive truth-conditions alike. I shall not go through the arguments which prove the truth-conditions of '⊃' and '≡', given 4.2 and the definitions. Instead I sum up the **PC** interpretation rules by presenting the truth-conditions for all five PC connectives, primitive and non-primitive, in matrices:

T∨, T⊃, T≡ and others

σ	$\sim\sigma$		σ	τ	$\sigma \& \tau$	$\sigma \vee \tau$	$\sigma \supset \tau$	$\sigma \equiv \tau$
T	F		T	T	T	T	T	T
F	T		T	F	F	T	F	F
			F	T	F	T	T	F
			F	F	F	F	T	T

Each connective, when it is interpreted in these ways, gives a name to formulae (or sometimes sentences) having it as their main connective: for any well-formed formulae π and φ, $\sim\pi$ is called a negation, ($\pi \& \varphi$) a conjunction, ($\pi \vee \varphi$) a disjunction (or alternation, QUINE *MofL* p. 10; but HUGHES & LONDEY p. 33 use 'alternation' in another sense), ($\pi \supset \varphi$) a material conditional, and ($\pi \equiv \varphi$) a material biconditional. In 2.13 some of these names, 'negation', 'conjunction', and 'material conditional', were applied to propositions, but not in quite the same sense: formulae and sentences are negations etc. in virtue of containing a certain symbol which has been given a certain truth-condition, whereas propositions are negations etc. *of* other propositions in virtue of the *possibility* of expressing the former in sentences which affix those symbols to sentences expressing the latter.

Matrices are available as a way of presenting truth-conditions because of a feature which is peculiar to PC connectives, that they are interpreted as **truth-functional**. This means that the truth or falsity, in a context, of any sentence having one of them as its main connective is a function of (is determined by) the truth or falsity, in that context, of its remaining parts. In the other calculi interpretation rules still determine truth and falsity: so a right hand column of

4.6 Metatheorems on truth

'T's and 'F's could be constructed for each connective if only a eft hand column could. But the condition is not met, because truth and falsity are no longer determined *by* the truth and falsity of parts but by, for example, a sentence's being true-in-every-world or a predicate's being true of something. It follows that the arguments proving truth-conditions for the non-primitive connectives '∃' and '◇' cannot be displayed in generalised truth-tables, and we shall have to return to prose.

For '∃' the proof is this. Take a QC-context, domain and world, an open sentence in some variable v, and the closed sentence which results from it when v is uniformly replaced by some subject not already contained in it. There are two cases to consider: (i) ∃v followed by the open sentence is T in the context, domain and world; (ii) it is F in them. Since the argument is quite long it will save space to take the two cases jointly, bracketing the second. By Def∃ ∼∀v∼ followed by the open sentence is T(F). So by T∼ ∀v∼ followed by the open sentence is F(T). So by T∀ '∼' followed by the closed sentence, with subject in place of v, is F in some (T in all) unequivocal contexts differing from the QC-context at most as to the reference within the domain of the subject. So by T∼ again the closed sentence itself is T in some (F in all) such differing contexts. This shows that if ∃v followed by the open sentence is T(F), the closed sentence is T in some (F in all) such differing contexts. But the same joint argument works in the reverse direction too; so we can add 'and only if'. The metatheorem thus proved is: [T∃] for any v, in any QC-context, domain and world, ∃v followed by an open sentence in v is T or F according as the result of replacing v uniformly by some subject not already contained in the open sentence is T in some unequivocal context differing from the QC-context at most as to the reference within that domain of the subject, or F in every such context.

Proof of the truth-condition for '◇' is along similar lines. Take an S5-(QS5-) context, domain and world, and a sentence σ, and suppose that ◇σ is T(F) in that context, domain and world. By Def◇ ∼□∼σ is T(F) in them. So by T∼ □∼σ is F(T). So by T□ ∼σ is F in some world (T in every world). So by T∼ σ is T in some world (F in every world). The joint argument works in the reverse direction too. So the truth-condition is: [T◇] for any sentence σ, ◇σ is T or F in any S5-(QS5-) context, domain and world according as σ is T in some world or F in every world, in that context and domain.

4.7 Other people's rules

I shall discuss seven ways in which other people's interpretation rules differ significantly from those of 4.1 and 4.2.

(1) Although we have seen in 2.5 that the use of formulae to reveal form is little affected by interpretation of letters as dummies rather than schematic, still that alternative has repercussions on 4.3 and 4.5. The proof that all well-formed formulae turn out as schematic will be replaced by a proof that they turn out as sentences, mostly with unfixed meanings. The model-theoretic language in 'v('p') = 1', 'v('a') = Napoleon' and the like will accordingly have to be fleshed out in terms of meaning not fitting, e.g. as 'in v 'p' is declared synonymous with some sentence which is T' and 'in v 'a' is declared synonymous with some subject which can be used to refer to Napoleon'. This accounts for the use in MATES (pp. 54–6) and MASSEY (p. 19 note) of the word 'interpretation' as an alternative to 'assignment' or 'valuation': pairings of values with a formula are explicated as interpretations if they are explicated as fixing *ad hoc* meanings to the formula's constituent letters. Interpretations, in this usage, are not determined by the interpretation rules; rather those rules, by interpreting (in one sense) letters as expressions of unfixed meaning, deliberately leave us free to interpret (in the new sense) each such expression on each occasion of its use. Hence interpreting letters and interpreting connectives become less alike in one way, more alike in another; less alike because only connective-interpretation is the business of the interpretation *rules*, more alike because in both cases to interpret is to assign a meaning (whereas the interpretation rules for letters, whether they make them schematic or dummies, do not assign them meanings).

(2) The word 'interpretation' is subject to further vagaries. According to QUINE (*MofL* p. 29) "by interpretation of the letter '*p*' (or '*q*' etc.) may be meant specification of an actual [indicative sentence] which is to be imagined in place of the letter". Here letters are schematic and 'interpreting' them is replacing them by sentences or other expressions which fit them. So when QUINE says

4.7 Other people's rules

(*MofL* p. 35) that a truth-functional schema is called valid "if it comes out true under every interpretation of its letters" he means 'if every T or F sentence PC-fitting it is T' which, restricted to eternal sentences and generalised over PC-contexts, domains and worlds, holds just when it is PC-valid in the sense of 2.13 (3); see 7.1. In Mates 'true under all interpretations' for 'valid' more nearly means what it seems to say, but still not quite. No formula is true under *all* interpretations: e.g. '$P \supset P$' is not T in a language in which 'P' abbreviates 'Paris' and '$\supset$' means 'is larger than'. Rather the sense is ' "$P \supset P$" is true under all l-interpretations' where l is some logical language containing T $\supset$ and the convention that 'P' abbreviates sentences, so that all that remains for an 'l-interpretation' to do is to specify which sentence 'P' abbreviates.

(3) Interpretation rules stated in the manner of the pure semantics of 4.5 are sometimes left in a perilously abstract state, through failure to explicate 'valuation', 'domain' and 'world'. There is nothing objectionable about such abstract semantics as a subject of mathematical study; it constitutes a kind of logistic system in which relations are explored not between formulae or sequents but between ordered pairs (or triples) each joining a formula and a value (and a world). It is even possible, and from this mathematical point of view desirable, to get by without identifying any of the values, and in particular without indicating that '1' and '0' are to abbreviate 'truth' and 'falsity'. But abstract semantics is not yet semantics at all, since metalogical formulae like '$v(\pi) = 1$' can only serve to interpret the connectives if the metalogical word 'valuation' and the metalogical symbol '1' have themselves been first explicated.

(4) One possible way of explicating '$v('p') = 1$' would be 'in v 'p' is declared to be a name of truth', and another similar way would be 'in v 'p' is replaced by a name of truth'. The temptation to regard the values of every logical letter as things named by the letter, or named by expressions replacing it, comes from the treatment of functions in mathematics. We have seen on p. 98 that when a binary relation is such that nothing has it to more than one thing it is called a (unary) function: squaring to, or having for a square, is an example among numbers, since the square—unlike the square root—of each number is unique. We can form a name or

designation of the second thing by taking a 'functor' or 'function sign' (cf. p. 255, MATES p. 158) such as '_^{2}' and fitting into its gap a name of the first thing; for example since 9 is the (only) square of 3 the expression '3^2' can be used as a name of 9 (and of no other number; so can '$(-3)^2$' be used as a name of 9 and of no other number). Function-signs are thus subject-forming operators on subjects. Frege suggested that we might regard truth-functional sentence-connectives as a species of function-sign, forming names of truth-values from names of truth-values. The mathematician says that x^2 has the 'value' 9 for the 'argument' 3, and $x - y$ has the 'value' 5 for the 'arguments' 7 and 2 in that order, i.e. for $\langle 7, 2 \rangle$; just so Frege proposed to say that '(p & q)' has the value truth for the argument $\langle$truth, truth$\rangle$ (this is how the expression 'truth-value' originated). It is then a short step to the notation 'if p = T and q = T, p & q = T', which looks like one row in the truth table of 'p & q' (LEMMON *BL* p. 65). But there is a high price to pay for this assimilation. Sentence-connectives form sentences out of sentences; so they can be a species of function-signs, forming subjects out of subjects, only if sentences are a species of subjects— in particular they will be, according to Frege's suggestion, names of truth and falsity. Once out in the open the suggestion is seen to be wrong: if 'Men eat frogs' were a name of truth, then 'Men eat frogs is stranger than fiction' should be a way of saying that truth is stranger than fiction, but it is not even grammatical. So we must reject notations like 'p = 1' as ungrammatical, and we must be careful to explicate 'v('p') = 1' not as 'in v 'p' is (replaced by) a sentence naming truth' but rather as 'in v 'p' is (replaced by) a sentence possessing truth, i.e. a T sentence' (see PRIOR, *OT* pp. 30–1). Hence the contrast stressed in 4.5 between 'v('p') = 1' and 'v('a') = Napoleon'; the latter does get explicated as 'in v 'a' is replaced by a name of Napoleon', because 'a' is to be interpreted as a subject letter replaceable by subjects not sentences. Hence too any attempt to find the same relation expressed in ' 'p' is paired with truth' as in ' 'a' is paired with Napoleon' will conflict with the intention to connect 'a' and 'p' with expressions belonging to exclusive grammatical categories. Such conflict is threatened by MATES' claim (p. 55) that sentence letters 'stand for' or 'denote' truth-values, and by MASSEY'S claim (pp. 25–6) that truth-values are the 'referents' of sentences.

4.7 Other people's rules

(5) In mathematical usage values are non-linguistic entities—numbers, truth-values, people etc. But logicians who follow the schematic interpretation without much mathematical apparatus sometimes treat values as linguistic entities, namely as those expressions which replace schematic letters when sentences are formed out of schemata. HUGHES & LONDEY, for example, write "We can get a proposition from 'if p, then q' only by replacing 'p' and 'q' by propositions ... 'p' is said to take propositions as values" (p. 2); and here, it seems, 'proposition' must mean 'indicative sentence' since it is sentences that replace letters (cf. p. 280 footnote "values whose substitution for the predicate variables"). This usage, which understands 'value of' as 'replacement for', is confusing because of its divergence from that of the mathematician, who says for example that the value of x^2 for the 'argument' 3 is the number 9, not the numeral '9'. Just as one must be alive to the distinction between a number and the numerals that name it, so one must also be alive to the distinction between a truth-value, truth or falsity, and the sentences that (do not name but) possess it. HUGHES & LONDEY not only mislead here but are themselves misled; for on the same page 2 they speak of numbers rather than numerals as values of numerical subject letters, and falsely claim that such letters are *replaced* by numbers. (The same confusion infects an expression not used in this book, 'value of a variable'; see QUINE, *RPM* p. 180).

(6) According to the formation rules of 3.2 'fab' and 'fa' are both well-formed; consequently '$(fab \supset fa)$' is well-formed; consequently it is interpreted as a schema fitted by sentences. But probably none of the sentences QC-fitting it can be used in a QC-context to express a proposition, true or false. For (i) the fitting conventions require that 'f' should be replaced in each of its two occurrences by the same predicate, and (ii) the context requires that the predicate should be used unequivocally. The sentence 'The car broke the wall $\supset$ the car broke' meets condition (i), but not (ii) since 'broke' shifts from a transitive to an intransitive meaning; the sentence 'She drank the potion $\supset$ she drank' meets condition (i), but probably not (ii) since 'drank' shifts from implying no supplementation to implying the supplementation 'something'. So probably '$fab \supset fa$' has no QC-instances; or if it does it is probably not QC-valid; and the same goes for the sequent $\langle \{`fab\text{'}\}, `fa\text{'} \rangle$. In general it is best to

avoid using the same predicate letter with a varying number of subject letters in a single formula or sequent, and to be content instead with the fact that the proposition expressed in the breaking example QC-instantiates '$fab \supset ga$', which is QC-invalid, and the proposition expressed in the drinking example QC-instantiates '$fab \supset \exists x fax$', which is QC-valid. Uncertainty about the status of formulae like '$fab \supset fa$' could be removed by banning them as ill-formed, through a formation rule requiring different styles of predicate letter for each number of following letters or variables. In this spirit 'R' is sometimes reserved as a more-than-one-place, or as a two-place, predicate letter (LEMMON *BL* p. 180). The resources of the alphabet are of course unequal to providing different styles for every number of places, so that if such are wanted some device like superscript numerals has to be used, as in 'f^1a', '$\exists x f^2 bx$', '$f^4 bbbc$'. Then for example $\langle \{'f^2 ab'\}, 'f^2 a' \rangle$ will contain an ill-formed formula, while $\langle \{'f^2 ab'\}, 'f^1 a' \rangle$ will be no harder to interpret than its unfestooned counterpart $\langle \{'fab'\}, 'ga' \rangle$. Furthermore '$p$', '$q$', '$r$' etc. can be replaced by 'f^0', 'g^0', 'h^0' etc. This is the notation of MATES (pp. 45, 51) and MASSEY (p. 230) who require superscript numerals but indemnify their elision. HUGHES & LONDEY (p. 296) have a similar formation rule.

(7) Some authors replace truth-conditions by satisfaction-conditions. This is particularly appropriate for systems in which there are well-formed formulae containing free variables, interpreted as open sentences or open schemata. Like predicates open sentences may be true or false *of* ordered sets of things but they cannot be T or F. Satisfaction is designed to encompass this kind of case. As a preliminary to stating satisfaction conditions the expression 'is satisfied by' needs first to be explicated, as follows: a closed sentence is satisfied by all or no ordered sets (of members of a domain in a context and world) according as it is T or F (in the domain, context and world)—here the reference to ordered sets idles; an open sentence is satisfied by an ordered set (of members of a domain in a context and world) if and only if the result of replacing its alphabetically first variable by a subject which refers (in the context) to the first member of the set, its alphabetically second variable by a subject which refers to the second member, and so on through all its alphabetically distinct variables, is a closed sentence

that is T (in the context, domain and world). In Quine's examples "The open sentence 'x walks' is satisfied [in English] by each walker and nothing else. The open sentence '$x > y$' is satisfied by each descending pair of numbers and no other pairs". The quotation is from *PofL* pp. 36–42, in which interpretation rules for the predicate calculus are stated in this way; see also MASSEY p. 386. Satisfaction may also be written into the definition of validity, 'π is an l-valid formula' becoming short for 'In any l-context, domain and world all open and closed sentences l-fitting π are satisfied by all ordered sets of members of the domain'.

Assuming Bivalence (see p. 165) a well-formed formula is valid by this definition if and only if its '$\forall$'-closure is valid by definition 2.13 (3), where the '$\forall$'-**closure** of a formula is the result of prefixing $\forall v$ for each v which occurs free in it, if any (MASSEY p. 305; cf. pp. 6–7 and the somewhat different definition of 'closure' in MATES p. 134; 'if any' indicates that the '$\forall$'-closure of a closed well-formed formula is itself; an '$\exists$'-**closure** similarly is the result of prefixing $\exists v$ for each free occurrence of v, if any). The notion of being satisfied by an ordered set is related to the model-theoretic notion, which I shall mention in 7.4, of being satisfied by a valuation; but the latter belongs to pure semantics.

CHAPTER FIVE

Derivation Rules for Sequents

5.1 Natural deduction

The logician who looks for patterns of correct argument has many ways of stating his results. We saw in Chapter 2 that a metalogical assertion such as

(A) The sequent $\langle\{`p\ \&\ q\text{'}\}, `p\text{'}\rangle$ is valid

refines

> The inference-schema 'p and q; so p' is valid.

The latter is perhaps more naturally formulated, in the manner of Aristotle, as

> Given that p and q, it follows that p

where we are left to supply the gloss 'This is T whatever sentences are put uniformly for "p" and "q" in it'. Other possibilities are

> The inference from 'p and q' to 'p' is correct
> 'p' is deducible from 'p and q'.

These last are ambiguous. If we understand the same tacit gloss, now operating through quotation marks, the second of them has the same force as is conveyed in the metalogical open sentence 'σ is deducible from $\ulcorner\sigma$ and $\tau\urcorner$'; it is a schema about sentences, gloss elided. Alternatively we can read it without gloss as a sentence about the schemata 'p and q' and 'p', synonymous with

> The schema 'p' is deducible from the schema 'p and q'.

(The basic case of this metalogical ambiguity is ' "p" is a sentence', which might be a (valid) schema about sentences or a (false) sentence about a schematic letter; some authors ban the former reading by refusing to let the required gloss operate through quotation marks).

5.1 Natural deduction

Finally, making the jump back to connectives, a pattern of correct argument might be reported in the words

(B) The formula 'p' is deducible from the formula 'p & q'.

The purpose of this section is to explore the relation between (A), which is stated in language I have explained, and (B), which is not. The trouble with (B) is that it imputes the relation of deducibility, the converse of entailment, not to propositions nor even to sentences (as in 'σ is deducible from ⌜σ and τ⌝') but to formulae. Deduction was explained in 2.4 in terms of truth and necessity; yet how can formulae be true or necessary? At this point the logician has a choice. One alternative is to point to the fact that formulae get interpreted, either as schemata or as sentences. It would be possible to extend the idea of deduction to cover sentences, or extend it through sentences to cover schemata, hence giving a meaning to (B) in terms of the interpretation of its symbols. The aim would be to manage the extension in such a way that (B) turned out to say the same thing as (A); and therefore deducibility, like validity, would have to be made relative to a logical language. The other alternative is to forget the connection of formulae with sentences and schemata, forget their possible interpretations altogether, and define instead a sense of deduction between formulae which is in no way beholden to the ordinary sense. The study of this kind of deduction will then be perfectly abstract, 'non-semantic', and it will be an open question, to be settled at a later stage, how the new relation connects with validity in any logical language.

As I forecast in the first two chapters. current logical practice favours the second alternative, and in construing (B) ignores the tenuous thread running back from it to (A). We are invited to understand (B) as a metatheorem inferred from the rules of some abstract system. Quine's 'deduction' rules (*MofL* p. 201 ff.) are perhaps not thus abstract; but Mates' 'inference rules' are so, in spite of the name (p. 97), as are Lemmon's 'derivation rules' (*BL* p. 8). As a help towards freeing assertions like (B) from association with the ordinary idea of deducibility I shall follow Mates and Lemmon in appropriating the word 'derivable' for the relation (B) attributes; all connection between deriving and deducing or inferring must be ignored. Before the end of this section 'derivability' will have become the name of a property of sequents;

but for the moment it is the name of a relation between formulae. Although in (B) itself this relation holds from one formula to another there will be cases in which it holds from more than one formula, and cases in which it holds from the empty set of formulae. So it is to be defined as a relation from sets of formulae, perhaps empty, to formulae, and (B) is to be rewritten as

(C) 'p' is derivable from {'p & q'}

A system using the relation of derivability might introduce it, as the property of well-formedness was introduced, by a recursive definition, which might have various categorical clauses such as 'π is derivable from $\{\pi\}$ (π well-formed)', 'π is derivable from $\{\pi$ & $\varphi\}$ (π and φ well-formed)', and also the hypothetical clause 'If π is derivable from a set of formulae Δ and every member of Δ is derivable from some subset of a set of formulae Γ, then π is derivable from Γ' (compare the 'transitivity' of entailment, p. 31). These clauses would state metalogical rules, which would have metalogical consequences provable as metatheorems. One metatheorem in many systems is the so-called Deduction Theorem (MASSEY p. 145, but in MATES p. 67 the Deduction Theorem is different, being semantic): if φ is derivable from the union of Γ and $\{\pi\}$, $\pi \supset \varphi$ is derivable from Γ. The Deduction Theorem stands at a junction in the network of logistic systems. On the one hand it has as a special case that if φ is derivable from $\{\pi\}$ alone, $\pi \supset \varphi$ is derivable from the empty set; and this suggests that we might replace all the categorical clauses of the form 'φ is derivable from $\{\pi\}$' by clauses of the form '$\pi \supset \varphi$ is derivable from the empty set', and we might state all the rules in terms of derivability from the empty set. That way leads to so-called 'axiomatic' systems which will be the subject of Chapter 6. On the other hand it is possible to promote various hypothetical metatheorems, perhaps including the Deduction Theorem itself, into the status of unproved rules and correspondingly to demote the rather cumbersome 'transitivity' rule and most of the categorical rules except 'π is derivable from $\{\pi\}$'. This last is Lemmon's rule A (MATES P, MASSEY RP), and the Deduction Theorem is Lemmon's CP (MASSEY Cd, but C in MATES is slightly different). Both become parts, by this second process, of what may be called, in a wide sense, a system of Natural Deduction.

5.1 Natural deduction

In the modern development of logistic systems 'axiomatic' versions, in which all formulae mentioned in the rules are derivable from the empty set, came first in time; and systems of natural deduction arose in response to the search for alternative rules which, while leaving the same formulae derivable from the same sets of formulae, resembled more closely the principles of reasoning used in actual deductions of conclusions from premisses. In the presentation of these systems there has been a tendency to exaggerate the resemblance, treating the rules as if they were not only *natural* but literally rules for *deduction*. In this spirit a student of natural deduction may be invited to 'assume' any formula, say '$p \mathbin{\&} q$', as a 'premiss', and to use the rule 'π is derivable from $\{\pi \mathbin{\&} \varphi\}$' in order to 'deduce' the 'conclusion' 'p'. But this is unsatisfactory for two reasons. First, if 'p' is an uninterpreted formula, it cannot literally be assumed or deduced: you might as well try to assume an ink-blot. Secondly, every natural deduction system contains at least one hypothetical rule which, like the Deduction Theorem, permits 'assumptions' to be cancelled; for example if 'p' is derivable from '$p \mathbin{\&} q$', the Deduction Theorem permits us to conclude that '$p \mathbin{\&} q \supset p$' is derivable from no 'assumptions'. So it is necessary to keep track of 'assumptions', and to know at each stage of a derivation not only what has been 'deduced' but also what it has been 'deduced' from. A simple chain of formulae, e.g.

$p \mathbin{\&} q$
p
$p \mathbin{\&} q \supset p$

hides these vital dependencies, and needs to be replaced by a chain showing at each stage the 'assumptions' remaining uncancelled. One way of doing so is to list uncancelled 'assumptions' in the left margin, as follows:

$\{p \mathbin{\&} q\} \quad p \mathbin{\&} q$
$\{p \mathbin{\&} q\} \quad p$
$\phantom{\{p \mathbin{\&} q\}} \quad p \mathbin{\&} q \supset p$

Putting these two criticisms together we can see that the first two stages in the above chain are not adequately licensed by the rules 'any formula may be assumed as premiss' and 'π is derivable from $\{\pi \mathbin{\&} \varphi\}$'.

There are various ways of making good the deficiency. One, similar to Quine's in *MofL*, adds supplementary rules about cancelling and explanations of the word 'assume' etc. Another, along the lines of LEMMON *BL*, changes the rules to 'any formula is derivable from the empty set, depending on itself' and 'π is derivable from $\{\pi \ \& \ \varphi\}$, depending on the same formulae as $\pi \ \& \ \varphi$ depended on'. A third possibility, which I prefer even though it moves away from the original conception of natural deduction, is to treat derivability as running, so to speak, horizontally rather than vertically: each formula is to be derivable not from preceding formulae in the chain (if any) but from the set of formulae to its left, on which it 'depends'. Then the rules become 'Any formula is derivable from itself (i.e. π is derivable from $\{\pi\}$)' and 'If $\pi \ \& \ \varphi$ is derivable from a set of formulae Γ, π is derivable from Γ'.

In this third method we have the now familiar pattern of recursive definition: a categorical rule masquerading as the 'rule of premisses' and a rule for eliminating '&' which is hypothetical like the Deduction Theorem. Each rule concerns the relation of derivability from some set of formulae Γ to some formula π. But what results differs still in two ways from the formulation to be used in this book. First, to say that derivability holds from Γ to π is the same as to say that it holds of the ordered set $\langle \Gamma, \pi \rangle$. Such an ordered set is a sequent. So instead of regarding derivability as a relation among formulae we can regard it more simply as a property of sequents, and we can reformulate (C) as

(D)   The sequent $\langle \{'p \ \& \ q'\}, \ 'p' \rangle$ is derivable.

Secondly, it is technically convenient (as forecast in 1.10) to define this property indirectly, rather than through a recursive specification. So the derivation rules will be directions for constructing items called sequent-derivations; and 'derivable sequent' will be defined as 'sequent which appears last in some sequent-derivation'.

5.2   *Formulating the rules*

A **sequent-derivation** in a calculus is a finite and non-empty ordered set of sequents, constructed according to the following rules, which are summarised in Appendix Two.

In the propositional calculus there are to be five sequent-rules,

5.2 Formulating the rules

one of them categorical, the rest hypothetical. The categorical rule is: [A] any PC-formula preceded by (the set consisting just of) itself may be entered in a sequent-derivation. By analogy with the formula system to come in Chapter 6 we may describe sequents licensed under categorical rules as sequent-axioms. Since A is the only axiom-licensing rule of the calculus (in QC another will be added) it is best to think of its name as standing for '**Axiom Rule**'. In Lemmon it means 'Rule of Assumptions', which is misleading for the reasons given in 5.1. In stating the hypothetical rules it would be tedious to forgo metalogical symbolism altogether, and I shall help myself to 'π' and 'φ' from the start. Many hypothetical sequent-rules come in pairs, one for introducing and one for eliminating some connective in the last formula in a sequent. The '&'-**Elimination** rule runs: [&E] for any formulae π and φ, if (π & φ) preceded by any (set of) formulae has been entered in a sequent-derivation, then π so preceded may be entered in it, and also φ so preceded may be entered in it. As the 'and' indicates this rule contains two parts, the first of which, like A, was anticipated in 5.1 The '&'-**Introduction** rule is: [&I] for any formulae π and φ, if π and φ each preceded by any (set of) formulae have both been entered in a sequent-derivation, then (π & φ) preceded by (the union of the sets of) those formulae may be entered in it. The union is formed by pooling: see p. 10. '$\sim$'-**Elimination** provides for eliminating double '$\sim$': [$\sim$E] for any formula π, if $\sim\sim\pi$ preceded by any (set of) formulae has been entered in a sequent-derivation, then π so preceded may be entered in it. The pair to this rule, '$\sim$'-Introduction, will be proved as a metatheorem in 5.4 and does not need to be included among the primitive rules; in Lemmon $\sim$E and $\sim$I are lumped together under the name 'Double Negation rule'. The last of the five propositional rules, **Reductio ad Absurdum**, corresponds to the following principle of reasoning: if a set of premises entail a contradiction, then one of the premises—any one—can be negated ('blamed' as some say) and deduced from the remaining premises. The rule states: [RAA] for any formulae π and φ, if (φ & $\sim\varphi$) preceded by (a set consisting of) π and any other formulae has been entered in a sequent-derivation, then $\sim\pi$ preceded by the (set of) other formulae may be entered in it. This is the only primitive rule to provide for reduction in the membership of the set of formulae with which a sequent begins. In Mates' system rule C has that role; in Massey's Cd; in Lemmon's RAA shares it with CP. Since it is possible by use of RAA to reduce membership of an initial set of formulae in a sequent to nil, the sets mentioned in this and every other hypothetical rule may be empty. On the other hand the sets which come in by the only categorical rule, A, are one-membered; and although &I provides for their enlargement by pooling we can never get by this process beyond a finite membership. Everything generated by the rules is therefore a finite sequent.

Statement of the rules can be shortened by adding metalogical symbolism from set theory: '{ }' for sets, '⟨ ⟩' for ordered sets, and '∪' for union of sets. I shall also continue the practice begun in the last section of using 'Γ', 'Δ' as metalogical variables ranging over sets of formulae. Then the PC rules become: for any formulae π, φ and sets of formulae Γ, Δ, in any sequent-derivation, if π is a PC-formula $\langle \{\pi\}, \pi \rangle$ may be entered; if $\langle \Gamma, \pi \& \varphi \rangle$ has been entered, $\langle \Gamma, \pi \rangle$ and also $\langle \Gamma, \varphi \rangle$ may be; if $\langle \Gamma, \pi \rangle$ and $\langle \Delta, \varphi \rangle$ have been entered, $\langle \Gamma \cup \Delta, \pi \& \varphi \rangle$ may be; if $\langle \Gamma, \sim\sim\pi \rangle$ has been entered, $\langle \Gamma, \pi \rangle$ may be; and if $\langle \Gamma \cup \{\pi\}, \varphi \& \sim\varphi \rangle$ has been entered, $\langle \Gamma, \sim\pi \rangle$ may be.

The predicate calculus with identity includes the same five rules, now adapted to QC-formulae and sequents of them; and adds four new rules, two for '=' and two for '∀'. I shall distinguish the '∀'-introduction rule as ∀I-S, because it has an analogue ∀I-F in the formula system of Chapter 6. Among the new rules one, for '='-**Introduction**, is categorical, and moreover stipulates for the first time a one-formula sequent, a formula preceded by the empty set. It is: [=I] for any subject letter a, $a = a$, preceded by (the set containing) nothing, may be entered in a sequent-derivation. All the other new rules involve substitution, of subject letters for subject letters, subject letters for variables, and variables for subject letters. '='-**Elimination** goes like this: [=E] for any subject letters a, β, and formula π containing a, if $a = \beta$ and π each preceded by any (set of) formulae have both been entered in a sequent-derivation, then the result of substituting β for at least one occurrence of a in π, preceded by (the union of the sets of) those formulae, may be entered. As in the formation rules reference here to substitution can be replaced by reference to stencils; then the rule provides that if Γ followed by $a = \beta$ and Δ followed by a stencil

5.2 Formulating the rules

filled up with α have both been entered, $\Gamma \cup \Delta$ followed by the same stencil filled up with β may be entered. Notice that nothing prevents the letter α which fills up a stencil from already being present elsewhere in the unfilled stencil. When that happens, filling it up with β will have the effect of substituting β for some but not all the occurrences of α in the original formula; and that is allowed. For example it follows from the rule that if $\langle\{$ '$a=b$'$\}$, '$a=b$'$\rangle$ and $\langle\{$'faa'$\}$, 'faa'$\rangle$ have been entered, then $\langle\{$'$a=b$', 'faa'$\}$, 'fba'$\rangle$ may be; in fact by choosing in turn the stencils 'f_a', '$fa\_$' and '$f\_\_$' we can successively enter the sequents ending 'fba', 'fab', 'fbb'. In the rule for '∀'-**Elimination** this liberty has to be curtailed. The reason is that we want every entered sequent to be well-formed; hence when $\forall v$ is eliminated from a sequent's last formula, no v may remain. If the rule is formulated in terms of substitution, this means that 'every occurrence' must replace 'at least one occurrence', as in : [∀E] for any subject letter α, variable v, and formula π, if any (set of) formulae followed by $\forall v\pi$ has been entered in a sequent-derivation, then that set followed by the result of substituting α for every occurrence of v in π may be entered in it. And the stencil formulation is: if Γ followed by $\forall v$ prefixing a stencil filled up with v has been entered, then Γ followed by the same stencil filled up with α may be, provided that the stencil contains no v. In the final rule, for '∀'-**Introduction**, the same proviso is needed in order to block formulae that are ill-formed on account of vacuous quantification. Although this proviso gives no trouble in practice, because one quickly gets an eye for ill-formed formulae, it is joined in the '∀'-Introduction rule by another, absent from ∀E, which is more tricky. I begin by explaining its motivation. The general idea of the rule is to license a sequent $\langle \Gamma, \forall v \varphi \rangle$ as enterable when $\langle \Gamma, \pi \rangle$ has been entered and π differs from φ in containing a subject letter wherever (old proviso) φ contains v. But there are two kinds of case we need to block if the rule is eventually to turn out sound, never leading from valid to invalid sequents. One case would arise if the rule were so framed as to permit passage from e.g. $\langle\{$ 'fa' $\}$, 'fa'$\rangle$ to $\langle\{$ 'fa'$\}$, '$\forall xfx$'$\rangle$ —it is obvious that the former sequent is valid but not the latter. To block this, it has to be stipulated that the letter 'bartered' for the variable v, here 'a', does not appear in the licensed sequent's *initial* set of formulae. The second case would arise if the rule were so framed as to permit passage from e.g.

⟨{ '∀xfxx'}, 'faa'⟩ to ⟨{ '∀xfxx'}, '∀xfxa'⟩. The former sequent is obviously QC-valid; but the latter is not, for it has as a QC-instance 'Everyone is the same age as himself; so everyone is the same age as Methuselah', an argument with true premiss and untrue conclusion. To block this, the ∀I rule will stipulate that the letter bartered for the variable *v*, here '*a*', does not appear in the licensed sequent's *last* formula. The joint effect of these restrictions is that when any variable *v* is introduced by the rule the subject letter bartered for it must appear *nowhere* in the sequent which emerges. This effect can be secured by stating the rule thus: [∀I-S] for any subject letter *a*, variable *v*, and formula π containing *a* but not *v*, if any (set of) formulae *not* containing *a*, followed by π, has been entered in a sequent-derivation, then that set followed by the result of substituting *v* for *every* occurrence of *a* in π and prefixing ∀*v* may be entered in it. In terms of stencils: if Γ followed by a stencil filled up with *a* has been entered, then Γ followed by ∀*v* prefixing the same stencil filled up with *v* may be, provided that Γ contains no *a* and the stencil contains neither *v* nor *a*.

It cannot be denied that these predicate calculus sequent rules, and particularly ∀I-S, are harder to understand and manipulate than any of the formation and interpretation rules; in fact they are the hardest indispensable rules in the book. Metalogical symbolism, now with 'ϕ' ranging over stencils and 'Λ' for the empty set, certainly makes it possible to state them more briefly, which may help. They become: for any subject letter *a*, variable *v*, stencil ϕ, and sets of formula Γ, Δ, in any sequent-derivation, $\langle \Lambda, a = a \rangle$ may be entered; if $\langle \Gamma, a = \beta \rangle$ and $\langle \Delta, \phi a \rangle$ have been entered, then $\langle \Gamma \cup \Delta, \phi\beta \rangle$ may be; if ϕ contains no *v* and $\langle \Gamma, \forall v \phi v \rangle$ has been entered, then $\langle \Gamma, \phi a \rangle$ may be; and if ϕ contains no *v* and neither ϕ nor Γ contains *a* and $\langle \Gamma, \phi a \rangle$ has been entered, then $\langle \Gamma, \forall v \phi v \rangle$ may be.

The sequent rules of S5 and QS5 result by adapting to S5-formulae and QS5-formulae the rules of PC and QC respectively and adding to each set a rule for '$\Box$'-**Elimination** and a rule for '$\Box$'-**Introduction**. The former is quite unproblematic, and goes like this: [$\Box$E] for any formula π, if $\Box\pi$ preceded by any (set of) formulae has been entered in a sequent-derivation, then π so preceded may be entered in it. '$\Box$'-**Introduction**, distinguished as $\Box$I-S because it too will have an analogue in the formula system of Chapter 6, stands in the same relation to its counterpart elimination

5.2 Formulating the rules

rule as ∀I-S did to the elimination rule for the universal quantifier, and hence needs a proviso corresponding to the requirement that a sequent licensed by ∀I-S should exclude all occurrences of the bartered subject letter. The corresponding requirement is that in a sequent licensed by □I-S all formulae must be **fully modalised**, which means that every propositional letter, every predicate letter, and every '=' which they contain must lie within the scope of '□' or '◇' (for example '□ ($p \supset a=a$)' and '□$p \supset$ ◇($a=a$)' are fully modalised, but '□$p \supset a=a$' is not). The final formula in a sequent licensed by the rule is bound to be fully modalised, because '□' will be its main connective; so the proviso in the rule will concern the initial formulae. The rule is: [□ I-S] for any formula π, if π preceded by any (set of) formulae, all fully modalised, has been entered in a sequent-derivation, then □π so preceded may be entered in it. Without the proviso nothing would prevent passage from the valid ⟨{'p'}, 'p'⟩ to the invalid ⟨{'p'}, '□p'⟩.

The same metalogical symbolism as before permits the S5 and QS5 modal rules to be stated in the form: for any formula π and set of formulae Γ, in any sequent-derivation, if ⟨Γ, □π⟩ has been entered, then ⟨Γ, π⟩ may be; and if all members of Γ are fully modalised and ⟨Γ, π⟩ has been entered, then ⟨Γ, □π⟩ may be.

Finally, the symbolic definitions are all allowed to function as rules for constructing sequent-derivations. That is: for any π, ♀ and Γ, if ♀ results from π by one of the symbolic definitions, and ⟨Γ, π⟩ has been entered in a sequent-derivation, then ⟨Γ, ♀⟩ may be entered in it.

The set of derivable sequents in each calculus is now to be defined in terms of these rules. A sequent is derivable in the propositional calculus, **PC-derivable** for short, when it is the last entry in a PC sequent-derivation, i.e. in some derivation constructed according to the five PC rules plus the definitions; a **QC-derivable** sequent is the last entry in some QC sequent-derivation; and similarly in the other cases.

5.3 Sequent-derivations

The purpose of derivation rules is to afford a method of proving derivability. The method is: construct a sequent-derivation in which the sequent to be proved derivable is the last entry. In this section I shall illustrate the method and then comment briefly on it.

Here is an example of a PC sequent-derivation, the order of its four sequents running from left to right:

(E) $\langle\{`p\ \&\ q`\}, `p\ \&\ q`\rangle, \langle\{`p\ \&\ q`\}, `q`\rangle,$
         $\langle\{`r`\}, `r`\rangle, \langle\{`p\ \&\ q`, `r`\}, `q\ \&\ r`\rangle$

(E) is a sequent-derivation of PC (and also of QC, S5 and QS5) because it is a finite and non-empty ordered set of sequents, its first and third sequents are licensed by A, its second is a result (one of two that are possible) of applying &E to its first, and its fourth is a result (again one of two possible) of applying &I to its second and third. The third sequent could have been placed earlier, but the second sequent required previous entry of the first, and the fourth required previous entry of the second and third. By definition a sequent-derivation is just an ordered set of sequents constructed according to the rules. But in order to make for ease of construction, and of checking, it is useful to adopt some extra conventions that are not part of the definition. There will be five of them (all in standard use). (i) Each sequent in a derivation will be entered on a separate line. So (E) becomes:

$\langle\{`p\ \&\ q`\}, `p\ \&\ q`\rangle$
$\langle\{`p\ \&\ q`\}, `q`\rangle$
$\langle\{`r`\}, `r`\rangle$
$\langle\{`p\ \&\ q`, `r`\}, `q\ \&\ r`\rangle$

(ii) The lines will be numbered, thus:

(1) $\langle\{`p\ \&\ q`\}, `p\ \&\ q`\rangle$
(2) $\langle\{`p\ \&\ q`\}, `q`\rangle$
(3) $\langle\{`r`\}, `r`\rangle$
(4) $\langle\{`p\ \&\ q`, `r`\}, `q\ \&\ r`\rangle$

(iii) Instead of writing out an expression for each sequent on its line, only the last formula in it will be written, each of the other formulae in it, if there are any, being indicated in the left hand margin of its line by means of an index number; and the index number will be the number of some earlier (or not later) line in which that formula is the last formula, i.e. in which it is actually written. So (E) becomes:

{1}   (1)   '$p \& q$'
{1}   (2)   'q'
{3}   (3)   'r'
{1,3} (4)   '$q \& r$'

Here '1' in the left hand margin of lines (1), (2) and (4) refers to the formula *written* in (1), viz. '$p \& q$', and '3' in the left hand margin of lines (3) and (4) refers to 'r'. This convention makes the structure of a derivation much more perspicuous. The convention is possible—index numbers are always available—because according to the rules of 5.2 no formula can get into a properly constructed derivation except as the last formula of the sequent that introduces it. (iv) Next, the curly brackets and quotation marks will be elided, thus:

1   (1) $p \& q$
1   (2) q
3   (3) r
1,3   (4) $q \& r$

(v) Finally, most derivations will be *annotated* by citing in the right hand margin of each line the derivation rule or definition which justifies its entry at that point in the derivation, together with the numbers of any previous lines in the derivation to which the rule or definition has been applied. In (E) the first and third entries are justified by A, the second by applying &E to (1), and the fourth by applying &I to (2) and (3). So it becomes:

1   (1) $p \& q$ A
1   (2) q &E   1
3   (3) r A
1,3   (4) $q \& r$ &I   2,3

Notice that although line (4) is justified by lines (2) and (3), its indexed formulae on the left are not 2 and 3 themselves but—as &I requires—the formulae indexed in them, viz. 1 and 3: its written formula 'depends' on what theirs 'depended' on. Notice too that whereas the citations on the right are discretionary annotation, what mathematicians call an analysis of the derivation, the index numbers on the left are *part of the sequents entered*, and so cannot be omitted although they might be replaced by actually writing out the formulae they refer to.

Any reader to whom the idea of a derivation is quite new will need to supplement the above explanation by reference to some other book or by working through examples. I shall do no more here than to give a few further examples of annotated derivations, two more from PC, and one each from QC, S5 and QS5.

(F) 1   (1) $p \& \sim p$ A
         (2) $\sim(p \& \sim p)$ RAA 1
         (3) $p \supset p$ Def$\supset$ 2

Here the first entry is $\langle\{\text{'}p \& \sim p\text{'}\}, \text{'}p \& \sim p\text{'}\rangle$, a sequent-axiom by A; the second is $\langle \Lambda, \text{'}\sim(p \& \sim p)\text{'}\rangle$, which comes by RAA from the first entry because that sequent's last formula was a case of $\varphi \& \sim \varphi$, allowing (the only) one formula from its initial set to be negated and written as last formula following the (empty) remainder of the set; the final entry is $\langle \Lambda, \text{'}p \supset p\text{'}\rangle$, which comes from line 2 by applying Def$\supset$ to that line's last formula. For the remaining examples I give less commentary; they need to be pondered line by line.

(G) 1   (1) $p \supset q$ A
     2   (2) p A
     3   (3) $\sim q$ A
     2,3   (4) $p \& \sim q$ &I   2,3
     1   (5) $\sim(p \& \sim q)$ Def$\supset$ 1
     1,2,3 (6) $(p \& \sim q) \& \sim(p \& \sim q)$ &I   4,5
     1,2   (7) $\sim\sim q$ RAA   6
     1,2   (8) q $\sim$E 7

This uses all the primitive PC rules except &E. Notice how the set of indexed formulae on the left is built up by applications of &I and then diminished by an application of RAA. I shall return to (G) in the next section.

(H) 1   (1) fa A
     2   (2) $\forall x \sim fx$ A
     2   (3) $\sim fa$ $\forall$E 2
     1,2 (4) $fa \& \sim fa$ &I   1,3
     1   (5) $\sim \forall x \sim fx$ RAA 4
     1   (6) $\exists x fx$ Def$\exists$ 5

It will be obvious by now that no entry is determined by its precursors; there are always alternatives, if only fresh applications of A. For example after line 4 in (H), even granted the decision to apply RAA, it was permissible to have entered

| | 2 | (5a) | $\sim fa$ | | RAA | 4 |

'blaming' 1 instead of 2 for the 'contradiction'.

(I)
1	(1)	$\Box p \vee \Box q$	A	
1	(2)	$\sim(\sim\Box p \& \sim\Box q)$	Def$\vee$	1
3	(3)	$\sim p \& \sim q$	A	
3	(4)	$\sim p$	&E	3
5	(5)	$\Box p$	A	
5	(6)	p	$\Box$E	5
3,5	(7)	$p \& \sim p$	&I	4,6
3	(8)	$\sim\Box p$	RAA	7
3	(9)	$\sim q$	&E	3
10	(10)	$\Box q$	A	
10	(11)	q	$\Box$E	10
3,10	(12)	$q \& \sim q$	&I	9,11
3	(13)	$\sim\Box q$	RAA	12
3	(14)	$\sim\Box p \& \sim\Box q$	&I	8,13
1,3	(15)	$(\sim\Box p \& \sim\Box q) \& \sim(\sim\Box p \& \sim\Box q)$	&I	2,14
1	(16)	$\sim(\sim p \& \sim q)$	RAA	15
1	(17)	$p \vee q$	Def$\vee$	16
1	(18)	$\Box(p \vee q)$	$\Box$I-S	17

Here the application of $\Box$I-S is correct in line 18 because the (only) formula in the set indexed there is fully modalised. The converse sequent $\langle\{`\Box(p \vee q)`\}, `\Box p \vee \Box q`\rangle$ is not derivable (cf. ARISTOTLE, *De Int.* 9.19^{a}28–9), although both $\langle\{`\Diamond(p \vee q)`\}, `\Diamond p \vee \Diamond q`\rangle$ and its converse are derivable.

(J)
	1	(1)	$a = b$	A	
		(2)	$a = a$	= I	
		(3)	$\Box(a = a)$	$\Box$I-S	2
	1	(4)	$\Box(a = b)$	= E	1,3

All members of the initial set in line 3 are fully modalised, because there are none. In the application of = E the eliminated '=' is in

'$a = b$', and the stencil, which happens to contain another '$=$', is '$\Box(a = \_\_)$'.

I end with two comments about the use of derivations to prove derivability. (i) A derivation is not an argument (it contains no sentences). But it does, at least if annotated, show or *display* the steps by which to argue that all its entries deserves their place, and therefore that its last entry is derivable. Notice that what is thus proved in a derivation is not a sequent, but *that a sequent is derivable*. 'Provable' is not synonymous with the technical sense of 'derivable', though is might be used as a lazy shorthand for 'provably derivable'. (ii) The rules of 5.2 for constructing derivations have a feature not shared by Quine's rules of natural deduction, namely that any initial segment of a derivation is a derivation, or in other words if you cut off the last entry in a derivation you are always left with a derivation, down to the limit where only one entry remains (which must be a sequent-axiom). This feature is definitive of 'logistic system' (MASSEY p. 274). It follows from it, by the definition of 'derivable', that not only the last but every entry in a derivation is a derivable sequent.

5.4 *Metatheorems on derivability*

An effective method could be devised for constructing a sequent-derivation whose last entry is any desired sequent, if it is derivable (MATES pp. 147–50, not in 1st edition; cf. MASSEY p. 300). But there is no effective method of constructing, for each derivable sequent, a short derivation—let alone the shortest—whose last entry it is; this requires practice, tactical instruction, and ingenuity. The appeal of the method, and also its advantage over the formula-derivations to be discussed in 6.3, arise mainly from the fact that most of the derivation rules for sequents mirror principles of reasoning which we all use, even if unconsciously. In this section I shall show how, on the basis of the rules of 5.2 together with the symbolic definitions (mostly absent from LEMMON) it is possible to prove various metatheorems which likewise mirror principles of reasoning. The metatheorems will not be directives for constructing sequent-derivations; but in the next section I shall extend the idea of a sequent-derivation so that we can make use of them. In what follows '⊢' abbreviates 'is derivable'.

5.4 *Metatheorems on derivability*

Modus Ponendo Ponens for Sequents [MPP-S]. For any π, φ, Γ, Δ, if $\vdash\langle\Gamma, \pi \supset \varphi\rangle$ and $\vdash\langle\Delta, \pi\rangle$, then $\vdash\langle\Gamma \cup \Delta, \varphi\rangle$.

Proof. Take some π, φ, Γ, Δ, and suppose that $\langle\Gamma, \pi \supset \varphi\rangle$ and $\langle\Delta, \pi\rangle$ are derivable; that is (using numbered lines for a reason which will appear shortly):

(1) $\vdash\langle\Gamma, \pi \supset \varphi\rangle$ supposition
(2) $\vdash\langle\Delta, \pi\rangle$ supposition

Since the chosen φ, and therefore $\sim\varphi$, must be well-formed under the first supposition, it follows from rule A that $\langle\{\sim\varphi\}, \sim\varphi\rangle$ is derivable for the chosen φ; that is

(3) $\vdash\langle\{\sim\varphi\}, \sim\varphi\rangle$ A

Similarly it follows from &I that, for the chosen π, φ, Γ, Δ, if $\langle\Delta, \pi\rangle$ and $\langle\{\sim\varphi\}, \sim\varphi\rangle$ are derivable, so is $\langle\Delta \cup \{\sim\varphi\}, \pi \,\&\, \sim\varphi\rangle$; therefore from lines 2 and 3 we can infer:

(4) $\vdash\langle\Delta \cup \{\sim\varphi\}, \pi \,\&\, \sim\varphi\rangle$ &I   2,3

From (1) by Def$\supset$ we get

(5) $\vdash\langle\Gamma, \sim(\pi \,\&\, \sim\varphi)\rangle$ Def$\supset$ 1

From &I it follows again that if 4 and 5 then 6 below; so from 4 and 5 we can infer

(6) $\vdash\langle\Gamma \cup \Delta \cup \{\sim\varphi\}, (\pi \,\&\, \sim\varphi) \,\&\, \sim(\pi \,\&\, \sim\varphi)\rangle$ &I   4,5

From RAA it follows that if 6 then 7 below; so

(7) $\vdash\langle\Gamma \cup \Delta, \sim\sim\varphi\rangle$ RAA   6

From $\sim$E it follows that if 7 then 8 below; so

(8) $\vdash\langle\Gamma \cup \Delta, \varphi\rangle$ $\sim$E   7

Thus for the chosen π, φ, Γ, Δ, whatever they are—i.e. for any π, φ, Γ, Δ—if the suppositions are true, then $\langle\Gamma \cup \Delta, \varphi\rangle$ is derivable. Q.E.D.

It is no accident that this metalogical proof runs nearly parallel to derivation (G) in the last section. In fact it results from (G) by the following five operations: (i) replace '*p*' and '*q*' by the metalogical variables 'π' and 'φ' respectively; (ii) replace the index numbers '1' and '2' in (G) by the metalogical variables 'Γ' and 'Δ' respectively; (iii) record lines 1 and 2 as 'suppositions'; (iv) add to each line the metalogical abbreviation '⊢'; (v) prefix 'for any π, φ, Γ, Δ' to the whole proof. But these changes are more than a formality; by inserting '⊢', i.e. 'is derivable', in each line they convert the line from a sequent into a metalogical open sentence about sequents, and by prefixing metalogical quantifiers to the whole array they convert it from a set of sequents into a generalised argument about sequents, which could be expressed in English rather than the metalogical symbols that are used for brevity. Because this sort of conversion is always possible it will be instructive to write the remaining proofs of this section, like that of MPP-S, in numbered and annotated lines; but they are proofs about derivability, not derivations according to the definition of 'derivation' in 5.2. Of course each proof may build on those that precede, using their results as well as the primitive rules and definitions.

Modus Tollendo Tollens [MTT]. For any π, φ, Γ, Δ, if ⊢⟨$\Gamma, \pi \supset \varphi$⟩ and ⊢⟨$\Delta, \sim\varphi$⟩, then ⊢⟨$\Gamma \cup \Delta, \sim\pi$⟩.

One proof, using MPP-S, results by converting Lemmon's derivation 55 on p. 62 of *BL*.

Modus Ponendo Tollens [MPT]. For any π, φ, Γ, Δ, if ⊢⟨$\Gamma, \sim(\pi \& \varphi)$⟩ and ⊢⟨$\Delta, \pi$⟩, then ⊢⟨$\Gamma \cup \Delta, \sim\varphi$⟩; also if ⊢⟨$\Gamma, \sim(\pi \& \varphi)$⟩ and ⊢⟨$\Delta, \varphi$⟩, then ⊢⟨$\Gamma \cup \Delta, \sim\pi$⟩.

Proof of first version. For any π, φ, Γ, Δ

(1) ⊢⟨$\Gamma, \sim(\pi \& \varphi)$⟩   supposition
(2) ⊢⟨Δ, π⟩   supposition
(3) ⊢⟨{φ}, φ⟩   A
(4) ⊢⟨$\Delta \cup \{\varphi\}, \pi \& \varphi$⟩   &I   2,3
(5) ⊢⟨$\Gamma \cup \Delta \cup \{\varphi\}, (\pi \& \varphi) \& \sim(\pi \& \varphi)$⟩   &I   1,4
(6) ⊢⟨$\Gamma \cup \Delta, \sim\varphi$⟩   RAA   5

Modus Tollendo Ponens [MTP]. For any π, φ, Γ, Δ, if ⊢⟨$\Gamma, \pi \vee \varphi$⟩ and ⊢⟨$\Delta, \sim\pi$⟩, then ⟨$\Gamma \cup \Delta, \varphi$⟩; also if ⊢⟨$\Gamma, \pi \vee \varphi$⟩ and ⊢⟨$\Delta, \sim\varphi$⟩, then ⊢⟨$\Gamma \cup \Delta, \pi$⟩.

The proof is straightforward by Def∨, Def⊃ and MPP-S.

5.4 Metatheorems on derivability

'$\sim$'-**Introduction** [$\sim$I]. For any π, Γ, if $\vdash\langle\Gamma,\pi\rangle$, then $\vdash\langle\Gamma,\sim\sim\pi\rangle$.

Proof. For any π, Γ
(1) $\vdash\langle\Gamma, \pi\rangle$ supposition
(2) $\vdash\langle\{\sim\pi\}, \sim\pi\rangle$ A
(3) $\vdash\langle\Gamma\cup\{\sim\pi\}, \pi\,\&\sim\pi\rangle$ &I   1,2
(4) $\vdash\langle\Gamma, \sim\sim\pi\rangle$ RAA   3

Conditional Proof [CP]. For any π, φ, Γ, if $\vdash\langle\Gamma\cup\{\pi\}, \varphi\rangle$ then $\vdash\langle\Gamma, \pi\supset\varphi\rangle$.

Proof. For any π, φ, Γ

(1) $\vdash\langle\Gamma\cup\{\pi\}, \varphi\rangle$ supposition
(2) $\vdash\langle\{\pi\,\&\sim\varphi\}, \pi\,\&\sim\varphi\rangle$ A
(3) $\vdash\langle\{\pi\,\&\sim\varphi\}, \sim\varphi\rangle$ &E   2
(4) $\vdash\langle\Gamma\cup\{\pi, \pi\,\&\sim\varphi\}, \varphi\,\&\sim\varphi\rangle$ &I   1,3
(5) $\vdash\langle\Gamma\cup\{\pi\,\&\sim\varphi\}, \sim\pi\rangle$ RAA   4
(6) $\vdash\langle\{\pi\,\&\sim\varphi\}, \pi\rangle$ &E   2
(7) $\vdash\langle\Gamma\cup\{\pi\,\&\sim\varphi\}, \pi\,\&\sim\pi\rangle$ &I   5,6
(8) $\vdash\langle\Gamma, \sim(\pi\,\&\sim\varphi)\rangle$ RAA   7
(9) $\vdash\langle\Gamma, \pi\supset\varphi\rangle$ Def$\supset$ 8

'$\vee$'-**Introduction** [$\vee$I]. For any π, φ, Γ, if $\vdash\langle\Gamma, \pi\rangle$ then $\vdash\langle\Gamma, \pi\vee\varphi\rangle$ and also $\vdash\langle\Gamma, \varphi\vee\pi\rangle$.

Proof of first half. For any π, φ, Γ

(1) $\vdash\langle\Gamma, \pi\rangle$ supposition
(2) $\vdash\langle\{\sim\pi\,\&\sim\varphi\}, \sim\pi\,\&\sim\varphi\rangle$ A
(3) $\vdash\langle\{\sim\pi\,\&\sim\varphi\}, \sim\pi\rangle$ &E   2
(4) $\vdash\langle\Gamma\cup\{\sim\pi\,\&\sim\varphi\}, \pi\,\&\sim\pi\rangle$ &I   1,3
(5) $\vdash\langle\Gamma, \sim(\sim\pi\,\&\sim\varphi)\rangle$ RAA   4
(6) $\vdash\langle\Gamma, \pi\vee\varphi\rangle$ Def$\vee$ 5

The other half of the proof is the same except that '$\sim\varphi\,\&\sim\pi$' replaces '$\sim\pi\,\&\sim\varphi$' throughout.

'$\vee$'-**Elimination** [$\vee$E]. For any π, φ, ρ, Γ, Δ, E, if $\vdash\langle\Gamma, \pi\vee\varphi\rangle$ and $\vdash\langle\Delta\cup\{\pi\},\rho\rangle$ and $\vdash\langle E\cup\{\varphi\},\rho\rangle$, then $\vdash\langle\Gamma\cup\Delta\cup E,\rho\rangle$.

For use of this metatheorem see LEMMON *BL* pp. 22–5; I omit its proof.

The preceding metatheorems concern derivability in all four calculi, but those which now follow belong to QC and QS5 only.

'∃'-**Introduction** [∃I]. For any α, ν, φ not containing ν, and Γ, if ⊢⟨Γ, φα⟩, then ⊢⟨Γ, ∃νφν⟩.

The proof parallels (H) in the last section, with 'ν' for 'x', 'α' for 'a', and 'φ' for 'f'. The proviso that φ contain no ν is required for the use of ∀E in line 3 of it. This proof is analogous to that of ∨I, as will be the proof of ◇I.

'∃'-**Elimination** [∃E]. For any π, α, ν, φ, Γ, Δ (no ν in φ, no α in π, φ or Δ), if ⊢⟨Γ, ∃νφν⟩ and ⊢⟨Δ ∪ {φα}, π⟩ then ⊢⟨Γ ∪ Δ, π⟩.

This difficult metatheorem is analogous to ∨E. The provisos in it are required for the use of ∀I-S in its proof which, although I omit it, can be divined from (L) on p. 136. There are some comments on use of the metatheorem on p. 247. In S5 and QS5 '◇'-rules analogous to the two '∃'-rules are provable. I state them here without proof.

'◇'-**Introduction** [◇I]. For any π, Γ, if ⊢⟨Γ, π⟩ then ⊢⟨Γ, ◇π⟩.

'◇'-**Elimination** [◇E]. For any π, ϙ, Γ, Δ (π and Δ fully modalised), if ⊢⟨Γ, ◇ϙ⟩ and ⊢⟨Δ ∪ {ϙ}, π⟩, then ⊢⟨Γ ∪ Δ, π⟩.

Among the infinity of other metatheorems that could be proved I choose one hard one, which is like MATES' Replacement Metatheorem (p.136) and also like HUGHES & LONDEY's Rule for Substitution of Equivalents (p. 117). The pairs of formulae with which it deals I shall call 'interderivable', reserving 'equivalent' for a semantic rather than proof-theoretic meaning (see p. 189). Two formulae π and ϙ are **interderivable** when the '∀'-closure (p. 111) of their biconditional is derivable from the empty set, i.e. when there are n variables $v_1 \ldots v_n$ such that $\langle \Lambda, \forall v_1 \ldots \forall v_n(\pi \equiv \text{ϙ}) \rangle$ is a derivable sequent. If $n = 0$, π and ϙ must be well-formed and the sequent is just $\langle \Lambda, \pi \equiv \text{ϙ} \rangle$, but it is useful to have a definition that counts pairs like 'fx' and '$\sim\sim fx$' as interderivable too, even though they are not well-formed.

Interderivability metatheorem. When for any part of the last formula of a derivable sequent an interderivable part is substituted, the result is still a derivable sequent if still well-formed.

Here 'part' is to be understood in such a way that atomic formulae contain no parts; e.g. 'fa' is not a part of 'fab'. Absence of this

5.4 Metatheorems on derivability

restriction would further complicate the proof, which is lengthy anyhow, and in three stages. I give them for QS5; they can readily be adapted to S5, QC (as in MATES) or PC (as in HUGHES & LONDEY). In the first stage it is to be proved that for any π, φ, ρ, ν, and ϕ and ψ containing no ν,

(a) If π is interderivable with φ, so is $\sim\pi$ with $\sim\varphi$

(b) If π is interderivable with φ, so is $\pi \,\&\, \rho$ with $\varphi \,\&\, \rho$, and so is $\rho \,\&\, \pi$ with $\rho \,\&\, \varphi$

(c) If $\phi\nu$ is interderivable with $\psi\nu$, so is $\forall\nu\phi\nu$ with $\forall\nu\psi\nu$

(d) If π is interderivable with φ, so is $\Box\pi$ with $\Box\varphi$.

Proofs. (a) The supposition is that for some n

(1) $\vdash \langle \Lambda, \forall\nu_1 \ldots \forall\nu_n(\pi \equiv \varphi) \rangle$ supposition

It follows by n applications of $\forall$E that $\vdash \langle \Lambda, \pi_n \equiv \varphi_n \rangle$, where π_n and φ_n are the results of putting a_1 for ν_1, ... a_n for ν_n in π and φ, and π and φ themselves contain none of $a_1, \ldots a_n$.

For ease of reading I drop the subscripts and write this as

	(2)	$\vdash \langle \Lambda, \pi \equiv \varphi \rangle$	$\forall$E n times	1
so	(3)	$\vdash \langle \Lambda, (\pi \supset \varphi) \,\&\, (\varphi \supset \pi) \rangle$	Def $\equiv$	2
	(4)	$\vdash \langle \Lambda, \pi \supset \varphi \rangle$	&E	3
	(5)	$\vdash \langle \{\sim\varphi\}, \sim\varphi \rangle$	A	
	(6)	$\vdash \langle \{\sim\varphi\}, \sim\pi \rangle$	MTT	4,5
	(7)	$\vdash \langle \Lambda, \sim\varphi \supset \sim\pi \rangle$	CP	6

Similarly from line 3

(8)	$\vdash \langle \Lambda, \varphi \supset \pi \rangle$	&E	3
(9)	$\vdash \langle \{\sim\pi\}, \sim\pi \rangle$	A	
(10)	$\vdash \langle \{\sim\pi\}, \sim\varphi \rangle$	MTT	8,9
(11)	$\vdash \langle \Lambda, \sim\pi \supset \sim\varphi \rangle$	CP	10

So from lines 7 and 11

(12)	$\vdash \langle \Lambda, (\sim\pi \supset \sim\varphi) \,\&\, (\sim\varphi \supset \sim\pi) \rangle$	&I	7,11
(13)	$\vdash \langle \Lambda, \sim\pi \equiv \sim\varphi \rangle$	Def $\equiv$	12

Restoring the subscripts, we then use n applications of ∀I-S to get

(14) $\vdash \langle \Lambda, \forall\nu_1 \ldots \forall\nu_n(\sim\pi \equiv \sim\wp)\rangle$ ∀I-S n times   13

Q.E.D. The proofs of (b), (c) and (d) are along similar lines, and are left to the reader.

In the second stage (elided in HUGHES & LONDEY p. 120) it is to be proved that for any well-formed formula π, the formula which results by substituting for any part of it an interderivable part is interderivable with it; or in other words, given any pair of interderivable formulae, a well-formed formula containing the first of the pair is interderivable with the formula which results by substituting the second. The proof is by strong mathematical induction on the length of formulae. Take some pair of interderivable formulae. Abbreviate 'formula π whose '∀'-closure is well-formed and which contains the first of the pair as a part' to '$\underline{\pi}$', and abbreviate 'formula which results from $\underline{\pi}$ by substituting the second of the pair for the first' to '$\underline{\underline{\pi}}$'; similarly for '$\wp$' etc. Then take some such formula $\underline{\pi}$. Suppose (the inductive supposition) that every such $\underline{\wp}$ shorter than $\underline{\pi}$ is interderivable with $\underline{\underline{\wp}}$. The cases to be surveyed divide into three kinds, the third subdividing. First the interderivable part in $\underline{\pi}$ may be the whole of $\underline{\pi}$. Then trivially $\underline{\pi}$ and $\underline{\underline{\pi}}$ are interderivable. Secondly $\underline{\pi}$ or $\underline{\underline{\pi}}$ may be in non-primitive notation. In that case they are interderivable if and only if their primitive versions are. Thirdly the interderivable part in $\underline{\pi}$ may be less than the whole of it, $\underline{\pi}$ and $\underline{\underline{\pi}}$ being in primitive notation. Then because of the sense given to 'part' in the Metatheorem π cannot be atomic, and there remain four cases to consider. (i) $\underline{\pi}$'s main connective is '$\sim$', i.e. it is $\sim\underline{\wp}$ for some $\wp$ whose '∀'-closure is well-formed. Then the part for substitution is in $\underline{\wp}$, so that $\sim\underline{\wp}$ is $\sim\underline{\underline{\wp}}$. By the inductive supposition $\underline{\wp}$, being shorter than $\underline{\pi}$, is interderivable with $\underline{\underline{\wp}}$. Hence by (a) of the first stage of the proof $\sim\underline{\wp}$ s interderivable with $\sim\underline{\underline{\wp}}$. But $\sim\underline{\underline{\wp}}$ is $\underline{\underline{\sim\wp}}$, i.e. $\underline{\underline{\pi}}$. (ii) $\underline{\pi}$ is $\wp \& \rho$, for some $\wp$ and ρ whose '∀'-closures are well-formed. Then $\underline{\wp \& \rho}$ is $\underline{\wp} \& \rho$ or $\wp \& \underline{\rho}$. By the inductive supposition $\underline{\wp}$ is interderivable with $\underline{\underline{\wp}}$ and $\underline{\rho}$ with $\underline{\underline{\rho}}$. Hence by (b) $\wp \& \rho$ is interderivable with both $\underline{\underline{\wp}} \& \rho$ and $\wp \& \underline{\underline{\rho}}$. But $\underline{\underline{\wp \& \rho}}$, i.e. $\underline{\underline{\pi}}$, is one of these. (iii) $\underline{\pi}$ is $\forall\nu\phi\nu$ for some $\phi\nu$ whose '∀'-closure is well-formed. Then $\underline{\forall\nu\phi\nu}$ is $\forall\nu\underline{\phi\nu}$.

5.4 Metatheorems on derivability

By the inductive supposition $\underline{\phi\nu}$ is interderivable with $\underline{\phi\nu}$ (this is the clause for the sake of which the supposition must extend beyond well-formed formulae). Hence by (c) $\forall\nu\underline{\phi\nu}$ is interderivable with $\forall\nu\underline{\phi\nu}$. But this is $\forall\nu\underline{\phi\nu}$, i.e. $\underline{\underline{\pi}}$. (iv) $\underline{\pi}$ is $\square\varphi$ for some φ whose '$\forall$' closure is well-formed. The same argument applies as in (i), now appealing to (d). This completes the survey of cases, proving that for any pair of interderivable formulae and for any π containing the first of the pair whose '$\forall$'-closure is well-formed, if every formula containing the first of the pair whose '$\forall$'-closure is well-formed and which is shorter than π is interderivable with the result of substituting the second, so is π itself with the result of that substitution. Then by the principle of strong mathematical induction it follows that *every* formula containing the first of the pair whose '$\forall$'-closure is well-formed is interderivable with the result of substituting the second. A well-formed formula is the '$\forall$'-closure of a well-formed formula (itself). Hence in particular every *well-formed* formula containing the first of the pair is interderivable with the result of substituting the second, which was to be proved in the second stage.

In the third stage it is to be proved that for any π and φ that are well-formed and interderivable, if a derivable sequent has π for the *whole* of its last formula, then the result of substituting φ for it is still a derivable sequent. Proof. Take some Γ and well-formed π and φ, and suppose that π and φ are interderivable and $\langle\Gamma, \pi\rangle$ is derivable. Since π and φ are well-formed and interderivable,

(1) $\vdash\langle\Lambda, \pi \equiv \varphi\rangle$ by definition of 'interderivable'
so (2) $\vdash\langle\Lambda, (\pi \supset \varphi)\,\&\,(\varphi \supset \pi)\rangle$ Def≡ 1
(3) $\vdash\langle\Lambda, \pi \supset \varphi\rangle$ &E 2
(4) $\vdash\langle\Gamma, \pi\rangle$ supposition
(5) $\vdash\langle\Gamma, \varphi\rangle$ MPP-S 3,4

The conclusions of the second and third stages can now be put together. Suppose that for some π, φ, Γ (i) φ results from π by substituting an interderivable part, (ii) $\langle\Gamma, \pi\rangle$ is derivable, and (iii) $\langle\Gamma, \varphi\rangle$ is well-formed. By (ii) π is well-formed, and by (iii) φ is well-formed. So by the second stage π and φ are themselves interderivable. So by the third stage $\langle \Gamma, \varphi \rangle$ is derivable. Q.E.D.

In order to use this metatheorem we need to be supplied with pairs of interderivable formulae. Among such pairs are π and $\sim\sim\pi$, $\forall v \forall \mu \pi$ and $\forall \mu \forall v \pi$, and $\exists v \exists \mu \pi$ and $\exists \mu \exists v \pi$, for any π which is such that the '$\forall$'-closures of those formulae are well-formed; the proofs of interderivability are quite easy. So we get as consequences of the metatheorem that [$\sim$ Int] the result of inserting or deleting '$\sim\sim$' anywhere in the last formula of a derivable sequent is a derivable sequent, provided that insertion preserves well-formedness; and [$\forall$Int and $\exists$Int] the result of re-arranging adjacent occurrences of '$\forall$'-plus-variable or of '$\exists$'-plus-variable in the last formula of a derivable sequent is a derivable sequent (cf. HUGHES & LONDEY p. 269); the occurrences must be adjacent, not separated even by a bracket. $\sim$ Int looks a bit like Lemmon's Double Negation, the conjunction of $\sim$E and $\sim$I. But it is much more than that, for it covers occurrences of '$\sim\sim$' anywhere in a sequent's last formula, not just at the beginning. A better comparison would be with the symbolic definitions, which likewise apply to any part of a well-formed formula. $\forall$Int and $\exists$Int are examples of **quantifier shift rules**, or rules of passage, which allow the scope of a quantifier, under certain conditions, to be extended or diminished. In '$\forall x \forall y f x y$', for instance, the scope of the second '$\forall$' is '$\forall y f x y$'; and according to $\forall$Int it is interderivable with '$\forall y \forall x f x y$', in which the scope of the '$\forall$' binding 'y' has been widened. Formulae in which all quantifiers have greater scope than any other connective are called prenex; and every well-formed formula containing quantifiers is interderivable with some prenex formula. But the rules of prenexing (QUINE *MofL* pp. 124-9) are complicated since in many cases a quantifier shifted to the left must change from universal to existential or vice versa; e.g. though '$\forall x f x \ \& \ p$', '$p \ \& \ \forall x f x$' and '$p \supset \forall x f x$' are interderivable with '$\forall x(fx \ \& \ p)$', '$\forall x(p \ \& \ fx)$' and '$\forall x(p \supset fx)$' respectively, '$\forall x f x \supset p$' is interderivable with '$\exists x(fx \supset p)$', and the same is true with '$\exists$' for '$\forall$' and '$\forall$' for '$\exists$' (compare derivation (L) on pp. 136-7). More confusingly still, a quantifier outranked by '$\equiv$' cannot in general be prenexed without doubling; e.g. '$\forall x f x \equiv p$' is interderivable with '$\forall x \exists y((fy \supset p) \ \& \ (p \supset fx))$', but not with '$\forall x(fx \equiv p)$' or '$\exists x(fx \equiv p)$'. Once quantifiers have been prenexed their order is

5.4 Metatheorems on derivability

not indifferent; for ∀Int and ∃Int do not cover mixed runs of '∀' and '∃', which are freely rearrangeable only in sequents in which all predicate letters are one-place (QUINE *MofL* pp. 118–23).

5.5 Abridged derivations

It would be tedious and absurd if every sequent-derivation had to start again at the beginning, making no use of those that precede it. One way of avoiding that necessity while still keeping within the definition of 'sequent-derivation' given in 5.2 would be to count each derivation as part of a single long one, extending over a whole book, or course of lectures, or examination script, or whatever seemed to be the appropriate unit (accordingly derivation lines might be numbered in a single continuous series). But such a fused derivation would still need to contain many seemingly redundant parts; for example the inclusion of (H) in it, which proved the derivability of $\langle\{`fa`\}, `\exists x fx`\rangle$, would not dispense us from going through exactly parallel proofs if we wished at some later stage to establish the derivability of $\langle\{`gb`\}, `\exists x gx`\rangle$ or $\langle\{`\sim(faa \& q)`\}, `\exists y \sim(fya \& q)`\rangle$. Metatheorems come to the rescue, in one of two ways. Either we can prove a Substitution Metatheorem, permitting entry of a sequent in a derivation whenever it is a 'substituend' of some sequent already proved derivable; this, which is the way of Lemmon's Rule of Sequent Introduction (*BL* p. 58), I shall not adopt though I shall describe it in 5.6 (7). The other way is to use, and if necessary to enlarge, the battery of metatheorems proved in 5.4. Either course involves changing the definition of 'sequent-derivation' so as to permit the metatheorems to justify entries. But the change does not open up any new destinations that could not have been reached by the rules of 5.2; it only shortens journeys to the old destinations. This is because an entry justified by a metatheorem can always be reached more lengthily by going through the steps that were used in proving the metatheorem, steps which of course relied on nothing except rules already adopted. Hence in derivations metatheorems may function as Short Cut rules (MATES p. 120, 'admissible rules' LAMBERT & VAN FRAASSEN p. 38).

I shall now illustrate the power of metatheorems to shorten derivations, and their dispensability. A licence to justify an entry by the Interderivability Metatheorem makes it possible to get to the last entry of the following derivation in five lines instead of twenty (and compare the nine-line derivation in MATES p. 126):

(K)
1	(1)	$\sim\forall x \exists y \forall z f x y z$	A
1	(2)	$\sim\forall x \sim\forall y \sim\forall z f x y z$	Def∃ 1
1	(3)	$\exists x \forall y \sim\forall z f x y z$	Def∃ 2
1	(4)	$\exists z \forall y \sim\forall z \sim \sim f x y z$	∼Int 3
1	(5)	$\exists z \forall y \exists z \sim f x y z$	Def∃ 4

The effect is to shift '∼' past three quantifiers, each of which changes from '∀' to '∃' or '∃' to '∀'. The next example illustrates the dispensability of metatheorems by recording, in boxes, the steps which MPP–S, ∃E, and CP shortcut (the shortest route using the 5.2 rules alone is in fact shorter than the route through the boxes, but still fifteen lines long).

(L)
1	(1)	$\forall x(fx \supset p)$	A			
2	(2)	$\exists x f x$	A			
3	(3)	fa	A			
1	(4)	$fa \supset p$	∀E	1		
5	(5)	$\sim p$	A			
3,5	(6)	$fa \,\&\, \sim p$	&I	3,5		
1	(7)	$\sim(fa \,\&\, \sim p)$	Def⊃	4		
1,3,5	(8)	$(fa \,\&\, \sim p) \,\&\, \sim(fa \,\&\, \sim p)$	&I	6,7		
1,3	(9)	$\sim\sim p$	RAA	8		
1,3	(10)	p	∼E	9	MPP–S	4,5
1,3,5	(11)	$p \,\&\, \sim p$	&I	5,10		
1,5	(12)	$\sim fa$	RAA	11		
1,5	(13)	$\forall x \sim fx$	∀I-S	12		
2	(14)	$\sim\forall x \sim fx$	Def∃	2		
1,2,5	(15)	$\forall x \sim fx \,\&\, \sim\forall x \sim fx$	&I	13,14		
1,2	(16)	$\sim\sim p$	RAA	15		
1,2	(17)	p	∼E	16	∃E	2,10
18	(18)	$\exists x f x \,\&\, \sim p$	A			
18	(19)	$\sim p$	&E	18		
1,2,18	(20)	$p \,\&\, \sim p$	&I	17,19		
1,18	(21)	$\sim \exists x f x$	RAA	20		
18	(22)	$\exists x f x$	&E	18		

5.5 Abridged derivations

1,18	(23)	$\exists x fx\ \&\ \sim \exists x fx$	&I	21,22		
1	(24)	$\sim(\exists x fx\ \&\ \sim p)$	RAA	23		
1	(25)	$\exists x fx \supset p$	Def⊃	24	CP	17

It is unreasonable in general to use a metatheorem in a derivation without first proving it. Otherwise every derivation could be shortened to its last entry, justified by merely asserting the metatheorem whose proof parallels its other entries. Sequent-derivations may be abridged, but we have to be careful that the abridgments still *display* the method of proving that their last entries are derivable—and it is doubtless sometimes a debatable matter whether that condition has been met.

5.6 Other people's rules

I shall mention nine ways in which other people's rules of derivation differ from those adopted in the present chapter.

(1) In MATES '$\langle \Gamma, \pi \rangle$ is derivable' is replaced by 'π is derivable from Γ'. We have seen in 5.1 that this is a trifling difference.

(2) Authors prescribe various ways of 'keeping track of assumptions'. Usually, as in 5.3, the method involves citing 'assumptions' in the left-hand margin of a derivation, so that a derivation not only displays the derivability of some sequent but consists of a string of sequents, one to each line (so MATES, MASSEY, LEMMON *BL*). In this method only the last formulae of successive sequents, the ones written on successive lines, mirror the pattern of actual reasoning. So it is not surprising that there exist even more 'natural' methods of 'deduction' in which successive lines are merely formulae; of this kind are the methods of QUINE (*MofL* chs. 30, 37) and FITCH (ch. 2, cf. LAMBERT & VAN FRAASSEN).

(3) In the method of MASSEY, modelled on QUINE, the rules corresponding to ∀I-S and ∃E are so formulated that not every sequent in a derivation is derivable, with the result that not every initial segment of a derivation is a derivation. Rogue sequents have consequently to be 'flagged', and rules have to be stated for

telling when a derivation is 'finished' (QUINE *MofL* pp. 204-5, MASSEY pp. 285-90).

(4) In QUINE, MASSEY and MATES the rules for introducing quantifiers are called UG and EG, for 'universal generalisation' and 'existential generalisation'. The rules for eliminating quantifiers are called US and ES in MATES ('S' for 'specification'), UI and EI in QUINE and MASSEY ('I' for 'instantiation'—it is unfortunate that this conflicts with its use for 'introduction').

(5) If the primitive, i.e. undefined, connectives are different, not just notationally, the primitive, i.e. unproved, derivation rules must be different too, to secure the same set of derivable sequents. The general requirement turns out to be that a sequent system needs a rule for introducing and a rule for eliminating each of its primitive connectives. The system of 5.2 meets the requirement in spite of not containing ∼I as primitive, because RAA fulfils the function of introducing '∼'. ∼I could of course be added, superfluously, to the list of rules, as LEMMON *BL* superfluously adds it; but it cannot replace RAA, if only because no other rule in 5.2 reduces the number of formulae in a sequent's initial set. In MATES, where in effect '∼', '⊃', '∀' are sole primitive connectives, MPP-S is used for eliminating and C for introducing '⊃' and, because of a feature of C which distinguishes it from the Deduction Theorem, CP on p. 129, there is only a single '∼' rule; but this latter, MT, again differs from MTT on p. 128. LEMMON uses only one definition, Def≡, and so needs many more primitive derivation rules, though not quite so many as for his own reasons he actually provides.

(6) When MATES passes from the propositional to the predicate calculus (p. 112) he discards all but A and C from his propositional rules and substitutes T, which amounts to 'if $\langle\{\pi_1, \ldots \pi_n\}, \wp\rangle$ is well-formed and PC-valid and each of $\langle \Gamma_1, \pi_1\rangle, \ldots \langle \Gamma_n, \pi_n\rangle$ has been entered, $\langle \Gamma_1 \cup \ldots \Gamma_n, \wp\rangle$ may be entered'; and MASSEY (p. 276) concurs. This course does not threaten the soundness in QC of the predicate calculus system, since every QC-sequent which is PC-valid is also QC-valid (see pp. 194-5). And for the same reason rule T could be introduced in S5, QS5 and, of course, PC itself. The motive for its introduction is the existence of methods

for proving **PC**-validity directly, without recourse to propositional derivation rules (see 7.2). Hence, the argument goes, if the purpose of logistic systems is eventually to provide proofs of validity in certain logical languages, and **PC**-valid sequents that are well-formed in those systems are all valid in those languages, why not make use of the direct methods instead of bothering with propositional derivations which are not always short or easy to find? The resulting natural deduction systems of MATES and MASSEY are *impure* in that their reference to validity presupposes an interpretation of the symbols they manipulate (but they could be purified by substituting '**PC**-select', in the sense of 7.3, for '**PC**-valid').

(7) Natural Deduction systems may contain a Rule of Substitution. Although this could of course be among the primitive rules, it is more often cited as a metatheorem, e.g. by Lemmon who gives a proof of it for the propositional calculus (S2 on p. 55 of *BL*). The rule states, with deceptive simplicity, that any substituend (or 'substitution-instance') of a derivable sequent is derivable. I I shall not prove it, but on pp. 158–9. I shall explain the meaning of 'substituend of a formula', from which the extension to 'substituend of a sequent' is easy. The rule, once proved, can be used for shortening derivations by permitting entry of any sequent which is a substituend of some sequent previously proved derivable; and its use can supplant that of other metatheorems on derivability. For example if it is desired to prove the derivability of $\langle\{'p'\}, '\sim\sim p'\rangle$ and also $\langle\{'q'\}, '\sim\sim q'\rangle$, then instead of first proving $\sim$I we can use the following abridged sequent-derivation:

(M) 1   (1) p A
     2   (2) $\sim p$ A
     1,2   (3) $p \& \sim p$ &I   1,2
     1   (4) $\sim\sim p$ RAA   3
     q (5) $\sim\sim q$ substituend of (4)

Notice that the substitution in line 5 affects the initial set in that line, which becomes $\{'q'\}$, as well as the written formula, which becomes '$\sim\sim q$'. LEMMON's Rule of Sequent Introduction (*BL* p. 58, cf. MATES p. 101) is a bit more complex, partly because steps of CP and MPP-S are needed to prove it from the Substitution Rule and partly because it is stated specifically as a rule of construction. It goes like this: if $\langle\{\pi_1, \ldots \pi_n\}, \varphi\rangle$ is a substituend of some sequent proved derivable in a previous derivation and each of $\langle \Gamma_1, \pi_1\rangle$, $\ldots \langle \Gamma_n, \pi_n\rangle$ has been entered, $\langle \Gamma_1 \cup \ldots \Gamma_n, \varphi\rangle$ may be entered.

(8) In place of '$\langle \Gamma, \pi\rangle$ is derivable when it is the last entry in some derivation' MATES in effect substitutes '$\langle \Gamma, \pi\rangle$ is derivable when for some subset Δ of $\Gamma \langle \Delta, \pi\rangle$ is the last entry in some derivation' (MATES pp. 98, 113). Since infinite sets have finite subsets this admits infinite sequents as derivable (though they are not well-formed under the formation rules of the present book). The generality thus gained is not of practical value outside mathematics and would complicate the proof of soundness in 7.5.

(9) LEMMON and HUGHES & LONDEY call proved rules 'derived rules', which loses the virtue claimed for the word 'derivable' on p. 113, that its links with the ordinary concept of deduction are tenuous and easy to ignore. Lemmon's usage may suggest that derived rules are derivable in the same sense as derivable sequents are. They are not. A 'derived' rule is a metatheorem, a metalogical truth about sequents provable from the primitive derivation rules. A sequent is not a metalogical truth, because it is not a truth; it may be proved derivable but it cannot be derived in the *sense* 'proved' (p. 126).

CHAPTER SIX

Derivation Rules for Formulae

6.1 *Axiomatic systems*

In 5.1 I sketched a logistic system which started with various categorical rules and added the hypothetical rule 'if π is derivable from Δ and every member of Δ is derivable from some subset of Γ, π is derivable from Γ'. Then I exchanged it for a sequent system whose rules were fully stated in 5.2. The sequent system differed from its sketched precursor in two ways, one more important than the other. The less important difference was that I chose to substitute derivability as a property of sequents for derivability as a relation from sets of formulae to formulae, replacing 'π is derivable from Γ' by '$\langle \Gamma, \pi \rangle$ is derivable'. The more important difference was that the sequent system, even for the propositional calculus, contained not one but four hypothetical rules and only a single categorical rule (two in QC). In the present chapter I shall move away from the sketched system in the other direction, keeping its preponderance of categorical rules but discarding its application to sequents.

The change is effected in two steps. First the derivation rules, both categorical and hypothetical, are made to apply only to formulae which are derivable from the empty set of formulae, Λ. The fact that some formula π is derivable from the empty set can still, of course, be stated by saying that a sequent is derivable, namely the sequent $\langle \Lambda, \pi \rangle$; but it is simpler now to leave out reference to sequents and to say merely that π is a derivable formula. As in 5.1 it was possible but unnecessary to think of '$\langle \Gamma, \pi \rangle$ is a derivable sequent' as meaning 'π is derivable from Γ', so in the new system it will be possible but unnecessary to think of 'π is a derivable formula' as meaning 'π is derivable from Λ'. The second step in the transformation will be to frame rules for constructing derivations in such a way that every entry in a derivation must be a formula

141

derivable from the empty set, i.e. a derivable formula. This means that the Deduction Theorem, which refers essentially to formulae derivable from non-empty sets, will not be provable in the logistic system of this chapter—a feature which distinguishes it from Massey's system P (MASSEY p. 125 ff.).

Many authors use the word 'theorem' in place of 'derivable formula' (MATES pp. 127, 166, LEMMON *BL* p. 50, MASSEY p. 128, QUINE *MofL* p. 72); and many describe theorems that are derivable in virtue of categorical rules as 'axioms' (MATES p. 165, QUINE *MofL* p. 72, MASSEY p. 126; an alternative terminology restricts the word 'theorem' to derivable formulae that are not axioms, HUGHES & LONDEY p. 88). Consequently logistic systems in which only formulae and no (other) sequents are derivable are often distinguished as 'axiomatic'. But the name is misleading for two reasons. First, sequent systems also must contain what I have called sequent-axioms such as $\langle \{`p`\}, `p` \rangle$, i.e. formulae derivable from sets of formulae in virtue of categorical rules, and may even contain formula-axioms such as $\langle \Lambda, `a = a` \rangle$, i.e. formulae derivable from the empty set in virtue of categorical rules; the former are like, and the latter actually are, axioms in the logician's traditional sense. Secondly, use of the words 'axiom' and 'theorem' may suggest too close an analogy with what MATES (p. 183) calls a deductive theory, QUINE (*MofL* p. 74) a postfoundational axiom system, and MASSEY (p. 307) a postulate system. Deductive theories in this sense—Euclid's geometry is the most famous specimen—differ from logistic systems in two crucial respects: they are interpreted, and moreover must be interpreted in such a way that they consist of sentences not schemata; and their theorems are entailed by their axioms. By contrast the relation among formulae in a system of derivable formulae—that the other theorems are derivable if the axioms are—holds whether or not the formulae are interpreted and regardless of what the interpretation may be; and even if a system's formulae are made by some interpretation into sentences, its axioms might fail to entail its theorems without reproach to the system as such—failure would merely attest the system's unsoundness under *that* interpretation. A third, less definite, difference is that logistic systems are usually developed, as in this book, in the course of a *study* of entailment: they reveal, if sound, patterns of deductively correct inference. That is why derivation rules get called—too

6.1 Axiomatic systems

hastily, as we saw on p. 113—rules of inference. But in a deductive theory like Euclid's, interest centres on the special subject matter and inferences, though of course drawn, are not examined systematically, if at all.

Because the formula systems of this chapter are no more 'axiomatic' than the sequent systems of Chapter 5 I shall avoid that name for them. But I shall defer to tradition in calling their categorically derivable formulae axioms, in spite of the big difference between uninterpreted formulae and the propositions taken as axioms in a deductive theory. Once 'axiom' has been permitted there would be no objection to 'theorem', though I shall continue to use 'derivable formula' instead. Most logicians now guard against confusion between derivable formulae and provable assertions about them by distinguishing the latter as 'metatheorems'; but HUGHES AND LONDEY are an exception, and the Deduction Theorem is commonly so called.

As in Chapter 5, I shall formulate the rules as rules for constructing a formula-derivation.

6.2 Formulating the rules

A **formula-derivation** in a calculus is a finite and non-empty ordered set of formulae, constructed according to the following rules which are summarised in Appendix Two.

As in the sequent system, there are to be five propositional rules, but this time four of them are categorical. The first is **Iteration for '&'**: [It&] for any PC-formula π, $\pi \supset \pi \& \pi$ may be entered in a formula-derivation. Its mate **Simplification for '&'**, is closely analogous to &I of the sequent system: [Simp&] for any PC-formulae π and φ, $\pi \& \varphi \supset \pi$ may be entered in a formula-derivation. Analogy between elimination-rules and simplification-rules will run right through the two sets of systems. The former are, in a way, more powerful. For one thing '$\pi \& \varphi \supset \varphi$ is derivable' is not incorporated in Simp&, though it can be proved, eventually, in the formula system; whereas &E contained a part corresponding to that version too. For another thing, and more fundamentally, the formula system affords no means of gaining the generality of &E's reference to sets of formulae Γ; as forecast in 6.1 all such initial sets now have to be empty. Notice that π and φ must be well-formed, to guarantee that $\pi \& \phi \supset \pi$ is; in the hypothetical &E this work was done by the supposition that $\langle \Gamma, \pi \& \phi \rangle$ is derivable. The third rule is **Commutation for '&'**, so called because it corresponds roughly to the provable semantic rule 'if ⌜$\sigma \& \tau$⌝ is T, so is ⌜$\tau \& \sigma$⌝' which is a law of commutation; but the formula system requires a negated and categorical version as primitive, the unnegated and hypothetical version being eventually provable: [Com&] for any PC-formulae π and ϕ, $\sim(\pi \& \phi) \supset \sim(\phi \& \pi)$ may be entered in a formula-derivation. The final axiom rule, which I call '**Summation for '&'** on the analogy of Summation in *Principia Mathematica* (WHITEHEAD & RUSSELL p. 97), runs like this: [Sum&] for any PC-formulae π, ϕ, ρ, $(\pi \supset \phi) \supset (\sim(\phi \& \rho) \supset \sim(\pi \& \rho))$ may be entered in a formula-derivation. To these four is added a single hypothetical rule, **Modus Ponendo Ponens for Formulae**. This is just the special case of MPP-S in which both Γ and Δ are empty: [MPP-F] for any formulae π and ϕ, if $\pi \supset \phi$ and π have both been entered in a formula-derivation, then ϕ may be entered in it.

For abbreviating the statement of these rules I shall here, though not in Appendix Two, write '$(\pi \& \phi)$' etc. as '$\pi\phi$' etc. and '$\sim$' as a bar surmounting the formula within its scope. This, the notation of Quine (*MofL* p. 9), brings great economy to the formulation of rules in a propositional formula system in which '$\sim$' and '&' are primitive. The five rules become: for any PC-formulae π, ϕ, ρ, in any formula-derivation, $\pi \supset \pi\pi$, $\pi\phi \supset \pi$, $\overline{\pi\phi} \supset \overline{\phi\pi}$, and $(\pi \supset \phi) \supset (\overline{\phi\rho} \supset \overline{\pi\rho})$ may be entered; and if $\pi \supset \phi$ and π have been entered, then ϕ may be.

In the predicate calculus with identity the same five rules reappear, adapted to QC-formulae, and four new ones are added, two each for '=' and '∀'. Of the four newcomers '='-**Introduction** is the very same rule as in the sequent system, now expressed in the words: [=I] for any subject letter a, $a = a$ may be entered in a formula-derivation. The next rule, also categorical, I call **Simplification for '='** because of a resemblance, admittedly slight, with Simp&: each contains an occurrence to the left of '$\supset$' of the symbol it is named after, and no occurrence to the right (hence each can be used in conjunction with MPP-F for eliminating its symbol, and Simp= stands to =E as we found that Simp& stands to &E). The

6.2 Formulating the rules

rule is: [Simp=] for any subject letters α and β and QC-formulae π and φ, $\alpha = \beta \supset (\pi \supset \varphi)$ may be entered in a formula-derivation if φ differs from π only in containing β in at least one place where π contains α. In the language of stencils the rule becomes: $\alpha = \beta \supset (\phi\alpha \supset \phi\beta)$ may be entered provided that $\phi\alpha$ is a QC-formula. Of the two '∀'-rules **Simplification for '∀'** continues the process of converting hypothetical elimination rules for sequents into categorical rules for formulae. One formulation would be: [Simp∀] for any subject letter α, variable ν, formula π containing ν and QC-formula φ, $\forall\nu\pi \supset \varphi$ may be entered in a formula-derivation if φ differs from π only in containing α in every place where π contains ν. As in the sequent system this is unlike Simp= in requiring substitution of α for ν throughout π. So its stencil version must insist on a stencil not already containing ν, and must take the form: for any α, ν and ϕ, $\forall\nu\phi\nu \supset \phi\alpha$ may be entered provided that $\phi\alpha$ is a QC-formula and ϕ contains no ν. The final rule, '∀'-**Introduction**, is hypothetical, and like ∀I-S requires that the formula licensed should contain no occurrence of the 'bartered' subject letter. In terms of substitution: [∀I-F] for any subject letter α, variable ν, QC-formula π containing no α, and QC-formula φ containing α but not ν, if $\pi \supset \varphi$ has been entered in a formula-derivation, then $\pi \supset \forall\nu$ followed by the result of substituting ν for every occurrence of α in φ may be entered in it. In terms of stencils: if $\pi \supset \phi\alpha$ has been entered, then $\pi \supset \forall\nu\phi\nu$ may be, provided that π contains no α and ϕ contains neither ν nor α.

In 6.4 I shall show how on the basis of ∀I-F the simpler but less powerful metatheorem 'if ⊢$\phi\alpha$, then ⊢$\forall\nu\phi\nu$' can be proved (ϕ still containing no α or ν). Notice, though, that this is by no means the same as proving the categorical metatheorem '⊢$\phi\alpha \supset \forall\nu\phi\nu$'. There is a contrast here with Simp∀, which is categorical and can be proved in the sequent system from the hypothetical ∀E as follows:

(1) ⊢⟨{∀ν$\phi\nu$}, ∀ν$\phi\nu$⟩   A
(2) ⊢⟨{∀ν$\phi\nu$}, $\phi\alpha$⟩   ∀E   1
(3) ⊢⟨Λ, ∀ν$\phi\nu \supset \phi\alpha$⟩   CP   2

provided $\phi\alpha$ is well-formed and ϕ contains no ν. An attempt to reproduce this proof with '$\phi\alpha$' and '∀ν$\phi\nu$' exchanged would founder in line 2, where ∀I-S would require that the initial set of formulae contain no α. In fact the categorical metatheorem cannot be proved from the rules of either the formula system or the sequent system; which is just as well because for most α, ν, ϕ, $\phi\alpha \supset \forall\nu\phi\nu$ is QC-invalid, and so a logistic system containing the rule would be QC-unsound. This is a suitable point therefore at which to draw attention to the vital difference, in any system, between metatheorems of the form '$\vdash\pi \supset \varphi$' and of the form 'if $\vdash\pi$, then $\vdash\varphi$'. The latter can be inferred from the former in a system containing MPP, but the former cannot in general be inferred from the latter (different again is the categorical form '$\vdash\langle\{\pi\}, \varphi\rangle$', which some would write as '$\pi \vdash \varphi$'; this entails and is entailed by '$\vdash\pi \supset \varphi$' in systems containing A, MPP and the Deduction Theorem).

With full metalogical abbreviation as before the four extra predicate calculus rules become: for any subject letters α and β, variable ν, stencil ϕ and QC-formula π, in any formula-derivation, $\alpha = \alpha$ may be entered; if $\phi\alpha$ is a QC-formula, $\alpha = \beta \supset (\phi\alpha \supset \phi\beta)$ may be entered; if $\phi\alpha$ is a QC-formula and ϕ contains no ν, $\forall\nu\phi\nu \supset \phi\alpha$ may be entered; if ϕ contains no ν and neither ϕ nor π contains α and $\pi \supset \phi\alpha$ has been entered, then $\pi \supset \forall\nu\phi\nu$ may be.

The formula-rules of S5 and QS5 result by adapting to S5-formulae and QS5-formulae the rules of PC and QC respectively, and adding to each set a pair of rules analogous to Simp∀ and ∀I-F. **Simplification for '□'**, which is categorical, is: [Simp□] for any S5-(QS5-)formula π, $\square\pi \supset \pi$ may be entered in a formula-derivation. **'□'-Introduction for Formulae** remains hypothetical and carries over from the sequent system the requirement that every formula licensed by it should be fully modalised (see p. 121). Its statement is: [□I-F] for any S5-(QS5-) formulae π and φ, if $\pi \supset \varphi$ has been entered in a formula-derivation, then $\pi \supset \square\varphi$ may be entered in it, provided that π is fully modalised. Without the proviso nothing would prevent passage from the S5-valid '$p \supset p$' to the S5-invalid '$p \supset \square p$'. As in QC the simpler and less powerful metatheorem 'if $\vdash\varphi$, then $\vdash\square\varphi$ (φ fully modalised)' is provable from □I-F; and in contrast with ∀I-F the categorical '$\vdash\varphi \supset \square\varphi$' is also provable, provided still that φ is fully modalised (see p. 153).

Abbreviated, the modal rules are: for any S5-formulae π and φ, in any formula-derivation, $\square\pi \supset \pi$ may be entered; and if π is fully modalised and $\pi \supset \varphi$ has been entered, then $\pi \supset \square\varphi$ may be. Similarly for QS5.

Finally, the symbolic definitions are allowed to function as rules

6.2 Formulating the rules

for constructing formula-derivations. That is: for any π, φ, if φ results from π by one of the symbolic definitions, and π has been entered in a formula-derivation, then φ may be entered in it.

The set of derivable formulae in each calculus is now to be defined in terms of these rules. A formula is derivable in the propositional calculus, **PC-derivable** for short, when it is the last entry in some PC formula-derivation, i.e. in some derivation constructed according to the five PC rules plus the definitions; a **QC-derivable** formula is the last entry in some QC formula-derivation; and similarly in the other cases.

6.3 Formula-derivations

A formula-derivation, like a sequent-derivation, does not infer that a formula is derivable by argument from premisses, but rather displays that fact in a structure made according to rules. For better display I adopt the following fairly standard conventions: (i) each formula in a derivation will be written on a separate line; (ii) the lines will be numbered; (iii) the derivation rule or definition which justifies each entry will be cited to its right.

Here are some derivations by way of example. In the first I resume the convention introduced in 6.2 of writing $\ulcorner(\pi \,\&\, \varphi)\urcorner$ as $\ulcorner\pi\varphi\urcorner$, so as to make the shape of each formula plainer. The reference '(N)' continues the series begun in Chapter 5.

(N) (1) $(p \supset pp) \supset (\sim(pp \,\&\sim p) \supset \sim(p \,\&\sim p))$ Sum&
  (2) $(p \supset pp) \supset ((pp \supset p) \supset (p \supset p))$ Def$\supset$ twice 1
  (3) $p \supset pp$ It&
  (4) $(pp \supset p) \supset (p \supset p)$ MPP-F   2,3
  (5) $pp \supset p$ Simp&
  (6) $p \supset p$ MPP-F   4,5

Notice that It&, used in line 3, requires the same formula thrice repeated, while Simp&, used in line 5, permits without requiring that. The layout is simpler than in sequent-derivations because, each line being a formula rather than a sequent, no sets of formulae need to be cited in the left hand margin (or: the citation is 'Λ' throughout). But it is typical of 'axiomatic' methods that (N) is twice the length of (F) on p. 124 which ended '$\langle \Lambda, `p \supset p`\rangle$'. Also, results in the formula systems rely much more heavily on use of preceding derivations. Whereas for example the rules of 5.3 permit a nine-line sequent-derivation ending '$\langle \Lambda, \text{'}fa \supset \exists x fx\text{'}\rangle$', the formula '$fa \supset \exists x fx$' can be reached in a formula-derivation only through a complex set of propositional moves leading to '$(\forall x \sim fx \supset \sim fa) \supset (fa \supset \sim \forall x \sim fx)$', whence it emerges by Simp$\forall$, MPP-F and Def$\exists$ (cf. '$\exists$'-Introduction on p. 152). Similarly the sequent whose validity shows that '$=$' expresses a transitive relation, $\langle \Lambda, \text{'}a = b \supset (b = c \supset a = c)\text{'}\rangle$, can be reached in eight lines in a sequent-derivation, but its last formula needs a much longer formula-derivation, even though two very similar-looking versions are axioms and so arrive in one line each:

(O) (1) $a = b \supset (a = c \supset b = c)$ Simp=

(P) (1) $a = b \supset (c = a \supset c = b)$ Simp=

(in (O) the stencil is ' $= c$', in (P) '$c = \_\_$').

In S5 and QS5 there is the same problem of length. But one interesting S5-derivable formula emerges fairly quickly:

(Q) (1)

.

.

.

(6) $\Diamond p \supset \Diamond p$ by steps as in (N)
(7) $\Diamond p \supset \Box \Diamond p$ $\Box$I-F 6

Line 7 is correct because '$\Diamond p$' is fully modalised. This formula is sometimes called the 'characteristic S5 axiom', because its derivability distinguishes S5 from various weaker modal systems. That it is not an axiom of S5 in the present book illustrates the familiar fact that one and the same system can be axiomatised in different ways.

6.4 *Metatheorems on derivability*

In this section I select some among the infinitely many metatheorems provable in the formula systems of 6.2. Because the metalogical proofs of these rules virtually copy, as in Chapter 5, the steps of derivations, they tend to be lengthy and to rely on their precursors: and for these reasons I shall leave several of them incomplete.

6.4 Metatheorems on derivability

Syllogism [Syll]. For any well-formed π, φ, ρ, $\vdash(\pi \supset \varphi) \supset ((\varphi \supset \rho) \supset (\pi \supset \rho))$; also if $\vdash \pi \supset \varphi$, then $\vdash(\varphi \supset \rho) \supset (\pi \supset \rho)$; also if $\vdash \pi \supset \varphi$ and $\vdash \varphi \supset \rho$, then $\vdash \pi \supset \rho$.

This is three different metatheorems under the same name, the first of them categorical like Sum&, the other two hypothetical. HUGHES & LONDEY call the first 'Syll' and the last 'Derived Rule 2' (p. 106). The proof of the categorical version is this: for any well-formed π, φ, ρ,

(1) $\vdash(\pi \supset \varphi) \supset (\sim(\varphi \,\&\, \sim\rho) \supset \sim(\pi \,\&\, \sim\rho))$ Sum&
(2) $\vdash(\pi \supset \varphi) \supset ((\varphi \supset \rho) \supset (\pi \supset \rho))$ Def⊃ twice   1

The hypothetical versions can then be reached by appending:

(3) $\vdash \pi \supset \varphi$ supposition
(4) $\vdash(\varphi \supset \rho) \supset (\pi \supset \rho)$ MPP-F   2,3

and then

(5) $\vdash \varphi \supset \rho$ supposition
(6) $\vdash \pi \supset \rho$ MPP-F   4,5

Both categorical and hypothetical versions have their uses, and so it is with most of the other metatheorems I shall state.

Double Negation for Formulae [DN-F]. For any well-formed π, $\vdash \sim\sim\pi \supset \pi$; also $\vdash \pi \supset \sim\sim\pi$; also $\vdash \pi$ if and only if $\vdash \sim\sim\pi$.

I shall prove the two categorical versions (lines 6 and 13 below); the other follows easily from them as in Syll. For any well-formed π,

(1) $\vdash \pi \supset \pi$ proof parallels (N) on p. 147
(2) $\vdash \sim(\pi \,\&\, \sim\pi) \supset \sim(\sim\pi \,\&\, \pi)$ Com&
(3) $\vdash(\pi \supset \pi) \supset \sim(\sim\pi \,\&\, \pi)$ Def⊃   2
(4) $\vdash \sim(\sim\pi \,\&\, \pi)$ MPP-F   1,3
(5) $\vdash \sim(\sim\sim\pi \,\&\, \sim\pi)$ special case of (4)
(6) $\vdash \sim\sim\pi \supset \pi$ Def⊃   5
(7) $\vdash \sim\sim\sim\pi \supset \sim\pi$ special case of (6)

(8) $\vdash(\sim\sim\sim\pi \supset \sim\pi) \supset (\sim(\sim\pi \,\&\, \pi)$
$\supset \sim(\sim\sim\sim\pi \,\&\, \pi))$ Sum&
(9) $\vdash \sim(\sim\pi \,\&\, \pi) \supset \sim(\sim\sim\sim\pi \,\&\, \pi)$ MPP-F   7,8
(10) $\vdash \sim(\sim\sim\sim\pi \,\&\, \pi)$ MPP-F   4,9
(11) $\vdash \sim(\sim\sim\sim\pi \,\&\, \pi) \supset \sim(\pi \,\&\, \sim\sim\sim\pi)$
    Com&
(12) $\vdash \sim(\pi \,\&\, \sim\sim\sim\pi)$ MPP-F   10,11
(13) $\vdash \pi \supset \sim\sim\pi$ Def⊃   12

Transposition [Transp]. For any well-formed π, φ, $\vdash(\pi \supset \varphi) \supset (\sim\varphi \supset \sim\pi)$; also $\vdash(\sim\varphi \supset \sim\pi) \supset (\pi \supset \varphi)$; also $\vdash \pi \supset \varphi$ if and only if $\vdash \sim\varphi \supset \sim\pi$.

I prove the first version: for any well-formed π, φ

(1) $\vdash \sim\sim\pi \supset \pi$ DN-F
(2) $\vdash(\pi \supset \varphi) \supset (\sim\sim\pi \supset \varphi)$ Syll   1
(3) $\vdash \sim(\sim\sim\pi \,\&\, \sim\varphi) \supset \sim(\sim\varphi \supset \sim\sim\pi)$ Com&
(4) $\vdash(\sim\sim\pi \supset \varphi) \supset (\sim\varphi \supset \sim\pi)$ Def⊃ twice   3
(5) $\vdash(\pi \supset \varphi) \supset (\sim\varphi \supset \sim\pi)$ Syll   2,4

Here Syll is used in two versions, the first hypothetical version in line 2, which therefore cites one preceding line, and the second hypothetical version (HUGHES & LONDEY's DR2) in line 5, which therefore cites two preceding lines. The proof of the converse categorical version of Transp is similar, but uses the converse categorical version of DN-F. Transp is otherwise called 'Contraposition'. From this point I shall abandon proofs for a bit, merely stating results in the order in which they come out. With the help of Transp it is quite easy to prove that for any well-formed π, φ, ρ, $\vdash \pi \,\&\, \varphi \supset \varphi \,\&\, \pi$ (Pure Com&), $\vdash(\pi \supset \varphi) \supset (\pi \,\&\, \rho \supset \varphi \,\&\, \rho)$ (Pure Sum&) and $\vdash \pi \,\&\, \varphi \supset \varphi$ (an alternative Simp&). Then we can get

Simplification for '⊃' [Simp⊃]. For any well-formed π, φ, $\vdash \pi \supset (\varphi \supset \pi)$; also if $\vdash \pi$, then $\vdash \varphi \supset \pi$.

Next an ingenious and difficult proof leads to

6.4 Metatheorems on derivability

Association for '&' [Assoc&]. For any well-formed π, φ, ρ, $\vdash((\pi \mathbin{\&} \varphi) \mathbin{\&} \rho) \supset (\pi \mathbin{\&} (\varphi \mathbin{\&} \rho))$; also $\vdash(\pi \mathbin{\&} (\varphi \mathbin{\&} \rho)) \supset ((\pi \mathbin{\&} \varphi) \mathbin{\&} \rho)$; also $\vdash(\pi \mathbin{\&} \varphi) \mathbin{\&} \rho$ if and only if $\vdash \pi \mathbin{\&} (\varphi \mathbin{\&} \rho)$.

The structure of the proof can be divined from HUGHES & LONDEY p. 131, where a proof of the corresponding Assoc ∨ is given in the formula system of WHITEHEAD & RUSSELL, which has '∼' and '∨' as primitive connectives. It is not surprising that Whitehead and Russell failed to find the proof of Assoc ∨ and so included it needlessly among their axiom-rules.

Importation and Exportation. For any well-formed π, φ, ρ [Imp] $\vdash(\pi \supset (\varphi \supset \rho)) \supset (\pi \mathbin{\&} \varphi \supset \rho)$; also [Exp] $\vdash(\pi \mathbin{\&} \varphi \supset \rho) \supset (\pi \supset (\varphi \supset \rho))$; also $\vdash \pi \supset (\varphi \supset \rho)$ if and only if $\vdash \pi \mathbin{\&} \varphi \supset \rho$.

Proof of Imp. For any well-formed π, φ, ρ

(1) $\vdash \sim(\pi \mathbin{\&} \sim\sim(\varphi \mathbin{\&} \sim\rho)) \supset \sim(\sim\sim(\varphi \mathbin{\&} \sim\rho) \mathbin{\&} \pi)$ Com&
(2) $\vdash(\pi \supset (\varphi \supset \rho)) \supset \sim(\sim\sim(\varphi \mathbin{\&} \sim\rho) \mathbin{\&} \pi)$ Def⊃ twice 1
(3) $\vdash(\varphi \mathbin{\&} \sim\rho) \supset \sim\sim(\varphi \mathbin{\&} \sim\rho)$ DN-F
(4) $\vdash((\varphi \mathbin{\&} \sim\rho) \supset \sim\sim(\varphi \mathbin{\&} \sim\rho)) \supset$
    $(\sim(\sim\sim(\varphi \mathbin{\&} \sim\rho) \mathbin{\&} \pi) \supset \sim((\varphi \mathbin{\&} \sim\rho) \mathbin{\&} \pi))$ Sum&
(5) $\vdash \sim(\sim\sim(\varphi \mathbin{\&} \sim\rho) \mathbin{\&} \pi) \supset \sim((\varphi \mathbin{\&} \sim\rho) \mathbin{\&} \pi)$ MPP-F 3,4
(6) $\vdash(\pi \supset (\varphi \supset \rho)) \supset \sim((\varphi \mathbin{\&} \sim\rho) \mathbin{\&} \pi)$ Syll 2,5
(7) $\vdash \sim((\varphi \mathbin{\&} \sim\rho) \mathbin{\&} \pi) \supset \sim(\pi \mathbin{\&} (\varphi \mathbin{\&} \sim\rho))$ Com&
(8) $\vdash(\pi \supset (\varphi \supset \rho)) \supset \sim(\pi \mathbin{\&} (\varphi \mathbin{\&} \sim\rho))$ Syll 6,7
(9) $\vdash((\pi \mathbin{\&} \varphi) \mathbin{\&} \sim\rho) \supset (\pi \mathbin{\&} (\varphi \mathbin{\&} \sim\rho))$ Assoc&
(10) $\vdash \sim(\pi \mathbin{\&} (\varphi \mathbin{\&} \sim\rho)) \supset \sim((\pi \mathbin{\&} \varphi) \mathbin{\&} \sim\rho)$ Transp 9
(11) $\vdash(\pi \supset (\varphi \supset \rho)) \supset \sim((\pi \mathbin{\&} \varphi) \mathbin{\&} \sim\rho)$ Syll 8,10
(12) $\vdash(\pi \supset (\varphi \supset \rho)) \supset (\pi \mathbin{\&} \varphi \supset \rho)$ Def⊃ 11

The proof of Exp is similar. Then the 'if and only if' version comes by applications of MPP-F.

Permutation [Perm]. For any well-formed π, φ, ρ, $\vdash(\pi \supset (\varphi \supset \rho)) \supset (\varphi \supset (\pi \supset \rho))$; also if $\vdash \pi \supset (\varphi \supset \rho)$, then $\vdash \varphi \supset (\pi \supset \rho)$.

This comes quite easily from Imp and Exp. All the foregoing metatheorems are provable in all four calculi. I shall now state a few that are provable only in QC and QS5.

'$\exists$'-Introduction for Formulae. For any a, v, and ϕ not containing v, if ϕa is well-formed, then $\vdash \phi a \supset \exists v \phi v$; also if $\vdash \phi a$, then $\vdash \exists v \phi v$.

Proof of categorical version: for any such a, v, ϕ,

(1)	$\vdash \forall v \sim \phi v \supset \sim \phi a$	Simp$\forall$	
(2)	$\vdash \sim \sim \forall v \sim \phi v \supset \forall v \sim \phi v$	DN-F	
(3)	$\vdash \sim \exists v \phi v \supset \forall v \sim \phi v$	Def$\exists$	2
(4)	$\vdash \sim \exists v \phi v \supset \sim \phi a$	Syll	1,3
(5)	$\vdash \phi a \supset \exists v \phi v$	Transp	4

Pure '$\forall$'-Introduction for Formulae. For any a, v, and ϕ containing neither, if $\vdash \phi a$, then $\vdash \forall v \phi v$.

Proof: for any such a, v, ϕ,

(1)	$\vdash \phi a$	supposition	
(2)	$\vdash \phi a \supset ((p \supset pp) \supset \phi a)$	Simp$\supset$	
(3)	$\vdash (p \supset pp) \supset \phi a$	MPP-F	1,2
(4)	$\vdash (p \supset pp) \supset \forall v \phi v$	$\forall$I-F	3
(5)	$\vdash p \supset pp$	It&	
(6)	$\vdash \forall v \phi v$	MPP-F	4,5

The trick here is to choose some axiom which is like '$p \supset pp$' in containing no a—any such will do. The metatheorem differs from '$\exists$'-Introduction in having, as explained on p. 146, no categorical version. Two other useful metatheorems are

Distribution for '$\forall$' and '$\exists$'. For any a, v, and ϕ and ψ containing no v, [Dist$\forall$] if ϕa and ψa are well-formed, $\vdash \forall v (\phi v \supset \psi v) \supset (\forall v \phi v \supset \forall v \psi v)$; also [Dist$\exists$] if ϕa and ψa are well-formed, $\vdash \forall v (\phi v \supset \psi v) \supset (\exists v \phi v \supset \exists v \psi v)$; also if $\vdash \forall v (\phi v \supset \psi v)$, then both $\vdash \forall v \phi v \supset \forall v \psi v$ and $\vdash \exists v \phi v \supset \exists v \psi v$.

Proof of the categorical versions: for any such a, v, ϕ, ψ

(1)	$\vdash \forall v \phi v \supset \phi a$	Simp$\forall$	
(2)	$\vdash (\phi a \supset \psi a) \supset (\forall v \phi v \supset \psi a)$	Syll	1
(3)	$\vdash \forall v (\phi v \supset \psi v) \supset (\phi a \supset \psi a)$	Simp$\forall$	
(4)	$\vdash \forall v (\phi v \supset \psi v) \supset (\forall v \phi v \supset \psi a)$	Syll	2,3

(5) $\vdash \forall v(\phi v \supset \psi v) \& \forall v \phi v \supset \psi a$	Imp	4
(6) $\vdash \forall v(\phi v \supset \psi v) \& \forall v \phi v \supset \forall v \psi v$	$\forall$I-F	5
(7) $\vdash \forall v(\phi v \supset \psi v) \supset (\forall v \phi v \supset \forall v \psi v)$	Exp	6

(1) $\vdash \forall v(\phi v \supset \psi v) \supset (\phi a \supset \psi a)$	Simp$\forall$	
(2) $\vdash (\phi a \supset \psi a) \supset (\sim \psi a \supset \sim \phi a)$	Transp	
(3) $\vdash \forall v(\phi v \supset \psi v) \supset (\sim \psi a \supset \sim \phi a)$	Syll	1,2
(4) $\vdash \forall v(\phi v \supset \psi v) \supset \forall v(\sim \psi v \supset \sim \phi v)$	$\forall$I-F	3
(5) $\vdash \forall v(\sim \psi v \supset \sim \phi v) \supset (\forall v \sim \psi v \supset \forall v \sim \phi v)$	Dist$\forall$	
(6) $\vdash \forall v(\phi v \supset \psi v) \supset (\forall v \sim \psi v \supset \forall v \sim \phi v)$	Syll	4,5
(7) $\vdash (\forall v \sim \psi v \supset \forall v \sim \phi v) \supset (\sim \forall v \sim \phi v \supset \sim \forall v \sim \psi v)$	Transp	
(8) $\vdash (\forall v \sim \psi v \supset \forall v \sim \phi v) \supset (\exists v \phi v \supset \exists v \psi v)$	Def$\exists$ twice	7
(9) $\vdash \forall v(\phi v \supset \psi v) \supset (\exists v \phi v \supset \exists v \psi v)$	Syll	6,8

Because of the close analogy between the quantifier rules, Simp$\forall$ and $\forall$I-F, and the modal rules, Simp$\square$ and $\square$I-F, modal metatheorems analogous to the above three are provable in S5 and QS5, namely:

'$\diamond$'-**Introduction for Formulae.** For any π, if π is well-formed, then $\vdash \pi \supset \diamond \pi$; also if $\vdash \pi$, then $\vdash \diamond \pi$.

Pure '$\square$'-Introduction for Formulae. For any π, if $\vdash \pi$, then $\vdash \square \pi$; also if π is well-formed and fully modalised, $\vdash \pi \supset \square \pi$.

Distribution for '$\square$' and '$\diamond$'. For any π and ρ, [Dist$\square$] if π and ρ are well-formed, $\vdash \square(\pi \supset \rho) \supset (\square \pi \supset \square \rho)$; also [Dist$\diamond$] if π and ρ are well-formed, $\vdash \square(\pi \supset \rho) \supset (\diamond \pi \supset \diamond \rho)$; also if $\vdash \square(\pi \supset \rho)$, then both $\vdash \square \pi \supset \square \rho$ and $\vdash \diamond \pi \supset \diamond \rho$.

The one failure of analogy with QC, forecast on p. 146, is that Pure '$\square$'-Introduction has a categorical version. Its proof is: for any well-formed and fully modalised π

(1) $\vdash \pi \supset \pi$	proof parallels (N) on p. 147	
(2) $\vdash \pi \supset \square \pi$	$\square$I-F	1

It is because of the possibility of proving this metatheorem that the 'characteristic S5 axiom' '$\diamond p \supset \square \diamond p$' is derivable in the S5 and QS5 systems, as is '$\square p \supset \square \square p$', the characteristic axiom of the weaker modal system S4; moreover from the former we can prove, e.g. by '$\Diamond$'-Introduction and Syll, the derivability of '$p \supset \Box\Diamond p$' (p. 161), the characteristic axiom of another weaker system B; see HUGHES & CRESSWELL pp. 46, 49, 57.

In QS5 metatheorems are provable concerning the relationship between modal connectives and quantifiers. The three which follow are the most interesting (see BARCAN p. 2, and BURIDAN p. 130).

Barcan Metatheorem. For any v, and ϕ not containing v, if $\forall v \phi v$ is well-formed, $\vdash \forall v \Box \phi v \supset \Box \forall v \phi v$; also if $\vdash \forall v \Box \phi v$, then $\vdash \Box \forall v \phi v$; also if $\exists v \phi v$ is well-formed, $\vdash \Diamond \exists v \phi v \supset \exists v \Diamond \phi v$; also if $\vdash \Diamond \exists v \phi v$, then $\vdash \exists v \Diamond \phi v$.

Proof of first version: for any v, and ϕ not containing v, if $\forall v \phi v$ is well-formed, then for any α not in ϕ

(1) $\vdash \Box \phi \alpha \supset \phi \alpha$ Simp$\Box$
(2) $\vdash \forall v (\Box \phi v \supset \phi v)$ Pure $\forall$I   1
(3) $\vdash \forall v \Box \phi v \supset \forall v \phi v$ Dist$\forall$ 2
(4) $\vdash \forall v \Box \phi v \supset \Box \forall v \phi v$ $\Box$I-F   3

I omit proof of the other versions, as of the next rule.

Converse Barcan Metatheorem. For any v, and ϕ not containing v, if $\forall v \phi v$ is well-formed, $\vdash \Box \forall v \phi v \supset \forall v \Box \phi v$; also if $\vdash \Box \forall v \phi v$, then $\vdash \forall v \Box \phi v$; also if $\exists v \phi v$ is well-formed, $\vdash \exists v \Diamond \phi v \supset \Diamond \exists v \phi v$; also if $\vdash \exists v \Diamond \phi v$, then $\vdash \Diamond \exists v \phi v$.

Buridan Metatheorem. For any v, and ϕ not containing v, if $\exists v \phi v$ is well-formed, $\vdash \exists v \Box \phi v \supset \Box \exists v \phi v$; also if $\vdash \exists v \Box \phi v$, then $\vdash \Box \exists v \phi v$; also if $\forall v \phi v$ is well-formed, $\vdash \Diamond \forall v \phi v \supset \forall v \Diamond \phi v$; also if $\vdash \Diamond \forall v \phi v$, then $\vdash \forall v \Diamond \phi v$.

Proof of first version: for any v, and ϕ not containing v, if $\exists v \phi v$ is well-formed, then for any α not in ϕ

(1) $\Box \phi \alpha \supset \phi \alpha$ Simp$\Box$
(2) $\forall v (\Box \phi v \supset \phi v)$ Pure $\forall$I   1
(3) $\exists v \Box \phi v \supset \exists v \phi v$ Dist$\exists$ 2
(4) $\exists v \Box \phi v \supset \Box \exists v \phi v$ $\Box$I-F   3

I omit proof of the other versions. There is no converse Buridan metatheorem, and such formulae as '$\Box \exists x f x \supset \exists x \Box f x$' are not

6.4 *Metatheorems on derivability*

QS5-derivable (nor QS5-valid). I shall return to these three metatheorems in 10.7 and 10.8.

6.5 *Abridged derivations*

It will be proved in outline on p. 192 that π is a valid formula of one of the four calculi if $\langle \Lambda, \pi \rangle$ is a valid sequent of that calculus. This being so, and given also the soundness of the formula and sequent systems, there are always two logistic methods available for proving the validity of a formula π: find a formula-derivation ending π, or find a sequent-derivation ending $\langle \Lambda, \pi \rangle$. In practice the latter method is nearly always the handier of the two. Nevertheless it is worth describing ways of improving the former method, by abridgment of formula-derivations. (i) We shall need the same kinds of short cut as in sequent-derivations, namely use of substitution or other metatheorems or both. And of course there is the same justification as before for relaxing the definition of 'formula-derivation' so as to license these abridgments: every entry reachable by them could have been reached without them. It is also customary, and highly desirable, to permit other abridgments: (ii) entries justified by categorical rules can be elided when it is sufficiently obvious what they are, and (iii) two or more applications of MPP-F or Syll can be run together. Here is an example in which short cuts of all three kinds are used:

(R) (1) $\sim\sim(q \,\&\, \sim p) \supset (q \,\&\, \sim p)$ DN-F
    (2) $\sim\sim(q \,\&\, \sim p) \supset \sim p$ Syll   1, Pure Com&, Simp&
    (3) $p \supset \sim(q \,\&\, \sim p)$ Transp 2
    (4) $p \supset (q \supset p)$ Def$\supset$ 3

After line 1 entries of '$(q \,\&\, \sim p) \supset (\sim p \,\&\, q)$' and '$(\sim p \,\&\, q) \supset \sim p$' are elided, so that the annotation of line 2 refers not to them but to the categorical version of Pure Com& and the categorical rule Simp& which justify them: line 1 together with the former yields '$\sim\sim(q \,\&\, \sim p) \supset (\sim p \,\&\, q)$' by Syll, and that together with the latter then yields line 2 by another application of Syll; these two applications are run together so as to make line 1 plus the two elided formulae yield line 2 directly. More important than the saving by elision is the use of metatheorems DN-F, Syll, Pure Com& and

Transp, without which the derivation would need more nearly forty than four lines. In the next example Syll affords a modest abridgment of formula-derivation (N) from p. 147:

(S) (1) $p \supset pp$ It&
     (2) $pp \supset p$ Simp&
     (3) $p \supset p$ Syll 1,2

These are considerable economies. The trouble is that facility in using and following them demands practice, without which the methods of Chapter 5 are undoubtedly easier. Just how far to let abridgment go is, as in sequent-derivations, a matter for discretion. It would be possible for example, and perhaps sufficiently perspicuous, to contract (S) still further into the single line

(1) $p \supset p$ Syll   It&, Simp&

or as others would write it (cf. QUINE *MofL* p. 73)

(1) It& $\supset$ (Simp& $\supset$ ($p \supset p$))   Syll

6.6 *Other people's rules*

(1) There are various ways of changing the axiom-rules while leaving exactly the same formulae derivable. Eight alternative sets of such rules for propositional systems in which only '$\sim$' and '&' are primitive (called KN systems after the Polish notation) have been examined by PORTE. They include a set due to Curry which differs from that of 6.2 in substituting '$\vdash(\pi \supset \varphi) \supset (\overline{\rho\varphi} \supset \overline{\rho\pi})$' for Sum&, which was '$\vdash(\pi \supset \varphi) \supset (\overline{\varphi\rho} \supset \overline{\pi\rho})$'; and a set due to Rosser which replaces Com& and Sum& by the single rule '$\vdash(\pi \supset \varphi) \supset (\overline{\varphi\rho} \supset \overline{\rho\pi})$' (ROSSER p. 55; also in COPI, p. 177). To prove that these changes do not affect the set of derivable formulae it is necessary to show that the primitive rules of each system are either primitive or provable in the others—a laborious business.

(2) If the primitive connectives are different the minimum list of primitive derivation rules must be different too. Modus Ponendo Ponens is commonly the only primitive hypothetical rule in versions of the propositional calculus (though its '$\pi \supset \varphi$' will have different definitional expansions according as '&' or '$\vee$' is primitive, and no expansion if '$\supset$' is). AN systems, in which only '$\sim$' and '$\vee$' are

6.6 Other people's rules

primitive in the propositional calculus, can start with rules corresponding to A1, A2, A3 and A5 of HUGHES & LONDEY (p. 102), or with a shorter set in which A3 and A5 are combined as Rosser combines Com& and Sum& (see PRIOR FL p. 305, 6.12(6)). CN systems, with '$\sim$' and '$\supset$' primitive, may start from the three propositional rules in MATES (p. 165, I-III) or from three corresponding to the rules in QUINE (*MofL* pp. 72-3, (1)-(3)); both these sets are due to Łukasiewicz. Many other possibilities are noted by Prior (*FL*, appendix 1) including several with only a single axiom-rule. Proof that all these make the same formulae derivable is again by showing that the primitive rules of each are either primitive or provable in the others; except that in such cases what is primitive in one system must be written out in the system's primitive notation before submitting to proof in another system.

(3) Various alternatives to the two '$\forall$'-rules are known. One replaces $\forall$I-F by its pure version and adds the categorical rule '$\vdash \forall v(\pi \supset \phi v) \supset (\pi \supset \forall v \phi v)$, if π and $\forall v \phi v$ are well-formed and π contains no v'. Mates dispenses with a hypothetical '$\forall$'-rule by admitting free variables in well-formed formulae and stating his rules under the rubric 'the '$\forall$'-closures of the following are axioms' (MATES p. 165). Then instead of justifying argument from, say, "$\vdash$ '$fa \supset fa$' " to "$\vdash$ '$\forall x(fx \supset fx)$' " the rules ensure that the same argument which shows that $\vdash$ '$fa \supset fa$' shows also that the '$\forall$'-closure of '$fx \supset fx$' is derivable, i.e. that $\vdash$ '$\forall x(fx \supset fx)$'.

(4) A common alternative to the '$\square$'-rules which keeps the same formulae derivable, i.e. which is a set of S5 rules, retains Simp$\square$ and replaces $\square$I-F by its pure form together with three categorical rules stating that $\vdash \square(\pi \supset \varphi) \supset (\square \pi \supset \square \varphi)$—i.e. Dist$\square$—, $\vdash \square \pi \supset \square \square \pi$ and $\vdash \pi \supset \square \diamond \pi$ (or '$\vdash \diamond \pi \supset \square \diamond \pi$' in place of the last two, MASSEY p. 106). The motive for the larger set is comparison with other modal systems: if '$\vdash \pi \supset \square \diamond \pi$' is dropped from it we get the system S4; if '$\vdash \square \pi \supset \square \square \pi$' is dropped, the system B; and if both are dropped, the system T, otherwise called M.

(5) Formula systems may, like sequent systems, contain a Rule of Substitution stating that every substituend of a derivable formula is derivable. The rule can, with difficulty, be proved as a metatheorem in the systems of 6.2, just as its analogue was provable in

the systems of 5.2. But in formula systems a very common alternative, adopted by HUGHES & LONDEY (p. 102), QUINE (*MofL* pp. 72–3) and MASSEY (p. 126), is to make the Rule of Substitution primitive and to replace the axiom-rules by a finite list of formulae that are axioms. In the propositional calculus it is fairly easy to see how this transformation leaves the same formulae derivable. We start by defining a PC-substituend thus:

'φ is a PC-substituend of π' is to mean 'φ is the result of one or more successive operations in which a PC-formula is substituted for a propositional letter uniformly throughout π'

(where uniformity as usual demands the same formula for the same letter and permits it for different letters). Since propositional letters are themselves PC-formulae the following are all PC-substituends of '$p \& q \supset p$': itself, '$p \& p \supset p$', '$q \& r \supset q$', '$(q \supset r) \& \sim p \supset (q \supset r)$'; and so on. It follows from this definition that the axiom-rule Simp& is true if and only if every PC-substituend of '$p \& q \supset p$' is derivable (and obviously such a formula as '$q \& p \supset q$' would serve here in place of '$p \& q \supset p$' since it has the same PC-substituends, though such a formula as '$(p \& p) \& q \supset (p \& p)$' would not since it has fewer). From this it is fairly clear, though the matter would take some proving, that Simp& has the same effect in the propositional calculus as the conjunction of ' "$p \& q \supset p$' is derivable' with the hypothetical Rule of Substitution 'if φ is a PC-substituend of π and π is derivable, so also is φ'. Hence it is possible to reformulate the derivation rules of the propositional calculus by adding that Rule of Substitution to MPP-F as a second primitive hypothetical rule and replacing the axiom-rules by "The following are derivable: '$p \supset pp$', '$pq \supset p$', '$\overline{pq} \supset \overline{qp}$', '$(p \supset q) \supset (\overline{qr} \supset \overline{pr})$' ".

The same change is easily made in S5; in QC and QS5 it becomes much more complex because of the need to permit substitution for subject letters and variables and predicate letters. The Rule of Substitution itself is simple enough: every QC-substituend of a QC-derivable formula is QC-derivable (and similarly for QS5). But the business of defining 'QC-substituend' is fairly formidable. Here is one way. We allow a stencil to contain gaps marked by different numerals, e.g. '$\forall x(fx①② \& g②①a)$'. We say that such a stencil is *filled* when some letter is uniformly inserted once into

6.6 Other people's rules

each gap marked '①', some letter, the same or different, is uniformly inserted once into each gap marked '②', and so on. We define an atomic stencil as a stencil that becomes an atomic formula when all its gaps are filled by subject letters, and a well-formed stencil, e.g. a QC-stencil, as a stencil that becomes a well-formed formula, e.g. a QC-formula, when all its gaps are filled by subject letters (the latter is close to Mates' definition of 'stencil' itself (MATES p. 178)). Then

> '♀ is a QC-substituend of π' is to mean '♀ is the result of one or more successive operations in which a QC-formula is substituted for a propositional letter, or a subject letter for a subject letter, or a variable for a variable (provided that no variable ν is substituted for a different variable already in the scope of $\forall \nu$ or $\exists \nu$), or a QC-stencil for an atomic QC-stencil (provided that no stencil containing ν is substituted for a different atomic stencil already in the scope of $\forall \nu$ or $\exists \nu$), uniformly throughout π'.

For alternative ways of stating this definition, and for use of the predicate calculus Substitution Rule, see MATES pp. 179–80 and LEMMON *BL* pp. 150–2. Because the definition is so complicated it is not surprising that most logicians prefer to avoid making the Rule of Substitution primitive in the predicate calculus, and use instead universal axiom-rules like those of 6.2, so called axiom-schemata.

(6) Some authors, including HUGHES & LONDEY (p. 102), present derivation rules for formulae as a recursive definition of 'derivable formula' rather than directions for constructing a formula-derivation. For example in place of '♀ may be entered if $\pi \supset$ ♀ and π have been' MPP-F becomes '♀ is derivable if $\pi \supset$ ♀ and π are'. See pp. 14, 180.

(7) Although we may think of a derivable formula as one that is derivable from the empty set, the formula systems of 6.2 do not define 'derivable from' except in this special case. It could be defined for PC, however, in the following way (cf. MASSEY p. 144). Add to the PC derivation rules 'any well-formed formula may be entered in a formula-derivation as an "assumption"'. Then define

'π is derivable from Γ' to mean 'There is a formula-derivation whose last entry is π and whose assumptions are the members of Γ (or: of a subset of Γ)', and define 'π is a derivable formula' to mean 'π is derivable from Λ'. The same formulae remain PC-derivable as by the rules of 6.2. Because of ∀1-F and □I-F more complex manoeuvres would be needed to work the extension into the other three formula systems; see for example MASSEY pp. 206, 414–5.

Such an extension allows formula-derivations to be used in proving the derivability of sequents. For example the following formula-derivation has '$p \,\&\, q$' as sole assumption and 'p' as last entry, and so proves that 'p' is derivable from '$p \,\&\, q$', i.e. that $\vdash \langle \{`p \,\&\, q`\}, `p`\rangle$:

(1) $p \,\&\, q$ 'assumption'
(2) $p \,\&\, q \supset p$ Simp&
(3) p MPP-F   1,2

Notice that the 'assumption' here is a formula, not the proposition that that formula is derivable; so what is proved is that 'p' is derivable from '$p \,\&\, q$', not that 'p' is derivable—from nothing—if '$p \,\&\, q$' is. Finally the formula-derivation becomes a sequent-derivation if we use the device of Chapter 5 for 'keeping track of assumptions':

1   (1) $p \,\&\, q$ 'assumption'
   (2) $p \,\&\, q \supset p$ Simp&
1   (3) p MPP-F   1,2

The rules of Chapter 5 allow the same sequent to be proved derivable more briefly, by means of

1   (1) $p \,\&\, q$ A
1   (2) p &E   1

and that is why they are preferable, even though the presence of RAA and CP in them requires, as the formula rules do not, some device for keeping track of assumptions.

(8) Methods of annotating derivations, and methods of abridgment, vary a good deal. Here is a formula-derivation using the rule '$(q \supset r) \supset (p \vee q \supset p \vee r)$ is an axiom' (WHITEHEAD & RUSSELL's Summation, HUGHES & LONDEY's A5), the Rule of Substitution,

6.6 Other people's rules

and the definition '$(\pi \supset \varphi)$ is short for $(\sim\pi \vee \varphi)$', which I call for the nonce 'Df⊃'. First I set out the derivation in full in the style of 6.3; then as it would be formulated and abridged by three other authors.

Style of 6.3:

(1) $(q \supset r) \supset (p \vee q \supset p \vee r)$ Summation
(2) $(q \supset r) \supset (\sim p \vee q \supset \sim p \vee r)$ Substitution   1
(3) $(q \supset r) \supset ((p \supset q) \supset (p \supset r))$ Df⊃   2

WHITEHEAD & RUSSELL p. 100:

$\left[\text{Sum } \dfrac{\sim p}{p}\right]$ $\vdash :. q \supset r . \supset : \sim p \vee q . \supset . \sim p \vee r$ (1)

$[(1) . (\text{Df}\supset)]$ $\vdash :. q \supset r . \supset : p \supset q . \supset . p \supset r$

HUGHES & LONDEY pp. 105, 108:

Sum $(\sim p/p): (q \supset r) \supset ((\sim p \vee q) \supset (\sim p \vee r))$ (1)
$(1) \times \text{Df}\supset : (q \supset r) \supset ((p \supset q) \supset (p \supset r))$ (2)

PRIOR, *FL* p. 27:

Sum $p/Np \times \text{Df}\supset = (1)$

(1) $CCqrCCpqCpr$

Another style is proof trees, in which the tips of the branches are axioms and the final formula is at the base of the trunk. Here is a proof in that style ending with the 'characteristic B axiom' '$p \supset \square\lozenge p$'.

```
                    ─────────DN-F   ─────────Simp□
~~□~p ⊃ □~p           □~p ⊃ ~p
─────────                              ─────────Syll                    ─────────Simp&
~~□~p ⊃ ~p                                                  ◇p & ◇p      ◇p & ◇p ⊃ ◇p
─────────Transp                                             ─────────────────────────Syll
p ⊃ ~□~p                                                              ◇p ⊃ ◇p
─────────Def◇                                                         ─────────□I-F
p ⊃ ◇p                                                                ◇p ⊃ □◇p
──────────────────────────────────────────────────────────────────────────────Syll
                                p ⊃ □◇p
```

Derivation Rules for Formulae

Every formula must have a bar above it, marked with a rule justifying its entry on the basis of what is entered, if anything, above it. So only categorical rules justify bars with nothing above them. Formula-derivations with 'assumptions' can be represented by trees in which some tips have no superposed bar, and sequent-derivations can be written that way too, except that some means has to be found for showing when an 'assumption' has been cancelled by RAA or CP, e.g. the square brackets in this example:

$$
\begin{array}{c}
 [\Diamond p] \\
 \overline{} \,\Box\text{I-S} \\
[p] \Box\Diamond p \\
\overline{} \,\Diamond\text{I} \overline{} \text{ CP cancelling '}\Diamond p\text{'} \\
\Diamond p \Diamond p \supset \Box\Diamond p \\
\overline{} \text{MPP-S} \\
\Box\Diamond p \\
\overline{} \text{CP cancelling '}p\text{'} \\
p \supset \Box\Diamond p
\end{array}
$$

But it would be closer to the spirit of Chapter 5 to write sequent trees with strings of formulae, indicating sequents, on each line, e.g. like this:

$$
\begin{array}{c}
 \overline{} \,\text{A} \\
 \Diamond p \vdash \Diamond p \\
\overline{} \,\text{A} \overline{} \,\Box\text{I-S} \\
p \vdash p \Diamond p \vdash \Box\Diamond p \\
\overline{} \,\Diamond\text{I} \overline{} \text{ CP} \\
p \vdash \Diamond p \vdash \Diamond p \supset \Box\Diamond p \\
\overline{} \text{MPP-S} \\
p \vdash \Box\Diamond p \\
\overline{} \text{CP} \\
\vdash p \supset \Box\Diamond p
\end{array}
$$

(9) I end with a comment on the name 'Transformation Rule' for what I call hypothetical derivation rules. Hughes & Londey adopt it in preference to 'Rule of Inference' on the ground that the latter 'would tend to impose an interpretation' (HUGHES & LONDEY p. 96, compare p. 113 above). But the name has two drawbacks of its own. It stresses a distinction *within* the derivation rules—between categorical and hypothetical—which is also present but

6.6 Other people's rules

unmarked within the formation rules. And it suggests that the relation between formation rules and derivation rules is like that between the rules for setting the board at chess and the rules for moving pieces; whereas in unextended axiomatic systems it is the axioms rather than the formation rules which correspond to rules for setting the board, since well-formed formulae that are not derivable never get on to the board at all.

CHAPTER SEVEN

Proving Validity

7.1 *Bivalence*

Although proofs of validity follow many different routes, all the routes converge on to a single main highway for the last part of the journey. In the case of valid formulae the point of convergence is the point at which it is proved, for some logical language l and well-formed formula π, that

(1) No sentence l-fitting π is F in any l-context, domain or world.

A sentence is F in an l-context, domain and world when it can be used in that l-context and domain to express a proposition which would be false given that world (p. 87). So (1) is true if and only if

> No proposition expressible in any l-context and domain in a sentence l-fitting π would be false given any world.

A proposition expressible in an l-context and domain in a sentence l-fitting π is, by 2.13 (2), an l-instance of π. Hence (1) is true if and only if

> No l-instance of π would be false given any world, i.e.
>
> No l-instance of π would be false, whatever the facts.

So far so good. But there remains a gap to be bridged between this and 'π is l-valid'; for the latter, by 2.13 (3), means

(2) Every l-instance of π would be true whatever the facts.

It may appear that the gap can be bridged by inferring from (1) to

(3) Every sentence l-fitting π is T in every l-context, domain and world

and then inferring from (3) to (2). But neither inference

would be correct. (1) does not entail (3) without the extra stipulation that every sentence l-fitting a formula is T or F in every l-context, domain and world. Many logicians make the stipulation. In Quine, for example, formulae are schemata for 'statements', where a statement is a T or F sentence ("Each actual statement has a specific truth value" QUINE *MofL* p. 29); and in MATES (p. 56) and MASSEY (p. 25) formulae are directly interpreted as T or F sentences. But this is not enough on its own, since (3), which amounts to

> In every l-context and domain, for every sentence σ l-fitting π, some necessary truth is expressible in σ,

does not entail (2), which amounts to

> In every l-context and domain, for every sentence σ l-fitting π, only necessary truths are expressible in σ.

Here again extra stipulations could come to the rescue: restrict sentences to eternal sentences (whose truth-value is constant in a language, see p. 49) and worlds to the actual world (see pp. 56–7). Then (3) becomes 'Eternal sentences l-fitting π are T in every domain', which does entail 'Eternal sentences l-fitting π can only express truths in any domain'. This is the procedure of Quine, who makes (3) thus shorn his definition of 'π is l-valid' (QUINE *MofL* p. 35).

I shall adopt a different stipulation, the Principle of Bivalence:

7.1 (4) Every l-instance of a formula would, whatever the facts, be true or false.

Strictly speaking this is a schema of many principles, one for each logical language l. The relativity to languages is avoidable: since every l-instance of a formula is a proposition, the gap between (1) and (2) could equally well have been bridged by the more sweeping assertion that every proposition would, whatever the facts, be true or false, and the Principle of Bivalence is often stated that way (cf. W. & M. KNEALE p. 47, LEMMON *BL* p. 64).

The Principle needs defence. At least its more sweeping version is vulnerable to objections of quite various sorts, some of which can be illustrated by the following examples of propositions that might be alleged to be neither true nor false (henceforward 'neuter'):

(A) Derivability is or is not ambitious
(B) If Hougoumont had fallen, Wellington would have lost Waterloo
(C) The Pope never beats his wife
(D) France is hexagonal
(E) Proposition (E) is false

Since 'proposition' is a semi-technical term, it would have been possible—and consistent with the usage explained in 2.6—to stipulate that if any of (A)–(E) is neuter it is not a proposition. But if that stipulation is combined with the theses adopted in Chapter 2 that all premisses and conclusions are propositions and that all arguments consist of premisses and conclusions, the result would be to exclude from logical appraisal, as not being arguments, many items which one might well hope to catch under some calculus or other. 7.1 (4) itself can similarly be saved by fiat, and even more reasonably because 'l-instance' is a wholly technical term. But the effect is still restrictive. The definition of 'material conditional' on p. 63 leaves it unclear whether any material conditionals with a neuter component are true or false. If none are, or not all are, arguments containing premisses or conclusions like (A)–(E) will at least sometimes, by 7.1 (4), correspond to material conditionals which are not l-instances of any formula, and so will not be testable by any of the calculi covered by 'l'. It is not satisfactory therefore to adopt Bivalence, even in the form of 7.1 (4), unless we can show that the restrictions thereby imposed on use of calculi are either unimportant or illusory or excessively difficult to avoid. This I shall now try to do.

Exclusion of arguments containing (A) from appraisal by a calculus is surely unimportant, since (A) exhibits a kind of nonsense or meaninglessness (not lexical or grammatical but a 'category mismatch', see STRAWSON *Cat.* p. 194ff.), and "meaningless sentences really have no business in logic; for their meaninglessness unfits them for any interesting role in (valid) inference" (HAACK, p. 117). Exclusion of arguments containing the subjunctive conditional (B) is unimportant for a different reason. Although such

7.1 Bivalence

conditionals might turn up as instances of an atomic formula in a valid sequent, an argument featuring them is much more likely to require, for its appraisal, some calculus which can reveal their internal structure, and so which contains a connective answering to 'If it were the case that . . ., it would be the case that . . .' There exist such calculi, but the four in this book are not among them; see p. 197. In any case, the view that subjunctive conditionals are neuter is not obviously correct (though defended e.g. in MACKIE pp. 105–8), and without it the exclusion of (B) is illusory. As for (C), 9.3 and 9.6 will suggest that if it expresses a proposition at all it expresses a true or false one. That leaves (D), a case of vagueness (the example is from AUSTIN, p. 142), and (E), a case of antinomy (it is a version of the Liar Paradox). Both have claims to be propositions—(D) at least a strong one—and both have claims to be brought within the scope of simple logic. But the price of doing so is high. Since neither of them seems aptly describable as true or false, we should need, in the absence of 7.1 (4), to devise a calculus in which there were methods of proving for some formulae not just that no instances of them are false in any world but that no instances of them are false or neuter in any world. One way of doing this is to rewrite the interpretation rules of PC with three-value in place of two-value matrices, e.g. (putting 'is N' for 'is a sentence that can be used to express a neuter proposition')

(i)

	$\sim$
T	F
N	N
F	T

or (ii)

	$\sim$
T	F
N	T
F	T

or (iii)

	$\sim$
T	F
N	F
F	T

together with

(iv)

&	T	N	F
T	T	N	F
N	N	N	F
F	F	F	F

or (v)

&	T	N	F
T	T	N	F
N	N	N	N
F	F	N	F

and analogously for the interpretation rules of QC etc. Unfortunately these revisions turn out to be unhelpful, for two reasons. First, it becomes hard to discern the meanings assigned to the connectives by the new rules, and therefore hard to formalise arguments into symbols. This problem shows up in unexpected valuations. For example a propositional calculus defined by (i) and (iv) or (i) and (v) and still containing Def ∨ will license valuations in which $v('p \vee \sim p') = N$, so that '$p \vee \sim p$' will be invalid in it (the Law of Excluded Middle will fail). Substitution of (ii) or (iii) for (i) avoids this curiosity—so showing that the Law of Excluded Middle can survive abandonment of Bivalence—but yields the metatheorem for (ii) (and for (iii) in brackets) that if $v('p') = v('q') = N, v('p \vee q') = F(T)$; and one may wonder whether it is possible to have a grasp of the meaning of '∨' when a context in which 'France is hexagonal' can only express a neuter proposition is one in which 'France is hexagonal ∨ France is hexagonal' can only express a false (true) proposition. Although this first difficulty might be circumvented by a more radical departure from the truth-conditions of 4.2—e.g. by adding extra primitive connectives, or by admitting more than three values, or by abandoning truth-functionality (see VAN FRAASSEN, pp. 94–6)—a second difficulty remains. If there are vague propositions like 'France is hexagonal' for which it is unreasonable to choose between the appraisals 'true' and 'false', why should there not be others for which it is unreasonable to choose between 'true' and 'neuter' or between 'neuter' and 'false'? In a similar way the objections against counting (E) as true or false are quite closely paralleled by objections against counting

(F) Proposition (F) is either false or neuter

as either true or false or neuter. This shows that it is impossible to devise any calculus, or at least any reasonably simple one, within which all arguments containing propositions of the kinds illustrated by (D) and (E) can be appraised; so that their exclusion from the scope of the calculi of this book, though real and regrettable, would not be easily cured. In general, then, the ban on appraisal of arguments containing (A)–(E) which 7.1 (4) imposes or seems to impose is in no case a good reason for abandoning that Principle and rewriting interpretation rules in such a way as to make proofs of validity independent of it.

7.1 Bivalence

Parallel reasoning shows the need for Bivalence in the case of valid sequents:

7.1 (5) Every l-instance of a sequent has premisses and conclusion all of which would, whatever the facts, be true or false.

7.1 (4) and 7.1 (5) are to be stipulated as part of the definitions of 'l-instance', parallel to but independent of the stipulation (which I do not adopt) that every sentence l-fitting a formula is T or F in every l-context, domain and world.

7.2 Semantic methods

As was forecast in 2.12, the methods of proving validity which this book is chiefly concerned to explain go through the notion of derivability and so involve proof of the soundness of logistic systems. But there are other methods, 'semantic' in the sense that they ignore derivability. In particular it would be absurd to conceal the semantic methods available in the propositional calculus, which have the advantage in practice over formula-derivations and sequent-derivations of being 'effective'—not only do they always lead in a finite number of steps to the conclusion that a PC-formula or PC-sequent is PC-valid, when it is, but they also present at each step instructions as to what to do next (whereas to construct reasonably short derivations one must use one's ingenuity). As a matter of fact the semantic methods in the propositional calculus constitute 'decision procedures' for the PC-validity of PC-formulae and PC-sequents, i.e. they are effective methods of deciding about any such thing whether *or not* it is PC-valid; for they also lead by an effective procedure to the conclusion that a PC-formula or PC-sequent is PC-invalid, when it is.

Let us consider the case of formulae first. Given Bivalence, a formula is PC-valid if—and, it may be added, only if—no sentence PC-fitting it is F in any PC-context, domain and world. I shall now describe two of the most simple and familiar ways of deciding, for a PC-formula, whether or not this condition is met. The first method, truth-tabling, proceeds by trying to fit an F sentence to a PC-formula in a PC-context, domain and world, and demonstrating that failure is inevitable; the other, *reductio*, proceeds by supposing that an F sentence can be fitted and demonstrating that the supposition leads to self-contradiction.

The method of truth-tabling starts by taking a PC-context, domain and world and the PC-formula to be tested, and then reasons as follows. If an F sentence is to replace the formula, each of the formula's constituent letters must by the truth-conditions and fitting conventions of PC be uniformly replaced by a T or F sentence. Since these latter sentences fall into just two kinds, T and F, and there are 2^n permutations of the kinds for a formula containing n different letters, the various attempts to fit an F sentence to the formula can be classified into 2^n kinds of replacement; and by using the PC truth-conditions we can compute, for each kind, whether it succeeds in replacing the whole formula by a sentence which is F in the chosen PC-context, domain and world. If we find that that happens for none of the 2^n permutations—because all fit a T sentence to the formula—we shall then have shown that no sentence PC-fitting the formula is F. All this can be set out diagrammatically in a truth-table. Each row of the table represents at the left hand side all those sentences PC-fitting the n letters of the formula which share the same T-or-F rating; and there are 2^n rows. In each row computation of the T-or-F rating of successively larger parts of the sentences is recorded under the corresponding parts of the formula, as in the generalised truth-tables of 4.6. And the column under the whole formula, showing ratings for the complete sentences fitting it, will contain no Fs if and only if the formula is PC-valid. Here is an example:

(1) p	(2) q	(3) $p \supset q$	(4) $\sim p$	(5) $\sim p \supset q$	(6) $(p \supset q) \& (\sim p \supset q)$	(7) $q \equiv (p \supset q) \& (\sim p \supset q)$
T	T	T	F	T	T	T
T	F	F	F	T	F	T
F	T	T	T	T	T	T
F	F	T	T	F	F	T
		from (1) and (2) by T $\supset$	from (1) by T $\sim$	from (4) and (2) by T $\supset$	from (3) and (5) by T &	from (2) and (6) by T $\equiv$

The parts of each row to the left of the leftmost vertical line, i.e. under letters, are best written in a standard order, as follows: start with a row of Ts; to convert each row into the next lower one replace its last T with an F and any Fs succeeding that T with Ts;

7.2 Semantic methods

you will end with a row of Fs (see HUGHES & LONDEY p. 57). Space can be saved, at the cost of hiding the order of computation, by omitting the intermediate formulae and transferring the ratings that go with them to places under their main connectives in the final formulae, thus (the columns are numbered for cross-reference):

p	q	$q \equiv (p \supset q) \,\&\, (\sim p \supset q)$
T	T	T T T F T
T	F	T F F F T
F	T	T T T T T
F	F	T T F T F

(1) (2)   (7) (3) (6) (4) (5)

The formula is PC-valid if and only if it has no 'F's under its own main connective. Truth-tabling is often said to 'evaluate' a formula.

The conclusions proved by means of truth-tables are more general than they look. Admittedly each table evaluates only one formula, unlike the generalised truth-tables of 4.6. But what a table allows us to assert about its formula is that *no* sentence PC-fitting it is F in any PC-context, domain and world. For the first row of the specimen table justifies the general assertion that σ is T in *every* PC-context, domain and world and for *every* sentence σ PC-fitting the specimen formula which is such that the parts fitting 'p' and 'q' in it are both T; and the other rows similarly. The success of the proof of validity depends on the fact that these four general assertions exhaust the possibilities, and so entail that no sentence at all which PC-fits the formula is F in any PC-context, domain and world.

Every PC-formula can be tested for PC-validity by the truth-table method. The proof is this: (i) because every PC connective has a PC matrix, each row in a PC-formula's truth-table must yield a rating under the formula's main connective; (ii) because every PC-formula is of finite length, the number n of its different constituent letters must be finite, and so the number 2^n of rows in its truth-table must be finite. On the other hand since the number of rows rises exponentially with the number of different letters, a truth-table may be very long. Hence not only does the method become exceedingly tedious for a formula with four or more different letters (and so 16 or more rows), but it is also highly susceptible to human error—though machines love it. So the *reductio* method is often preferable.

In the *reductio* method (HUGHES & LONDEY pp. 58–61, MASSEY pp. 58–60) we begin by taking a PC-context, domain and world and a sentence PC-fitting the PC-formula to be tested, and we suppose that the sentence is F in that context, domain and world. PC matrices are then used to compute backwards to the T-or-F ratings of constituent parts of the sentence. We aim to find that however the computation proceeds the PC truth-conditions force different ratings on to parts fitting the same part of the formula. If they do, we can reason as follows: by the PC fitting conventions, those parts must be the same sentence; but if the same sentence has different ratings there is equivocation; so the context is not a PC-context, contrary to supposition; and if every attempt to fit an F sentence to the formula is forced into such contradiction, there can be no F sentence PC-fitting it and the formula must be PC-valid. The computational part of the argument may again be represented diagrammatically, by putting 'F' under the formula's main connective and calculating outwards. Here is how it works on the same formula as before.

$$q \equiv (p \supset q) \& (\sim p \supset q)$$
$$\text{F}$$

At once the argument divides into two cases (often this can be avoided); for by T≡

either (i) $q \equiv (p \supset q) \& (\sim p \supset q)$ or (ii) $q \equiv (p \supset q) \& (\sim p \supset q)$
 T F T F T F F F T F

Here the entries under the first occurrence of '*q*' are repeated under the other occurrences, as non-equivocation requires.

Taking (i) first, T⊃ forces

$$q \equiv (p \supset q) \& (\sim p \supset q)$$
$$\text{T F} \text{T T F} \text{T T}$$

7.2 Semantic methods

Then **T&** forces an equivocal rating for '$(p \supset q) \& (\sim p \supset q)$', contrary to supposition:

(A) $\quad q \equiv (p \supset q) \& (\sim p \supset q)$
T F $\quad$ T T F $\quad\quad$ T T
T

Case (ii) also leads to self-contradiction. By **T&** we get

$\quad q \equiv (p \supset q) \& (\sim p \supset q)$
$\quad$F F $\quad$ T F T $\quad\quad$ T F

Whence by **T⊃** twice

$\quad q \equiv (p \supset q) \& (\sim p \supset q),$
$\quad$FF F T F T F $\quad$ T F

whence by **T∼** 'p' gets an equivocal rating:

(B) $\quad q \equiv (p \supset q) \& (\sim p \supset q)$
FF F T F T FT T F

(A) and (B) are attempts to construct an entry in the formula's truth-table which puts 'F' under the main connective; neither succeeds, because in each case there is an equivocal rating. The two together suffice to prove **PC**-validity because at no stage after the first did the truth-conditions permit further division. The general assertion justified by (A) and (B) is: if in any **PC**-context domain and world any sentence **PC**-fitting the formula is F, then either (A) or (B) results.

These methods can easily be extended to sequents. Just as a **PC**-formula is **PC**-valid if and only if no sentence **PC**-fitting it is F in a **PC**-context, domain and world, so, granted Bivalence, a **PC**-sequent is **PC**-valid if and only if there is no way of **PC**-fitting sentences to its formulae in a **PC**-context, domain and world so that the sentence fitting the last formula is F and none of the others are F. To test for this property by the truth-table method, just construct tables for each formula in the sequent (LEMMON *BL* p. 75); to test for it by the *reductio* method, suppose that some F sentence replaces the sequent's last formula and some T sentence each of its others (if any). Here are proofs by both methods of the PC-invalidity of the two-formula sequent $\langle\{`p \supset (q \supset r)'\}, `(p \supset q) \supset r'\rangle$:

p q r	$p \supset (q \supset r)$	$(p \supset q) \supset r$
T T T	T T	T T
T T F	F F	T F
T F T	T T	F T
T F F	T T	F T
F T T	T T	T T
F T F	T F	T F
F F T	T T	T T
F F F	T T	T F

$p \supset (q \supset r) \quad (p \supset q) \supset r$
$\quad\quad\; T \quad\quad\quad\quad\quad T \quad F \; F$

The second proof has been left incomplete; but enough is filled in to make it clear that if 'F' is next put under 'p', either 'T' or 'F' may be put under 'q' without forcing equivocation. The two permutations which result are rows 6 and 8 in the truth-table; so in these two cases attempts to fit an F sentence to the sequent's last formula and a T sentence to its other formula succeed, and the sequent is accordingly not PC-valid. Notice that although these methods constitute a decision procedure for the PC-validity of PC-sequents, they would not suffice, without further argument, if PC-sequents could be infinite (the further argument is known as proof of 'compactness', QUINE *MofL* p. 173, MASSEY pp. 376–8).

Other decision procedures for the PC-validity of PC-formulae are QUINE'S truth-value analysis (*MofL* pp. 29–32), reduction to normal form (LEMMON *BL* pp. 189–200, QUINE *MofL* pp. 58–71, HUGHES & LONDEY pp. 72–9, MASSEY pp. 64–74), and semantic tableaux (MASSEY pp. 358–64). All can easily be adapted to PC-sequents. Well-formed formulae and sequents of them that are PC-valid are often called 'tautologous' (LEMMON *BL* p. 68, MATES p. 89).

The S5-validity of S5-formulae and finite sequents of them is also decidable, and can be tested by an extension of the truth-table method (MASSEY pp. 163–81) or of the *reductio* method (HUGHES

7.2 Semantic methods

& CRESSWELL pp. 82–104, 115–6) or of normal forms (ib. pp. 116–21) or of semantic tableaux. Although the existence of these extensions is of theoretical interest, their extra complexity means that our purposes—which require proofs of validity but not invalidity—are better served in S5 by non-semantic methods. As regards the predicate calculus, the QC-validity of certain sub-sets of QC-formulae, and finite sequents of them, is decidable, again by extensions of the propositional calculus methods (QUINE *MofL* pp. 129–33, 155–60, HUGHES & LONDEY pp. 183–210, 232–241, MASSEY pp. 343–50). But there is no general decision procedure for QC-validity, and provably not (given a plausible assumption, see QUINE *MofL* pp. 180–5, MASSEY pp. 335–42, HUGHES & LONDEY pp. 299–300). It follows that there is no general decision procedure for QS5-validity either (in fact the case is worse, see HUGHES & CRESSWELL p. 148), and in QC and QS5 we are forced to rest content with methods of proving validity but not invalidity. Semantic tableaux can still be used for this one-sided work: they yield a result *if* the formula or sequent is valid, but if it is invalid they may go on for ever, so never demonstrating its invalidity (MASSEY p. 369, LAMBERT & VAN FRAASSEN p. 114). But logistic methods are generally preferable in the predicate calculus and in QS5, because easier.

7.3 Logistic methods

A proof by logistic methods that some formula or sequent is valid in some calculus goes through two stages: a derivation, which displays the formula or sequent as derivable in the calculus; and a proof of soundness, which argues that all formulae or sequents derivable in the calculus are valid in it. The next two sections will give proofs of the soundness of the formula systems and sequent systems of QC, S5 and QS5; they could easily be adapted to PC which I leave out only because semantic methods are easier there.

The governing idea of the proofs is this: that all derivable formulae and sequents will be valid if everything generated by the derivation rules is valid, that is, if the axioms are all valid and the hypothetical derivation rules 'preserve' validity, never leading from the valid to the invalid (HUGHES & LONDEY p. 83). Although it is fairly obvious that most of the derivation rules have this character it is not quite obvious that all of them do, and in any case rigorous proofs are desirable. The central part of each proof will be a strong mathematical induction, and this will prove, not precisely that all derivable formulae and sequents are valid, but that all entries in a derivation have a property allied to validity, which I shall call selectness (the word is from MENDELSON, p. 38, cf. 'Φ-valid' HUGHES & LONDEY pp. 133–4). So each induction must be supplemented by two other parts, one connecting 'derivable' with 'entry in a derivation' and the other connecting 'select' with 'valid'. The main division in the proofs will be between the sequent systems of Chapter 5 and the formula systems of Chapter 6.

There are two preliminary matters to be dealt with in this section. The first of them is to introduce the idea of selectness. This is a 'semantic' idea, but abstract, belonging to an extension of the pure semantics sketched in 4.5. As that section explained, a valuation in a calculus is an ordered set pairing values with every well-formed formula of the calculus (perhaps relative to every world in a set of worlds) and with every other letter, except variables, in the well-formed formulae of the calculus. According to the rules stated in 4.5 the values paired with formulae, including propositional letters, have to be truth and falsity, denoted by '1' and '0'; but there might have been other rules involving more or other values, and in a purely abstract development the metalogical symbols for values, such as '1' and '0', would be left unexplicated. In any case there would have to be some set of values for pairing with formulae; and within that set we are now to imagine a subset called the **designated** values. When a valuation pairs one of these designated values with a formula (perhaps relative to a world) it is said to 'satisfy' the formula (in the world) or, in the usage of MATES (p. 60) and MASSEY (p. 248), to be a 'model' of it. A formula is **select** when it is satisfied by every valuation (and world) in every domain (and set of worlds), i.e. when every valuation pairs a designated value with it in every domain (and relative to every world). Similarly a sequent is **select** when every valuation (and world) in every domain (and set of worlds) which satisfies all of its non-last formulae satisfies its last formula, i.e. when every valuation which pairs a designated value with its non-last formulae in any domain (and relative to any world) pairs a designated value with its last formula in that domain (and relative to that world).

In order to determine whether a formula or sequent is select in

7.3 Logistic methods

some calculus we need two pieces of information about the calculus: its value rules, and the list of values designated in it. The value rules for QC, S5 and QS5 (and PC) were stated in 4.5. I now add the designation rule

The value 1, and no other, is QC-designated

and likewise for S5 and QS5 (and PC). In consequence of this rule a formula π is QC-select if and only if for every QC-valuation v and domain, v pairs 1 with π—i.e. $v(\pi) = 1$; and it is S5-select (QS5-select) if and only if for every S5-valuation (QS5-valuation) v and world w (and domain), $v(\pi, w) = 1$. Similarly for sequents: a sequent $\langle\{\pi_1, \ldots \pi_n\}, \varphi\rangle$ is QC-select if and only if for every QC-valuation v and domain, if $v(\pi_1) = \ldots v(\pi_n) = 1$, then $v(\varphi) = 1$; and it is S5-select (QS5-select) if and only if for every S5-valuation (QS5-valuation) v and world w (and domain), if $v(\pi_1, w) = \ldots v(\pi_n, w) = 1$, then $v(\varphi, w) = 1$.

As a second preliminary I give proofs of three lemmata (subsidiary theses) which will be needed in the main inductions of 7.4 and 7.5.

Lemma (a) For any QC-valuation v, subject letters α and β, and QC-stencil ϕ, if $v(\alpha) = v(\beta)$, then $v(\phi\alpha) = v(\phi\beta)$.

The proof is by induction on the length (number of symbols) of formulae. Take some α and β, some QC-valuation v such that $v(\alpha) = v(\beta)$, some length, and some QC-formula $\phi\alpha$ of that length, and suppose (the inductive supposition) that for all QC-valuations v_1 such that $v_1(\alpha) = v_1(\beta)$ and QC-formulae $\psi\alpha$ of less than that length, $v_1(\psi\alpha) = v_1(\psi\beta)$. (i) If $\phi\alpha$ is atomic and contains a predicate letter δ, it is $\delta a_1 \ldots a_n$ for some $a_1, \ldots a_n$ at least one of which is α. Then $\phi\beta$ is $\delta\beta_1 \ldots \beta_n$ where $\langle\beta_1, \ldots \beta_n\rangle$ differs from $\langle a_1, \ldots a_n\rangle$ only in containing β in at least one place where the latter contained α. Hence $\langle v(\beta_1), \ldots v(\beta_n)\rangle$ differs from $\langle v(a_1), \ldots v(a_n)\rangle$ only in containing $v(\beta)$ in at least one place where the latter contained $v(\alpha)$. But since $v(\alpha) = v(\beta)$ this is no difference. So $\langle v(a_1), \ldots v(a_n)\rangle = \langle v(\beta_1), \ldots v(\beta_n)\rangle$. So by VP of p. 99 $v(\delta a_1 \ldots a_n) = v(\delta\beta_1 \ldots \beta_n)$. (ii) If the main connective of $\phi\alpha$ is '=', $\phi\alpha$ is $a_1 = a_2$ for some a_1 and a_2 at least one of which is α. The argument is parallel. (iii) If the main connective of $\phi\alpha$ is '∀', it is ∀νψαν for some ν and QC-stencil ψ containing places marked '①' and '②' (see pp. 158–9 for such marked stencils and for QC-stencils). Then $\phi\beta$ is $\forall\nu\psi\beta\nu$. Take some subject letter γ distinct from α and β. Then for all v_1 that differ from v at most in what they pair with γ, $v_1(\alpha) = v_1(\beta)$. So by the inductive supposition $v_1(\psi\alpha\gamma) = v_1(\psi\beta\gamma)$. So by V∀ of p. 99 $v(\forall\nu\psi\alpha\nu) = v(\forall\nu\psi\beta\nu)$. (iv) If the main connective of $\phi\alpha$ is '∼', it is $\sim\psi\alpha$ for some QC-stencil ψ. Then $\phi\beta$ is $\sim\psi\beta$. By the inductive supposition $v(\psi\alpha) = v(\psi\beta)$. So by V∼ $v(\sim\psi\alpha) = v(\sim\psi\beta)$. (v) For other main connectives, primitive and not primitive, the argument is parallel. This proves that for any α, β and length, if for all QC-valuations v_1 such that $v_1(\alpha) = v_1(\beta)$, and QC-formulae $\psi\alpha$ of less than that length, $v_1(\psi\alpha) = v_1(\psi\beta)$, then for all QC-valuations v such that $v(\alpha) = v(\beta)$, and QC-formulae $\phi\alpha$ of that length, $v(\phi\alpha) = v(\phi\beta)$. Whence the conclusion follows by the Principle of Strong Induction.

Lemma (b) For any subject letter α and QC-formula π containing no α, if two QC-valuations differ at most in what they pair with α, they pair the same value with π.

Proof. Take some α, some length, some QC-formula π of that length containing no α, and two such differing valuations v and v_1, and suppose (the inductive supposition) that for all QC-formulae φ of less than that length containing no α any two such differing valuations pair the same value with φ. (i) If π is atomic, it is either some propositional letter φ or $\alpha_1 = \alpha_2$ or $\delta\alpha_3 \ldots \alpha_n$ for some $\alpha_1, \ldots \alpha_n$ none of which is α and some predicate letter δ. Since pairings with letters other than α are the same in v and v_1, $v(\varphi) = v_1(\varphi)$; also $v(\alpha_1) = v_1(\alpha_1)$ and $v(\alpha_2) = v_1(\alpha_2)$, so that by V= $v(\alpha_1 = \alpha_2) = v_1(\alpha_1 = \alpha_2)$; also $v(\alpha_3) = v_1(\alpha_3), \ldots$ and $v(\alpha_n) = v_1(\alpha_n)$, and $v(\delta) = v_1(\delta)$, so that by VP $v(\delta\alpha_3 \ldots \alpha_n) = v_1(\delta\alpha_3 \ldots \alpha_n)$. (ii) If the main connective of π is '∀', π is $\forall\nu\phi\nu$ for some ν and QC-stencil ϕ containing no α. Take some subject letter β distinct from α, and suppose that $v(\forall\nu\phi\nu) = 0$. Then by V∀ $v^*(\phi\beta) = 0$ for some valuation v^* which differs from v at most in what it pairs with β. Take the valuation v_1^* which analogously differs from v_1 at most in what it pairs with β and which pairs the same value with β as v^* does. Then v_1^* differs from v^* at most in what it pairs with α. So by the inductive supposition, since $\phi\beta$ contains no α, $v^*(\phi\beta) = v_1^*(\phi\beta)$. So $v_1^*(\phi\beta) = 0$. So by V∀ again $v_1(\forall\nu\phi\nu) = 0$. The same argument works with 'v' and 'v_1'

exchanged. So $v(\forall \nu \phi \nu) = v_1(\forall \nu \phi \nu)$. (iii) If the main connective of π is '$\sim$', π is $\sim\wp$ for some well-formed $\wp$ containing no a. By the inductive supposition $v(\wp) = v_1(\wp)$. So by V$\sim$ $v(\sim\wp) = v_1(\sim\wp)$. (iv) For other main connectives, primitive and not primitive, the argument is parallel. This completes the induction and proves the lemma.

Lemma (c) For any QS5-formula π, QS5-valuation v, and worlds w and w_1 in a set, if π is fully modalised, then $v(\pi, w) = v(\pi, w_1)$.

Proof. Take some QS5-valuation v and worlds w and w_1, some length, and some fully modalised QS5-formula π of that length, and suppose (the inductive supposition) that for all QS5-valuations v_1 and fully modalised QS5-formulae $\wp$ of less than that length $v_1(\wp, w) = v_1(\wp, w_1)$. (i) Since π is fully modalised it is not atomic. (ii) If the main connective of π is '$\forall$', π is $\forall \nu \phi \nu$ for some fully modalised QS5-stencil ϕ. By the inductive supposition $v_1(\phi a, w) = v_1(\phi a, w_1)$ for all QS5-valuations v_1 and subject letters a. So by V$\forall$ $v(\forall \nu \phi \nu, w) = v(\forall \nu \phi \nu, w_1)$. (iii) If the main connective of π is '$\Box$', π is $\Box \wp$ for some QS5-formula $\wp$. Suppose that $v(\Box \wp, w) = 0$. Then by V$\Box$ $v(\wp, w^*) = 0$ for some w^* in the set of worlds. So by V$\Box$ again $v(\Box \wp, w_1) = 0$. The same argument works with 'w' and 'w_1' exchanged. So $v(\Box \wp, w) = v(\Box \wp, w_1)$. (iv) If the main connective of π is '$\sim$', π is $\sim \wp$ for some fully modalised QS5-formula $\wp$. By the inductive supposition $v(\wp, w) = v(\wp, w_1)$. So by V$\sim$ $v(\sim \wp, w) = v(\sim \wp, w_1)$. (v) For other main connectives, primitive and not primitive, the argument is parallel. This completes the induction and proves the lemma.

We can now proceed to the soundness proofs themselves, starting with the formula systems of Chapter 6, which are in one or two ways easier to tackle than the sequent systems of Chapter 5.

7.4 *Soundness of the formula systems*

The proof is in three stages:

(1) Every derivable formula is an entry in a formula-derivation
(2) Every entry in a formula-derivation is select
(3) Every select formula is valid.

180   *Proving Validity*

Stage (1). By the definition of 'derivable' (p. 147) a derivable formula is the last entry in some formula-derivation. So it is an entry. (It was for the sake of this stage that the derivation rules were presented as rules for *constructing* formula-derivations.)

Stage (2) is to be proved by mathematical induction, starting with QC. Take some entry in some QC formula-derivation and suppose (the inductive supposition) that all earlier entries in that derivation, if any, are QC-select. Then consider the various ways in which the formula could have got into the derivation. There are thirteen of them, one for each derivation rule and one for each definition. In what follows I use 'for all (some) v' to abbreviate 'for every (some) QC-valuation v in every (some) domain'.

(i)–(iv) The formula got in by one of the categorical rules It&, Simp&, Com&, Sum&. In that case it is easy to check that it is QC-select. A *reductio* argument is simplest. For example if the formula got in by It&, it is $\pi \supset \pi \& \pi$, for some QC-formula π. Suppose for *reductio* that $\pi \supset \pi \& \pi$ is not QC-select; then for some v $v(\pi \supset \pi \& \pi) = 0$; then by V$\supset$ $v(\pi) = 1$ and $v(\pi \& \pi) = 0$, which is impossible by V&. Similarly for the other axioms.

(v) The formula got in by MPP-F. In that case it is some QC-formula φ and (because MPP-F is hypothetical) there are previous well-formed entries $\pi \supset \varphi$ and π; by the inductive supposition $\pi \supset \varphi$ and π are QC-select, i.e. $v(\pi \supset \varphi) = v(\pi) = 1$ for all v; then by V$\supset$ $v(\varphi) = 1$ for all v, i.e. φ is QC-select.

(vi) The formula got in by =I. Then it is $\alpha = \alpha$ for some α. But by V= $v(\alpha = \alpha) = 1$ for all v, i.e. $\alpha = \alpha$ is QC-select.

(vii) The formula got in by Simp=. Then it is $\alpha = \beta \supset (\phi\alpha \supset \phi\beta)$ for some α, β, and QC-stencil ϕ. Suppose for *reductio* that for some v $v(\alpha = \beta \supset (\phi\alpha \supset \phi\beta)) = 0$; then by V$\supset$ $v(\alpha = \beta) = 1$ and $v(\phi\alpha \supset \phi\beta) = 0$. Then by V= $v(\alpha) = v(\beta)$; whence by lemma (a) of the previous section $v(\phi\alpha) = v(\phi\beta)$; whence by V$\supset$ $v(\phi\alpha \supset \phi\beta) = 1$, which is impossible.

(viii) The formula got in by Simp∀. Then it is $\forall v \phi v \supset \phi\alpha$ for some α, v, and QC-stencil ϕ not containing v. Suppose for *reductio*

7.4 Soundness of the formula systems

that for some v $v(\forall \nu \phi \nu \supset \phi a) = 0$; then by $V \supset v(\forall \nu \phi \nu) = 1$ and $v(\phi a) = 0$; then by $V\forall$ $v_1(\phi a) = 1$ for all v_1 which differ from v at most in what they pair with a; so in particular $v(\phi a) = 1$, which is impossible.

(ix) The formula got in by $\forall$I-F. Then for some a, ν, QC-formula π containing no a, and QC-stencil ϕ contain no a or ν, the formula is $\pi \supset \forall \nu \phi \nu$ and (because $\forall$I-F is hypothetical) there is a previous entry $\pi \supset \phi a$. Suppose for *reductio* that for some v $v(\pi \supset \forall \nu \phi \nu) = 0$; then by $V \supset v(\pi) = 1$ and $v(\forall \nu \phi \nu) = 0$; then by $V\forall$ $v_1(\phi a) = 0$ for some v_1 which differs from v at most in what it pairs with a; by lemma (b) of the previous section, since π contains no a $v_1(\pi) = v(\pi) = 1$; so by $V \supset v_1(\pi \supset \phi a) = 0$; but by the inductive supposition $\pi \supset \phi a$ is QC-select, so that $v_1(\pi \supset \phi a) = 1$.

(x)–(xiii) The formula got in by one of the definitions. Then a definitional expansion or abbreviation of it is a previous entry which, by the inductive supposition, is QC-select. So the formula is QC-select.

This completes the proof that in a QC formula-derivation if every entry before a certain point is QC-select, so is the entry at that point; whence it follows by the principle of strong induction that every entry in a QC formula-derivation is QC-select, which is (2) for QC.

In proving (2) for S5 and QS5 we need to adapt part or all of the inductive proof to assignments which pair values with formulae relative to a world, and also to add clauses for Simp☐, ☐I-F and Def◇. I shall sketch the result for QS5. Take some formula which occurs as an entry in some QS5 formula-derivation, and suppose that all earlier entries in that derivation are QS5-select. Then consider the various ways in which the formula could have got in to the derivation. 'For all (some) v', now abbreviates 'for every (some) set of worlds and every (some) QS5-valuation v in every (some) domain'.

(i) The formula got in by It&. Then it is $\pi \supset \pi \& \pi$ for some QS5-formula π. Suppose for *reductio* that for some v and w in the set $v(\pi \supset \pi \& \pi, w) = 0$; then by $V \supset v(\pi, w) = 1$ and $v(\pi \& \pi, w) = 0$, which is impossible by V&.

(ii)–(xiii) are adapted in the same way from the QC proof (notice that lemmata (a) and (b) also need adaptation).

(xiv) The formula got in by Simp$\Box$. Then it is $\Box\pi \supset \pi$ for some QS5-formula π. Suppose for *reductio* that for some v and w in the set $v(\Box\pi \supset \pi, w) = 0$; then by $V\supset v(\Box\pi, w) = 1$ and $v(\pi, w) = 0$; then by $V\Box\ v(\pi, w_1) = 1$ for all worlds w_1 in the set, and so in particular $v(\pi, w) = 1$, which is impossible.

(xv) The formula got in by $\Box$I-F. Then for some QS5-formula φ and fully modalised QS5-formula π it is $\pi \supset \Box\varphi$ and (because $\Box$I-F is hypothetical) there is a previous entry $\pi \supset \varphi$. Suppose for *reductio* that for some v and w in the set $v(\pi \supset \Box\varphi, w) = 0$; then by $V\supset v(\pi, w) = 1$ and $v(\Box\varphi, w) = 0$, whence by $V\Box\ v(\varphi, w_1) = 0$ for some w_1 in the set; by lemma (c), since π is fully modalised, $v(\pi, w) = v(\pi, w_1) = 1$; so by $V\supset v(\pi \supset \varphi, w_1) = 0$; but by the inductive supposition $\pi \supset \varphi$ is QS5-select, so that $v(\pi \supset \varphi, w_1) = 1$, which is impossible.

(xvi) The same argument applies to Def$\Diamond$ as to the other definitions. This completes the induction, proving (2) for QS5. Adaptation to S5 (and PC) is straightforward.

Stage (3). The QC value-rules together with the stipulation that 1 alone is QC-designated can be regarded as giving a definition of 'QC-select'; and similarly for S5 and QS5 (and PC). Some authors present these rules as definitions of validity, but that would be improper here because we already have in 2.13 (3) a definition of 'valid formula'. Rather it needs now to be *proved* that all QC-select formulae are QC-valid, and similarly in the other cases. But the proof cannot get going while the metalogical symbol '1' and the metalogical word 'valuation' remain unexplicated. Accordingly the remaining tasks are first to explicate these expressions and then to show that under the explication all select formulae are valid in the sense of 2.13 (3). I start with QC (the argument applies to PC too).

The explication is as on pp. 100–2. It follows that '$v(\pi) = 1$ for every QC-valuation v in every domain' cashes out as 'π is replaced by a sentence which is T in every replacement of well-formed formulae by T or F sentences that conforms to the QC-fitting conventions and in every QC-context and domain and world' which, put more

7.4 Soundness of the formula systems

simply, is 'in a QC-context and domain and world a sentence QC-fitting π is either not F or T'.

The second task is to show that any formula which is QC-select under the above explication is QC-valid in the sense of 2.13 (3); actually the converse holds too, but we shall not need it. If a formula π is QC-select, then for every QC-valuation v and domain $v(\pi) = 1$; hence by the explication a sentence QC-fitting π is either not F or T, in any QC-context and domain and world. Since QC-contexts ban equivocation, a sentence which is T in one is not F in it; so a sentence which is either not F or T in one is in any case not F in it. So if π is QC-select under the explication, no sentence QC-fitting π is F in any QC-context, domain and world. This means that no proposition expressible, in a QC-context and domain, in a sentence QC-fitting π would be false given any facts; whence by definition 2.13 (2) of 'instance' no QC-instances of π would be false whatever the facts. It then follows by Bivalence, 7.1 (4), that every QC-instance of π would be true whatever the facts, i.e. that π is QC-valid in the sense of 2.13 (3).

It remains to extend the proof to S5 and QS5. If a formula π is S5-select, then for every S5-valuation v and world w $v(\pi, w) = 1$; hence by the explication of p. 102 a sentence S5-fitting π is either not F or T, in any S5-context and domain and world. Likewise if a formula π is QS5-select, then for every QS5-valuation v and domain and world w, $v(\pi, w) = 1$; hence by the explication a sentence QS5-fitting π is either not F or T, in any QS5-context and domain and world. The inferences to validity are as before. This completes the proof of stage (3) for QC, S5, QS5 (and PC). From (1), (2) and (3) together it then follows that

7.4 (4) All QC-derivable formulae are QC-valid; similarly for S5 and QS5 (and PC).

7.5 Soundness of the sequent systems

The proof is again in three stages:

(1) Every derivable sequent is an entry in a sequent-derivation
(2) Every entry in a sequent-derivation is select
(3) Every select sequent is valid.

Stage (1). By the definition of 'derivable' on p. 121 a derivable sequent is the last entry in some sequent-derivation. So it is an entry.

Stage (2), starting with QC. Take some sequent which occurs as an entry in some QC sequent-derivation, and suppose (the inductive supposition) that all earlier entries in that derivation, if any, are QC-select. Then consider the various ways in which the sequent could have got into the derivation. There happen to be the same number as in the QC formula system, thirteen. In what follows 'for all (some) v', again abbreviates 'for every (some) QC-valuation v in every (some) domain'. Most of the proofs will be direct, unlike the *reductio* proofs of the previous section.

(i) The sequent got in by A. Then it is $\langle\{\pi\}, \pi\rangle$ for some QC-formula π. But trivially if $v(\pi) = 1$, $v(\pi) = 1$, for all v; so the sequent is QC-select.

(ii) The sequent got in by &E. Then it is $\langle\{\pi_1, \ldots \pi_n\}, \varphi\rangle$ for some QC-formulae $\pi_1, \ldots \pi_n, \varphi$, and there is a previous entry in the derivation $\langle\{\pi_1, \ldots \pi_n\}, \varphi \& \rho\rangle$ or $\langle\{\pi_1, \ldots \pi_n\}, \rho \& \varphi\rangle$, for some QC-formula ρ. By the inductive supposition the previous entry is QC-select; so for all v, if $v(\pi_1) = \ldots v(\pi_n) = 1$, then $v(\varphi \& \rho) = 1$ or $v(\rho \& \varphi) = 1$. In either case $v(\varphi) = 1$ by V&. So the sequent is QC-select.

(iii)–(iv) Similarly for &I and $\sim$E, since by V& if $v(\varphi) = v(\rho) = 1$, $v(\varphi \& \rho) = 1$, for all v, and by V$\sim$ if $v(\sim\sim\varphi) = 1$, $v(\varphi) = 1$, for all v.

(v) The sequent got in by RAA. Then it is $\langle\{\pi_1, \ldots \pi_n\}, \sim\varphi\rangle$ for some QC-formulae $\pi_1, \ldots \pi_n, \varphi$, and there is a previous entry in the derivation $\langle\{\pi_1, \ldots \pi_n, \varphi\}, \rho \& \sim\rho\rangle$ for some QC-formula ρ. By the inductive supposition the previous entry is QC-select; so for all v, if $v(\pi_1) = \ldots v(\pi_n) = v(\varphi) = 1$, then $v(\rho \& \sim\rho) = 1$. But for all v $v(\rho \& \sim\rho) = 0$, by V$\sim$ and V&. So if $v(\pi_1) = \ldots v(\pi_n) = 1$, $v(\varphi) \neq 1$, and therefore $= 0$. But in that case $v(\sim\varphi) = 1$, by V$\sim$. Hence the sequent is QC-select.

7.5 Soundness of the sequent systems

(vi) The sequent got in by =I. Then it is $\langle \Lambda, \alpha = \alpha \rangle$ for some α. But by V= $v(\alpha = \alpha) = 1$ for all v; so the sequent is QC-select.

(vii)–(viii) The cases of =E and ∀E are again similar to (ii), the salient facts being that if $v(\alpha = \beta) = v(\phi\alpha) = 1$, $v(\phi\beta) = 1$, by V= and lemma (a); and if $v(\forall v \phi v) = 1$, $v(\phi \alpha) = 1$, by V∀.

(ix) The sequent got in by ∀I-S. Then for some α, v, QC-formulae $\pi_1, \ldots \pi_n$ containing no α and QC-stencil ϕ containing no α or v it is $\langle \{\pi_1, \ldots \pi_n\}, \forall v \phi v \rangle$ and there is a previous entry in the derivation $\langle \{\pi_1, \ldots \pi_n\}, \phi \alpha \rangle$. Suppose for *reductio* that the sequent is not QC-select; then for some v $v(\pi_1) = \ldots v(\pi_n) = 1$ and $v(\forall v \phi v) = 0$. Then by V∀ $v_1(\phi \alpha) = 0$ for some v_1 that differs from v at most in what it pairs with α. By lemma (b), since $\pi_1, \ldots \pi_n$ contain no α $v_1(\pi_1) = \ldots v_1(\pi_n) = 1$ also; but by the inductive supposition the previous entry is QC-select, so that $v_1(\phi \alpha) = 1$, which is impossible.

(x)–(xiii) The same argument applies to the definitions as in 7.4.

This completes the proof that in a QC sequent-derivation if every entry before a certain point is QC-select, so is the entry at that point; whence it follows by the principle of strong induction that every entry in a QC sequent-derivation is QC-select.

Adaptation to S5 and QS5 is exactly as in 7.4 except that the new inductive clauses now refer to the sequent rules □E and □I-S. Here is a sketch of the result for QS5.

(i)–(xiii) Adapted from QC.

(xiv) The case of □E is similar to (ii) since by V□ if $v(\Box \pi, w) = 1$, $v(\pi, w) = 1$, for all v and w in the set of worlds.

(xv) The sequent got in by □I-S. Then for some QS5-formula ϙ and fully modalised QS5-formulae $\pi_1, \ldots \pi_n$ it is $\langle \{\pi_1, \ldots \pi_n\}, \Box ϙ \rangle$ and there is a previous entry in the derivation $\langle \{\pi_1, \ldots \pi_n\}, ϙ \rangle$. Suppose for *reductio* that the sequent is not QS5-select; then for some v and w in the set v $(\pi_1, w) = \ldots v(\pi_n, w) = 1$ and $v(\Box ϙ, w) = 0$. Then by V□ $v(ϙ, w_1) = 0$ for some w_1 in the set.

By lemma (c), since $\pi_1, \ldots \pi_n$ are fully modalised $v(\pi_1, w_1) = \ldots v(\pi_n, w_1) = 1$ also; but by the inductive supposition the previous entry is QS5-select, so that $v(\varphi, w_1) = 1$, which is impossible.

(xvi) Def$\diamondsuit$ is dealt with like the other definitions.

This completes the induction, proving (2) for QS5. Adaptation to S5 (and PC) is straightforward.

Stage (3). It remains to prove that if a sequent is QC-select it is QC-valid, and similarly for S5 and QS5. Take some sequent $\langle \{\pi_1, \ldots \pi_n\}, \varphi \rangle$ and suppose that it is QC-select, i.e. for every QC-valuation v if $v(\pi_1) = \ldots v(\pi_n) = 1$, then $v(\varphi) = 1$. By the same metalogical explication as in 7.4 this cashes out as: in any ordered set of sentences successively QC-fitting the formulae of the sequent, if the non-last members, fitting $\pi_1 \ldots \pi_n$, are all either not F or T, the last member, fitting φ, is either not F or T, in any QC-context and domain and world. Hence if the non-last members are T, the last member is either not F or T. Since QC-contexts ban equivocation, a sentence that is either not F or T in one is in any case not F in it. So if the non-last members in any such set are T, the last member is not F, in any QC-context and domain and world. Now start from the other end, supposing for *reductio* that the chosen sequent is not QC-valid. By definition 2.11 (2) of 'valid' and the definition of 'strictly implies' (p. 32) this means that for some world w there is a QC-instance of the sequent with premisses that would be true given w and a conclusion that would not be true given w. By Bivalence, 7.1 (5), the conclusion would be false given w. And by definition 2.11 (1) of 'instance' the premisses and conclusion are expressible in some QC-context and domain in a set of sentences which, when ordered with the conclusion-sentence last, QC-fit the successive formulae of the chosen sequent. Premisses and conclusions are propositions. So for some QC-context and domain and for some ordered set of sentences successively QC-fitting the formulae of the sequent, the non-last sentences in the set can express propositions which would be true, i.e. are T sentences, in w, and the last sentence can express a proposition which would be false, i.e. is an F sentence, in w. But we have seen that in any such set, if the non-last members are T in a QC-context

7.5 Soundness of the sequent systems

and domain and world, the last member is *not* F in them. This ends the *reductio*, and so proves that any QC-select sequent is QC-valid.

Extension of stage (3) to the modal calculi follows the same lines as in 7.4, completing the proof of (3) for QC, S5 and QS5 (and PC). From (1), (2) and (3) we can infer

7.5 (4) All QC-derivable sequents are QC-valid; similarly for S5 and QS5 (and PC).

CHAPTER EIGHT

Some More Metatheory

8.1 *Some more metalogical properties*

In this section I introduce various properties and relations which, like validity, belong to formulae relative to interpretation, i.e. in some logical language l. A formula is called **consistent** in a language l, l-consistent for short, when it has some true l-instance (cf. QUINE *MofL* p. 35), and l-inconsistent otherwise, i.e., given Bivalence, when all its l-instances are false (HUGHES & LONDEY p. 6, LEMMON *BL* p. 68). Hence every valid formula with instances is consistent and none is inconsistent. In a language containing T∼ a formula π is inconsistent if and only if $\sim\pi$ is valid (l-inconsistency is l-validity of the negation). This is, unfortunately, not the only sense of 'inconsistent' used in logic. Some authors call a formula inconsistent when its negation is derivable (rather than valid—so making consistency a proof-theoretic rather than semantic property, cf. MASSEY p. 149, MATES p. 142). The word is also applied to other things than formulae: a proposition is called inconsistent, or self-contradictory, when its negation, i.e. contradictory, is a necessary truth (see p. 29); and a system is called inconsistent in various senses alluded to in 8.2. A formula such as 'p' with some true and some false l-instances falls between l-validity and l-inconsistency, and is sometimes called **contingent** (HUGHES & LONDEY p. 5, LEMMON *BL* p. 68, MASSEY pp. 20–1). In this book 'invalid' means 'not valid', but in MASSEY (p. 20) it has the sense here given to 'inconsistent'; so according to Massey's usage contingent formulae fall between the valid and the invalid.

A formula φ is called an **l-consequence** of a set of formulae Γ when the sequent $\langle \Gamma, \varphi \rangle$ is l-valid (MATES pp. 63–4, cf. MASSEY p. 57; but some authors, e.g. LAMBERT & VAN FRAASSEN p. 29, use 'consequence of' proof-theoretically, to mean 'derivable from'). In the special case where φ is a consequence of $\{\pi\}$, i.e. where Γ

8.1 Some more metalogical properties

contains only one member, we can say that ♀ is a consequence of the *formula* π, or alternatively that ♀ is **l-implied** by π (LEMMON *BL* p. 69, cf. QUINE *MofL* p. 39, MASSEY p. 56). In a language containing T ⊃ ♀ is a consequence of π if and only if π ⊃ ♀ is valid (l-implication is l-validity of the material conditional, QUINE *MofL* p. 40). Two sets of formulae Γ and Δ are called **l-equivalent** when ⟨Γ, ♀⟩ is l-valid for all ♀ in Δ and also ⟨Δ, π⟩ is l-valid for all π in Γ. In the special case where {π} is equivalent to {♀}, i.e. where Γ and Δ each contain only one member, we can say that the *formulae* π and ♀ are l-equivalent (this, the normal, kind of l-equivalence is mutual l-implication). In a language containing T ≡ π and ♀ are equivalent if and only if π ≡ ♀ is valid (l-equivalence is l-validity of the material biconditional, QUINE *MofL* p. 52). It is important to distinguish the consequence relation (and the technical 'implication') from entailment, and equivalence from mutual entailment: sets of premisses entail conclusions and propositions entail one another, but sets of formulae have formulae for l-consequences and formulae are l-equivalent to one another. Admittedly it would be possible in view of principles 2.4 (1) and 2.11 (2) to make entailment include the l-consequence relation (MASSEY p. 57) and to make mutual entailment include l-equivalence; but the price would be to reverse the decisions of 2.5 and 2.6—that is, to identify premisses and conclusions as sentences not propositions (then entailment would become language-relative) and to treat each l as a language in which formulae are interpreted as sentences not schemata.

Such assimilation of consequence to entailment and equivalence to mutual entailment is not possible when, as sometimes happens, these semantic properties of formulae are defined within model theory in terms of valuations and designated values, and the model-theoretic notions are left at an abstract level. We saw on p. 182 that some authors define 'π is l-valid' as 'v(π) = 1 for all v (i.e. every l-valuation v in every domain)'—the sense I there gave to 'π is l-select'. Just so 'π is l-consistent' may be defined as 'v(π) = 1 for some v', '♀ is an l-consequence of Γ' as 'for all v, if v(π) = 1 for all π in Γ, then v(♀) = 1', and 'π is l-equivalent to ♀', as 'for all v, v(π) = 1 if and only if v(♀) = 1' (in modal languages the definitions would need to be relativised to worlds.) Assuming that the value 1 alone is designated in l a formula is l-consistent in this model-theoretic sense if and only if some l-valuation satisfies it (see p. 176);

hence the word 'consistent' is often replaced by '**satisfiable**'. Furthermore a *set* of formulae Γ is called satisfiable, and its members simultaneously satisfiable, when there is some v such that $v(\pi) = 1$ for all π in Γ: for example although 'p' and '$\sim p$' are each **PC**-satisfiable formulae, the set $\{'p', '\sim p'\}$ is not a **PC**-satisfiable set.

It is almost inevitable to label some of these semantic properties of formulae with words which have another logical use at the pre-technical, non-symbolic, level. The words 'valid', 'consistent', 'contingent', 'consequence' and 'equivalent' witness my surrender to this temptation, the words 'entail', 'imply' that of others. The dangers of these double meanings are well illustrated in LEMMON (*BL* p. 69–70), who presents the word 'implication' and several others as naming relations which hold between propositions, but defines them in such a way that they name relations which hold between formulae.

8.2 *Some more metalogical truths*

In this section I state a number of other metatheorems, but without proving them.

The converse property to soundness is completeness, and a calculus is called **complete** when all its valid formulae or sequents are derivable (sometimes 'statement-complete' for the case of formulae, 'argument-complete' for that of sequents). Under the definitions of 'valid' and 'derivable' adopted in this book none of the four calculi is complete in precisely the above sense, both because many ill-formed formulae and sequents of them are valid (as having no instances) but none are derivable, and because some infinite sequents of well-formed formulae are valid but none are derivable. If the requirements of well-formedness and finitude were added, either in the definitions of 'valid' or in the statement of the completeness metatheorems, the calculi would turn out complete; that is

8.2 (1) All **PC**-valid **PC**-formulae are **PC**-derivable; similarly for **QC**, **S5** and **QS5**.

8.2 (2) All **PC**-valid **PC**-sequents are **PC**-derivable; similarly for **QC**, **S5** and **QS5**.

8.2 Some more metalogical truths

8.2 (1) and 8.2 (2) are much harder to prove than the soundness metatheorems. Sometimes the kind of completeness asserted in them is distinguished as weak completeness; for the strong varieties see HUGHES & LONDEY p. 139. Proof of 8.2 (1) for PC, the easiest case, is given in HUGHES & LONDEY pp. 139–41 (Theorem I), and of 8.2 (2) for PC in LEMMON pp. 84–90 (Metatheorem III).

Both soundness and completeness are defined relative to interpretation rules: they connect the logistic or 'syntactic' notion of derivability in a system with the 'semantic' notion of validity in a language. Hence completeness is sometimes called 'semantic completeness' to distinguish it from other properties, not altogether unrelated, which a system may possess uninterpreted (MATES p. 184). In the same way soundness is sometimes called 'semantic consistency' (MATES p. 186) or even just 'consistency'. HUGHES & LONDEY (pp. 137–8) distinguish three other senses in which systems —as opposed to formulae—are called consistent, all making consistency a purely proof-theoretic property, not relative to any interpretation rules. I shall mention only one of the three, the one in which to assert consistency of the systems of Chapters 5 and 6 is to assert the metatheorems

8.2 (3) For any formula π, if π is PC-derivable, $\sim\pi$ is not; similarly for QC, S5 and QS5

8.2 (4) For any formula π, if $\langle \Lambda, \pi \rangle$ is PC-derivable, $\langle \Lambda, \sim\pi \rangle$ is not; similarly for QC, S5 and QS5.

In place of 8.2 (4) Lemmon has '$\langle \Lambda, \pi \,\&\, \sim\pi \rangle$ is not derivable' (*BL* p. 80). These metatheorems are true, and follow easily, given T$\sim$, from the soundness and completeness metatheorems, since by T$\sim$ if any well-formed π is valid, $\sim\pi$ is not; similarly for $\langle \Lambda, \pi \rangle$ and $\langle \Lambda, \sim\pi \rangle$. It is clear that the sense of 'consistent' explicated in 8.2 (3) and 8.2 (4) applies only to systems which contain the symbol '$\sim$' or something that can be taken as a notational variant of it.

In Chapters 5 and 6 my policy was, adequately for the purposes of this book, to present sequent-metatheorems independently of formula-metatheorems. But of course there are close connections between them. For example

8.2 (5) For any PC-formulae $\pi_1 \ldots \pi_n$, φ, $\pi_1 \& \ldots \pi_n \supset \varphi$ is a PC-valid formula if and only if $\langle \{\pi_1, \ldots \pi_n\}, \varphi \rangle$ is a PC-valid sequent; similarly for QC, S5 and QS5.

This is proved quite simply by means of T& and T⊃; and it has as a special consequence, where $n=0$, that π is valid in each of the four calculi if and only if $\langle \varLambda, \pi \rangle$ is. Hence incidentally it also follows, given soundness and completeness, that any two well-formed formulae are interderivable in the sense of p. 130 if and only if they are equivalent. Similarly

8.2 (6) For any formulae $\pi_1, \ldots \pi_n$, φ, $\pi_1 \& \ldots \pi_n \supset \varphi$ is a PC-derivable formula if and only if $\langle \{\pi_1, \ldots \pi_n\}, \varphi \rangle$ is a PC-derivable sequent; similarly for QC, S5 and QS5.

The derivability result is not so easy to prove independently, but again follows given soundness and completeness. Its special consequence that ⊢π if and only if ⊢$\langle \varLambda, \pi \rangle$ makes each of the formula systems part of the same calculus as the corresponding sequent system, according to the criterion of identity for calculi adopted in 1.12.

A point worth noting is that surprisingly small changes to the interpretation rules would overturn the 'only if' in 8.2 (5), thus (given 8.2 (6)) destroying the soundness of the sequent systems but not of the formula systems: intuitionist interpretation rules for '~' and '&', if combined with Def ⊃ unchanged, are an example. For this reason sequent systems are sometimes called stronger than formula systems; but they are no stronger relative to the classical interpretation rules of Chapter 4.

There are also, of course, connections among the four formula systems and among the four sequent systems. Both sorts can be arranged in the following pattern

$$\begin{array}{c} \text{PC} \\ \nearrow \uparrow \nwarrow \\ \text{QC} \quad\quad \text{S5} \\ \nwarrow \uparrow \nearrow \\ \text{QS5} \end{array}$$

where the arrows convey a threefold meaning: (i) QC *includes* PC (and similarly for the other arrows) in the sense that every PC-

8.2 Some more metalogical truths

derivable formula and sequent is QC-derivable; (ii) QC is an *extension* of PC (and similarly for the other arrows) in the sense that the inclusion goes just one way, i.e. not every QC-derivable formula or sequent is PC-derivable; and (iii) QC is a *conservative* extension of PC (and similarly for the other arrows) in the sense that the new derivable formulae and sequents added by QC are none of them even well-formed in PC, i.e. every QC-derivable PC-formula and PC-sequent is PC-derivable. Given soundness and completeness these results carry over from derivability in the systems to validity of well-formed formulae and sequents in the logical languages.

Each rule in the sets of primitive derivation rules of 5.2 and 6.2 is not only unproved in this book but unprovable from the remainder of its set. For if any were provable from the remainder, its addition to the remainder would license no extra formulae or sequents as derivable; whereas in each case extra formulae or sequents are licensed. That is, each rule is **independent** of the others in its set in the sense that some formulae or sequents are derivable with the rule but not without it. The method of proving that a rule is independent in its set is to find some property of formulae or sequents that is 'preserved' by all the rules in the set except the independent one; different properties being needed for each independent rule. Usually the property sought is selectness in some specially devised model theory with its own values, designated values, and value-rules. Once the property has been found, the reasoning is this. Those derivation rules which preserve it form a truncated logistic system which is 'sound' relative to the property, i.e. all of whose derivable formulae or sequents have the property; whereas the rule which fails to preserve it leads from formulae or sequents having it (or, if categorical, from nothing) to a formula or sequent lacking it. Since the latter lacks the property it is not derivable in the 'sound' truncated system. But it was derivable in the original system. So some formulae or sequents are derivable with the rule but not without it. See QUINE *MofL* pp. 73–4, HUGHES & LONDEY ch. 18, MASSEY pp. 134–41.

CHAPTER NINE

Formalising: PC and QC

9.1 Introduction

I showed in 2.14 that proofs of an argument's correctness divide into two main operations: formalising, i.e. finding some sequent which the argument instantiates or some formula instantiated by its corresponding material conditional; and proving that the sequent or formula is valid (cf. the description in ACKERMANN p. 6: abstracting an appropriate logical problem and solving it). These two operations are not much alike. Proofs of validity, whether direct or indirect, deal only in symbols, though interpreted symbols, and can be checked or even discovered mechanically; on the other hand in looking for a sequent or formula that is instantiated by a given argument or its corresponding material conditional we are involved in the greater complexity of working with symbols and words together—symbols in the sequent or formula, words in the initial statement of the argument—and there is no mechanical check on success. It is because of the former feature, their extra conceptual complexity, that I have postponed treatment of the problems of formalising to this late stage of the book, even though in use it is natural to make sure that one's sequent or formula is indeed instantiated by the argument under examination or its corresponding material conditional before testing for validity.

The process of formalising is a transformation from words into symbols which can be broken down into the following seven stages.

(1) *Reordering*. The sentences in which the argument is initially stated may need to be stripped of intermediate conclusions, and the result may need reordering with the conclusion-sentence last.

(2) *Rewording, or paraphrasing*. The sentences may need to be reworded, i.e. replaced by others which express the same premisses

9.1 *Introduction*

and conclusion. Any connecting particles between them, e.g. 'for', 'therefore', 'nevertheless', must be deleted.

(3) *Rectifying*. Any wrong usage will have to be eliminated, and so will equivocation, i.e. repetitions of sentences, subjects or predicates with inconstant content, reference or meaning (plus supplementation) respectively.

(4) *Translating*. Variables may need to be introduced, and connectives will supplant words such as 'not', 'and', 'if', 'necessarily' and prefixes such as 'everything . . . is such that . . .'. Sentences may have to be reorganised into the predicate-leading construction. Brackets may be needed for grouping.

(5) *Domain-restriction*. Explicit restrictions on the range of variables, as in 'everyone x' or 'every formula y', may be suppressed when they are uniform over the whole argument, so that the argument becomes an instance relative to the domain so restricted.

(6) *Schematising*. All remaining word-groups in the sentences must be replaced uniformly by schematic letters of the appropriate grammatical categories.

(7) *Making a single sequent or formula*. If a valid sequent is aimed at, the resulting formulae must be appropriately cased in angled and curly brackets; if a valid formula, they must be assembled into a single formula instantiated by the argument's corresponding material conditional.

It is not necessary, of course, to write down the result of each of these successive transformations separately; nor is it necessary to perform them in precisely the above order.

Notice that none of the seven stages of transformation need preserve sameness of meaning. Reordering will not if there are intermediate conclusions to be excised. Rewording demands that substituted sentences express the same propositions as those they replace, but to do so they need not have the same meanings; see p. 37. Rectifying requires sameness of meaning only in the case of predicates. As for what I call translating, pp. 96–7 showed that for purposes of testing correctness the standard of accuracy required when putting connectives for words is no higher than sameness of truth-conditions. (5) will change meaning by relativisation to domains, and (6) will destroy meaning by exchanging sentences for formulae interpreted as schematic, i.e. as replaceable by meaningful sentences (this would be different if we interpreted the letters as dummies). Finally (7) may replace an inference-pattern by a conditional sentence-pattern. One might be tempted to think of the whole process of formalising as a kind of translation from words into symbols; but because the steps in it do not have to preserve sameness of meaning they are translations of a special kind, and in particular schematising is far from coming under the ordinary idea of translating.

Chapter 11 will exemplify the process. In this chapter and the next I shall examine various systematic, or at least recurrent, problems that arise in it. They do not arise equally at every stage. There is nothing hard about reordering. The rewording involved in stage (2) calls for a certain amount of care and a certain amount of sensitivity to linguistic idiom. I shall say something about it in 9.4. Rectifying is straightforward. Translating gives rise to the problems which will occupy most of this chapter and the next, problems of deciding whether and when certain English words have the same truth-conditions as were assigned to the logical connectives in 4.2. Domain-restriction is mainly straightforward, but see 10.7. 9.2 and 9.3 will discuss schematising, which is a matter of recognising grammatical categories. There is nothing hard about stage (7) for sequents nor, given $T \supset$ and $T\&$, for formulae: to assemble a string of formulae into a single formula instantiated by the argument's corresponding material conditional just put '$\supset$' after the penultimate formula in the string and '&' after each of that one's precursors, if any.

9.2 *Importing propositional letters*

In order to transform a set of sentences into a sequent or formula which it fits by the **PC** or **S5** fitting conventions we need to be able to recognise, for supplanting by 'p', 'q' etc., components in the set which are functioning as indicative sentences; and for transformation in accordance with the **QC** or **QS5** fitting conventions

9.2 Importing propositional letters

we may need also to be able to recognise, for supplanting by 'a', 'b' etc. and 'f', 'g' etc., components functioning as subjects and predicates. In this section I shall discuss sentences, in the next subjects. Predicates pose no special problem, for they are just whatever is left when one or more subjects are dropped from an indicative sentence.

There is rarely doubt whether an expression is functioning as an indicative sentence; and when doubt exists its resolution is rarely vital for logical purposes. That the resolution *might* be vital can be seen by considering arguments like this,

> If it were raining, the witch-doctor would be dancing;
> so if the witch-doctor did not dance, it would not rain,

which looks vaguely like a **PC**-instance of $\langle\{`p \supset q\text{'}\}, `\sim q \supset \sim p\text{'}\rangle$. If the argument were such an instance, it would be correct, since the sequent is **PC**-valid. But it is not correct, because the truth of its premiss requires at most that the witch-doctor dances in response to rain while the truth of its conclusion requires that his dancing produces rain. One thing which prevents the argument from in fact instantiating the proposed sequent is that at least some of its component clauses, 'it were raining' and so on, cannot be reexpressed in indicative sentences. But even if that objection were waived, two other features block the instantiation: in such subjunctive 'if'-sentences, 'if' has a different truth-condition from that assigned to '$\supset$' by $\mathbf{T} \supset$ (see 9.5), and anyhow uniform replacement of component clauses by 'p' and 'q' would demand prior rewording into something like '. . . so if the witch-doctor would not be dancing, it were not raining', which is impossible. In order to deal with subjunctive 'if'-sentences as a class it would be necessary to add to **PC** a new connective, say '$\square\!\!\rightarrow$', with the interpretation 'if it were the case that . . ., it would be the case that . . .'. In this richer logical language the argument would indeed be an instance of $\langle\{`p\square\!\!\rightarrow q\text{'}\}, `\sim q\square\!\!\rightarrow \sim p\text{'}\rangle$; but that sequent, unlike the **PC**-sequent, is invalid in the new language (see LEWIS p. 35). A somewhat similar case is

> If anyone can swim, he can float; so if anyone can swim, anyone can float,

which, though plainly incorrect, might be taken for a **PC**-instance of the trivially **PC**-valid sequent $\langle\{`p \supset q'\}, `p \supset q'\rangle$. In this example there is genuine doubt whether the component clauses function as indicative sentences, doubt which cannot altogether be allayed by the consideration that one rewording of the argument replaces some of the clauses by open sentences, thus: 'everyone x is such that if x can swim, x can float; so everyone x is such that if x can swim, everyone y is such that y can float'. Yet, as with the previous example, rejection of indicative status is not needed to block the instantiation; for in such general 'if'-sentences 'if' has different truth-conditions from those assigned to '$\supset$' by **T**$\supset$ (see 9.5), and anyhow uniform replacement of component clauses by 'p' and 'q' would demand that the difference in wording between the argument's premiss and conclusion be paraphrased away, which is impossible in a statement of that argument. In order to deal with general 'if'-sentences we need the predicate calculus, in which the argument **QC**-instantiates the sequent $\langle\{`\forall x(fx \supset gx)'\}, `\forall x(fx \supset \forall y gy)'\rangle$ but the sequent is **QC**-invalid. Similar considerations apply to the claim that

> Every marriage ends in death or divorce; not every marriage ends in death; so every marriage ends in divorce

is a **PC**-instance of the **PC**-valid sequent $\langle\{`p \vee q', `\sim p'\}, `q'\rangle$.

9.3 Importing subject letters

The category of subject, like the other grammatical categories, is defined by function not grammatical form; and although form remains here a guide to function, it is a less sure guide than in the case of indicative sentences. Moreover philosophers disagree about the defining function.

I start with a rough account. Obviously, subjects in English are to be found only among noun phrases. But not all noun phrases inside a predicate are subjects—e.g. 'a ship' in 'is a ship'—and this explains why logicians use the word 'subject' rather than 'object'. On the other hand some grammatical objects are subjects in the logician's sense; for example all three noun phrases in 'James smelt gas in the kitchen' are at least candidates for that status. This suggests the following guide in English, which possesses a definite

9.3 *Importing subject letters*

and an indefinite article. Singular noun phrases with no article generally function as subjects; these include proper names like 'James', pronouns like 'he', demonstratives like 'that', stuff-names like 'gas', 'snow', 'linen', and abstract nouns like 'courage', 'mankind'. Singular noun phrases with the definite article often, but not always, function as subjects; these are called **definite descriptions** and among them are to be included phrases beginning with possessives like 'my' and demonstratives like 'this', which can be thought of as abbreviating 'the'-phrases ('my uncle'—'the uncle of me', 'this hat'—'the hat here'). The remaining singular noun phrases, those beginning with the indefinite article, usually do not function as subjects; nor in general do plural noun phrases, since 'subject' means, in this book, 'singular referring expression'. But for a more accurate account we need to turn from form to function.

An expression has the status of a subject, in the logical sense, when it is used as a singular referring expression, i.e. used to make an identifying reference to some one thing (STRAWSON *Ind.* p. 16, *IRT*). Proper names are rightly taken to be the paradigm of words apt for such use, and that explains why some authors apply the label 'proper name' to every expression when it has such use, i.e. to every subject (in Lemmon's book 'proper name' is further extended to subject *letters*). Referring is here to be understood as an activity that cannot be engaged in unintentionally. But this leaves two questions about identifying reference: exactly what intention is necessary for use of an expression to be such a referring use?, and must the intention, besides occurring, succeed in some way before we can speak of such a use? Over both these questions there is much dispute, which is best solved, for our limited purposes, by stipulation. First, then, I shall stipulate that an intention to refer is an intention to identify—i.e. pick out for oneself or another—some one thing as a subject of discourse by means of an expression. So it will be absent when, for example, a conjuror says 'Is that your watch?' in order to draw attention away from his own hands but not towards anything in particular. Secondly, I shall stipulate that the intention is present but unsuccessful only in the case when there is nothing, so to speak, at its 'target' (GEACH *LM* p. 147), as may happen if someone says 'The King of France is bald' under the misapprehension that France is a monarchy (STRAWSON *OR* p. 13, a "spurious use" which "fails to mention anybody") or when someone says 'Mr

Glass must have offended Todhunter' in comment on Todhunter's misheard exclamation 'Damn it! Missed a glass' (cf. CHESTERTON p. 17, cited by GEACH *LM* p. 157). This requirement is often presented as a requirement of existence: just as, for example, a man's intention to resign from office can be successful only if what he intends to resign from is an existing office of his, so—the argument goes—a man's intention to refer can be successful only if what he intends to refer to is an existing thing of some sort. The argument construes reference as one among the many relations which hold, if at all, between two currently existing things. But not all relations are like that. Although I cannot be the husband, I can be the son, of someone who exists no longer; and although I cannot comfort or cherish, I can esteem or emulate or worship, a thing which exists at no time. Referring—like intending itself—is most naturally placed in the last of these groups, a group in which the requirement of identifiability breaks free of the requirement of sometime existence; hence a reference, like an attitude of worship, may have a determinate target, and so escape being 'spurious', without having as its target anything that did or will exist (BARNES p. 48). Accordingly we are free to rule, as I shall, that (i) fulfilment of an intention to refer, while demanding reference to something, does not demand reference to anything that ever did or will exist. Furthermore (ii) the conditions of success which I stipulate allow an intention of reference to be successful even though the reference departs from right usage, as when an intention to refer by means of 'The King of France' or 'Louis' has a target, but a target which—whether the speaker knows it or not—that description is not true of or that name is not a name of (DONNELLAN p. 287); and (iii) the conditions allow an intention of reference to be successful even though it is misunderstood, or not understood, by its audience, so that the speaker fails to 'secure uptake' (AUSTIN p. 116) and fails to identify in the hearer's sense of 'identify' (STRAWSON *Ind.* p. 16). Finally if a speaker succeeds in referring, then what he refers to is always what he intends to refer to.

We can now return from function to grammatical form. The stipulations confirm, what was said earlier, that *proper names* generally function as subjects. But sometimes e.g. 'Bethlehem' may be short for 'the city which is called Bethlehem', and such abbreviated 'the'-phrases raise the same problems as other definite descriptions. According to Russell's Theory of Descriptions (RUSSELL *OD* p. 51, *IMP* p. 173) no *definite description* functions as a subject. But this theory is dissonant with the above conditions for subjecthood, and its espousal by Russell was almost certainly due to his adopting—rightly or wrongly—more stringent conditions. I suggest that matters are as follows. Some definite descriptions have actually become proper names, as 'the King's Arms', 'the Tower of London', 'Rufus's Oak', 'the morning star' (the test of proper name status is highly complex, but capital letters are suggestive in English, and certainly a description has become a proper name when it is conventionally used of something it is not true of, as Beethoven's Second Piano Concerto has that name even though composed and performed first). In using a sentence like 'The housewife is hardworking', a speaker could intend reference to some particular housewife (or, exceptionally, non-housewife) or could intend the general assertion that all or most housewives are hardworking. 'The winner will receive a subscription to *Men Only*' and 'The author of *Waverley* maunders' are ambiguous in a somewhat similar way: because it is not usually known in advance who, if anyone, will win, and was not known for some time after publication who wrote *Waverley*, these sentences may well be, or have been, used with the meaning 'whoever wins . . .', 'whoever wrote *Waverley* . . .'; and such uses have been distinguished from the referential as 'attributive' (see DONNELLAN). *Pronouns* in referential use might be called 'systematically variable names' (STRAWSON *SPLG* p. 60). Their use in the role of logical variables is equally common and, of course, different: contrast, for example, the two occurrences of 'it' in

> If anything is true it is reasonable; so
> if Christianity is true it is reasonable,

an argument which is not a **QC**-instance of $\langle\{`fa \supset ga`\}, `fb \supset gb`\rangle$ (cf. GEACH *R&G* p. 125, QUINE *W&O* pp. 113–14). The same divergence appears between the occurrences of 'himself' in 'Satan loves himself' and 'only Satan loves himself'; the former can be reworded with 'Satan' for 'himself', but the latter cannot since it restricts the class of self-lovers where 'only Satan loves Satan' restricts the class of Satan-lovers (the example is due, I think, to Geach). 'No news is good news' is exceptional in having a 'no'-phrase as subject, and normal uses of 'everything', 'nobody', 'some number' etc. are obviously not referential; otherwise for example we should expect 'Everyone loves everyone' to have the same truth-condition as 'Everyone loves himself' (QUINE *MofL* p. 141).

9.4 Importing variables and brackets

The formula '$\forall x(fx \supset gx)$' could be abbreviated without ambiguity into '$\forall(f \supset g)$'; and in general a predicate calculus which is monadic, in the sense of confining its predicate letters to marking places for one-place predicates, can get by without variables (HUGHES & LONDEY chs. 23–36, QUINE *MofL* chs. 18–20). But more-than-one-place predicates bring with them the need to indicate not only how many gaps follow a predicate letter but also which gaps are linked with which preceding quantifier in inextricably nested quantifications such as '$\forall x \exists y fxy$' and '$\exists z(\forall y fyz \lor gz)$'. Variables prevent ambiguities in this *linkage*. In a similar way marks of internal punctuation prevent the ambiguities of *grouping*, or scope, which infect such formulae as '$p \supset q \supset p$'. In English and other natural languages neither kind of ambiguity is actually prevented by rules of syntax, and the ways of avoiding them are multifarious. For both reasons problems can arise when the operation of translating words into symbols presents choices of linkage or of grouping.

I exploited the ambiguous linkage in 'Everyone praised Rex to his mother' when introducing variables in 1.3. Even when ambiguity is absent transformation of a sentence of natural language into the language of quantified variables often calls for reflection, and for attention to niceties of idiom. For example 'Every father has a father' means 'For everything x, if x is a father of something, something is a father of x', and so QC-instantiates '$\forall x(\exists y fxy \supset \exists y fyx)$' rather than the repetitious '$\forall x(\exists y fxy \supset \exists y fxy)$'. Or again the sentence 'If anything causes itself, something is its effect' would change in meaning if we substituted '... is its own effect'; the former QC-instantiates '$\forall x(fxx \supset \exists y gyx)$', the latter '$\forall x(fxx \supset \exists y gyy)$' or equivalently '$\exists x fxx \supset \exists x gxx$'; for 'its own', like 'itself', generally picks up the nearest available antecedent.

9.4 Importing variables and brackets

Ambiguous grouping was known to Aristotle as ambiguity of composition (*Soph. El.* 4.166^{a}23). A famous example (JOSEPH pp. 582–3) is 'Children of both sexes are admitted free', which might QC-instantiate (relative to the domain of children) either '$\forall x(fx \supset hx)$ & $\forall x(gx \supset hx)$' or, as the showman insisted, '$\forall x(fx$ & $gx \supset hx)$'. One of Aristotle's examples, 'It is possible for someone who is not writing to write', is ambiguous at least in its Greek version between a QS5-instance of '$\exists x \Diamond(\sim fx \& fx)$' and of '$\exists x(\sim fx \& \Diamond fx)$'. Another case, due to Strawson (*SPLG* p. 8), is 'Both Tom and William are either mad or lying', where it is not clear whether 'and' or 'or' has wider scope. But often, as with linkage, attention to idiom will dispel any initial doubts about correct grouping. Strawson points out that the sentence 'Either Tom or William rides and drinks', superficially parallel to his other example, cannot idiomatically be used to say that at least one of them rides and at least one of them drinks but ought to mean that at least one of them does both, so QC-instantiating '$(fa \& ga) \lor (fb \& gb)$' rather than '$(fa \lor fb) \& (ga \lor gb)$'. Here is a more complex illustration of the power of English idiom to reduce, if not remove, ambiguities in the scope of propositional connectives:

> If you lengthen the agenda then a second meeting will be needed, or else some of the business will be skimped and members will complain that their views have not been properly heard.

The status of main connective is in competition between three words, 'if', 'or' and 'and'; and two of the choices permit variant grouping within the remainder of the sentence. But of the five notional possibilities only one is at all plausible, and the sentence should be understood as expressing a PC-instance of '$p \supset (q \lor (r \& p_1))$' (compare Quine's similar example, *MofL* p. 50).

Since the quantifiers, and the unary connectives '$\sim$', '$\Box$' and '$\Diamond$', display their relative scope by order rather than bracketing, some grouping-ambiguities lead to alternative orderings of two such connectives, and some grouping-mistakes result in wrong ordering. For example 'All prices are not stable' may mean 'Not all prices are stable' or 'All prices are unstable (no prices are stable)', and so may QC-instantiate, relative to the domain of prices, either '$\sim \forall x fx$' or '$\forall x \sim fx$'. On the other hand, 'Anyone can win' certainly expresses a **QS5**-instance, relative to the domain of persons, of '$\forall x \Diamond fx$' rather than '$\Diamond \forall x fx$', and likewise, almost certainly, does 'Everyone can win'. 'Everything has a cause' means 'For everything x, at least one thing causes x', so expressing a **QC**-instance of '$\forall x \exists y fyx$'. The corresponding **QC**-instance of '$\exists y \forall x fyx$', which differs in grouping but not linkage, states that for at least one thing y, y causes everything; and this cannot be rendered in English by 'Everything has a cause' but requires something like 'Everything has a cause in common' (or perhaps 'Everything has the same cause', which however suggests that everything has just one cause in common or even, differently again, that everything has its only cause in common). Combinations of 'every' or 'necessarily' with 'some' or 'possibly' seem to produce real ambiguity only when the leading word is from the latter pair, as in 'Some girl is loved by every boy' which is ambiguous between 'Each boy has a girl-beloved' and 'All the boys share a girl-beloved'. We have seen in previous chapters that these last three pairs of formulae make valid sequents when put together in one order, invalid when put in the converse order: for $\langle \{``\forall x \sim fx"\}, ``\sim \forall x fx" \rangle$, $\langle \{``\Diamond \forall x fx"\}, ``\forall x \Diamond fx" \rangle$ and $\langle \{``\exists y \forall x fyx"\}, ``\forall x \exists y fyx" \rangle$ are all valid, their converses all invalid. Moreover arguments which instantiate the invalid versions are frequently incorrect; hence Geach's label 'boy-and-girl fallacy' for the last case (GEACH *LM* pp. 1–13).

9.5. *Importing propositional connectives*

It is obvious that given **T**$\sim$, **T**& and the truth-conditions provable from them by Def$\lor$, Def$\supset$ and Def$\equiv$ the five propositional connectives roughly translate 'not', 'and', 'or', 'if' and 'if and only if'. How rough are these translations? Syntactical constraints on the symbolic connectives account for quite a lot of the difference in meaning between them and their English counterparts. Provided that 'not' can be worked into phraseology in which it governs the whole of some closed or open sentence, and the sentence is indicative, '$\sim$' will translate it (but 'not' in that syntactical role rarely has initial position, whereas '$\sim$', like the phrase 'it is not the case that', must have). Similarly '&' may be used in symbolisations of 'John and Jane are liars' or 'John and Jane are neighbours', because those sentences must say the same as 'John is a liar and Jane is a

9.5 Importing propositional connectives

liar' and 'John is a neighbour of Jane and Jane is a neighbour of John', in each of which '&' can supplant 'and'. But this transformation will not work in examples such as 'John and Jane are husband and wife', 'York lies between London and Edinburgh', 'The flag is black and white' (ACKERMANN p. 64), where parallel rewording changes or destroys the meaning. Since translation by a connective only requires sameness of truth-conditions, '&' will commonly serve to render other conjunctions than 'and', such as 'but' and 'although'; and for the same reason it will render 'and' even when that word carries a suggestion of temporal order as in 'They got married and had a baby', provided that the suggestion does not affect truth-conditions (see pp. 96–7).

In practice the only difficult cases involve '$\supset$' (and its definitional derivative '$\equiv$' which I shall not discuss separately). We have seen in 9.2 that '$\supset$' cannot supplant 'if' in *subjunctive* 'if'-sentences, whose components do not fit propositional letters. But some such sentences, e.g. 'If 3 were even, it would be divisible by 2', may be symbolised with '$\supset$' as subordinate connective to '$\Box$'; see pp. 240–1. Likewise '$\supset$' cannot always supplant 'if' in *general* 'if'-sentences, whether or not their components are judged to be syntactically suitable. For according to T$\supset$ the sentence 'Anyone can swim $\supset$ he can float' must be usable in an English context to express a truth, since its component 'Anyone can swim' is usable in an English context to express a falsehood; and this truth-condition is not shared by the parent sentence 'If anyone can swim he can float'. However, general 'if'-sentences can be symbolised with '$\supset$' as subordinate connective to a universal quantifier (QUINE *MofL* p. 20). The really troublesome cases are the singular indicative 'if'-sentences, like 'If you strike the match forthwith, it will light'. This example is typical in implying some sort of connection—the match's flammability—between antecedent and consequent, which would make the truth of the antecedent a reason for thinking that the consequent is true. In order to know whether 'if' can be supplanted by '$\supset$' in such a case we therefore need to know whether the implication contributes to the sentence's truth-condition (cf. FREGE *SuB* pp. 75–6). If it does, the implication will be truth-carrying, so that when what is implied is false—e.g. the match is wet—the 'if'-sentence will itself express a falsehood. That blocks the proposed translation into '$\supset$', for T$\supset$ ensures that 'You strike the match forthwith ⊃ it will light' is *true* even of an unlightable match, provided that you do not strike it: the fourth line of the '⊃'-matrix applies (hence T⊃ and T& ensure that whenever 'You strike the match ⊃ it will light' is T in a PC-context and domain and world, so also is 'The match is wet & you strike it forthwith ⊃ it will light'; see STEVENSON p. 279). The same goes for many other examples, e.g. 'If Locke and Russell were contemporaries, so were Locke and Spinoza', whose '⊃'-version states a truth even though its implication of common dates for Russell and Spinoza is false. If on the other hand these implications are merely suggestions ('implicatures', GRICE *CTP* pp. 90–5) contributing at most to the tone of a singular 'if'-sentence and not to its truth-condition, we can agree that such 'if''s share the truth-condition of '⊃' and we can ignore any residual difference of meaning. There are other less typical examples where the implication is absent or hard to discern, e.g. 'If France is in Australia then the sea is salt' (QUINE *MofL* p. 21). In such cases trouble could be shirked by deeming the sentence to express no proposition at all (on one view indeed the characteristic use of an 'if'-sentence is not to assert a conditional proposition but to assert a proposition—the consequent—conditionally on the fulfilment of the antecedent, so that 'conditionals' with false antecedents are not true or false but void, like conditional bets). A more systematic and, I believe, more plausible judgment is that the falsity of the antecedent expressed in such an 'unconnected' sentence, or the truth of its consequent, is enough on any occasion of use to ensure that the sentence is true, though not enough to ensure that it is felicitous or appropriate. This assigns the truth-condition of '⊃' to the 'unconnected' cases of 'if'. But it must be admitted that the assignment is less reasonable in the 'connected' cases, and there is much to be said for the view that 'If you strike the match forthwith, it will light' is F in contexts of reference to a wet match even if unstruck by you. In any case the truth-conditions assigned to '⊃' by T⊃ cannot, as we have seen, be extended to cover all general or subjunctive 'if'-sentences (see MACKIE pp. 74–81).

9.6 *Importing the predicate-leading construction*

From the PC interpretation rules I now turn to the question: what constraints are imposed by TP on translation from ordinary English

9.6 Importing the predicate-leading construction

subject–predicate constructions into the artificial construction which gathers subjects at the end of the sentence? It will be sufficient to deal with one-place predicates, since the others add no extra problems.

Given the meaning stipulated in 9.3 for 'refer' and the general requirement (in the logical interpretation rules) of right usage, TP for one-place predicates may be reformulated in these three parts: a sentence of the predicate-leading construction is T(F) in a QC-context and domain and world if and only if (a) in the context there is something x to which the component subject is intended to refer and of which the subject is in fact a name or description or other designation (as I shall say: to which the subject 'applies'), (b) x is a member of the domain and (c) the component predicate is true (false) of x in that context and domain and world. The two requirements in part (a), without which a sentence so constructed is neither T nor F in a QC-context, are clearly separable. We might have waived, at this point, the demand for right usage, substituting (a1) 'there is something to which the subject is intended to refer'. I shall distinguish the more stringent version in TP itself as (a2). Or we might have made truth and falsity independent of speaker's intention. This could be done in various ways. One could be (a3) 'There is just one thing to which it would be natural and reasonable, in the context, to take the subject as being intended to refer, and the subject applies to that thing'. Notice too that these three versions could be presented as alternative accounts of what make an intention to refer successful; and they are so presented by STRAWSON (*SPLG* p. 62). Other possibilities are (a4) 'There is just one thing to which the subject applies' and (a5) 'There is at least one thing to which the subject applies'. Finally, whichever of these requirements were adopted we could have ruled that failure to satisfy it leads to falsehood rather than lack of truth-value, so banning 'truth-value gaps'.

How does TP as it stands, viz. (a2) plus (b) and (c), compare with the truth-condition for the subject–predicate construction in unsupplemented English? We need not, fortunately, consider every kind of English sentence so constructed. Because of the definition of 'subject' in 9.3 and because instances must be rightly expressible in sentences fitting a sequent or formula, a candidate for transformation into the predicate-leading construction will already fulfil two conditions; there will be something that its component subject is intended (in the context) to refer to, and the subject will apply to that thing. This means that if requirement (a1) or (a2) or one of their variants banning truth-value gaps is met by any English sentence of the candidate class, then requirement (a2) is met by it; and so is requirement (b), since a speaker's intended reference, if successful, counts as part of his subject matter. Ignoring (c) for the moment we can therefore conclude that all such sentences share the truth-conditions of **TP** and so can be translated into the predicate-leading construction.

But there may remain English sentences for which the right truth-conditions include one of the clauses (a3)–(a5), perhaps varied so as to ban truth-value gaps. In particular Russell's Theory of Descriptions held that (a4) so varied is right for all definite descriptions: Russell proposed that sentences of the form 'the f is g' are T or F according as there is or is not something of which alone 'f' is true and of which 'g' is true. This proposed truth-condition (which Russell combined with the quite independent thesis that definite descriptions do not function as subjects) rests on the view that '*the*, when it is strictly used, involves uniqueness' (RUSSELL *OD* p. 44), which is faulty in confounding 'the' with 'the only' (SEARLE pp. 83–4): there need be no departure from the strictest canons of English usage when 'The policeman is drunk' is used to express a truth in our world of many policemen, and after the Tay Bridge was blown down there were still many bridges over the Tay. Neither do proper names involve uniqueness: it is false that 'Everest' names at most one thing, though 'At most one thing is Everest' is F in no context (cf. STRAWSON *OR* p. 23). Relaxation of (a4) to (a5) would remove this fault by assigning the same truth-condition to the definite 'The f is g' as to the indefinite 'An f is g', which is implausible though not inconsistent with their retaining different meanings. But even if (a4) and (a5) are implausible, (a3) remains in serious competition with (a1) and (a2) as an account of the truth-conditions of some English sentences containing subjects, both definite descriptions and proper names. For example it is in virtue of (a3) that we count 'George I died in 1760' as F even when it is said in intended reference to George II; in these circumstances (a1) would yield the verdict 'T', (a2) 'neither T nor F'. The example involves misnaming, but the competition survives restriction to

9.6 Importing the predicate-leading construction

right usage, as in the following case. In an essay on the philosopher Plato an undergraduate inserts the sentence 'Plato was a comic playwright'; he knows that there was a comic playwright of that name, and intends reference to him rather than the philosopher; but he gives no indication of this change of reference. (a2) yields the verdict that his sentence is T, for the thing to which he intends reference was called Plato and was a comic playwright. But (a3)'s verdict, which goes the other way, is surely preferable. In such cases, which are doubtless marginal, translation into the predicate-leading construction would change truth-value, and therefore would be wrong.

What of requirement (c)? By the technical definition of 'true (false) of' (p. 90) it expands into 'The component predicate can be used to attribute a property, defined over the domain, which holds (does not hold) of x'. The meaning of this expansion is somewhat elusive, and there is a philosophical puzzle which gives some support to the suggestion that one meaning is appropriate for the predicate-leading construction, another for constructions of ordinary English. I shall now describe the puzzle, and defend a solution which does not have that effect.

Consider the two following arguments, the second of them due to Quine (*R&M* p. 139):

(A) The youngest member of the rugby team is the tallest; the youngest member of the rugby team is the youngest member of the Jones family; so the youngest member of the Jones family is the tallest.

(B) Giorgione was so called because of his size; Giorgione was Barbarelli; so Barbarelli was so called because of his size.

These arguments apparently QC-instantiate the QC-valid sequent $\langle \{`fa\text{'}, `a = b\text{'}\}, `fb\text{'} \rangle$; but they cannot really do so because they are plainly incorrect. The puzzle is: why do they not? One solution, which was tried out by Russell in *OD*, holds in effect that the expressions 'the youngest member of the rugby team', 'the youngest member of the Jones family', 'Giorgione' and 'Barbarelli' do not function in these arguments as subjects. But the suggestion is implausible at least in (B). A second solution is this. The property of being so called because of his size cannot be said to hold or not to hold of Giorgione *simpliciter*: rather it holds of him *qua* Giorgione but not *qua* Barbarelli, and similarly for (A). To justify the validity of the valid sequent $\langle\{`fa`, `a = b`\}, `fb`\rangle$, and so the soundness of the derivation rule =E, it is necessary to understand requirement (c) in the sense 'can be used to attribute a property which holds of x *qua* everything (nothing)'; but with the ordinary English sentence 'Giorgione was so called because of his size' it is enough for truth that the property should hold of him *qua* Giorgione. This suggestion too is implausible, for although a relation may hold from Giorgione to one thing and not another, surely no property can both hold and not hold of him (hence a principle attributed to Leibniz, and sometimes called Leibniz' Law, survives (A) and (B), namely that if a is the same thing as b, any property of a is a property of b; see CARTWRIGHT *I&S* pp. 119–21). Another possibility is that what blocks the proposed instantiation is not a mismatch of truth-conditions between ordinary subject–predicate constructions and TP, but a failure to eliminate equivocation from the sentences in (A) and (B). The equivocation could lie in either of two places. Frege's solution, the third in this survey, was to the effect that 'Giorgione' (and similarly 'Barbarelli'), though a genuine subject in (B), has inconstant reference, referring on its second occurrence to Giorgione, the customary or direct reference of the name, but on its first occurrence to something else, the customary 'sense' of the name, whatever that may be (FREGE *SuB* pp. 58–9, MATES pp. 23–4). I shall recur to this in connection with example (C) below, more like Frege's own; here it is enough to say that his proposal, queer enough for (C), would be ludicrous for (A) and (B). (Hence a different, and metalinguistic, version of Leibniz' principle, the Law of Substitutivity which states that co-referring expressions can be substituted *salva veritate*, is false for English.) Fourthly and finally then we must locate the equivocation in the predicates 'is the tallest' and 'was so called because of his size'. These have a common characteristic: they require supplementation from the subject to which they are attached. Thus in (A) the first occurrence contracts 'is the tallest in the rugby team' while the second contracts 'is the tallest in the Jones family'; and in (B) the first occurrence stands in for 'was called "Giorgione" because of his size', the second for 'was called "Barbarelli" because of his size'. When occurrences of a predicate require different supplementations, there is equivocation. Hence neither (A) nor (B) satisfies

9.6 Importing the predicate-leading construction

the conditions for being a QC-instance of the given sequent (see pp. 49, 58).

The problem is less tractable when it is due to indirect discourse, introduced by 'propositional attitude' verbs of believing, wanting, hoping, doubting and the like (QUINE, *QPA*), for example:

(C) Oedipus wanted to marry Jocasta; Jocasta was his mother; so he wanted to marry his mother.

Here it is natural to say that Oedipus wanted to marry his mother under one description but not under another, *qua* Jocasta perhaps but anyhow not *qua* his own mother. Yet this is still not serious support for the suggestion that the property of having been wanted as a wife by Oedipus both holds, *qua* one thing, and does not hold, *qua* another, of Jocasta. Nor are the solutions of Russell and Frege much more attractive here than for (A) and (B), although it was examples involving indirect discourse which engaged their attention; for surely 'his mother' does, or might, function in (C) as a subject, and surely it refers therein to his mother. On the other hand the solution favoured above for (A) and (B) now looks rather far-fetched: what are the different supplementations implied by the two occurrences of 'Oedipus wanted to marry . . .'? Perhaps none is implied by the first occurrence, 'in the belief that she bore him' by the second. Or perhaps we should say, following the suggestion made on p. 38, that argument (C) is actually correct; that its conclusion is true although infelicitously expressed (URMSON pp. 116–22); and that the contradictory of its conclusion—that Oedipus did not want to marry his mother—only appears true because it is confused with the truth that he wanted not to marry her (he wanted two things whose joint fulfilment was impossible, but it was not impossible for him, at least while ignorant, to want both of them). Or it may be that none of these solutions is adequate.

Although it is therefore not quite clear that (C) and its like do constitute exceptions to the Law of Substitutivity—that co-referring expressions can be substituted *salva veritate*—it is clear that if they do so the cause is some propositional attitude verb. Occurrences of these verbs can be reworded into unary sentence connectives on the pattern of 'Oedipus wanted it to be that . . .' and 'Tom believes that . . .', and such of these connectives as convert a sentence within which co-referring expressions can be substituted *salva veritate* (e.g. 'Oedipus is married to his mother') into a sentence within which they cannot (e.g. perhaps 'Oedipus wanted it to be that Oedipus is married to his mother') have been called **referentially opaque** contexts (QUINE *R&M* p. 142, 3 *Grades* p. 158). By an easy extension we may describe as referentially opaque any predicate in attachment to which co-referring subjects cannot always be substituted *salva veritate*, whether it contains such a connective (e.g. perhaps 'Oedipus wanted it to be that Oedipus is married to . . .') or not (e.g. '. . . was so called because of his size'). 'Non-Shakespearean' is another label for these predicates, alluding to 'A rose by any other name would smell as sweet' (GEACH *LM* p. 139); and 'intensional' is yet another, which, however, spreads itself over different senses also (KNEALE *I&I* pp. 76–7; PRIOR *I&I* pp. 91–2). If it is right to say that all such predicates seek supplementation, and get it from the subject to which they are attached, then a common feature of them all is to force attached subjects into contributing to their meaning and so into having more than a referring role. It would then follow that *purely* referring expressions with the same reference can be substituted *salva veritate* (QUINE *R&M* p. 140, LOAR pp. 50–1), and the way of eliminating equivocation that is due to opaque predicates would be to purify the subjects attached to them. The difficulty lies not in performing this operation but in knowing when it needs to be performed.

I am inclined to think that this fourth solution works generally—that opacity never survives the removal of equivocation. But if it does *not* work generally, we should need to buttress it by a fifth solution, as follows. Because of their opacity, predicates like 'Oedipus wanted it to be that Oedipus is married to . . .' do not attribute properties at all; hence they are not, under the definitions of p. 90, true or false of anything; hence they cannot be transformed into the predicate-leading construction, and arguments not expressible without them cannot be appraised with the help of **TP**. This is the cautious policy of MASSEY (pp. 228–30, 233–4) and MATES (p. 77, where the word 'predicate' is itself defined to mean 'transparent, i.e. non-opaque, predicate').

A further alleged example of referential opacity will be examined in 10.5.

9.7 Importing quantifiers

Quantifiers play the role which traditional logic assigned to 'syncategorematic' words of natural language such as 'omnis', 'all', 'some'. In that logic four forms of categorical proposition were recognised and distinguished under the labels A,E,I and O. The schemata below give a version of each form, together with the QC-formulae they apparently translate into when quantifiers and variables are put for the syncategoremetic words.

A	every f is a g	$\forall x(fx \supset gx)$
E	no f is a g	$\sim \exists x(fx \mathbin{\&} gx)$
I	some f is a g	$\exists x(fx \mathbin{\&} gx)$
O	not every f is a g	$\sim \forall x(fx \supset gx)$

Although it is no part of the purpose of this book to examine the rules of traditional logic, comparison of these schemata with their associated QC-formulae will be useful because the words they contain often turn up in English formulations of arguments. How close are the associations?

One difference concerns the functions of the schematic letters 'f' and 'g'. In the formulae these are, of course, predicate letters, replaceable by one-place predicates such as 'is a price', 'is stable' or 'fluctuates'. But in the traditional schemata they mark gaps for expressions of a slightly different grammatical category, terms (QUINE *MofL* p. 79), which are formed by first rewording one-place predicates into singular noun phrases preceded by 'is' (the copula), as in 'is a price', 'is a stable thing', 'is a thing that fluctuates', and then eliding 'is a'. Since such rewording is always possible—though not always natural—no confusion arises in practice from a licence to use the same logical letters both as one-place predicate letters and as term letters; and I have informally availed myself of this licence earlier in the book.

Another small difference concerns the I form. In the predicate calculus there is no difference in meaning between corresponding sentences QC-fitting '$\exists x(fx \mathbin{\&} gx)$' and '$\exists x(gx \mathbin{\&} fx)$'. But English sentences such as 'Some bird is chirping' and 'Something chirping is a bird' are not natural variants of one another (cf. STRAWSON, *SPLG* p. 108) and we should therefore expect the I versions of these, 'Some bird is a thing that is chirping' and 'Some thing that is chirping is a bird', not to be counted as interchangeable. Traditional logic evades this issue in the manner of 4.4, by ruling that the schemata 'Some f is a g' and 'Some g is an f' have the same truth-conditions (hence its derivation rules license 'conversion' of the I form), and ignoring any residual difference of meaning between them. We are therefore to think of translation into the I form as exactly parallel to translation into a sentence QC-fitting '$\exists x(fx\ \&\ gx)$'; it is 'translation' only in the sense of preserving truth-conditions, part by part, and any instance of 'Some f is a g' will be an instance, more or less directly, of its converse 'Some g is an f'. In a rather similar way 'Some f is a g' can have instances in which it is not natural to use the English word 'some' at all, like Strawson's example 'I've just been stung by a wasp' (*SPLG* p. 111). In general 'Some f is a g' should be regarded as a specimen schema, for which 'An f is a g' would often be an acceptable substitute sharing the same truth-condition though differing in subtle respects. When that substitution is in order, both 'Some f is a g' and 'An f is a g' can be translated into the predicate calculus '$\exists$'-form. Even the plural 'Some fs are gs' can be so translated when its suggestion of 'at least two' is not serious enough to affect truth-conditions; for '$\exists$' means, of course, 'at least one', given Def$\exists$ together with T $\sim$ and T$\forall$. Exactly the same considerations apply to the traditional E form 'No f is a g'.

There is however a significant difference between the A form and '$\forall x(fx \supset gx)$'. 'Every f is a g' competes for the role of specimen A schema with 'Any f is a g', 'Each f is a g', 'All fs are gs', 'All the fs are gs', and doubtless others. But the first and last of these alternative schemata differ not only in conditions of appropriateness but in truth-conditions; for (speaking schematically) the truth of 'Any f is a g' does not require that there be an f (e.g. Newton's first law of motion does not require that there be a moving body not acted on by external forces, STRAWSON *ILT* p. 164), whereas the truth of 'All the fs are gs' does require that there be an f ("It would seem grotesque to maintain that anyone saying 'All the books in his room are by English authors' had made a true statement if the room referred to were empty of books", STRAWSON *ILT* p. 148). Traditional logic chose to interpret 'every' in the sense 'all the', and as a result the I form is a consequence, in the sense of 8.2, of the A form; i.e. $\langle\{$'every f is a g'$\}$, 'some f is a g'$\rangle$ is a valid sequent of traditional logic. By contrast T∀ ties '∀' to 'any'; and ⟨{'∀x(fx ⊃ gx)'}, '∃x(fx & gx)'⟩ is not QC-valid, since the truth of a sentence QC-fitting its second, but not its first, formula requires the truth of the corresponding sentence QC-fitting '∃xfx'. Exactly the same feature distinguishes the O form from '~ ∀x(fx ⊃ gx)': in traditional logic O is a consequence of E, but the sequent ⟨{'~ ∃x(fx & gx)'}, '~ ∀x(fx ⊃ gx)'⟩ is not QC-valid since again the truth of a sentence QC-fitting its second, but not its first, formula requires the truth of the corresponding sentence QC-fitting '∃xfx'. Forms with this requirement, and thus all four traditional forms, are said to have 'existential import'.

Though 'any' and 'all the' clearly diverge in truth-conditions, 'every', 'each' and 'all' sit rather uneasily between them, and often it is unclear whether or not they have existential import. Consider the argument

All prices are stable; so some prices are stable.

Although any argument might be correct in spite of QC-instantiating a QC-invalid sequent, it is hard to see how this one could be correct if it is a genuine QC-instance of ⟨{'∀x(fx ⊃ gx)'}, '∃x(fx & gx)'⟩. So in this sort of case the predicate calculus is not in general helpful for testing correctness; rather we are forced to work the other way round, using intuitions about correctness to determine what sequent adequately represents the argument's form. However, there is a pitfall in this path. When the argument *is* judged correct, one may be tempted to write '⊃' rather than '&' in its conclusion, translating 'Some prices are stable' into '∃x(x is a price ⊃ x is stable)'. This is wrong because the formula '∃x(fx ⊃ gx)', though indeed a QC-consequence of '∀x(fx ⊃ gx)', abbreviates '~ ∀x ~~ (fx & ~gx)' and so, suppressing the double '~', is QC-instantiated by 'Not everything is an unstable price', whereas we wanted 'Not every price is an unstable price' (QUINE *MofL* p. 116, MATES p. 72). On the other hand these two do amount to the same thing when the domain is restricted to prices, so that relative to that domain the argument does QC-instantiate the QC-valid sequent ⟨{'∀x(fx ⊃ gx)'}, '∃x(fx ⊃ gx)'⟩. But also, relative to that domain, it can be expressed more briefly in 'Everything is stable; so something is stable' which QC-instantiates the shorter QC-valid sequent ⟨{'∀xgx'}, '∃xgx'⟩. Here then is one way, domain-restriction, of formalising the argument on the supposition that its 'all' has existential import. Another, which involves no special restriction on the domain, is to make the premiss's existential import explicit by splitting it into two premisses, respectively instantiating '$\forall x(fx \supset gx)$' and '$\exists x fx$'. Notice that the former way, through restricted domains, depends on prices being a genuine domain: there must be something at the target of our intention to talk about prices, so that the class of prices has a member (see pp. 54–5).

An independent point: notice that '$\exists x \exists y(fx \,\&\, fy)$' means 'something is f and something is f'; to capture the stronger claim that at least *two* things are f—'else' after the second 'something'—we should need '$\exists x \exists y(x \neq y \,\&\, fx \,\&\, fy)$' (cf. MATES p. 82, LEMMON *BL* p. 164).

9.8 *Existence and domains*

I now turn to a different problem which may be suggested by comparison between traditional logic and the predicate calculus. By means of Def$\supset$ and exchange of QC-equivalents it is possible to render all the traditional forms into QC-formulae which begin with an unnegated quantifier: A and I remain as before, E becomes '$\forall x(fx \supset \sim gx)$' and O becomes '$\exists x(fx \,\&\, \sim gx)$'. In traditional metalogical parlance the forms with '$\forall$' renderings, A and E, are described as universal, those with '$\exists$' renderings, I and O, as particular. But modern logicians, while taking over 'universal' for the '$\forall$' quantifier, usually substitute '*existential*' for 'particular' as the metalogical label for '$\exists$'. The very notation of '$\exists x$' is meant to suggest interpretation as 'there exists an x such that', whereas 'some' not 'exists' is the key word in the I form, and also in the O form if that is given as 'Some f is not a g'. In 4.5 T$\exists$ ignored this notational suggestion, interpreting '$\exists$' in terms of the words 'some member of the domain'; but the choice of wording would be unimportant if 'some' had the same truth-condition as 'an existing' and 'some existing'. Does it?

Since '$\exists$' is not a primitive connective in QC, the wording of T$\exists$ stems from that of T$\forall$; and if the former were to be changed to 'some existing member of the domain' the latter would have to become 'every existing member of the domain'. So the truth-conditions of these metalogical uses of 'some' and 'some existing'

9.8 Existence and domains

will be the same only if those of 'every' and 'every existing' are the same. It is clear enough that not every member of a domain need, literally speaking, be an existing member: for a thing may remain a fit subject for discourse after it has ceased to exist, or become one before it comes to exist. The domain of historical personages, for example, includes as members not only the living but the dead; and the dead must be *current* members in order to provide falsification for such currently false sentences as '$\forall x(x$ is famous $\supset x$ is alive)'. The falsity of this sentence, relative to the domain of historical personages, is due to its expressing in a QC-context the false proposition that all the so far famous (if any) are still living; and it would be absurd to limit the sentence to expressing in a QC-context the different proposition that all the so far famous who still exist (if any) are still living. Of course many things, such as numbers, never come into existence or cease to exist, and many domains consist of just such things. But since there is no good reason to prevent logic from testing arguments about what is creatable or perishable, domains must be permitted to include what has not yet been created or has already perished. The gloss on 'every member of the domain' must at least be relaxed to 'every sometime existing member of the domain' (cf. STRAWSON *ILT* pp. 150–1, MASSEY pp. 264–5, and the example in LAMBERT & VAN FRAASSEN p. 182; also, for a halfway house, PRIOR *PPF* p. 171 "The dead are metaphysically less frightening than the unborn").

But is this relaxation enough? When we turn from history to fiction the problem seems to break out again. Although things mentioned in fiction may be real (e.g. places, even in non-historical novels) they may be figments; and there seems to be a possibility of producing arguments, which logic might occasionally want to appraise, about all or some members of a domain embracing figments, e.g. arguments involving the Jules Verne character who attempted a journey to the centre of the earth. Here we face the difficulty of relating fiction to falsity. There are three kinds of sentence to consider: (D) a sentence in Verne's book meaning 'Someone has travelled beneath the earth from Iceland to Stromboli'; (E) a commentator's sentence 'One of Verne's characters travelled beneath the earth from Iceland to Stromboli'; (F) a pedantic commentator's sentence 'One of Verne's characters is said in the book to have travelled beneath the earth from Iceland to

Stromboli'. Common sense would suggest that in each case the speaker's subject matter must include figments at least if his sentence is to express a truth, and perhaps even if it is to express a falsehood. If so, there are only two ways of saving the thesis that what falls within a speaker's subject matter—i.e. is a member of some domain—must be a sometime existent: either none of (D)–(F) express truths (nor perhaps falsehoods) relative to any domain, or figments do in some sense exist. One may indeed plausibly hold that (D) expresses neither a truth nor a falsehood, but is a pretence of truth. Sentences like (E) have been thought true by some, e.g. BARNES p. 49, "Mr Slope was a devious chaplain", WOODS, p. 28 (provisionally) "Holmes is a man (or was), and he did live in London, and does not exist and never did", and false by others, e.g. GRICE *VN* p. 119, "If Pegasus does not exist. . . . 'Pegasus flies' will be false". The crucial case is (F) (cf. BARNES p. 50), which is certainly true. Relative to what domain? Russell's example 'The present King of France is bald' has accustomed philosophers to the idea that the subject matter of a proposition may be other than it seems; for in the context imagined by Russell the reference intended by 'the present King of France' does not succeed, so that "if we enumerated the things that are bald, and then the things that are not bald, we should not find the present King of France on either list" (RUSSELL *OD* p. 48). But given the stipulation of 9.3 that reference is among the relations which can hold to a never-existent object, there is no reason to deny the possibility of reference in the fictional case, nor therefore to deny that figments can be members of domains. Some philosophers accordingly cling to the dogma that even figments exist in some sense. But either the proposed kind of existence is bogus (e.g. being-something, i.e. being f for some f, which is compatible with non-existence, or existing-in-fiction, which is no more a way of existing than imagining yourself rich is a way of being rich, cf. WOODS p. 32) or else there is no reason, independent of the dogma, for thinking that figments have it. Much the same argument applies to hoaxes and superstitions as to fiction proper. It therefore seems reasonable to allow that a domain of discourse may include items, such as Zeus and Ossian and Verne's Professor Lidenbrock, which never did or will exist.

The words 'sometime existing' are absent from rules T∃ and T∀. If the above argument is right, their insertion would change the

9.8 Existence and domains

rules, and would detach the truth-conditions of '∀' and '∃' from those of the English words 'every' and 'some'. Consequently 'existential quantifier' is an inaccurate label for '∃' when that symbol is interpreted as in T∃, though I have adopted it in deference to modern logical usage; and T∃'s reading of '∃x' is not 'there exists something x such that' but rather 'something x is such that' or 'at least one thing x is such that' or perhaps 'there is something x such that'. (Similarly 'has existential import' is an inaccurate way of saying 'entails "some" '.)

I conclude this section by describing the changes in QC (and QS5) which would result if the truth-conditions for '∀' and '∃' were reworded in terms of sometime existent members of domains so that '∃' really deserved its name 'existential'. From the point of view of finding *instances* the changes would be slight, perhaps surprisingly so. The proposition that something is a figment would cease to be an instance, relative to any domain, of '∃xfx', since (i) '∃$x(x$ is a figment)' would express a falsehood relative to every domain but (ii) the proposition is a truth. Similarly no domain could be found relative to which '∃$x(x$ is a winged horse)' expressed a truth; but in this case—a more normal one—it is reasonable to hold that even the liberal domains admitted by T∃ contain no winged horses, on the ground that fictional or mythological horses are not horses (only real horses are really horses). If so, there is nothing to prevent the proposition that some horses have wings from instantiating '∃xfx' or '∃$x(fx \& gx)$' relative to a domain of sometime-existents, since the proposition is false (this goes with the doctrine that Santa Claus has no feet, PLANTINGA p. 154, and Holmes never lived in Baker Street). In general, cases in which the truth-conditions of 'some' and 'there exists (at some time)' come apart are rare. But from the point of view of *validity* there would be changes of two kinds. (1) The sequent $\langle\{`\forall xfx\text{'}\}, `fa\text{'}\rangle$ would cease to be valid, since a predicate fitting 'f' might be true of every sometime-existent member of every domain but not of every member, and then there would be false instances of 'fa' with no corresponding false instances of '∀xfx'. For a similar reason $\langle\{`fa\text{'}\},$ '∃xfx'$\rangle$ would cease to be valid, and so would substituends of both sequents. Versions of QC with these features are known as '(narrowly) free logics' (WOODS, p. 68, LAMBERT & VAN FRAASSEN ch. 6). But of course the validity of such sequents could easily be restored by adding a parallel existence-requirement to **TP**, so that fictional names like 'Pegasus' would cease to count as subjects for the purposes of **TP** (some logicians, as explained on p. 200, take the existence-requirement to be built into **TP** anyhow, as part of the requirement for success in an intention to refer). (2) The formula '$\exists x(x = a)$' would cease to be valid, since a subject fitting 'a' might refer to a never-existent member of some domain. In effect the formula would symbolise not 'a is the same thing as something' but 'a (is the same thing as something which) did or will exist' and so would be invalidated by the permanent non-existence of Pegasus, Zeus and so on. But again validity could be restored by adding an existence-requirement to **T=**, or by taking it that the success of an intended reference imposes that requirement.

Another possible departure from **QC** is to have two sets of quantifiers, one set interpreted in terms of existence, the other as in this book; see e.g. ROUTLEY.

9.9 Importing '='

In this section I shall discuss English sentences fitting the three following schemata: 'a is the same f as b', 'a is the same (thing) as b' and 'a is b'. Under what conditions, given **T=**, can these be translated into '$a = b$'?

The first form (in which 'f' is a term letter, see p. 213) appears in such sentences as 'John is the same age as Jack' and 'John's house is the same house as Jack's'. No one would imagine that '=' can supplant 'is the same f as' in the former of these examples, which can plainly be used to express a truth, relative to a domain, even when 'John' and 'Jack' refer to different members of the domain; here 'is the same age as' means 'is of, or has, the same age as'. On the other hand 'is the same house as' does seem to share the truth-condition assigned to '=' by **T=**. The contrast between 'same age' and 'same house' is traditionally described as a contrast between qualitative and numerical identity or sameness. *Qualitative identity* is similarity, which admits of degrees. '=' is a wrong translation of 'is the same age as' because sameness in age specifies a partial similarity which can hold between different things. But it is arguable that some partial similarities are identity-entailing, i.e. cannot hold between different things: for example those expressed by 'is

9.9 Importing '='

simultaneously at the same place as' and 'has the same origin as' (LOCKE, II. xxvii. 1.). Since the converse entailment certainly holds, it might be possible to translate a sentence such as 'John and Jack were born to the same parents at exactly the same time' into 'John and Jack were born to parents & John = Jack'. The objection to this translation is simply that the alleged identity-entailment of its partial similarity is open to dispute: obviously the translation would be improper, for example, in an argument designed to test Locke's principle. The highest degree of similarity is exact similarity, or indiscernibility. It is particularly plausible to maintain that exact similarity cannot hold between different members of any domain, i.e. that indiscernibles are identical (see QUINTON, pp. 24–8). Hence one can justify translating 'John and Jack are indiscernible' into 'John = Jack' if one can independently justify the Identity of Indiscernibles—together with its converse, which is the non-metalinguistic version of Leibniz' Law (see p. 210).

In the case of *numerical identity* problems arise about the choice of domains. Relative to the domain of people plus houses 'John's house is the same house as Jack's' translates uncontroversially into 'John's house = Jack's house', and likewise 'John and Jack live in the same house', if understood as meaning '... share at least one house', translates into '$\exists x \exists y$(John lives in x and Jack lives in y & $x = y$)'. But suppose we take a wider domain, such as material things. Then the suggested translation of the latter sentence would be '$\exists x \exists y(x$ is a house & y is a house & John lives in x & Jack lives in y & $x = y$)'; and in general it is suggested that the open schema 'x is (not) the same f as y' translates for the numerical identity cases into 'x and y are fs & (not) $x = y$'. This rendering has however been challenged on the ground that for some replacements of 'f' and 'g' there are ordered pairs of things which satisfy 'x is the same f as y & x is not the same g as y', whereas the suggested translation of this open schema, viz. 'x and y are fs and gs & $x = y$ & $x \neq y$', is, for all replacements of 'f' and 'g', inconsistent and satisfied by nothing. It is not here to the point, obviously, to cite replacements like 'age' or 'colour' or 'height', which no one would imagine express numerical identity. Rather the objection is that numerical identity and numerical difference themselves are not binary relations, holding or not holding of ordered pairs of members of a domain, but ternary relations which hold of ordered triples consisting of a member, a member, and a property of members—e.g. John's house, Jack's house, and the property of being a house. If this view is right, the ternary relation of identity cannot always be expressed by the two-place predicate which T= interprets '=' to be.

The 'ternary relation' view, which is Geach's (*LM* pp. 238-49), depends on a doctrine of counting. Consider the list

(G)   The north wind doth blow
(H)   The north wind doth blow

As Frege in effect pointed out (*GL* pp. 28-9) the question how many items there are in this list cannot be answered until we know what sort of items are to be counted: for there are two sentence-tokens in it (see p. 36) but one sentence-type. Geach infers that (G) is the same sentence-type as (H) but a different sentence-token. But this inference can be met with a dilemma (PERRY p. 188, cf. DUMMETT pp. 570-2). The letter '(G)' is being used to refer either to a sentence-type or to a sentence-token: if the former, then (G) is not a different sentence-token from (H) because it is not a sentence-token at all; if the latter, then (G) is the same sentence-type as (H) only in the sense 'token of the same sentence-type as', which does not predicate numerical identity at all. Similarly if we follow Geach in introducing the expression 'is the same surman as' with the meaning 'has the same surname as', and if we are then told that a room in which every man has a surname contains three men but two surmen, we must conclude that either surmen are not men (but perhaps groups of men) or, if they are, 'is the same surman as' does not predicate numerical identity of surmen. In general, Frege's point that the number you get depends on what things you are counting has no tendency to show that the number you get when you are counting things depends on what you are counting them as. This destroys Geach's objection against translating open sentences like 'x is the same house as y', 'x is the same man as y', 'x is—as opposed to 'is a token of'—the same sentence-type as y' into symbolic versions fitting the open schema 'x is an f & $x = y$'.

It is also common in English to abbreviate the form 'a is the same f as b' into 'a is the same (thing) as b'; and it follows that the latter transforms into '$a = b$' when the former expresses either numerical identity or an identity-entailing similarity. Likewise the '=' sign

9.9 Importing '='

in mathematics fulfils the truth-condition of $\mathbf{T}=$ relative to the domain of numbers; for it attributes equality, which is identity-entailing among numbers.

Finally, the word 'is' on its own sometimes abbreviates 'is the same thing as', and it has that role whenever it is a two-place predicate joining two subjects rather than a copula joining a subject and a term. Hence recognition of the identity-role of 'is' depends on recognition of subjects. When flanked by two proper names as in 'Jacob is Israel' 'is' normally has the relational identity-role, and so translates into '='; for the only interpretations which would block this translation are the unlikely 'Jacob is called Israel' or 'The thing called Jacob is (also called) Israel'. On the other hand when 'is' is flanked by two definite descriptions, or by one proper name or pronoun and one definite description, the alternatives to an identity interpretation are more plausible and more various. For example it seems to be a mere quirk of English that superlative and ordinal predicates such as 'is the highest . . .', 'is the first . . .' commonly use the definite article; and in French where the article is mandatory its function is nevertheless different from that of introducing an identifying reference. So the natural rendering of 'Everest is the highest mountain' would be 'No mountain is higher than Everest' or 'Everest is higher than every other mountain', instantiating '$\forall x(fx \supset \sim hxa)$' or '$\forall x(fx \ \& \ x \neq a \supset hax)$' rather than '$a = b$'. The same is true of descriptions of offices and relationships held by one thing at a time (within a given domain), e.g. 'the parson', 'the Vice-chancellor', 'the state capital of Michigan'. On the other hand right usage often permits a referential use even where it does not require one. Thus, for example, Russell was wrong to maintain (*OD* p. 51) that 'The author of *Waverley* was Scott' must have the meaning 'Scott alone wrote *Waverley*' and so must instantiate '$fab \ \& \ \forall x(fxb \supset x = a)$' rather than '$c = a$' (and in fact the problem which Russell sought to solve by this analysis, of non-substitutivity, cannot always be so solved since it also arises with proper names that are certainly functioning as subjects). In general if 'is' is flanked by an admitted subject and a definite description, or by two definite descriptions, then even assuming right usage it is likely to be speaker's intention which determines whether the definite descriptions are functioning as subjects, and hence whether the 'is' abbreviates 'is the same thing as'.

CHAPTER TEN

Formalising: *S5* and *QS5*

10.1 Importing '□': *Preliminaries*

The relationship between the connectives interpreted by T□ and Def◇ and the English words 'necessarily' and 'possibly' is still uncomfortably obscure. In traditional modal logic, mainly the work of Aristotle, and in the revival of the subject by C. I. Lewis in the 1920s, derivation rules were emphasised and interpretation remained vague. Recently Hintikka, Kripke and others have provided interpretation rules on the normal recursive pattern, as in 4.2, with the result that the validity of modal formulae and sequents can now be established either directly or through proofs of the soundness of various sets of modal derivation rules. These rules give us something definite against which to test the claim that such schemata as 'necessarily p' and 'a is necessarily f' share the truth-conditions of '□p' and '□fa', and likewise for 'possibly' and '◇'; but the test remains difficult, both because of ambiguities in the English words and because the interpretation rules for the symbols rely on the concept of a possible world, which needs explication.

The difficulty shows itself in the variety of alternatives to the modal interpretation rules of **S5** and **QS5** which are still in the field—alternatives studied not just for their own sake but as serious rivals in the project of capturing the truth-conditions of 'necessarily' and 'possibly'. Most rivals of **S5** alter only T□; those of **QS5** may also alter TP, T∀ and T=. My chief aim in this chapter is to defend, with some qualifications, the claim that 'necessarily' does share the **S5** and **QS5** truth-condition of '□'.

According to that truth-condition a sentence such as '□(Gold is a metal)' is T in a world (and l-context and domain) if and only if its embedded part 'Gold is a metal' is T in every world (in that l-context and domain); and this means that for any choice of l-context and domain and for any possible facts the former sentence

10.1 Importing '□': Preliminaries

is usable (in that I-context and domain) to express a proposition which would be true given those facts if and only if the latter sentence is usable (in that I-context and domain) to express a proposition which would be true whatever the facts. But 'would be true whatever the facts' means 'is a necessary truth' (p. 29); so 'is T in every world' means 'can be used to express a necessary truth'. In what follows I shall abbreviate the latter, and so the former, to 'is Nec': that is

> 'is Nec (in a language, context and domain)' is short for 'can be used (in that language, context and domain) to express a proposition which would be true whatever the facts'.

This being the cash-value of the truth part of the truth-condition for '□' in S5 and QS5, our remaining task will be to examine whether the same truth-condition holds for the English word 'necessarily', i.e. to examine the credentials of

(1) For any sentence σ and world w, ⌜necessarily σ⌝ is T in w, in an English context and domain, if and only if σ is Nec in that context and domain,

or put briefly, '⌜necessarily σ⌝ is T iff σ is Nec'. I shall assume that the corresponding falsity-condition stands or falls with (1).

10.2 An illusion of understanding

One way of defending (1), tempting but inadequate, would be to understand instances of the schema 'necessarily p' as no more nor less than covert instances of the metalinguistic schema ' "p" is Nec'. According to this suggestion the syntax of 'necessarily' is superficial. The word presents itself as an adverb or connective, forming sentences from sentences; but its occurrences can be systematically transformed into occurrences of a verb-phrase or predicate, forming sentences from names of sentences (quoted sentences). For example in place of the adverb 'necessarily' attached to the sentence 'Gold is a metal' we are to substitute the verb-phrase 'is Nec' attached to the noun-phrase 'the sentence "Gold is a metal"'. This suggestion is sometimes, in allusion to a mediaeval controversy, called 'taking necessity *de dicto*'. It is inadequate for at least the following reason. The connective 'necessarily' can operate not only on closed sentences as in 'necessarily for all x, if x is a bachelor, x is unmarried' but also on open sentences as in 'for all x, necessarily if x is a bachelor, x is unmarried'. The latter, like the former, is T in English; but the proposed rendering of it 'for all x, the sentence "if x is a bachelor, x is unmarried" is Nec' is not T in English, since its mentioned sentence, being open, is not Nec (in any 1-context and domain; nor even T, nor even F). On this see QUINE 3 *Grades* p. 170.

The same troubles afflict a related metalinguistic interpretation of 'necessarily' which is worth mentioning for historical reasons. I introduced ' "p" is Nec' as a schema, intended to be fitted by ' "All bachelors are unmarried" is Nec', ' "Gold is a metal" is Nec', and so on; thus a metalinguistic schema, about sentences. Another way of reading it—the only right way, according to some pedants, see p. 112—is as a sentence about the schema 'p'. Now schemata cannot be Nec, because they cannot (any more than open sentences) be T. But they can be valid. So an alternative suggestion would be to regard 'necessarily' as hiding the predicate 'is valid' ('⊩' for short), true of schemata rather than sentences. There is a good case for the view that this transformation, from 'necessarily p' to '⊩ "p"', motivated Lewis' introduction of the connective '□' for 'necessarily' (or rather, since he made '◇' primitive, that he read 'possibly p' as ' "p" is consistent' in the sense of 8.1); and furthermore that Lewis simply overlooked the difference between using schemata as in 'necessarily p' and talking about them as in '⊩ "p" '. Hence Quine's accusation that "modern modal logic was conceived in sin: the sin of confusing use and mention" (QUINE *RPM*, p. 175). Be this as it may, the version '⊩π' is as far as 'σ is Nec' from capturing the truth-condition of ⌜necessarily σ⌝; and farther, if formulae are not sentences.

10.3 *Some pitfalls*

From unsuccessful defence of (1) I now turn to unsuccessful attacks on it. Their want of success is due in most cases to confusion between the property of being Nec and other related properties. In this section I shall distinguish three other such properties which are fairly plainly different from it. The confusions to come in 10.4–7 will be more seductive, though equally fatal to the project

10.3 Some pitfalls

of overthrowing (1). In what follows I use 'context' as short for 'context of right and unequivocal usage'.

Being **Nec**, i.e. **T** in every world, (in a language, context and domain) differs from being **T** in every context (in a language, world and domain). The latter is a property of eternal sentences (p. 49). For example 'There are rainbows' is **T** in this world in every English context and suitable domain, but it can only express a contingent truth and so is not **Nec**.

Being **Nec** is perhaps more easily confused with being **T** in every language (in a world, context and domain). No sentence whatever is **T** in every language; for example 'All girls are female' could not be used to express a truth if 'girls' meant what 'children' does. Nevertheless that sentence is **Nec** in some English context and domain, since it can in some English context and domain be used to express a proposition which would be true whatever the facts; see PLANTINGA pp. 52–4. For the same reason 'is **T** in every world' differs from 'is **T** of necessity', meaning 'could in every world be used to express a truth'. Indeed the latter is probably just a misleading way of formulating 'is **T** in every language', languages being thought of as fixed by worlds.

A third possible confusion is with the property of being self-verifying. I call a sentence self-verifying (in a language and domain) when it could not in any context and world (relative to that language and domain) be used to express a proposition which would not be true in that world. Examples in English are 'I exist', 'at least one proposition is affirmative' (AYER *PofK* pp. 45–6, PRIOR *PTP*). These sentences are not **Nec** in every—if any—English context and domain.

The three distinctions save (1) from various purported counter-examples. Someone might allege, with reference to an English context and domain, that 'All girls are female' is not **Nec** while the result of prefixing 'necessarily' to it is **T**; but the sentence is **Nec**, though not **T** in every language. Conversely someone might allege that 'There are rainbows', 'I exist' and 'At least one proposition is affirmative' are **Nec** while the results of prefixing 'necessarily' to them are not **T** in our world; but the sentences are not **Nec**, though the first of them is **T** in every context and the other two are self-verifying. (1) survives such objections quite easily: I now turn to more formidable objections against it.

10.4 Necessity and accessible worlds

(1) has the consequence that for any σ, if ⌜necessarily σ⌝ is T it is **Nec**. Proof of this, which parallels part of lemma (c) on p. 179, is as follows. Take some sentence σ and world w, and English context and domain, and suppose that ⌜necessarily σ⌝ is T in w (in that context and domain). Then by (1) σ is **Nec** (in them). Then take some world w_1. By (1) in the reverse direction ⌜necessarily σ⌝ is also T in w_1 (in that context and domain). This follows for every choice of w_1, whether the same as w or not. So if ⌜necessarily σ⌝ is T in w (in some English context and domain), it is T in every w_1, i.e. is **Nec** (in that context and domain). The proof can be adapted to ⌜not necessarily not σ⌝ by extending (1) into a truth-and-falsity-condition. The two proofs trade on (1)'s claim that when ⌜necessarily σ⌝ can be used to express a proposition which would be true (false) given some possible facts, e.g. the actual facts, σ can be used to express a proposition which would (not) be true whatever the facts, i.e. is T in (not) every world; and this has been held by some to be objectionable on the ground that there might be worlds so 'remote' from ours that the truth (falsity) of σ in them is irrelevant to the truth (falsity) of ⌜necessarily σ⌝ in ours. According to the objection the truth or falsity of ⌜necessarily σ⌝ in a world depends only on whether σ is T in all worlds 'accessible' to that one (others say 'accessible from', or 'alternative to' HINTIKKA pp. 66–7, or 'relevant to' MASSEY p. 398). Hence it might be that ⌜necessarily σ⌝, though T in our world, is F in some other world, and so not **Nec**; the sentence might even be F in some world w accessible to ours, since σ might be F in a remoter world, accessible to w but not to ours. Consequently, the objection goes, the right hand side of (1) ought to be changed from 'is **Nec**' to (as I shall put it) 'is **Necac** in w', where

> 'is **Necac** in w' is short for 'is T in every world accessible to w'.

The first proof is thereby blocked unless accessibility is reflexive and transitive. With a parallel change in the falsity condition for 'necessarily', the second proof is also blocked unless accessibility is reflexive, transitive and symmetrical.

The objection seems to be motivated by the thought that necessary

10.4 *Necessity and accessible worlds*

truths might not have been necessary, i.e. that what would have been true whatever the facts would, given some possible facts, not have been something which would have been true whatever the facts. It is hard to make this plausible. The contingency of languages shows only that necessary truths might not have been expressible as they are, not that they might not have been necessary (see KRIPKE *I&N* p. 145, *N&N* p. 308; PLANTINGA pp. 52–4): a sentence may still be **Nec** though not **T** of necessity. The inference about some proposition 'It would be true whatever the facts; so it would, whatever the facts, be something which would be true whatever the facts would in that case be' seems as irresistible as the inference 'You wouldn't reach the sea today however fast you walked; so you wouldn't, however fast you walked, reach the sea today however fast you in that case walked'. Nor for that matter do I see how one could doubt that contingent truths would be contingent whatever the facts. (W. & M. KNEALE pp. 555–66 and HINTIKKA pp. 76–7 agree with this account; cf. LEMMON *ML* pp. 35–7, CARNAP pp. 174–5).

Moreover, the proposed emendation of (1) needs explication, for 'accessible', which comes in with the definition of 'is **Necac** in w', is a term of art. The explications most widely canvassed are that accessibility is (a) reflexive or (b) reflexive and transitive or (c) reflexive and symmetrical or (d) reflexive, transitive and symmetrical, i.e. an equivalence relation. A supporter of accessibility must defend some explication of it; and (d) collapses 'is **Necac** in w' into 'is **Nec**'.

Although I do not accept the emendation to (1), it is worth digressing to show how, if it were accepted, **T**□ could be changed so as to keep the truth-conditions of '□' and 'necessarily' in line. In place of **T**□ we should need

> In any l-context, domain and world w, ⌜□σ⌝ is **T** or **F** according as σ is **T** in every world accessible to w or **F** in some world accessible to w,

and in pure semantics

> $v(\Box \pi, w) = 1$ iff $v(\pi, w_1) = 1$ for all worlds w_1 in the set which are accessible to w.

Under this interpretation the S5 and QS5 logistic systems of Chapters 5 and 6 are no longer sound unless accessibility is explicated as an equivalence relation. If it is merely reflexive we should need the system T, also called M; if merely reflexive and symmetrical, the system B; if merely reflexive and transitive, the system S4 (see HUGHES & CRESSWELL, especially ch. 4).

10.5 *Necessity and reference*

Let 'P' abbreviate the sentence 'my favourite number is even'. It has been maintained, e.g. in CARTWRIGHT (*I&S* pp. 128–9) and QUINE (*W&O* pp. 195–200, 3 *Grades*), that there are English contexts and domains in which 'necessarily P' is T in our world but 'P' is not Nec. This is a complicated kind of case because 'my favourite number' will be a subject, i.e. referring expression, in some contexts but not others. Taking the non-referential contexts first, I assume that 'P' will then mean 'Just one number is my favourite, and that one is even', which is not Nec in a context of reference to me because I might have most favoured an odd number. But for the same reason 'necessarily P' will not be T in our world in such a context, since it will mean 'Necessarily just one number is my favourite and (necessarily) that one is even'. To be sure, it would be T in some world if it meant 'Just one number is my favourite, and that one is necessarily even'. But I do not think that this is a possible way of understanding 'necessarily P' in English, as opposed to the differently ordered sentence 'My favourite number is necessarily even'.

There is more doubt about the second kind of context for 'P', in which 'my favourite number' functions as a subject. I shall argue that in such a case the questions whether 'P' is Nec and 'necessarily P' is T alike turn on the question which, if any, is the favourite number of the person referred to by 'my'. But both these verdicts need investigation.

Suppose a referring context in which 'my' refers to Jones and Jones' favourite number is eight. In that case 'P' can be used to express the proposition that eight is even; the proposition is a necessary truth; therefore 'P' is Nec. One possible reason for doubting this conclusion is as follows. We have already on p. 227 seen the need to distinguish 'is Nec', i.e. 'can be used to express a

10.5 Necessity and reference

proposition which would be true whatever the facts', from 'is T of necessity', i.e. 'could whatever the facts be used to express a proposition which is true'. In between these two is the property I will call being **Necco**, defined by

> 'is **Necco** (in a language, context and domain)' is short for 'could whatever the facts be used (in that language, context and domain) to express a proposition which would be true given those facts'.

Some sentences are **Necco** in some English contexts, but '*P*' is not, even on the referential reading. For though, if Jones' favourite number is eight, '*P*' can be used by him in English to refer to eight and so to express a truth, it by no means follows that, if his favourite number were not eight, it could in that case be used by him in English to express what would in that case be a truth. Now someone who relied on the fact that '*P*' is not **Necco** on the referential reading as a reason for asserting that it is not **Nec** would need to invoke the thesis that 'my favourite number' "refers to one and the same individual . . . in all [possible] worlds" (HINTIKKA p. 73, cf. KRIPKE *I&N* p. 145, *N&N* pp. 269–70, 289). This seems to be the property which Kripke calls being a rigid designator: a designator is rigid (let us stipulate) if and only if anything to which it refers in an l-context and domain is a thing to which it would refer, in that l-context and domain, whatever the facts. If all subjects were rigid in this sense, I think it *would* follow that every sentence which is **Nec** in an l-context and domain is also **Necco** in them. Hence the evident fact that '*P*' as used by Jones is not **Necco**—his favourite number might have been twenty-three—*would* demonstrate that it is not **Nec** either. However the demonstration fails because 'my favourite number' is plainly not rigid in the sense stipulated.

Again I digress to consider what would happen if we tried to interpret the symbol '□' in terms of being **Necco** rather than **Nec**. One way is to redefine 'is T in w' as short for 'would, given w, express a proposition which would be true given w'; and similarly for 'F'. This change affects every truth-condition in a calculus. In particular TP would be replaced by this (schematically, for one-place predicates, eliding contexts and domains):

> '*fa*' is T or F in a world w according as '*a*' would in w refer to something of which '*f*' would be true or false in w,

and in pure semantics we should get

v(δα, w) = 1 iff ⟨v(α, w), w⟩ is a member of v(δ),

which differs from VP in having 'v(α, w)' for 'v(α)'. There must also be substantial changes to T= and T∀ (see HUGHES & CRESSWELL, pp. 196-9).

The variant truth-condition thus generated for '□' will detach it from 'necessarily', and so be pointless, if (1) survives. My purpose is now to show that (1) does survive: in the imagined context of reference to Jones whose favourite number is eight, in which we have seen that '*P*' is Nec, it is also the case that 'necessarily *P*' is T. The argument for the latter is: in that context 'necessarily *P*' expresses the proposition that necessarily eight is even, which is true. Here we need to rely on the doctrine that the truth-value of 'necessarily *P*' is fixed by the reference of its subject 'my favourite number', independently of the manner of that reference; in other words that 'necessarily . . . is even' is a referentially transparent predicate (p. 212). Quine has taken the contrary view (QUINE *W&O* pp. 197-9, cf. 3 *Grades* pp. 158-61, MATES p. 27, MASSEY pp. 228, 234); he holds that in a context of reference to a mathematical cyclist 'necessarily that mathematician is rational' is T but what results by substituting the co-referring expression 'that cyclist' is F. The cause of this alleged difference is "bias towards a background grouping" (QUINE *W&O* p. 199): the two sentences allude to different classes or groupings to which the mathematical cyclist belongs. In effect then 'necessarily that mathematician is rational' combines the assertion that he is rational with the true assertion that being rational follows from being a mathematician, whereas the sentence which results by substituting 'that cyclist' incorporates the falsehood that being rational follows from being a cyclist. The sentences imply respectively, '*qua* mathematician' and '*qua* cyclist', so that their subjects do not function as *purely* referring expressions. On Quine's view therefore we have opacity, and moreover we have the same explanation of it as on p. 210: like the predicate '. . . is so called because of his size' 'necessarily . . . is rational' risks equivocation through different *qua*-supplementations from its attached subject.

Opacity would bring out 'necessarily *P*' as F in every referring context; for being even does not follow from being anyone's

10.5 *Necessity and reference*

favourite number. It would thereby separate 'necessarily' from the interpretation given to '$\Box$' in this book, since T$\Box$ makes '$\Box$' transparent: schematically, if 'a' has the same reference as 'b' in a QS5-context and '$\Box fa$' is T, then '$\Box fb$' is T (which is why, through T=, '$a = b \supset (\Box fa \supset \Box fb)$' is QS5-valid). But the claim that 'necessarily' creates opacity is unconvincing to my ear (this retracts KIRWAN p. 45). Perhaps there is a *sense* of the word with that feature—a sense for which one might stipulate 'analytically' as an unambiguous synonym or which might be called *de dicto* in a further meaning of that overworked label (CARTWRIGHT *I&S* p. 129, HUGHES & CRESSWELL p. 199 footnote). More plausibly we might detect opacity in the differently ordered sentence 'my favourite number is necessarily even', where 'is necessarily' could mean 'is, and as such necessarily is'. But the natural truth-condition for 'necessarily *P*' is the transparent one: T if and only if 'necessarily . . . is even' is true of the thing referred to by 'my favourite number'.

I conclude that (1) survives for one sense of 'necessarily'; but in case there is another, opaque, sense, I shall qualify (1) when it appears in its final form on p. 240.

10.6 *Necessity and identity*

Let 'Q' abbreviate 'The mayor is the mayor'. Are there English contexts and domains in which 'necessarily Q' is T in some world and yet 'Q' is not Nec? Here the complications of the previous section are multiplied, since either one or both occurrences of 'the mayor' might be referential. In an l-context in which both are, 'is' means 'is the same as' and 'Q' expresses, about someone, the proposition that he is the same as himself. So it is Nec, and 'necessarily Q' is T in every world. If one or both occurrences are non-referential, then 'Q' expresses, about someone, the proposition that he alone is mayor, or expresses the proposition that someone alone is mayor. In either case it is not Nec, and 'necessarily Q' is not T in our world (of the actual members of the domain it might have been that none, or more than one, held the office of mayor).

The case may seem to change when two different expressions flank 'is', as in 'The shop steward is the mayor', 'R' for short. If both expressions are subjects, so that 'is' means 'is the same as', the sentence 'necessarily R' will be **T** in a world and context in which the two expressions refer to the same member of the domain. Yet 'R', unlike 'Q', seems not to be **Nec** in such a context and domain, but to express a contingent identity statement. At this point it is **T**= rather than **T**□ which appears to cause trouble for translation into symbols (so for the first time in this chapter, our problem is special to **QS5** rather than **S5**). For if 'the shop steward = the mayor' is **T** in a **QS5**-context, domain and world, it is **T** in that context and domain in every world: all true **QS5**-instances of '$a = b$' are necessary truths (hence '$a = b \supset \Box(a = b)$' is **QS5**-valid). It follows from this that if there are any contingently true identity statements, 'is the same as' does not share the truth-condition assigned to '=' by **T**=. But the reply is that there are no contingent identity statements, true or false; all the true ones are necessary truths, all the false ones necessary falsehoods. This is easy to doubt only because it is easy to misunderstand the requirements of identity and the requirements of necessity. 'R' will not be **Nec** in a context in which it means 'The shop steward holds (or alone holds) the office of mayor' or 'Someone holds (or alone holds) both offices' or other variants of these; but in those cases it does not express an identity statement (see 9.9). Even in a fully referential context, when it does express an identity statement, it will not be **Necco**, i.e. it will not be the case that 'R' could whatever the facts be used to express a proposition which would be true given those facts. But since 'the mayor' and 'the shop steward' are not rigid designators this does not prevent 'R' from being **Nec**, and it will be **Nec** given the 'is' of identity and sameness of reference, because in that case it will express the proposition that the mayor is himself.

This solution has affinities with KRIPKE *I&N* and *N&N*. But Kripke leaves it unclear whether definite descriptions are ever referential in my sense and yet is willing to treat many sentences embodying them as (expressing) identity statements (e.g. 'The first Postmaster General of the United States is identical with the inventor of bifocals', *I&N* p. 138). I think this second difference is only in nomenclature; there is no dispute that such sentences, although they contain 'is identical with' and can be formalised with '=', cannot be formalised into '$a = b$' unless their definite descriptions are referential.

10.7 Necessity and domains

It follows from the Barcan Metatheorem (p. 154) that '$\forall x \Box fx \supset \Box \forall x fx$', often called the Barcan formula, is QS5-valid, and it follows from the Converse Barcan Metatheorem that '$\Box \forall x fx \supset \forall x \Box fx$' is also QS5-valid. So '$\forall x \Box fx$' and '$\Box \forall x fx$' are QS5-equivalent, and any pair of sentences jointly fitting them, such as '$\forall x \Box$ green x' and '$\Box \forall x$ green x', have the same QS5 truth-conditions. Translation from 'necessarily' into '$\Box$' therefore seems to demand that the English sentences 'Everything is necessarily green' and 'Necessarily everything is green' likewise share the same truth-condition. Here is an argument that they do not.

Mediaeval logicians distinguished *necessitas consequentis*, exemplified in instances of '$p \supset \Box q$', from *necessitas consequentiae*, exemplified in instances of '$\Box(p \supset q)$'. A similar scope-difference accounts for the fact that

(A) Everything green is necessarily green

is F relative to many domains, whereas

(B) Necessarily everything green is green

is T relative to every domain. Now suppose we apply the procedure of 2.9 to (A) and (B), suppressing their first occurrences of 'green' in the hope of conveying the same propositions more economically by restricting the domain to green things. It seems to follow that the resulting 'Everything is necessarily green' remains F relative to the restricted domain, while 'Necessarily everything is green' remains T relative to it. So the truth-conditions for the two shortened sentences seem to differ.

The conclusion of this argument conflicts with (1). For suppose that the even simpler sentence 'Everything is green' is used relative to the domain of green things. It can express about the green things the proposition that they are all green, a proposition which, though true, would have been false given some possible facts (for the same reason as makes (A) F—not all the green things are necessarily green). Nor can the simple sentence express any other proposition about the green things, e.g. that they are green if green. So it is not Nec relative to the domain of green things. So according to

(1) 'Necessarily everything is green' is not **T** relative to that domain, contrary to the argument's conclusion.

This result casts doubt on the propriety of shortening (B) by domain restriction to 'Necessarily everything is green'. At any rate if the economising function of domains is to be preserved intact, (1) will have to be emended. The needed emendation substitutes (as I shall say) 'is **Nekky**' for 'is **Nec**' on its right hand side, where

> 'is **Nekky** in a domain **d** (and language and context)' is short for 'for any possible facts, can be used (in that language and context) relative to what would be in **d** given those facts to express a proposition which would be true given those facts'.

Under the new emendation to (1) 'necessarily everything is green' does come out **T** relative to the domain of green things, since its embedded part 'Everything is green', though not **Nec**, is **Nekky** in that domain, i.e. can be used to express a proposition which, whatever the facts, would be true about what would be in the domain; while the differently ordered 'Everything is necessarily green' still comes out **F**. The emendation also permits the converse. For example it might be true relative to the domain of things containing chlorophyll that every actual member cannot help being green though other things could be members without being green: then 'Everything is necessarily green' will be **T** relative to that domain, while 'Necessarily everything is green' will be **F**.

Is the emended truth-condition right for 'necessarily' in English? I think not. (A) and (B) do clearly differ in truth-condition, and 'Everything is necessarily green' is a suitable shorthand for (A). But 'Necessarily everything is green', if understood relative to the domain of green things, is best understood as alternative shorthand for (A), not for (B). The economising function of domains permits 'Everything green is green', to be expressed in 'Everything is green', but does not, I submit, permit 'Necessarily everything green is green' to be expressed in 'Necessarily everything is green'.

(1) can be defended more strongly than this against the proposed emendation. The economising function of domains is in any case to some extent an artificial device, recommended in the process of formalising for the technical purpose of shortening validity-proofs. We can simply stipulate as a rule governing this process that the

10.7 *Necessity and domains*

suppression of a predicate is forbidden, and so the restriction of a domain made valueless, when the predicate will after translation fall inside the scope of a modal connective. By this rule sentences fitting the schema 'Necessarily everything is f' must be understood as meaning what they say, and so as T only when the predicate fitting 'f' in them is genuinely true of everything, not just of everything under discussion. Alternatively, a restricted domain can be permitted even in modal arguments provided that its membership is the same in all worlds (these might be called rigid domains).

I shall end this section by digressing as in 10.4 and 10.5 to consider how, if one were to accept the new emendation of (1)— 'is Nekky' for 'is Nec'—a parallel change to T$\square$ could keep the truth-condition of '$\square$' in line with that of 'necessarily'. The trick is to associate domains with worlds by specifying a 'reflection' of each domain off each world. TP is then replaced as follows (schematically, for one-place predicates, eliding contexts):

> 'fa' is T or F in a world **w** and domain **d** according as 'a' refers to something common to **d** and its reflection off **w** and 'f' would be true or false in **w** of that thing.

Separate conditions for 'o' replace '$v(\pi,w) = 1$ or 0'. Half VP becomes

> $v(\delta a, w) = 1$ in **d** iff $v(a)$ is a member of **dw** and $\langle v(a), w \rangle$ is a member of $v(\delta)$, where **dw** is the reflection of **d** off **w**.

This is the semantics of page 172 in HUGHES & CRESSWELL, without their inclusion requirement. Reference to domains in T= and T∀ has to be adjusted consequentially. The revised rules invalidate both the Barcan formula '$\forall x \square fx \supset \square \forall x fx$' and its converse. Notice that the rules do not fully interpret the symbols until 'reflection of **d** off **w**' is explicated; and for alignment with 'is Nekky' the explication must be 'the things which would be in **d** given **w**'. HUGHES & CRESSWELL's version is 'the members of **d** which would exist given **w**', but (a) there is no reason why talk about a possible world should be confined to talk about things which would exist given that world, (b) if the Barcan formula or its converse are to be invalidated then, as HUGHES & CRESSWELL recognise, the reflection of **d** off **w** must not be forced to be a subset of **d**, and (c)

10.8 Essence

So far (1) has been defended as the correct truth-condition for the English word 'necessarily'. In this section I shall concede a fault in it.

We have seen that '$\forall x \Box fx$' and '$\Box \forall x fx$' are QS5-equivalent, and I have argued that this squares with translation between '$\Box$' and 'necessarily'. The pair '$\exists x \Box fx$' and '$\Box \exists x fx$' are more complicated to deal with. On the one hand they are not QS5-equivalent, since '$\Box \exists x fx \supset \exists x \Box fx$' is not QS5-valid; and correspondingly, for example, 'necessarily some things are axioms' is T while 'some things are necessarily axioms' is F (see pp. 204, 275). On the other hand '$\exists x \Box fx \supset \Box \exists x fx$', called the Buridan formula (PLANTINGA p. 58), is QS5-valid on account of the Buridan Metatheorem of p. 154; but in this case it becomes unclear again whether the behaviour of '$\Box$' in QS5 matches that of 'necessarily' in English. In the following passage Buridan provides the kernel of an argument against the English counterpart of his formula. "Again, this does not follow: it is possible that every being should be God, therefore every being has the possibility of being God. For the first is true; that is how things were before the creation of the world, and that is how things would be if God annihilated every creature. But the second is false because it is not possible for a creature to be God" (BURIDAN chapter 4 sophism 13, p. 130; cf. PRIOR *PPF* p. 138). Since there are creatures, not everything has the possibility of being divine, and 'Something is necessarily non-divine' is T; but since there need have been no creatures, it is possible that everything should have been divine, and 'Necessarily something is non-divine' is F. It might be objected that the reasons for these two verdicts conflict: if Caesar, for example, would be a creature whatever the facts, then surely whatever the facts something would be a creature. The easiest way to meet the objection, on Buridan's behalf, is by replying that 'Caesar is necessarily a creature' does not require Caesar's createdness in every possible world but only in every possible world in which he exists (presumably throughout his existence in it, and perhaps at all times in it). Then someone's

10.8 Essence

being necessarily a creature, sc. a creature in every possible world in which he exists, remains compatible as Buridan in effect urged with the possibility of creatureless worlds. Properties which hold necessarily in this way, i.e. are necessary to their owner's existence, are called essential; hence the thesis that 'Something is necessarily a creature' may be T in a context and domain in which 'Necessarily something is a creature' is F gets justified by the consideration that the former sentence may mean 'Something is essentially a creature'.

I think one must concede that 'necessarily' can be used in the way this thesis requires. If so, then (1) breaks down, since 'Something is essentially a creature' could be T even though there are creatureless possible worlds and hence nothing of which 'creature' would be true whatever the facts. It follows that if we wished to preserve translation from 'necessarily' to '$\Box$' even when 'necessarily' means 'essentially', the QS5 interpretation rules would need alteration after all. One recourse is to adopt Kripke's 1963 semantics for quantified modal logic (KRIPKE SC) which yields a free logic, invalidating not only the Buridan formula but the Barcan formula, the converse Barcan formula, and '$\forall x f x \supset f a$'. On the other hand any such alteration would face the objection that 'Something is necessarily a creature' *can* be read with the truth-condition implied by (1): T if and only if there is something of which 'creature' would be true whatever the facts. It therefore seems more economical (this retracts KIRWAN p. 43) to keep QS5 and to require that 'necessarily fa', when it means 'a is essentially f', be translated into '$\Box(a$ exists at some time $\supset fa)$'—which collapses into '$\Box fa$' only if we accept the dogma discussed in 9.8 that every member of a domain is sometime existent—or alternatively into '$\Box(a$ exists at some time $\supset a$ is f at that time)' or even '$\Box(a$ exists at some time $\supset a$ is f at some time)'.

It is worth adding by way of footnote that the label 'essential' is currently used in a number of senses. It applies most naturally, I submit, to the doctrine that 'a is essentially f' has some true instances, where this schema is understood in one of the three ways mentioned at the end of the last paragraph. But essentialism is sometimes understood as the doctrine that '$\Box fa$' has QS5-instances, or has true QS5-instances, or that '$\Box fa$ & ga & $\sim \Box ga$' has true QS5-instances; and there are other more complex possibilities (see QUINE 3 *Grades* p. 174, PARSONS).

The outcome of this section is that when 'necessarily' means 'essentially', ⌜necessarily σ⌝ may be T even though σ is not Nec. We found in 10.5 that the same may happen when, if ever, 'necessarily' is opaque. So (1) needs a double qualification, and must in the end be replaced by

10.8 (2) for any sentence σ and world w, ⌜necessarily σ⌝ is T in w, in a transparent English context ('necessarily' not meaning 'essentially') and domain if and only if σ is Nec in that context and domain.

This differs from the simpler truth-condition for '□' prescribed by S5 and QS5. Accordingly translation from 'necessarily' into '□' is wrong when '□' has its S5 or QS5 meaning and at the same time 'necessarily' means 'essentially' or creates opacity.

10.9 *Necessity and 'if'*

On p. 205 I commented that 'If 3 were even, it would be divisible by 2' can be symbolised with '⊃' as subordinate to '□'. This is because of two facts: that particular subjunctive conditional can also be expressed in the indicative by means of 'If 3 is even, it follows that 3 is divisible by 2'; and the English truth-conditions of ⌜If σ, then it follows that τ⌝ are the same as the S5 and QS5 truth-conditions of ⌜□(σ ⊃ τ)⌝. Here is a proof of the latter fact. Take two propositions, two English sentences σ and τ, a world w, and an S5-context (or QS5-context) and domain in which σ can be used to express the first proposition, τ the second. Suppose that the first proposition *entails* the second. Then on the one hand, the English sentence ⌜If σ, then it follows that τ⌝ is T in w in that context and domain (this relies on considerations parallel to 10.4). On the other hand, the first proposition could not have been true without the second being true, i.e. the second would be true in every world in which the first was. So τ is T, in the given context and domain, in every world in which σ is T in them. So by T⊃ ⌜σ ⊃ τ⌝ is T in every world, i.e. Nec, in them. So by T□ ⌜□(σ ⊃ τ)⌝ is T in w in them. Given the criterion of deductive correctness defended in 2.4—which is crucial here—the arguments work in the reverse direction also. Hence for any σ and τ, ⌜If σ, then it follows that

⌜τ⌝ is T in any S5-context (or QS5-context) and domain and world if and only if ⌜□(σ ⊃ τ)⌝ is T in them. Parallel arguments work for 'F'. Therefore any two such sentences have the same truth-conditions.

Even indicative 'if's can quite often be paraphrased into 'if__, it follows that . . .'. Whenever that paraphrase is in order, so is formalisation into ⌜□(π ⊃ φ)⌝, for some well-formed π and φ. See (G) of 11.1.

10.10 Importing '◇'

The previous sections have defended the view that the English adverb 'necessarily', when understood transparently and distinguished from 'essentially', shares the truth-condition assigned to '□' in S5 and QS5. If we look similarly for an English expression sharing the truth-condition assigned to '◇' (through T□, T~ and Def◇), the only serious candidates among adverbs are 'conceivably' and 'possibly'. But we shall find that both of these words have truth-conditions markedly divergent from T◇, although 'possibly' is acceptable as a conventional 'pronunciation' for '◇', less uncouth perhaps than 'lozenge' or 'diamond'.

If 'conceivably' were to do the job, it would have to have the following truth-condition, parallel to (1):

(3) ⌜conceivably σ⌝ is T in w if and only if σ can be used to express a proposition which would be true given some possible facts.

Neither the 'if' nor the 'only if' in (3) can be sustained. 'If' fails because what is possible may be inconceivable—at least to some people and why not to everyone? Some possible worlds may be too strange to conceive; so conceivability, unlike necessity, is affected by remoteness, and the truth-condition for ⌜conceivably σ⌝ would at least have to be changed to 'σ can be used to express a proposition which would be true in some world conceivable from w', with the understanding that what is conceivable from some world conceivable from w may nevertheless fail to be conceivable from w, i.e. conceivability is not transitive. This version brings in the accessibility relation, and gives it a fairly clear explication (see HUGHES & CRESSWELL, pp. 76–8). If we wished to align the truth-condition of '$\Diamond$' with that of 'conceivably' we should therefore need a modal calculus in which accessibility is non-transitive, e.g. B or T, invalidating the S5-theorems '$\Diamond\Box p \supset \Box p$' and '$\Diamond p \supset \Box\Diamond p$', and also invalidating the weaker S4-theorems '$\Diamond\Diamond p \supset \Diamond p$' and '$\Box p \supset \Box\Box p$'. 'Only if' relies on what Berkeley called the 'receiv'd axiom' that an impossibility cannot be conceived (BERKELEY p. 125). But the axiom's falsity follows from the really quite obvious fact that impossibilities, e.g. denials of mathematical and logical truths, can even be believed. This scotches both (3) and its accessibility-variant: ⌜conceivably σ⌝ may be T in w though no proposition expressible in σ would be true given any facts, nor therefore given any facts conceivable from w.

'Possibly', the other contender among adverbs, means 'not certainly not'. If this were to translate into '$\Diamond$', then by Def$\Diamond$ 'certainly' would have to translate into '$\Box$'; so 'certainly' and 'necessarily' would have to share the same truth-condition. The expression 'logically certain', used by some philosophers as a synonym for 'logically necessary', may encourage acquiescence in this consequence. But that usage is a barbarism since certainty, unlike necessity, is an epistemological notion to be analysed in terms of knowledge or confidence. The difference comes out if one reflects that the proposition that all of us will die is certain but not necessary, and conversely Goldbach's conjecture, the as yet unproved and unrefuted proposition that every even number is the sum of two primes, is perhaps necessary but not even perhaps certain (*pace* WHITE p. 83). Admittedly we do not know that Goldbach's conjecture is necessary, because its truth, and so its necessity, is not certain. But since it is a mathematical proposition we do know that it is necessary if true, whereas 'It is certain if true' would allow inference from its admitted uncertainty to its untruth. 'Possible' and its cognates are much to blame for this confusion between necessity and certainty (WHITE pp. 10–2). The adverb 'possibly' always, I think, means 'not certainly not'. For conveying the truth-condition of 'not necessarily not', and so of '$\Diamond$' in S5 and QS5, one must eschew adverbs in favour of a phrase such as 'it is possible that'. But even that phrase goes with 'possibly' when followed, as '$\Diamond$' must be, by an indicative sentence (WHITE p. 5). To have the right truth-condition it must be followed by 'should', or expanded into 'it is possible that it should be the case that' (contrast the consistent 'It is possible that he should be in London, but certain that he isn't' with the inconsistent 'It is possible that he is in London, but certain that he isn't'). Other phrases translatable into '$\Diamond$' are 'It is possible for it to be the case that' and 'It might have been the case that'—or perhaps 'might be', but not 'may be'. No less cumbrous ways exist, I believe, of conveying in English the meaning which T$\Diamond$ assigns to '$\Diamond$'.

CHAPTER ELEVEN

Applications

11.1 *Proofs of correctness*

This section shows the four calculi at work in proofs of the correctness of eight arguments. I give the proofs in a deliberately pedestrian and insipid way. In practice everyone applying logic will feel an urge to use short cuts, but they are dangerous until one has an eye for trouble. Formal methods sacrifice brevity and elegance to precision: if the precision is then put in jeopardy too hastily, one might as well not have used such methods in the first place—indeed better not, for they will only mystify.

(A) She won't be his companion and lover; she won't be his lover if she's not his companion; so she won't be his lover.

(i) Finding the sequent. Rewording. If the argument is to be correct we must understand 'won't' as expressing what will happen, not what she is willing should happen (for she might be willing to be his lover though unwilling to combine that with either of its possible accompaniments). So understood the argument is expressible in 'It is not the case that both she will be his companion and she will be his lover; if it is not the case that she will be his companion, it is not the case that she will be his lover; so it is not the case that she will be his lover'. Schematising. The component sentences fit schematic letters as follows:

'She will be his companion' fits 'p'
'She will be his lover' fits 'q'.

So the argument is expressible in sentences **PC**-fitting 'It is not the case that both p and q; if it is not the case that p, it is not the case that q; so it is not the case that q'. Translating. By $T\sim$, $T\&$ and $T\supset$ the argument is **PC**-expressible (i.e. expressible in some **PC**-incorporating language), relative to some domain, in sentences **PC**-fitting '$\sim(p\ \&\ q)$; $\sim p \supset \sim q$; so $\sim q$'. The sentences do not equivocate ('his' and 'she' have constant reference). So the argument is a **PC**-instance of the sequent $\langle\{`\sim(p\ \&\ q)\text{'},\ `\sim p \supset \sim q\text{'}\},$ $`\sim q\text{'}\rangle$. (ii) Proving validity. Since the **PC** sequent system is **PC**-sound, the sequent is **PC**-valid if it is **PC**-derivable. The following derivation proves that it is **PC**-derivable.

(A')	1	(1)	$\sim(p\ \&\ q)$	A	
	2	(2)	$\sim p \supset \sim q$	A	
	3	(3)	q	A	
	1,3	(4)	$\sim p$	MPT	1,3
	1,2,3	(5)	$\sim q$	MPP-S	2,4
	1,2,3	(6)	$q\ \&\ \sim q$	&I	3,5
	1,2	(7)	$\sim q$	RAA	6

The proof of derivability is incomplete in line (5) because too many formulae are indexed there. The argument's corresponding material conditional is a **PC**-instance of the formula '$\sim(p\ \&\ q)\ \&\ (\sim p \supset \sim q) \supset \sim q$'. Here is a proof that this formula is derivable in the **PC** formula system.

(A'')	(1)	$(\sim p \supset \sim q) \supset (q \supset p)$	Transp	
	(2)	$(q \supset p) \supset (\sim(p\ \&\ q) \supset \sim(q\ \&\ q))$	Sum&	
	(3)	$(\sim p \supset \sim q) \supset (\sim(p\ \&\ q) \supset \sim(q\ \&\ q))$	Syll	1,2
	(4)	$\sim(p\ \&\ q) \supset ((\sim p \supset \sim q) \supset \sim(q\ \&\ q))$	Perm	3
	(5)	$\sim(p\ \&\ q)\ \&\ (\sim p \supset \sim q) \supset \sim(q\ \&\ q)$	Imp	4
	(6)	$q \supset q\ \&\ q$	It&	
	(7)	$\sim(q\ \&\ q) \supset \sim q$	Transp	6
	(8)	$\sim(p\ \&\ q)\ \&\ (\sim p \supset \sim q) \supset \sim q$	Syll	5,7

(B) ARISTOTLE, *Top.* II 8.114^{a}19. 'A seeing is a perceiving; so a thing seen is a thing perceived.'

The correctness of (B) is too obvious to need proving by formal methods; it provides an exercise, not a problem. (i) Finding the sequent. Rewording. Since a thing seen or perceived is an object of seeing or perceiving, the argument is expressible in English combined with variables thus: 'For all x, if x is a seeing, x is a perceiving; so for all x, if for some y y is a seeing and x is an object of y, then for some y y is a perceiving and x is an object of y.' Schematising. The component predicates fit schematic letters as follows:

'___is a seeing' fits 'f___'
'___is a perceiving' fits 'g___'
'___is an object of . . .' fits 'h___. . .'

So the argument is expressible in sentences QC-fitting 'for all x, if fx, gx; so for all x, if for some y fy and hxy, then for some y gy and hxy'. Translating. By T$\forall$, T$\supset$, T$\exists$ and T& the argument is QC-expressible, relative to some domain, in sentences QC-fitting '$\forall x(fx \supset gx)$; so $\forall x(\exists y(fy \,\&\, hxy) \supset \exists y(gy \,\&\, hxy))$'. The sentences do not equivocate (there is room for doubt here: '___is an object of a seeing/perceiving' might share the referential opacity sometimes infecting the simpler predicates '___is seen' and '___is perceived' which they paraphrase, 'is' eliding 'is as such'; but I waive the doubt). So the argument is a QC-instance of the sequent $\langle\{`\forall x(fx \supset gx)'\}, `\forall x(\exists y(fy \,\&\, hxy) \supset \exists y(gy \,\&\, hxy))'\rangle$. (ii) Proving validity. Since the QC sequent system is QC-sound, the sequent is QC-valid if it is QC-derivable. The following derivation proves that it is QC-derivable:

(B')
1	(1) $\forall x(fx \supset gx)$	A		
2	(2) $\exists y(fy \,\&\, hay)$	A		
2	(3) $\sim\forall y\sim(fy \,\&\, hay)$	Def$\exists$	2	
4	(4) $\forall y\sim(gy \,\&\, hay)$	A		
4	(5) $\sim(gb \,\&\, hab)$	$\forall$E	4	
6	(6) $fb \,\&\, hab$	A		
6	(7) fb	&E	6	
1	(8) $fb \supset gb$	$\forall$E	1	
1,6	(9) gb	MPP-S	7,8	
6	(10) hab	&E	6	
1,6	(11) $gb \,\&\, hab$	&I	9,10	
1,4,6	(12) $(gb \,\&\, hab) \,\&\, \sim(gb \,\&\, hab)$	&I	5,11	
1,4	(13) $\sim(fb \,\&\, hab)$	RAA	12	
1,4	(14) $\forall y\sim(fy \,\&\, hay)$	$\forall$I-S	13	
1,2,4	(15) $\forall y\sim(fy \,\&\, hay) \,\&\sim\forall y\sim(fy \,\&\, hay)$	&I	3,14	
1,2	(16) $\sim\forall y\sim(gy \,\&\, hay)$	RAA	4	
1,2	(17) $\exists y(gy \,\&\, hay)$	Def$\exists$	16	
1	(18) $\exists y(fy \,\&\, hay) \supset \exists y(gy \,\&\, hay)$	CP	17	
1	(19) $\forall x(\exists y(fy \,\&\, hxy) \supset \exists y(gy \,\&\, hxy))$	$\forall$I-S	18	

Here is a shorter derivation, using $\exists$E and $\exists$I in place of Def$\exists$:

11.1 Proofs of correctness

(B″)
1	(1)	$\forall x(fx \supset gx)$	A		
2	(2)	$\exists y(fy \,\&\, hay)$	A		
3	(3)	$fb \,\&\, hab$	A		
3	(4)	fb	&E	3	
1	(5)	$fb \supset gb$	$\forall$E	1	
1,3	(6)	gb	MPP-S	4,5	
3	(7)	hab	&E	3	
1,3	(8)	$gb \,\&\, hab$	&I	6,7	
1,3	(9)	$\exists y(gy \,\&\, hay)$	$\exists$I	8	
1,2	(10)	$\exists y(gy \,\&\, hay)$	$\exists$E	2,9	
1	(11)	$\exists y(fy \,\&\, hay) \supset \exists y(gy \,\&\, hay)$	CP	10	
1	(12)	$\forall x(\exists y(fy \,\&\, hxy) \supset \exists y(gy \,\&\, hxy))$	$\forall$I-S	11	

In the application of $\exists$E α is 'b', ν is 'y', π is '$\exists y(gy \,\&\, hay)$' containing no 'b', ϕ is '$f\_ \,\&\, ha\_$' containing neither 'b' nor 'y' (so $\phi\alpha$ is 3), Γ is {2}, Δ is {1} containing no 'b'. The strategy for applying $\exists$E to the $\exists$-formula in line 2 is to introduce by A in line 3 a 'typical disjunct' of the $\exists$-formula, formed by dropping its '$\exists y$' and substituting a subject letter not already present in it for its remaining occurrences of 'y' (the 'typical disjunct' is so called by LEMMON, *BL* p. 112, because $\exists \nu \phi \nu$ may be thought of as an infinite disjunction $\phi\alpha \vee \phi\beta \vee \ldots$). The rule provides that what can be got, as in line 9, depending on (other formulae plus) the typical disjunct can be got, as in line 10, depending on (those formulae plus) what the $\exists$-formula depended on, in this case itself. The rule's proviso that neither ϕ, π nor Δ should contain α calls for these three cautions. (i) The letter introduced into the typical disjunct, here 'b', must be one which does not occur in the $\exists$-formula (it must be absent from ϕ and so from $\exists \nu \phi \nu$); thus line 3 will serve for $\exists$E in line 10, but $\langle \{{'fa \,\&\, haa'}\}, {'fa \,\&\, haa'} \rangle$, though of course derivable by A, would not have served. (ii) The letter introduced, here 'b', must have been removed from the written lines before $\exists$E is applied (it must be absent from π); in (B″) $\exists$I did this work of removal in line 9. (iii) The letter must also have disappeared from the indexed formulae of the derivation before $\exists$E is applied, except for its presence in the typical disjunct itself (α must be absent from the Δ part of $\Delta \cup \{\phi\alpha\}$); thus of the formulae indexed in line 9, 3 must, but 1 must not, contain 'b'.

Aristotle's actual words translate 'If a seeing is a perceiving, then a thing seen is a thing perceived', expressing a conditional proposition rather than an argument. The proposition can be proved to be a necessary truth by adding a final line of CP to the above derivations.

Logicians working within the Aristotelian tradition sometimes struggled to exhibit the correctness of arguments like 'Every ass is an animal; so every ass's tail is an animal's tail', which shares the form of (B). It cannot be done, because Aristotelian syllogistic has no room for two-place predicate letters as in 'hxy' (see LEMMON *BL* p. 131, QUINE *MofL* p. 138, WHITEHEAD & RUSSELL p. 291, and the instructive discussion in DUMMETT pp. 8–15). Nevertheless Aristotle's use of (B) suggests that he recognised it as having a valid form, even though his system could not prove the form's validity (see BOCHENSKI, p. 68).

The strategy of derivations (B') and (B") can be displayed by extracting the following sequents which are common to them:

2	(2)	$\exists y(fy \,\&\, hay)$	A
1,2		$\exists y(gy \,\&\, hay)$	
1		$\exists y(fy \,\&\, hay) \supset \exists y(gy \,\&\, hay)$	CP
1		$\forall x(\exists y(fy \,\&\, hxy) \supset \exists y(gy \,\&\, hxy))$	$\forall$I-S

The pattern of this string parallels the pattern of argument mentioned on p. 61 as characteristic of metalogical proof: supposing, inferring, conditionalising, and universalising.

(C)   Galileo said of the earth 'and yet it moves'. This looks like a scientific hypothesis, and yet the conclusion that the earth is moving *relative to something* is entailed by the following unexciting premisses: 'At least one thing is moving relative to something', 'Relative movement is symmetrical', 'Relative rest is transitive'.

(i) Finding the sequent. Rewording. 'Relative movement is symmetrical' means 'If one thing is moving relative to another, the latter is moving relative to the former'. 'Relative rest is transitive' means 'If one thing is at rest relative to a second, and the second relative to a third, then the first is at rest relative to the third'. '__is at rest relative to . . .' means '__is not moving relative to . . .'. So the argument is expressible in English plus variables thus: '(1) for some x and some y, x is moving relative to y; (2) for all x and y, if x is moving relative to y, y is moving relative to x; (3)

11.1 Proofs of correctness

for all x, y and z, if x is not moving relative to y, and y is not moving relative to z, then x is not moving relative to z; so (4) for some x, the earth is moving relative to x.' Schematising. The component expressions fit schematic letters as follows:

'___is moving relative to . . .' fits 'f___. . .'
'the earth' fits 'a'

So the argument is expressible in sentences QC-fitting 'For some x and y, fxy; for all x and y, if fxy then fyx; for all x, y and z, if not fxy and not fyz, then not fxz; so for some x, fax.' Translating. By T∃, T∀, T⊃, T~ and T& the argument is QC-expressible, relative to some domain, in sentences QC-fitting '$\exists x \exists y fxy$; $\forall x \forall y (fxy \supset fyx)$; $\forall x \forall y \forall z (\sim fxy \mathbin{\&} \sim fyz \supset \sim fxz)$; so $\exists x fax$.' The sentences do not equivocate. So the argument is a QC-instance of the corresponding sequent. (ii) *Proving validity*. The following derivation proves that the sequent is QC-derivable and so, by the soundness metatheorem, QC-valid (I omit some of the annotation):

(C′)	1	(1)	$\exists x \exists y fxy$		
	2	(2)	$\forall x \forall y (fxy \supset fyx)$		
	3	(3)	$\forall x \forall y \forall z (\sim fxy \mathbin{\&} \sim fyz \supset \sim fxz)$		
	4	(4)	$\forall x \sim fax$	A	
	4	(5)	$\sim fab$		
	2	(6)	$fba \supset fab$	∀E twice	2
	2,4	(7)	$\sim fba$	MTT	5,6
	4	(8)	$\sim fac$		
	2,4	(9)	$\sim fba \mathbin{\&} \sim fac$		
	3	(10)	$\sim fba \mathbin{\&} \sim fac \supset \sim fbc$	∀E three times	3
	2,3,4	(11)	$\sim fbc$		
	2,3,4	(12)	$\forall x \forall y \sim fxy$	∀I-S twice	11
	2,3,4	(13)	$\forall x \sim\sim \forall y \sim fxy$	~ Int	12
	1	(14)	$\sim \forall x \sim\sim \forall y \sim fxy$	Def∃ twice	1
	1,2,3,4	(15)	$\forall x \sim\sim \forall y \sim fxy \mathbin{\&} \sim \forall x \sim\sim \forall y \sim fxy$		
	1,2,3	(16)	$\sim \forall x \sim fax$		
	1,2,3	(17)	$\exists x fax$		

Line 12 is correct because 2, 3 and 4 contain no 'b' or 'c'.

(D) In the *Nicomachean Ethics* Aristotle says 'We do not choose everything for something else' (*EN* I 2.1094^{a}19-20, in an 'if' clause, but apparently endorsed by Aristotle). Later he says that *eudaemonia*, roughly happiness, is the most 'complete' end in that 'we choose it always on its own account and never on account of anything else' (I 7.1097^{b}1). And later still he says 'It is for the sake of this (*sc. eudaemonia*) that we do all the other things we do' (I 12. 1102^{a}2-3).

The last of these propositions follows from the other two on the assumptions (a) that nothing turns on the difference between 'choose' and 'do' or between 'on account of' and 'for the sake of', (b) that if one thing is chosen for the sake of another (or itself), the latter is chosen, and (c) that the first and second propositions respectively assert or entail that *everything* chosen is chosen for the sake of something chosen only for its own sake (all chains come to an end) and that nothing *except eudaemonia* is chosen only for its own sake (nothing else can end a chain).

It would be a good deal harder to convince a sceptic that this is the right interpretation of Aristotle's words than that the argument so extracted is a correct one. But if the latter task were necessary, here is how it could be discharged. (i) Finding the sequent. Rewording. 'Nothing except *eudaemonia*' means 'nothing not identical with *eudaemonia*'. So the argument is expressible in English plus variables thus: '(1) For all x, if x is chosen, then for some y, x is chosen for the sake of y and y is chosen only for its own sake; (2) For all x, if x is chosen and x is not identical with *eudaemonia*, x is not chosen only for its own sake; (3) For all x and y, if x is chosen for the sake of y, y is chosen; so (4) for all x, if x is chosen, x is chosen for the sake of *eudaemonia*.' Schematising. The component expressions fit schematic letters as follows:

'*eudaemonia*' fits 'a'
'__is chosen' fits 'f__'
'__is chosen for the sake of . . .' fits 'g__. . .'
'__is chosen only for its own sake' fits 'h__'

The last of these predicates could be broken down further, but does not need to be. So the argument is expressible in sentences QC-fitting 'For all x, if fx, then for some y, gxy and hy; for all x, if fx and x is not identical with a, then not hx; for all x and y, if gxy then

11.1 *Proofs of correctness*

fy; so for all x, if fx, then gxa.' Translating. By T∀, T⊃, T∃, T&, T~ and T= the argument is QC-expressible, relative to some domain, in sentences QC-fitting '$\forall x(fx \supset \exists y(gxy \,\&\, hy))$; $\forall x(fx \,\&\, x \neq a \supset \sim hx)$; $\forall x \forall y(gxy \supset fy)$; so $\forall x(fx \supset gxa)$.' The sentences do not equivocate. So the argument is a QC-instance of the corresponding sequent. (ii) Proving validity. The following derivation proves that the sequent is QC-derivable and so, by the soundness metatheorem, QC-valid:

(D')
1	(1) $\forall x(fx \supset \exists y(gxy \,\&\, hy))$			
2	(2) $\forall x(fx \,\&\, x \neq a \supset \sim hx)$			
3	(3) $\forall x \forall y(gxy \supset fy)$			
4	(4) fb	A		
1	(5) $fb \supset \exists y(gby \,\&\, hy)$			
1,4	(6) $\exists y(gby \,\&\, hy)$			
7	(7) $gbc \,\&\, hc$	A		
7	(8) hc			
7	(9) $\sim\sim hc$			
2	(10) $fc \,\&\, c \neq a \supset \sim hc$			
2,7	(11) $\sim(fc \,\&\, c \neq a)$	MTT	9,10	
2,7	(12) $fc \supset c = a$	Def ⊃	11	
7	(13) gbc			
3	(14) $gbc \supset fc$	∀E twice	3	
3,7	(15) fc			
2,3,7	(16) $c = a$			
2,3,7	(17) gba	=E	13,16	
18	(18) $\sim gba$	A		
2,3,7,18	(19) $gba \,\&\, \sim gba$			
2,3,18	(20) $\sim(gbc \,\&\, hc)$	RAA	7	
2,3,18	(21) $\forall y \sim (gby \,\&\, hy)$	∀I-S	20	
1,4	(22) $\sim \forall y \sim (gby \,\&\, hy)$	Def ∃	6	
1,2,3,4,18	(23) $\forall y \sim (gby \,\&\, hy) \,\&\, \sim \forall y \sim (gby \,\&\, hy)$			
1,2,3,4	(24) $\sim\sim gba$	RAA	18	
1,2,3,4	(25) gba			∃E 6,17
1,2,3	(26) $fb \supset gba$			
1,2,3	(27) $\forall x(fx \supset gxa)$			

The box shows how ∃E can be avoided; see p. 136.

(E) There is a class whose members are just those "sets" which are not members of themselves; so there is no universe class.

The premiss of this argument is itself entailed by a proposition commonly taken as an axiom of set theory ('axiom' in the postfoundational sense, see p. 142), to the effect that the schema 'There is a class whose members are just those "sets" which are f' is true for every replacement of 'f' by a predicate. In this Comprehension Axiom "set" has the special meaning 'class which is a member of something'. The bolder schema 'There is a class whose members are just those *classes* which are f' is known to be fitted by some false sentences; for example Russell's paradox leads to a proof that there is no class consisting just of the classes that are not self-membered (p. 52 and LEMMON *BL* pp. 209–10). But the Comprehension Axiom avoids this objection, and offers part of one —not the only—plausible starting point for set theory. Both the axiom and the argument should be understood as propounded relative to some domain of classes. In the argument's conclusion 'universe class' means 'class of which everything is a member'; often it is used for 'class of which all sets are members', and in that sense there is a universe class. (i) Finding the sequent. Rewording. In set theory it is usual to employ the symbol 'ε' with the fixed meaning 'is a member of'. So the argument is expressible in English with variables and 'ε', relative to the chosen domain, thus: 'For some x, for all y, $y\varepsilon x$ if and only if y is a "set" (i.e. for some z, $y\varepsilon z$) and not $y\varepsilon y$; so for no x is it the case that for every y $y\varepsilon x$.' Schematising. The component predicate fits a schematic letter as follows:

'$\_\varepsilon \ldots$' fits '$f\_ \ldots$'

So the argument is expressible, relative to the chosen domain, in sentences QC-fitting 'For some x, for all y, fyx if and only if for some z fyz and not fyy; so for no x is it the case that for every y fyx.' Translating. By T∃, T∀, T≡ and T∼ the argument is QC-expressible, relative to the domain, in sentences QC-fitting '$\exists x \forall y (fyx \equiv \exists z fyz \ \& \ {\sim}fyy)$; so $\forall x {\sim} \forall y fyx$.' The sentences do not equivocate. So the argument, whatever its domain, is a QC-instance of the corresponding sequent. (ii) Proving validity. The following derivation proves that the sequent is QC-derivable and so, by the soundness metatheorem, QC-valid:

11.1 Proofs of correctness

(E') 1	(1) $\exists x \forall y (fyx \equiv \exists z fyz \ \& \sim fyy)$		
2	(2) $\forall y fya$	A	
3	(3) $\forall y (fyb \equiv \exists z fyz \ \& \sim fyy)$	A	
3	(4) $fbb \equiv \exists z fbz \ \& \sim fbb$		
3	(5) $(fbb \supset \exists z fbz \ \& \sim fbb) \ \& \ (\exists z fbz$		
	$\qquad \& \sim fbb \supset fbb)$	Def$\equiv$	4
3	(6) $fbb \supset \exists z fbz \ \& \sim fbb$		
7	(7) fbb	A	
3,7	(8) $\exists z fbz \ \& \sim fbb$		
3,7	(9) $\sim fbb$		
3,7	(10) $fbb \ \& \sim fbb$		
3	(11) $\sim fbb$	RAA	7
2	(12) fba	$\forall$E	2
2	(13) $\exists z fbz$	$\exists$I	12
2,3	(14) $\exists z fbz \ \& \sim fbb$		
3	(15) $\exists z fbz \ \& \sim fbb \supset fbb$	&E	5
2,3	(16) fbb		
2,3	(17) $fbb \ \& \sim fbb$	&I	11,16
2	(18) $\sim \forall y (fyb \equiv \exists z fyz \ \& \sim fyy)$	RAA	17
2	(19) $\forall x \sim \forall y (fyx \equiv \exists z fyz \ \& \sim fyy)$		
1	(20) $\sim \forall x \sim \forall y (fyx \equiv \exists z fyz \ \& \sim fyy)$	Def$\exists$	1
1,2	(21) $\forall x \sim \forall y (fyx \equiv \exists z fyz \ \& \sim fyy)$		
	$\qquad \& \sim \forall x \sim \forall y (fyx \equiv \exists z fyz \ \& \sim fyy)$		
1	(22) $\sim \forall y fya$	RAA	2
1	(23) $\forall x \sim \forall y fyx$		

Digression on proofs in set theory. As in every use of formal methods, it is possible to interpret 'f' in the above derivation as a dummy rather than schematic letter, here assigned the *ad hoc* meaning 'is a member of'. Proofs in set theory commonly need no predicates besides 'is a member of', 'is identical with' and others definable in terms of this pair (indeed the latter of the pair is sometimes defined in terms of the former). So an alternative way of formalising such proofs is to vary **QC** by (a) dropping all its predicate letters and (b) introducing the symbol 'ε' as another *connective* (like '$=$') with the fixed meaning 'is a member of'. The resulting calculus is the same as **QC** except that FP and TP are replaced by suitably framed Fε and Tε. In this calculus the formulae '$\exists x \forall y (y \varepsilon x \equiv \exists z y \varepsilon z \ \& \sim y \varepsilon y)$' and '$\forall x \sim \forall y y \varepsilon x$' are well-formed; and being interpreted as sentences rather than schemata they are 'fitted' just by themselves (pp. 94–5). Hence argument (E) is not only a **QC**-instance of the sequent proved derivable in (E') but also an instance in the new calculus of the corresponding sequent with 'ε' for 'f'; and proof that the latter is derivable exactly parallels (E').

For work in set theory the variant calculus has one great advantage over **QC**: a useful range of extra expressions can be introduced into it by symbolic definition. For example the two-place predicate '$\subseteq$', meaning 'is a subclass of', has the definition: $\ulcorner \alpha \subseteq \beta \urcorner$ = $_{\text{def}}$ $\ulcorner \forall v(v\varepsilon\alpha \supset v\varepsilon\beta)\urcorner$ for some suitable v (i.e. for some variable v such that $\ulcorner \alpha \subseteq \beta \urcorner$ is not itself within the scope of a quantifier in v). Subjects can be introduced too. One way is to start from the *definite description* connective '$\imath$', with an interpretation by which $\ulcorner(\imath v\phi v)\urcorner$ means $\ulcorner$the sole v such that $\phi v\urcorner$. Since well-formed stencils of the new language contain no predicate letters but only the predicates 'ε' and '$=$' and others defined from them, $\ulcorner(\imath v\phi v)\urcorner$ will be capable of serving, for any v and many ϕs, as a subject, and the new language will therefore contain, in addition to subject letters 'a', 'b', 'c' etc., such symbolic subjects as '$(\imath x \sim \exists y y \varepsilon x)$' for 'the sole thing of which nothing is a member'; hence formulae like '$\sim a\varepsilon(\imath x \sim \exists y y \varepsilon x)$' must be admitted as well-formed, by the rule: for any v and well-formed π and ϕ, neither containing v, if π contains a subject letter, the result of substituting $\ulcorner(\imath v\phi v)\urcorner$ for that letter is well-formed. The interpretation of '$\imath$' here sketched is in terms of the English expression 'the sole'. An alternative (e.g. QUINE *MofL* p. 232) is to make $\ulcorner\psi(\imath v\phi v)\urcorner$ short for $\ulcorner\exists v(\psi v \ \& \ \forall \mu(\phi\mu \equiv \mu = v))\urcorner$ with suitable restrictions on ϕ, ψ and μ—i.e. to read it as 'Just one thing is ϕ and that is ψ'; but of course this alternative may yield different truth-conditions from the definition in terms of English, and it makes =I and ∀E unsound if '$(\imath x \forall y y \varepsilon x)$' etc. still function as subjects in the sense explained in 9.3. Given '$\imath$', by one of these routes, we can next introduce the *class abstract* connective $\ulcorner\{v: \ldots v \ldots\}\urcorner$, defined contextually, again with suitable restrictions on ϕ and μ, by: $\ulcorner\{v: \phi v\}\urcorner$ is short for $\ulcorner(\imath v\forall \mu(\mu\varepsilon v \equiv \phi\mu))\urcorner$, i.e. means $\ulcorner$the sole thing having for its members those things μ such that $\phi\mu\urcorner$ (QUINE *MofL* p. 239). This adds to the calculus such symbolic subjects as '$\{x: \exists y x \varepsilon y\}$' for 'the class of "sets"' and '$\{x: x = x\}$' for 'the class of things that are self-identical'. Some of these expressions may then be abbreviated by further symbolic definition: e.g.

11.1 Proofs of correctness

'Λ' for 'the empty class', may be introduced as short for '$\{x: x \neq x\}$'.

The definite description connective and the class abstract connective form subjects out of predicates and variables. Another useful device, again not exemplified in the calculi of this book, is the functor (p. 108, cf. MATES p. 158, MASSEY p. 325 ff.) which forms a subject from one or more other subjects: e.g. 'the father of ___' in English. Set theory employs many symbolic functors in addition to the symbolic predicates 'ε', '$\subseteq$' etc. and the symbolic subjects '$\{x: x \neq x\}$', 'Λ' etc. Here are some examples, contextually defined (these definitions follow LEMMON *IAST*; 'α' and 'β' now range over symbolic subjects, simple or complex, as well as subject letters). ⌜$\alpha \cup \beta$⌝, meaning ⌜the union of α and β⌝, is short for ⌜$\{x: x\varepsilon\alpha \vee x\varepsilon\beta\}$⌝; ⌜$\cup\alpha$⌝, meaning⌜ The sum of α, i.e. the union of α's members⌝, is short for ⌜$\{x: \exists y(x\varepsilon y \& y\varepsilon\alpha)\}$⌝; ⌜$\mathfrak{P}\alpha$⌝, meaning ⌜the power class of α, i.e. the class of all subsets of α⌝, is short for ⌜$\{x: \exists y x\varepsilon y \& x \subseteq \alpha\}$⌝; ⌜$\{\alpha\}$⌝, meaning ⌜the unit class of α, i.e. the class whose sole member if a set is α⌝, is short for ⌜$\{x: \exists y \alpha\varepsilon y \supset x = \alpha\}$⌝; ⌜$\{\alpha, \beta\}$⌝ is short for ⌜$\{\alpha\} \cup \{\beta\}$⌝; ⌜$\langle \alpha, \beta \rangle$⌝, meaning ⌜the ordered pair whose members if sets are α and β⌝, is short for ⌜$\{\{\alpha\}, \{\alpha, \beta\}\}$⌝; and ⌜$\alpha \times \beta$⌝, meaning ⌜the Cartesian product of α and β, i.e. the class of ordered pairs each consisting of a member of α followed by a member of β⌝, is short for ⌜$\{x: \exists y \exists z(x = \langle y, z \rangle \& y\varepsilon\alpha \& z\varepsilon\beta)\}$⌝.

Substitution of **Tε** for **TP** without any change in the QC derivation rules renders the new calculus incomplete. If for example the postfoundational Comprehension Axiom is true, then '$\exists x \forall y(y\varepsilon x \equiv \exists z y\varepsilon z \& y\varepsilon y)$' is valid in the new language; but it is not derivable in a system resulting from QC by substituting Fε for FP. Set theories may be seen as attempts to regain completeness by adding foundational axioms, especially existential ones, to those of QC. But none of the interesting theories has yet been proved sound, while it has been proved that if sound they are not complete (HUNTER p. 261, QUINE *MofL* ch. 46). This accounts for the currency of more than one set theory.

(F) In PLATO'S *Theaetetus* Socrates describes a theory which he 'dreamt', that knowledge is possible only of complexes, not elements (201d8–202c5). Then he offers a refutation of the dream theory by proving that it is not the case that some complexes are known but no elements are known. I take the premisses for the main part of the refutation to be as follows: if a complex is all its parts, then if it is known all its parts are known (203c4–7, d7–9; 205d7–9); if a thing has parts, it is all its parts (204a7–8; 205a8–9); if a complex has parts, its parts are just its elementary parts (205b11–13); and what has no parts is an element (205d4–5).

I shall comment on two of these premisses after first proving the correctness of the argument from them. (i) Finding the sequent. Rewording. An elementary part is just a part which is an element; so the third premiss can be simplified into 'any part of a complex is an element'. The argument is expressible in English plus variables thus: '(1) for all x, if x is a complex and x is all its own parts, then if x is known then for all y, if y is a part of x, y is known; (2) for all x, if for some y y is a part of x, then x is all its own parts; (3) for all x and y, if x is a complex and y is a part of x, then y is an element; (4) for all x, if for no y y is a part of x, then x is an element; so (5) it is not the case that both for some x x is a complex and x is known, and for no x x is an element and x is known.' Schematising. The component predicates fit schematic letters as follows:

'__is a complex' fits 'f__'
'__is all its own parts' fits 'g__'
'__is known' fits 'h__'
'__is a part of . . .' fits 'i__ . . .'
'__is an element' fits 'j__'

'i' and 'j' are not strictly QC letters (p. 71), but they read more easily than 'f_1', 'g_1'. This time I insert letters and connectives in a single operation. By T∀ and its fellows the argument is QC-expressible, relative to some domain, in sentences QC-fitting '$\forall x(fx \& gx \supset (hx \supset \forall y(iyx \supset hy)))$; $\forall x(\exists y i y x \supset g x)$; $\forall x \forall y(fx \& iyx \supset jy)$; $\forall x(\sim \exists y i y x \supset j x)$; so $\sim(\exists x(fx \& hx) \& \sim \exists x(jx \& hx))$'. If we may assume that 'is all its own parts' does not equivocate—for which see below—the argument is therefore a QC-instance of the corresponding sequent. (ii) Proving validity. The following derivation proves that the sequent is QC-derivable and so, by the soundness metatheorem, QC-valid:

11.1 Proofs of correctness

(F') 1	(1) $\forall x(fx \mathbin{\&} gx \supset (hx \supset \forall y(iyx \supset hy)))$		
2	(2) $\forall x(\exists y iyx \supset gx)$		
3	(3) $\forall x \forall y(fx \mathbin{\&} iyx \supset jy)$		
4	(4) $\forall x(\sim\exists y iyx \supset jx)$		
5	(5) $\exists x(fx \mathbin{\&} hx) \mathbin{\&} \sim\exists x(jx \mathbin{\&} hx)$ A		
5	(6) $\sim\exists x(jx \mathbin{\&} hx)$		
5	(7) $\sim\sim\forall x \sim(jx \mathbin{\&} hx)$	Def∃	6
5	(8) $\forall x \sim(jx \mathbin{\&} hx)$		
5	(9) $\sim(ja \mathbin{\&} ha)$		
10	(10) $fa \mathbin{\&} ha$		
10	(11) ha		
5,10	(12) $\sim ja$	MPT	9,11
4	(13) $\sim\exists y iya \supset ja$		
4,5,10	(14) $\sim\sim\exists y iya$	MTT	12,13
4,5,10	(15) $\exists y iya$		
2	(16) $\exists y iya \supset ga$		
2,4,5,10	(17) ga		
10	(18) fa		
2,4,5,10	(19) $fa \mathbin{\&} ga$		
1	(20) $fa \mathbin{\&} ga \supset (ha \supset \forall y(iya \supset hy))$		
1,2,4,5,10	(21) $ha \supset \forall y(iya \supset hy)$		
1,2,4,5,10	(22) $\forall y(iya \supset hy)$		
1,2,4,5,10	(23) $iba \supset hb$		
24	(24) iba		
1,2,4,5,10,24	(25) hb		
10,24	(26) $fa \mathbin{\&} iba$		
3	(27) $fa \mathbin{\&} iba \supset jb$	∀E twice	3
3,10,24	(28) jb		
1,2,3,4,5,10,24	(29) $jb \mathbin{\&} hb$		
5	(30) $\sim(jb \mathbin{\&} hb)$	∀E	8
1,2,3,4,5,10,24	(31) $(jb \mathbin{\&} hb) \mathbin{\&} \sim(jb \mathbin{\&} hb)$		
1,2,3,4,5,10	(32) $\sim iba$		
1,2,3,4,5,10	(33) $\forall y \sim iya$	∀I-S	32
4,5,10	(34) $\sim\forall y \sim iya$	Def∃	15
1,2,3,4,5,10	(35) $\forall y \sim iya \mathbin{\&} \sim\forall y \sim iya$		
1,2,3,4,5	(36) $\sim(fa \mathbin{\&} ha)$		
1,2,3,4,5	(37) $\forall x \sim(fx \mathbin{\&} hx)$		
5	(38) $\exists x(fx \mathbin{\&} hx)$		
5	(39) $\sim\forall x \sim(fx \mathbin{\&} hx)$	Def∃	38

258   *Applications*

| 1,2,3,4,5 | (40) $\forall x \sim (fx \ \& \ hx) \ \& \sim \forall x \sim (fx \ \& \ hx)$ |
| 1,2,3,4 | (41) $\sim (\exists x(fx \ \& \ hx) \ \& \sim \exists x(jx \ \& \ hx))$ |

Or the derivation could end more swiftly thus:

1,2,3,4,5,10,24	(30) $\exists x(jx \ \& \ hx)$	$\exists$I	29
1,2,3,4,5,10	(31) $\exists x(jx \ \& \ hx)$	$\exists$E	15,30
5	(32) $\exists x(fx \ \& \ hx)$		
1,2,3,4,5	(33) $\exists x(jx \ \& \ hx)$	$\exists$E	32,31
1,2,3,4,5	(34) $\exists x(jx \ \& \ hx) \ \& \sim \exists x(jx \ \& \ hx)$	&I	33,6
1,2,3,4	(35) $\sim (\exists x(fx \ \& \ hx) \ \& \sim \exists x(jx \ \& \ hx))$		

The second premiss of (F) appears in Plato's text as an intermediate conclusion supported by its own supplementary argument (see McDOWELL, pp. 244–6). Although I shall not examine the supplementary argument, I append a comment on the truth of the first two premisses of (F). Plato is in a dilemma. He could secure the truth—indeed necessary truth—of his first premiss ('If a complex is all its parts, then if it is known so are all its parts') by interpreting 'is all its parts' as 'is the same as each of its parts'. He could perhaps secure the truth of his second premiss ('All the parts are the same as the whole', 205d 9–10) by interpreting 'is all its parts' as 'is the same as the sum of its parts'. But with these divergent interpretations the argument will equivocate, while without them one of its premisses will be false (see McDOWELL, p. 243).

(G) If something has perfection, it follows that (it and therefore) something has perfection of necessity. It is possible that something should have perfection. So something does have perfection.

A proof of this conclusion might well be taken as proof of the existence of some kind of God, and indeed the argument is part of one such proof in HARTSHORNE (p. 51, misreported but well discussed in BARNES pp. 20–1). Whether the argument works as a proof I do not inquire; but at least it is correct. (i) Finding the sequent. Schematising. The component sentence fits a schematic letter as follows:

'Something has perfection' fits 'p'

11.1 Proofs of correctness

So the argument is expressible in sentences PC-fitting 'If p, then it follows that necessarily p; it is possible that it should be the case that p; so p'. Translating. By T$\Box$, T$\Diamond$ and the considerations in 10.9 the argument is S5-expressible in sentences PC-fitting, and so S5-fitting, '$\Box(p \supset \Box p); \Diamond p;$ so p.' The sentences do not equivocate. So the argument is an S5-instance of the corresponding sequent. (ii) Proving validity. The following derivation shows that the sequent is S5-derivable and so, by the soundness metatheorem, S5-valid:

(G')
1	(1)	$\Box(p \supset \Box p)$		
2	(2)	$\Diamond p$		
3	(3)	$\sim \Box p$	A	
1	(4)	$p \supset \Box p$	$\Box$E	1
1,3	(5)	$\sim p$	MTT	3,4
1,3	(6)	$\Box \sim p$	$\Box$I-S	5
2	(7)	$\sim \Box \sim p$	Def$\Diamond$	2
1,2,3	(8)	$\Box \sim p \ \& \ \sim \Box \sim p$		
1,2	(9)	$\sim\sim \Box p$		
1,2	(10)	$\Box p$		
1,2	(11)	p	$\Box$E	10

The argument's corresponding material conditional is an S5-instance of the formula '$\Box(p \supset \Box p) \ \& \ \Diamond p \supset p$'. I add for variety a proof that this formula is derivable in the S5 formula system:

(G'')
(1) $\Box(p \supset \Box p) \supset (\Diamond p \supset \Diamond \Box p)$	Dist $\Diamond$	
(2) $\sim \Box p \supset \Box \sim \Box p$	Pure $\Box$I-F	
(3) $\sim \Box \sim \Box p \supset \sim\sim \Box p$	Transp	2
(4) $\Diamond \Box p \supset \sim\sim \Box p$	Def$\Diamond$	3
(5) $\Diamond \Box p \supset \Box p$	Syll	4,DN-F
(6) $(\Diamond p \supset \Diamond \Box p) \supset ((\Diamond \Box p \supset \Box p)$ $\supset (\Diamond p \supset \Box p))$	Syll	
(7) $(\Diamond \Box p \supset \Box p) \supset ((\Diamond p \supset \Diamond \Box p)$ $\supset (\Diamond p \supset \Box p))$	Perm	6
(8) $(\Diamond p \supset \Diamond \Box p) \supset (\Diamond p \supset \Box p)$	MPP-F	5,7
(9) $\Box(p \supset \Box p) \supset (\Diamond p \supset \Box p)$	Syll	1,8
(10) $\Box(p \supset \Box p) \ \& \ \Diamond p \supset \Box p$	Imp	9
(11) $\Box p \supset p$	Simp$\Box$	
(12) $\Box(p \supset \Box p) \ \& \ \Diamond p \supset p$	Syll	10,11

(H) Some contingent truths (e.g. that I exist) cannot reasonably be doubted by me. So it is possible that some of the propositions I cannot reasonably doubt should be untrue.

The premiss was established by DESCARTES (*Meditation* 2, p. 25 ll. 12–3): it is a condition of doubting one's own existence that the doubt should be unfounded. The conclusion falls short of asserting that some not rationally dubitable propositions *are* untrue, but it shows that there is no necessity in their all being true. (i) Finding the sequent. Rewording. 'Is a contingent truth' means 'is true but is not necessarily true'. '*a* cannot reasonably be doubted' means 'It is not possible that *a* should be doubted with reason'. So the argument is expressible in English plus variables, relative to the domain of propositions, thus: 'For some x, x is true but not necessarily x is true, and it is not possible that I should doubt x with reason; so it is possible that for some x it should not be possible that I should doubt x with reason and yet x should not be true.' Schematising. The component expressions fit schematic letters as follows:

'__is true' fits 'f__'
I doubt__with reason' fits 'g__'

By T$\diamond$ 'it is possible that . . . should . . .' translates into '$\diamond$'. Hence, using T$\exists$, T&, T$\sim$, T$\square$ and T$\diamond$ and at the same time incorporating the schematic letters, we have: the argument is QS5-expressible, relative to the domain of people plus propositions, in sentences QC-fitting, and so QS5-fitting, '$\exists x((fx \ \& \sim \square fx) \ \& \sim \diamond gx)$; so $\diamond \exists x(\sim \diamond gx \ \& \sim fx)$.' The sentences do not equivocate ('I' and 'me' have the same reference). So the argument is a QS5-instance of the corresponding sequent. (ii) Proving validity. The following derivation proves that the sequent is QS5-derivable and so, by the soundness metatheorem, QS5-valid:

(H′) 1   (1) $\exists x((fx \ \& \sim \square fx) \ \& \sim \diamond gx)$
     2   (2) $\square \sim \exists x(\sim \diamond gx \ \& \sim fx)$ A
     2   (3) $\sim \exists x(\sim \diamond gx \ \& \sim fx)$
     2   (4) $\sim\sim \forall x \sim(\sim \diamond gx \ \& \sim fx)$
     2   (5) $\forall x \sim(\sim \diamond gx \ \& \sim fx)$
     2   (6) $\sim(\sim \diamond ga \ \& \sim fa)$
     2   (7) $\sim \diamond ga \supset fa$ Def$\supset$ 6

11.1 Proofs of correctness

8	(8)	$\sim\Diamond ga$	A	
2,8	(9)	fa		
2,8	(10)	$\Box fa$	$\Box$I-S	9
2	(11)	$\sim\Diamond ga \supset \Box fa$	CP	10
12	(12)	$(fa \,\&\, \sim\Box fa) \,\&\, \sim\Diamond ga$	A	
12	(13)	$\sim\Diamond ga$		
2,12	(14)	$\Box fa$		
12	(15)	$fa \,\&\, \sim\Box fa$		
12	(16)	$\sim\Box fa$		
2,12	(17)	$\Box fa \,\&\, \sim\Box fa$		
2	(18)	$\sim((fa \,\&\, \sim\Box fa) \,\&\, \sim\Diamond ga)$	RAA	17
2	(19)	$\forall x \sim((fx \,\&\, \sim\Box fx)) \,\&\, \sim\Diamond gx)$		
1	(20)	$\sim\forall x \sim((fx \,\&\, \sim\Box fx)) \,\&\, \sim\Diamond gx)$ Def∃		1
1,2	(21)	$\forall x \sim((fx \,\&\, \sim\Box fx)) \,\&\, \sim\Diamond gx)$		
		$\&\, \sim\forall x \sim((fx \,\&\, \sim\Box fx) \,\&\, \sim\Diamond gx)$		
1	(22)	$\sim\Box\sim\exists x(\sim\Diamond gx \,\&\, \sim fx)$	RAA	21
1	(23)	$\Diamond\exists x(\sim\Diamond gx \,\&\, \sim fx)$		

11.2 Beyond the methods of this book

(I) Aristotle died during the archonship of Philocles, July 322–July 321 B.C.; he died before Demosthenes, who died in October 322; he was 62 when he died; he was born during the archonship of Diotrephes, July 384–July 383; so he was born between July and October 384.

Though the correctness of (I) is not immediately evident, few would bother to test it by logical means. The best way is to fill in some intermediate conclusions: premisses one and two yield 'He died between July and October 322'; that and premiss three yield 'His 62nd birthday fell between July 323 and October 322'; from that arithmetic yields 'He was born between July 385 and October 384'; whence the conclusion follows with the help of premiss four.

(J) The battle of Waterloo lies in the past; so already in the past it lay in the past.

Suppose we add to PC the connective 'P' with the formation rule 'if π is well-formed, so is $P\pi$' and the interpretation 'it was the case that'. Then this little argument is an instance of $\langle\{`Pp\text{'}\}, `PPp\text{'}\rangle$, and its corresponding material conditional is an instance of '$Pp \supset PPp$'. Suppose further that we invent a formula system in which '$Pp \supset PPp$' is an axiom, or at least derivable. Would the system be sound under the interpretation, i.e. in the proposed extension of **PC**? This turns on whether '$Pp \supset PPp$' is valid under the interpretation. It is valid only if past time is dense, in the sense that between the present moment and any past moment (e.g. that at which the battle of Waterloo ended) there lies a third moment (at which the battle's end was already past). Tense logic, as this and similar extensions are called, is sometimes scorned on the ground that such questions belong to physics rather than logic. But there is a case to be made for the view that the density of time is a semantical question, to be answered by discovering the truth-condition of 'it was the case that' (and 'it will be the case that'). If so, the procedure of Chapters 9 and 10 can be followed: we can set up, as in modal logic, some truth-condition for 'P' under which '$Pp \supset PPp$' is provably valid, and then relegate to an extralogical stage the question whether the English phrase 'it was the case that' shares that truth-condition. Thus extensions of the calculi of this book are useful for testing arguments just so far as it remains plausible to hold that their connectives can be translated into reasonably familiar phrases of some natural language.

(K) 'In ordinary speech we move unhesitatingly from (e.g.) "Napoleon was a great general and McClellan was not", to "Napoleon was something that McClellan was not", yet . . . our entitlement to do so presupposes that the predicate generalised upon be thought of as naming in some way comparable to that required of singular terms [i.e. subjects] open to the parallel operation' of introducing quantifiers (FURTH p. 29).

There are three ways of dealing with arguments of the kind here cited. If we take seriously Furth's suggestion that the predicate 'was a great general' be thought of as naming in some way, we might construe it as covertly containing a name, e.g. the subject 'the class of great generals' attached to 'Napoleon' etc. by the two-place predicate 'is a member of'. This brings appraisal of the argument within the methods of the present book, as a QC-instance of the

11.2 Beyond the methods of this book

QC-valid sequent $\langle\{\text{'}fac\text{'} \ \&\ \sim fbc\text{'}\}, \text{'}\exists x(fax\ \&\ \sim fbx)\text{'}\rangle$. A second way is to permit quantification over predicates (higher-order quantification), by adding to QC a formation rule along the lines of 'If ϕf is well-formed, so is $\forall x \phi x$' (remember that a formula with any sort of gap in is a stencil, so that if ϕf is well-formed ϕ will have gaps suitable for filling with predicate letters, as in '$(\_aa \supset p)$' quantifying to '$\forall x(xaa \supset p)$'). The rule would need to be generalised from 'f' to all predicate letters and from 'x' to all variables; and clarity would be served by choosing a special style for predicate variables in place of 'x', 'y', 'z', e.g. bold-face '**f**' as in '$\forall \mathbf{f} \phi \mathbf{f}$'. The hope will be that, by combining this formation rule with a suitable interpretation of '$\forall \mathbf{f}$', '$\exists \mathbf{f}$' etc., it becomes possible to represent Furth's argument as an instance of $\langle\{\text{'}fa\ \&\ \sim fb\text{'}\}, \text{'}\exists \mathbf{f}(\mathbf{f}a\ \&\ \sim \mathbf{f}b)\text{'}\rangle$. But what is the interpretation to be? 'Something **f** is such that (**f** Napoleon)' seems to demand a name-like role for '**f**' in its first occurrence and a predicate-like role in its second—hence Furth's 'presupposition that predicates name in some way'. Similarly if T∀ and T∃ are applied without change to the new variables, they have such consequences as ' "∀**ff** Napoleon" is T in a context if and only if some predicate followed by "Napoleon" is T in every context differing at most as to the *reference* of the predicate'. Some predicates—what remain when subjects are deleted from a sentence—must therefore themselves be subjects, so that some sentences must consist of nothing but subjects. Logicians disagree whether these problems of interpretation can be resolved satisfactorily (for a sanguine view see PRIOR, *OT* pp. 31-43).

A third way of dealing with arguments such as that cited by Furth dispenses with predicate variables by allowing (schematic) predicate letters to be themselves bound by quantifiers: if ϕf is well-formed, so is $\forall f \phi f$. This requires a radically new interpretation of '$\forall$' and '$\exists$', which are now to attach to schemata such as 'f Napoleon' rather than open sentences such as '**f** Napoleon'. The interpretation will have consequences like this: ' "$\forall f f$ Napoleon" is T in a context, domain and world if and only if every one-place predicate followed by "Napoleon" makes a sentence that is T in them', or in other words 'if and only if every sentence fitting "f Napoleon" is T in them'. Because some logicians speak of expressions replacing a schematic letter as substituends of the letter, the interpretation is said to make quantification 'substitutional' (QUINE

E&Q pp. 104-6). The advantage of this account is to avoid the suggestion that predicates function like names.

Once predicate quantifiers have been somehow admitted it is an easy step to propositional quantifiers; indeed sentences can be thought of as no-place predicates (cf. p. 110). For 'Locke and Berkeley had some disagreements' we might try '∃p(Locke believed that **p** & Berkeley believed that ~**p**)' or on the substitutional account '∃*p*(Locke believed that *p* & Berkeley believed that ~*p*)'. Here is another example:

(L) Only guilty men don't tell the truth; so anyone who says he is guilty is guilty.

Argument (L) might be formalised with higher-order quantification in the following steps. It can be expressed in 'for all *x*, if for some **p** both not **p** and *x* says that **p**, then *x* is guilty; so for all *x*, if *x* says that *x* is guilty, *x* is guilty.' Schematising we get:

'__says that . . .' fits '*f*__. . .'
'__is guilty' fits '*g*__'

So we have the sequent ⟨{'∀*x*(∃**p**(~**p** & *fx***p**) ⊃ *gx*)'}, '∀*x*(*fxgx* ⊃ *gx*)'⟩. However (L) does not QC-fit this sequent, because '*f*' in it has to be replaced not by a predicate making sentences out of subjects but by the connective '__says that . . .', which makes a sentence out of a subject and another sentence (Prior proposed to call these 'connecticates'); so proof of the sequent's validity would require an extension of TP in addition to a satisfactory interpretation of '∃**p**'. '__says that . . .' naturally raises the same problem of referential opacity as the predicates like '__says that . . . is a spy' which can be made out of it (see pp. 211-2).

The foregoing extensions of QC and PC prompt a number of further comments. (i) Obviously substitutional quantification could replace the standard ('objectual') kind within QC itself. The easiest change would restate the truth part of T∀ thus: ∀*v* followed by an open sentence in *v* is T in a QC-context and domain and world if and only if every sentence which results from the open sentence by putting a subject for *v* is T in them (cf. LEBLANC & WISDOM pp. 145, 151-4). As with higher-order substitutional quantification this destroys the point of the distinction between open sentences and schemata, and so between variables and schematic letters. Hence a further simplification would yield '$\forall a$ followed by a schema containing a free but not bound is T in a context and domain and world if and only if every sentence fitting the schema is T in them', together with a parallel change in F$\forall$. (ii) The question arises whether this substitutional interpretation assigns the same truth-condition to '$\forall$' as T$\forall$ did. It does not, because domains might be larger than languages in the sense that a language might fail to provide enough subjects for referring without equivocation to each member of a domain. Indeed some domains are larger in this sense that any language could be: for a domain may have more members, but a language cannot have more subjects, than there are natural numbers. Relative to such an 'uncountable' domain it might happen that all sentences fitting e.g. 'brown a' are T in some context and world, and so '$\forall x$ brown x' is T in them under the substitutional truth-condition, even though some members of the domain are not brown in that world; for the context might be one in which no subject can unequivocally refer to any of the non-brown members. But T$\forall$ assigns the opposite truth-value to '$\forall x$ brown x' in that context: there will be a sentence, e.g. 'brown Jim', which though T in the context is F in some other, differing from it only in that 'Jim' now refers outside the brown members of the domain. The kernel of this argument is: given an uncountable domain of discourse each member can be reached by a subject in some context, but not all in the same one (cf. QUINE *RPM* pp. 180–1, *PofL* pp. 91–3). On the other hand this divergence of truth-conditions for sentences does not affect the validity of formulae or sequents: the QC derivation rules remain sound and complete (for formulae and finite sequents) under the substitutional truth-condition (see VAN FRAASSEN pp. 127–32). (iii) In a version of QC permitting free variables a formula may be counted valid just when its '$\forall$'-closure is valid, and a formula may be counted consistent in the sense of 8.1 just when its '$\exists$'-closure is consistent in that sense. Higher-order quantification draws attention to this point, and might make one wonder why quantification is necessary at all. In a free-variable version of QC the argument 'If anything is true, it is reasonable; Christianity is true; so it is reasonable' could be counted an instance of $\langle \{`fx \supset gx\text{'}, `fa\text{'}\}, `ga\text{'} \rangle$, and the different argument 'if anything is true, everything is reasonable; Christianity is true; so it is reasonable' could be counted an instance of $\langle \{`fx \supset gy\text{'}, `fa\text{'}\},$

'*ga*'⟩. But consider 'If everything is true, everything is reasonable; Christianity is true; so it is reasonable'. Unlike the other two arguments, this one is incorrect; hence it cannot be an instance of either of the given sequents, which are valid in the proposed version of QC. Rather its first premiss instantiates '$\forall x fx \supset gy$', or in QC itself '$\forall x fx \supset \forall y gy$'. The resulting sequent corresponds to the QC-invalid formula '$(\forall x fx \supset \forall y gy) \,\&\, fa \supset ga$'. This formula is QC-equivalent to '$\forall x \exists y ((fx \supset gy) \,\&\, fa \supset ga)$', which is neither an '$\forall$'-closure nor an '$\exists$'-closure of '$(fx \supset gy) \,\&\, fa \supset ga$'. That is why explicit quantification is indispensable (see QUINE *MofL* pp. 236–7).

(M) For any non-negative integer n, if all less-than-nth *f*s are *g*s, then all nth *f*s are *g*s; so all *f*s are *g*s.

This is a formulation of the Principle of Strong Mathematical Induction which was used but not proved in earlier chapters. Here it is formulated as a schema; so to accept it is to accept that all its instances with a true premiss have a true conclusion, i.e. that it is valid (in this world, at least). As it stands the schema is not valid: we require the further assumption that the *f*s are 'well-ordered', which means, or at least entails and is entailed by, 'every *f* has nth rank, for some non-negative integer n'.

Here is an informal proof that the schema so fortified is valid. Since by the assumption each *f* has nth rank for some n, one or more of the *f*s will be least (e.g. oth) in rank; so vacuously all less than those will be *g*s; so by the premiss-schema all those will be *g*s. If there remain further *f*s, some by the assumption will rank next (e.g. 1st); but we have proved that all less than them are *g*s; so by the premiss-schema again all the second group will be *g*s. In this way the argument can reach every group of *f*s which have nth rank for any n; and by the well-ordering assumption these are all the *f*s.

Can the proof be formalised? I shall show how the methods of this book are able to deal with inference-schemata that weaken (M)'s conclusion into 'All *f*s *up to such and such a rank* are *g*s', and are able to deal with them, in principle, however high a rank is chosen. Each weakened schema constitutes an initial segment of (M), and each of the infinitely many initial segments can be validated. But we shall see that this is too little for a proof of the validity of (M) itself.

11.2 Beyond the methods of this book

The first initial segment of (M) is 'For any n, if all the less-than-nth fs are gs, so are all the nth; so all the *least* fs are gs'. (i) Finding the sequent. Rewording. 'Less-than-nth' means 'mth, for some m less than n'; 'least' means 'nth, for any n such that for no m m is less than n'. The force of the variables 'n' and 'm', which here range over non-negative integers, can be captured by the unrestricted QC variables 'x' and 'y' if we express the first segment relative to the domain of non-negative integers, thus: 'for all x, if for any y less than x all the yth fs are gs, then all the xth fs are gs; so for all x such that for no y y is less than x all the xth fs are gs'. Schematising. Component predicates and predicate-schemata fit schematic letters as follows:

'__is less than . . .' fits 'h__. . .'
'all the __ th fs are gs' fits 'i__'

So the inference-schema is expressible, relative to the domain of non-negative integers, in schemata QC-fitting 'For all x, if for all y such that hyx, iy, then ix; so for all x such that for no y hyx, ix'. Translating. By the QC-interpretation rules the inference-schema is QC-expressible, relative to the domain, in schemata QC-fitting '$\forall x(\forall y(hyx \supset iy) \supset ix)$; so $\forall x(\sim \exists y hyx \supset ix)$'. The corresponding sequent can be proved derivable as follows:

(M')
1	(1)	$\forall x(\forall y(hyx \supset iy) \supset ix)$		
1	(2)	$\forall y(hya \supset iy) \supset ia$		
3	(3)	$\sim \exists y hya$	A	
4	(4)	$hba \mathbin{\&} \sim ib$	A	
4	(5)	hba		
4	(6)	$\exists y hya$	$\exists$I	5
3,4	(7)	$\exists y hya \mathbin{\&} \sim \exists y hya$		
3	(8)	$\sim(hba \mathbin{\&} \sim ib)$		
3	(9)	$hba \supset ib$	Def $\supset$	8
3	(10)	$\forall y(hya \supset iy)$		
1,3	(11)	ia		
1	(12)	$\sim \exists y hya \supset ia$		
1	(13)	$\forall x(\sim \exists y hyx \supset ix)$		

This proves the validity of the first segment of (M). For the second segment we need a sequent with the same first formula, but ending

268   *Applications*

'$\forall x(\sim \exists y hyx \lor \forall z(hzx \supset \sim \exists y hyz) \supset ix)$', instantiated by the conclusion that for every n which is least or is such that every m less than it is least, all the nth fs are gs—i.e. all the least or next to least fs are gs. The derivability of this second sequent is proved by extending the previous derivation thus:

(M″)	15	(15)	$\sim \exists yhyc \lor \forall z(hzc \supset \sim \exists yhyz)$	A	
	1	(16)	$\sim \exists yhyc \supset ic$	∀E	13
	17	(17)	$\sim ic$	A	
	1,17	(18)	$\sim\sim \exists yhyc$	MTT	16,17
	1,15,17	(19)	$\forall z(hzc \supset \sim \exists yhyz)$	MTP	15,18
	1,15,17	(20)	$hac \supset \sim \exists yhya$		
	21	(21)	hac	A	
	1,15,17,21	(22)	$\sim \exists yhya$		
	1,15,17,21	(23)	ia	MPP-S	12,22
	1,15,17	(24)	$hac \supset ia$		
	1,15,17	(25)	$\forall y(hyc \supset iy)$		
	1	(26)	$\forall y(hyc \supset iy) \supset ic$	∀E	1
	1,15,17	(27)	ic		
	1,15,17	(28)	$ic \ \& \sim ic$	&I	17,28
	1,15	(29)	$\sim\sim ic$		
	1,15	(30)	ic		
	1	(31)	$\sim \exists yhyc \lor \forall z(hzc \supset \sim \exists yhyz) \supset ic$		
	1	(32)	$\forall x(\sim \exists yhyx \lor \forall z(hzx \supset \sim \exists yhyz) \supset ix)$		

A third segment could now be added, and so on indefinitely. These successive applications of **QC** prove that successively greater parts of the class of fs are gs: the least fs, the least or next to least, and so on. Because of the well-ordering assumption we know that were this process continued to infinity it would cover all the fs; even if there were infinitely many of them, all have an nth rank, for some n, and so rank least or next to least or . . . But the disjunction of ranks cannot, if it is infinite, be handled in a single sequent-derivation, or in a finite number of them. We should have to go through an infinite number of derivations, which is impossible. Thus the Principle of Strong Mathematical Induction cannot be proved valid by the finitary methods of this book; and the same goes for its Weaker brethren which I have not described (there is a good

11.2 Beyond the methods of this book

treatment of the Principles in THOMASON ch. 14; see also MASSEY ch. 22).

11.3 Fallacies

In logical parlance fallacies are not false propositions but incorrect arguments (*non sequiturs*) which seem to be correct; and fallacy is not falsity but incorrectness. This section investigates what logic can do towards exposing fallacy.

I remarked on p. 65 that proofs of incorrectness do not invoke the technical concept of validity, under which formulae and sequents rather than arguments are valid or invalid. This needs two qualifications. In the first place an argument can be proved incorrect by logical means if each of its premisses can be shown to instantiate a valid *formula* and its conclusion an inconsistent formula. For that establishes that the premisses are necessary truths and the conclusion a necessary falsehood, whence *a fortiori* the premisses are true and the conclusion untrue, whence the argument is incorrect. But, plainly, few fallacious arguments are so parlously fallacious as to be caught by this method: many will have combinations of truth-values—some untrue premisses, or a true conclusion—which are compatible with correctness and incorrectness alike; and even when the premisses are true and the conclusion untrue, those facts will rarely be necessary, and still more rarely provable by logical means.

The second qualification is this. It is perfectly true that invalidity of *sequents* does not *prove* fallacy, since even a deductively correct argument may instantiate an invalid sequent: indeed every argument, when expressed with a single, if necessary conjunctive, premiss, PC-instantiates the PC-invalid sequent $\langle\{`p`\}, `q`\rangle$. Nevertheless invalidity proofs are useful as a challenge, which goes: 'Are you not assuming, when you accept the correctness of such and such an argument, that it is correct because it has such and such a form, instantiates such and such a sequent? If so, your reason is bad; for the sequent is invalid, and so has some incorrect instances, of which your argument may be one' (see POLLOCK pp. 159–62).

Although I shall not give much attention to methods of proving invalidity, the possibility of this challenge makes it worthwhile to sketch two of them. One is the method of **counterexamples**. If a formula is to be proved invalid, we reason: it, like all formulae, is invalid if it has some untrue instance: so find an untrue proposition instantiating it. Similarly if a sequent is to be proved invalid, we reason: it, like all sequents, is invalid if it has some instance with true premises and an untrue conclusion; so find an argument which instantiates it and has that offending combination. It is best that the instances chosen should be plainly instances, and best that their truth-values, or those of their component premises and conclusions, should also be plain.

The other method of proving invalidity I shall mention is **truth-tabling**, which has already been described in 7.1 as a method of proving PC-validity. It works for PC-invalidity too, since a PC-formula is PC-invalid if its truth-table contains at least one row showing 'F' under the main connective (this relies on the mild assumption that for each finite subset of the propositional letters and for each permutation of 'T' and 'F' among them there is a PC-context and domain and world in which sentences—not necessarily distinct—PC-fitting those letters have truth-values in that permutation). For example this partial truth-table is enough to show the PC-invalidity of the PC-formula '$p \supset (q \supset \sim p)$':

p	q	$p \supset (q \supset \sim p)$
T	T	F F F
T	F	
F	T	
F	F	

Similarly a PC-sequent is PC-invalid if its truth-table contains at least one row showing 'F' under the main connective of its last formula and 'T' under those of all its others. There are alternative methods of proving invalidity, available in the other calculi as well (not 'effective' of course in QC and QS5), but they are needlessly cumbersome for our purposes.

Where correctness is doubted proofs of invalidity, by counter-example or truth-tables or otherwise, buttress a challenge to it but not a refutation. I now turn to a more powerful procedure. An argument is incorrect at least by deductive standards if its premises could all have been true without its conclusion being true; and this joint possibility—of true premises with an untrue conclusion—may sometimes be verified by deduction from another more evident possibility (see SMULLYAN pp. 79–86). Then logic can be used if necessary to check the deduction. The procedure for a proof of incorrectness is therefore as follows: set out the premisses of the suspect argument and conjoin them with the negation of its conclusion. Then find some set x of propositions which is evidently possible, i.e. whose members could evidently have been true together; and demonstrate that x entails the conjunction. If need be, check the demonstration by logical means. Next, using the metalogical principle (which I am content merely to assert, but cf. Dist$\diamond$) that what is entailed by a possibility is itself possible, infer that the conjunction of the argument's premisses with the negation of its conclusion is itself possible, whence the premisses could all have been true though the conclusion was untrue, whence the argument is deductively incorrect. I append three comments on this proof procedure. Its kernel is the proof that the conjunction of some argument's premisses with the negation of its conclusion is entailed by some set x of propositions, in the limiting case by that conjunction itself. Let us call the propositions in this set the **rebutting propositions**, and the entailment the **rebutting argument**. Then the plan is to prove one argument deductively incorrect by proving another, rebutting, argument deductively correct. Secondly, rebuttal does not prove incorrectness, but only deductive incorrectness. Thirdly, it has to be assumed in each proof that the rebutting propositions *are* jointly possible. For the latter two reasons there is still an element of challenge in the rebuttal method: it is always open to an argument's champion to respond that deductive standards are inappropriately strict, or that what seemed possible to the challenger is not really possible (SMULLYAN p. 84).

I now turn to illustrations of these methods.

(N) If you take Prose composition without understanding Quintilian, you will not appreciate Roman oratory; unless you take Prose composition, you will not understand Quintilian; so you will appreciate Roman oratory only if you understand Quintilian.

We can attack this by the method of challenge as follows. (i) Finding a sequent. After some rewording (N) schematises into 'If p without its being the case that q, then not r; unless p, not q; so r only if q'.

272 *Applications*

'p without its being the case that q' translates into '$p \;\&\; \sim q$', 'unless p, not q' into '$\sim p \supset \sim q$', and 'r only if q' into '$r \supset q$'. So (N) is a PC-instance of the sequent $\langle\{\text{'}p \;\&\; \sim q \supset \sim r\text{'},$ '$\sim p \supset \sim q$'}, '$r \supset q$'$\rangle$. (ii) Proving invalidity.

p	q	r	$p \;\&\; \sim q \supset \sim r$	$\sim p \supset \sim q$	$r \supset q$
T	T	T			T
T	T	F			T
T	F	T	T T F F		F
T	F	F			T
F	T	T			T
F	T	F			T
F	F	T	F T T F	T T T	F
F	F	F			T

There is no need to fill in more of the table. The column for the last formula shows that an invalidating row, if there is one, must be row 3 or row 7; and the column for the first formula shows that it cannot be row 3. Row 7 discovers it. Testing for invalidity is useful here: one might have thought that the sequent was PC-valid and thence inferred that (N) was correct.

Yet (N) is not proved incorrect by this method. Suppose then that the challenge gets rejected: '(N) is correct in spite of PC-instantiating that PC-invalid sequent'. We can use the invalidity proof as a basis for finding a rebutting argument, as follows. First, reexpress (N) with PC connectives and dummy letters:

(N') $P \;\&\; \sim Q \supset \sim R$; $\sim P \supset \sim Q$; so $R \supset Q$

where 'P' abbreviates the sentence 'You will take Prose composition', 'Q' 'You will understand Quintilian' and 'R' 'You will appreciate Roman oratory'. Then the truth-table reveals that in any PC-context and domain and world the premiss sentences of (N') will be T and the conclusion-sentence F if 'P' and 'Q' are F and 'R' is T— hence if '$\sim P$', '$\sim Q$' and 'R' are all T. An adequate rebutting argument is therefore

(N") $\sim P$; $\sim Q$; R; so $(P \;\&\; \sim Q \supset \sim R) \;\&\; (\sim P \supset \sim Q) \;\&\; \sim (R \supset Q)$

11.3 Fallacies

That (N″) is correct is now sufficiently assured (but it could easily be checked by the methods illustrated in 11.1). Furthermore—and this is the vital extra that converts the challenge into a rebuttal—it is evident that the propositions expressed in '$\sim P$', '$\sim Q$' and 'R' are jointly possible. Hence the conclusion of (N″) is possible; hence (N) is deductively incorrect.

(O) 'In the observable world we discover an order of efficient causes, but no case is found, or ever could be found, of something efficiently causing itself . . . Now it is impossible to go on for ever in a series of efficient causes. For in every ordered series of efficient causes the first member of the series causes the intermediate member or members, which in turn cause the final member. If you eliminate a cause you eliminate its effect, so there will not be final or intermediate members in the series unless there is a first member . . . Therefore it is necessary to posit some first efficient cause, to which everyone gives the name "God" ' (AQUINAS, *ST* pars prima, qu. 2 art. 3, translated in KENNY, p. 34).

The argument seems to contain three premisses: (1) something causes something, i.e. there are causes; (2) nothing causes itself, i.e. causation is irreflexive; (3) if one thing (the 'first') causes another (the 'intermediate') and that causes a third (the 'final' or another intermediate), then the first causes the third, i.e. causation is transitive. Aquinas concludes that (4) something is an uncaused cause, i.e. causes something but is caused by nothing. A relation which is irreflexive and transitive is a 'partial ordering' relation in the sense of MENDELSON p. 170. The argument is incorrect if it is possible that everything should have a cause even though causation is a partial ordering relation. But I do not know how to demonstrate this possibility from another that is more evident. So we have to fall back on the method of challenge. Aquinas seems to be relying, in effect, on the QC-validity of the sequent $\langle \{$'$\exists x \exists y fxy$', '$\forall x \sim fxx$', '$\forall x \forall y \forall z (fxy \& fyz \supset fxz)$'$\}$, '$\exists x (\exists y fxy \& \sim \exists z fzx)$'$\rangle$. Yet that sequent is QC-invalid, as can be proved by counterexample, i.e. by finding another argument QC-instantiating it which has plainly true premisses and a plainly untrue conclusion. The argument that I choose as counterexample is one which can be expressed relative to the domain of non-negative integers thus: 'Some are greater than others; none is greater than itself; if one is greater than another and that than a third, the first is greater than the third; so some is greater than another but has none greater than itself (i.e. there is a greatest number)'. This proves the sequent's invalidity. But it is worth reiterating that (O) might be correct for all that: one is asked to regard the 'greater' relation, in the counterexample, as analogous to the causal relation, but there are no correct *arguments* from analogy. I append two comments. First, notice that the chosen counterexample has an infinite domain. This is necessary: the sequent is valid in every finite domain. Aquinas tries to ward off such counterexamples by proving as an intermediate conclusion that the domain of causes is finite: 'It is impossible to go on for ever in a series of efficient causes.' But the subsidiary argument fails because it "uses an equivocation between 'first = earlier' and 'first = unpreceded' to show that this series cannot be an infinite one" (KENNY p. 44). The second point is that Aquinas' conclusion, as I have interpreted it, hardly seems to justify theism, for which we should surely want 'Something causes *everything* except itself'. Even in a finite domain this will not follow without the extra premiss that one out of every pair of things causes the other, QC-instantiating '$\forall x \forall y (x \neq y \supset fxy \lor fyx)$'. The extra premiss makes causation out to be 'connected'; and a relation which is irreflexive, transitive and connected is a 'total ordering' relation in the sense of MENDELSON p. 170. It might seem, furthermore, that even the strengthened conclusion is short of monotheism, which should assert that *just one* thing causes everything except itself. But in fact this 'monotheist' thesis follows from the 'theist' one, given that the causal relation is at least a partial ordering; for the sequent $\langle \{$'$\forall x \sim fxx$', '$\forall x \forall y \forall z (fxy \ \& \ fyz \supset fxz)$', '$\exists x \forall y (x \neq y \supset fxy)$'$\}$, '$\exists x (\forall y (x \neq y \supset fxy) \ \& \ \forall z (\forall y (z \neq y \supset fzy) \supset z = x))$'$\rangle$ is QC-valid.

(P) 'I will not here trouble my self to prove that all Terms are not definable, from that Progress *in infinitum* which it will visibly lead us into, if we should allow that all Names could be defined. For if the Terms of one Definition were still to be defined by another, where at last should we stop?' (LOCKE, III iv 5).

11.3 *Fallacies*

In spite of the disclaimer Locke does offer a proof in his second sentence. It goes like this: suppose we try to define all terms; then we shall never get to an end (presumably we shall go round in an endless circle); so it is not possible that all terms should be defined; so not all terms are definable. The proof commits a fallacy in its last step, where Locke argues from 'It cannot be that all terms are defined' to 'Some terms cannot be defined'. Adequate rebutting propositions are: there are just two terms, each synonymous with the other; definition is possible by synonym, but in no other way; circular definition is impossible. These propositions entail that while all terms are capable of definition, it cannot be that all are defined. The propositions are possible. So what they entail is possible. So Locke's argument is incorrect. Here as in (N) we have a less evident possibility entailed by a (slightly) more evident one, only here there is little need to check the entailment by logical means. Once more the method of challenge is a useful alternative. Locke seems to be relying on the fact that his argument is a $QS5$-instance, relative to the domain of terms, of the sequent $\langle \{`\sim \Diamond \forall x fx'\}, `\exists x \sim \Diamond fx' \rangle$. The sequent can be proved $QS5$-invalid by this counterexample, due I think to Ryle: 'It is not possible that I should die on every day of the week; so there is some day of the week on which it is not possible that I should die.' Since the sequent's second formula is $QS5$-equivalent to '$\sim \forall x \Diamond fx$', the two of them differ, in effect, in the relative scope of '$\forall$' and '$\Diamond$'. For this ageless error see pp. 154, 204, and GEACH *LM* 1.1 especially pp. 4–5.

(Q) 'The name has to guarantee the existence of its object, in the sense that the failure of the object to exist deprives the name of significant use. But this entails that the object which a name denotes cannot be physical, since, on any tenable theory of perception, it is at least conceivable that the physical object which we suppose our demonstrative symbol to be indicating should not exist' (AYER *RM* p. 44).

Ayer is reporting, and apparently endorsing, an argument of Russell's. Its premisses are (1) 'Necessarily if a name names anything (has significant use), that thing exists' and (2) 'No physical thing exists of necessity'; its conclusion is (3) 'No physical thing has a name'. So the argument is deductively incorrect if it is jointly possible that some physical thing should have a name even though none need have existed and nothing could have had a name without existing. I do not see a more evident possibility from which to deduce this one. Nor am I sure that this is a possibility. For arguably (Q)'s first premiss is false (see p. 200); and if it is false it is impossible (by argument parallel to 'If ⌜necessarily σ⌝ is T, it is Nec', p. 228); and if (Q) contains an impossible premiss, it is deductively correct (see p. 30). On the other hand there is no comfort for Ayer in securing correctness at the price of a false premiss, and we can surely say that under the supposition of true premisses the possibility cited does obtain. Turning to the method of challenge, let (Q) be schematised as follows:

'___has a name' fits 'f___'
'___exists' fits 'g___'
'___is a physical thing' fits 'h___'.

Then the argument is a QC-instance of $\langle \{ `\Box \forall x(fx \supset gx)', `\sim \exists x(hx \& \Box gx)'\}, `\sim \exists x(hx \& fx)' \rangle$. Ayer seems to be relying on the QS5-validity of this sequent; but it is QS5-invalid, as the following counterexample shows: 'Necessarily if anyone is married to a person, that person is alive; no mortal person is necessarily alive; so no mortal person has anyone married to him.' The fallacy in (Q) is again a fallacy of scope, due to confusion between '$\Box \forall x(fx \supset gx)$' and '$\forall x(fx \supset \Box gx)$'. I do not think there is any doubt that Ayer's first premiss is an instance of the former; but only the latter would yield a QS5-valid sequent. Commenting on the original of Ayer's argument Geach has written "Russell's transition from 'A genuine proper name must name something' to 'Only a name that must name something is a proper name' is of course just a howler in modal logic; here he paid dearly for his lifelong neglect of the subject" (GEACH *LM* p. 155).

There is just the same howler in the transition from 'What is known must be true' to 'Only what must be true is known', and essentially the same one in the following simple anti-libertarian argument (many anti-liberterian arguments are as simple):

(R) He can't jump off the diving board unless he's courageous; he's not courageous; so he can't jump off the diving board.

11.3 Fallacies

This apparently relies on $\langle\{`\sim\Diamond(p\ \&\ \sim q)\text{'},\ `\sim q\text{'}\},\ `\sim\Diamond p\text{'}\rangle$ which is S5-invalid. From the given premisses all that follows is that he won't jump off the diving board, not that he can't. To get the conclusion asserted we should need to strengthen either the first premiss into 'he can't be (or isn't) *capable* of jumping off unless he's courageous' or the second premiss into 'He can't be courageous'. Actually it is an oversimplification to treat (R) as an S5-instance since its possibility is human, not absolute (p. 29). But whatever variant interpretation of '$\Diamond$' may be required to fit the human case it seems unlikely that the sequent thus instantiated would turn out valid under that interpretation. For if the interpretation keeps the PC truth-conditions and Def$\Diamond$, the sequent will still be valid under it only if $\langle\{`\sim\sim\Box(p\supset q)\text{'},\ `\sim q\text{'}\},\ `\sim\sim\Box\sim p\text{'}\rangle$ and so $\langle\{`\Box(\sim q\supset\sim p)\text{'}\},\ `\sim q\supset\Box\sim p\text{'}\rangle$ are. And even if this latter is valid in some other modal calculus than S5, at least it can be shown that $\langle\{`\Box(q\supset p)\text{'},\ `q\supset\Box p\text{'}\rangle$, of which it is a substituend, is not valid in any modal calculus which (a) is an extension of PC, (b) contains '$\Box(p\supset p)$' as valid and (c) contains '$\Box p\supset p$' as valid. For suppose it were valid in such a calculus. Then so also would be its substituend $\langle\{`\Box(p\supset p)\text{'}\},\ `p\supset\Box p\text{'}\rangle$, and thence by (b) $\langle\varLambda,\ `p\supset\Box p\text{'}\rangle$ and thence by (c) $\langle\varLambda,\ `p\equiv\Box p\text{'}\rangle$. So '$p$' and '$\Box p$' would be equivalent. But then '$\Box$' would do no work (there would be only one possible world), and the calculus would collapse into PC, contrary to (a) (HUGHES & CRESSWELL, p. 59). This is the price of confounding '$\Box(p\supset q)$', *necessitas consequentiae*, with '$p\supset\Box q$', *necessitas consequentis*.

(S) '(A3) Any Form can be predicated of itself. Largeness is large. F-ness is F.... (A4) If anything has a certain character, it cannot be identical with the Form in virtue of which we apprehend that character. If x is F, x cannot be identical with F-ness.... Substituting F-ness for x in (A4), we get: (A5) If F-ness is F, F-ness cannot be identical with F-ness. And since the consequent of (A5) is plainly false, because self-contradictory, at least one of the premisses from which it follows—(A3), (A4)—must be false' (VLASTOS *TMA* pp. 236–8).

The error here lies in Vlastos' double statement of (A4), which he calls the Nonidentity Assumption and which, like the Self-Predication Assumption (A3), he believes to have been in Plato's mind when Plato constructed the so-called Third Man argument against the unicity of Forms. Though Plato's argument concerns the Form Largeness it is evidently intended to be taken generally, and Vlastos seeks to make that generality explicit. In the first version of (A4) this work of generalising is done by 'anything' and 'character'. In the second version 'anything' is replaced by 'x', intended perhaps as a variable with universal quantification elided, and 'character' is replaced by 'F' intended as a schematic letter. What emerges is therefore a schema, not itself assessable as true or false, but conveying the claim that every sentence fitting it is true. Such introduction of symbols, whether schematic letters or variables, is of course a neat device for conveying generality, and one not confined to philosophical usage. But it can lead astray, and has done here, as a step by step translation from Vlastos' first version will show. Schematising that version and adding variables we get 'If anything x is F, x cannot be identical with the Form in virtue of which we apprehend x as F'. The phrase beginning 'the Form in virtue of which' is what might be called an open subject-schema constructed by means of a variable 'x' out of the functor-schema 'the Form in virtue of which we apprehend—as F'. Vlastos contracts this open subject-schema to 'F-ness', but that suppresses 'x': he should have had 'x's F-ness' (compare VLASTOS *TMA* p. 237 "If Largeness is large, then its Largeness cannot be identical with itself"). His argument is that (A4) and (A3) together generate a contradiction, and so are inconsistent with one another. But the contradiction disappears after this necessary revision of (A4). For what follows from it is not (A5) but 'If a thing's F-ness is F, its F-ness cannot be identical with its F-ness's F-ness', whose consequent is not self-contradictory. (The point was made in various critiques of VLASTOS *TMA*, and acknowledged in VLASTOS *TL* note 39.)

(S) reminds us that metalogical argument is itself not immune to logical error. Much of the metalogical argument in the present book is complex enough to risk such error. Some of it could be checked by the book's own methods, and some of the checks, assuming that their outcome is favourable, could prove that I have argued correctly—but only, of course, if the proof does not beg the question, by relying on what it seeks to vindicate. Equally, my arguments are open to the kind of challenge described in this final section.

APPENDIX ONE

Variant Notations

SCHEMATIC OR DUMMY LETTERS AND VARIABLES

	propositional letters	predicate letters	subject letters	variables
this book	$p, q, r \ldots$	$f, g, h \ldots$	$a, b, c \ldots$	$x, y, z \ldots$
QUINE *MofL* and MASSEY	$p, q, r \ldots$	$F, G, H \ldots$	none	$x, y, z \ldots$
LEMMON *BL*	$P, Q, R \ldots$	$F, G, H \ldots$	$a, b, c \ldots$ $m, n, o \ldots$	$x, y, z \ldots$
HUGHES & LONDEY	p, q, r $\ldots$	f, g, h $\ldots$	none	x, y, z $\ldots$
MATES	$A, B, C \ldots$	$A, B, C \ldots$	$a, b, c \ldots$	$x, y, z \ldots$

CONNECTIVES

The tables show variant connectives, but the letters here combined with them are all in the style of this book. The first table gives propositional connectives, the second the rest.

this book	$\sim p$	$p \& q$	$p \vee q$	$p \supset q$	$p \equiv q$
QUINE *MofL*	$\bar{p}$	pq	$p \vee q$	$p \supset q$	$p \equiv q$
LEMMON *BL* and MATES	$-p$	$p \& q$	$p \vee q$	$p \rightarrow q$	$p \leftrightarrow q$
HUGHES & LONDEY and MASSEY	$\sim p$	$p \cdot q$	$p \vee q$	$p \supset q$	$p \equiv q$
others	$\neg p$	$p \wedge q$			
Polish	Np	Kpq	Apq	Cpq	Epq

this book	$a = b$	$\forall x$	$\exists x$	$\Box p$	$\Diamond p$
QUINE *MofL* and MATES	$a = b$	(x)	$(\exists x)$		
LEMMON *BL*	$(a = b)$	(x)	$(\exists x)$		
HUGHES & LONDEY	$(a = b)$	Ux	$\exists x$		
MASSEY	$(a = b)$	(x)	$(\exists x)$	$\Box p$	$\Diamond p$
others		$\wedge x$	$\vee x$ Ex	Np	
Polish	Iab	Πx	Σx	Lp	Mp

Bibliography

There are many good books on elementary logic: see for example the bibliographies in MATES, HUGHES & LONDEY, and (with valuable comments) LEMMON *BL*. For a comprehensive list see *A Bibliography of Logic Books* by Michael Moss and Dana Scott, published by the Sub-faculty of Philosophy, 10 Merton Street, Oxford, July 1975. The list given here contains only books and articles cited in the text.

Abbreviations:

AE	*The Works of Aristotle translated into English*, Oxford University Press.
APQ	*American Philosophical Quarterly*
CRLT	*Contemporary Readings in Logical Theory*, edd. I. M. Copi and J. A. Gould, Macmillan 1967.
IandI	*Identity and Individuation*, ed. M. K. Munitz, New York University Press 1971.
LLP	*Logico-Linguistic Papers*, P. F. Strawson, Methuen 1971.
PAS	*Proceedings of the Aristotelian Society*.
PR	*Philosophical Review*
RandM	*Reference and Modality*, ed. L. Linsky, Oxford University Press 1971.
WofP	*The Ways of Paradox and other essays*, W. V. Quine, Random House 1966.

Where an entry in the bibliography mentions more than one source, page references in the text are to the first source listed.

ACKERMANN, R. J.: *Modern Deductive Logic*, Macmillan 1970.

ANDERSON, A. R.: 'An intensional interpretation of truth-values' in *Mind* 1972 pp. 348–71.

AQUINAS, ST. THOMAS, *ST*: *Summa Theologica*, Leonine edition, vol. 4, Rome 1888.

ARISTOTLE, *An. Pr.*: *Analytica Priora*, in *Aristotelis Analytica*, Oxford University Press 1964; translated in *AE* vol. 1, 1928.
— *De Int.*: *De Interpretatione*, in *Aristotelis Categoriae et Liber De Interpretatione*, Oxford University Press 1949; translated in *Aristotle's Categories and De Interpretatione* by J. L. Ackrill, Oxford University Press, 1963; also translated in *AE* vol. 1, 1928.
— *EN*: *Ethica Nicomachea*, Oxford University Press 1894; translated in *AE* vol. 9, 1925.
— *Soph. El.*: *Sophistici Elenchi*, in *Aristotelis Topica et Sophistici Elenchi*, Oxford University Press 1958; translated in *AE* vol. 1, 1928.
— *Top.*: *Topica*, references as for previous entry.
AUSTIN, J. L.: *How to Do Things with Words*, ed. J. O. Urmson, Oxford University Press 1962.
AYER, A. J., *PofK*: *The Problem of Knowledge*, Penguin 1956.
— *RM*: *Russell and Moore, the analytical heritage*, Macmillan 1971.
BARCAN, R. C. (MRS MARCUS): 'A functional calculus of first order based on strict implication' in *Journal of Symbolic Logic* 1946 pp. 1-16.
BARNES, JONATHAN: *The Ontological Argument*, Macmillan 1972.
BENNETT, JONATHAN: 'Entailment' in *PR* 1969 pp. 197-236.
BERKELEY, G.: 1st Draft of Introduction to the *Principles of Human Knowledge*, in *The Works of George Berkeley*, edd. A. A. Luce and T. E. Jessop, vol. 2, Nelson 1949; the draft was written in 1708.
BOCHENSKI, I. M.: *Ancient Formal Logic*, North-Holland 1957.
BURIDAN, JOHN: *Sophismata*, translated as *Sophisms on Meaning and Truth* by T. K. Scott, Appleton-Century-Crofts 1966.
CARNAP, RUDOLF: *Meaning and Necessity*, University of Chicago Press, 2nd edition 1956.
CARTWRIGHT, RICHARD, *I&S*: 'Identity and substitutivity' in *IandI*.
— *Prop*: 'Propositions' in *Analytical Philosophy* (1st series), ed. R. J. Butler, Blackwell 1962.
CHESTERTON, G. K.: 'The absence of Mr Glass' in *The Wisdom of Father Brown*, Tauchnitz 1928; first published 1913.
CHISHOLM, R. M.: 'Problems of identity' in *IandI*.
CHURCH, ALONZO: *Introduction to Mathematical Logic*, vol. 1, Princeton University Press, 2nd edition 1956.
COHEN, L. J.: *The Diversity of Meaning*, Methuen 1962.
COPI, I. M.: *Symbolic Logic*, Macmillan, 4th edition 1973.

DAVIDSON, DONALD, *DCT*: 'In defense of Convention T' in *Truth, Syntax and Modality*, ed. Hugues Leblanc, North-Holland 1973.
— *T&M*: 'Truth and meaning' in *Philosophical Logic*, edd. J. W. Davis, D. J. Hockney, and W. K. Wilson, Reidel 1969; reprinted from *Synthese* 1967 pp. 304-33.
DESCARTES, R.: *Meditationes de Prima Philosophia*, in *Oeuvres de Descartes*, edd. C. Adam and P. Tannery, vol. 7, Cerf 1904; translated in *The Philosophical Works of Descartes* by Elizabeth S. Haldane and G. R. T. Ross, vol. 1, Cambridge University Press 1911.
DONNELLAN, KEITH: 'Reference and definite descriptions' in *PR* 1966 pp. 281-304.
DUMMETT, MICHAEL: *Frege: Philosophy of Language*, Duckworth 1973.
FITCH, F. B.: *Symbolic Logic*, Ronald 1952.
VAN FRAASSEN, B. C.: *Formal Semantics and Logic*, Macmillan 1971.
FREGE, GOTTLOB, *BS*: *Begriffsschrift*, part of chapter 1 translated in *Philosophical Writings of Gottlob Frege* by P. T. Geach and M. Black, Blackwell 1952; the whole work translated in *From Frege to Gödel*, ed. J. van Heijenoort, Harvard University Press 1970; and in *Conceptual Notation*, by T. W. Bynum, Oxford University Press 1972; first published 1879.
— *GL*: *Die Grundlagen der Arithmetik: eine logisch-mathematische Untersuchung über den Begriff der Zahl*, reprinted with translation by J. L. Austin as *The Foundations of Arithmetic*, Blackwell, 2nd edition 1953; first published 1884.
— *SuB*: 'Über Sinn und Bedeutung', translated as 'On sense and reference' in *Philosophical Writings of Gottlob Frege* by P. T. Geach and M. Black, Blackwell 1952; also translated as 'On sense and nominatum' in *Readings in Philosophical Analysis*, edd. H. Feigl and W. Sellars, Appleton–Century–Crofts 1949; the latter translation reprinted in *CRLT*; originally in *Zeitschrift für Philosophie und philosophische Kritik* 1892 pp. 25-50.
FURTH, MONTGOMERY: 'Two types of denotation' in *Studies in Logical Theory*, *APQ* monograph no. 2, Blackwell 1968.
GEACH, P. T., *LM*: *Logic Matters*, Blackwell 1972.
— *R&G*: *Reference and Generality*, Cornell University Press 1962.
GENTZEN, GERHARD: 'Untersuchungen über das logische Schliessen', translated as 'Investigations into logical deduction' by M. E.

Szabo, *APQ* 1964 pp. 288–306; originally in *Mathematische Zeitschrift* 1935 pp. 176–221.

GRICE, H. P., *CTP*: 'The causal theory of perception' in *The Philosophy of Perception*, ed. G. J. Warnock, Oxford University Press 1967; reprinted from *PAS* supplementary volume 1961 pp. 121–68; also in *Perceiving, Sensing, and Knowing*, ed. R. J. Swartz, Doubleday 1965.

— *VN*: 'Vacuous names' in *Words and Objections*, edd. D. Davidson and J. Hintikka, Reidel 1969.

HAACK, SUSAN: *Deviant Logic*, Cambridge University Press 1974.

HAMBLIN, C. L.: *Fallacies*, Methuen 1970.

HARTSHORNE, C.: *The Logic of Perfection*, Open Court 1962.

HINTIKKA, JAAKKO: 'The modes of modality' in *Acta Philosophica Fennica* 1963 pp. 65–82.

HUGHES, G. E. & CRESSWELL, M. J.: *An Introduction to Modal Logic*, Methuen 1968.

HUGHES, G. E. & LONDEY, D. G.: *The Elements of Formal Logic*, Methuen 1965.

HUNTER, GEOFFREY: *Metalogic*, Macmillan 1971.

JESPERSEN, O.: *The Philosophy of Grammar*, Allen & Unwin 1924.

JOSEPH, H. W. B.: *An Introduction to Logic*, Oxford University Press, 2nd edition 1916.

KANT, I., *C*: *Critik der reinen Vernunft*, translated as *Critique of Pure Reason* by N. Kemp Smith, Macmillan, revised edition 1933; first published 1781.

— *L*: *Logik*, partly translated as *Kant's Introduction to Logic* by T. K. Abbott, Longmans 1885; first published 1800.

KENNY, ANTHONY: *The Five Ways*, Routledge 1969.

KIRWAN, CHRISTOPHER: 'How strong are the objections to essence?' in *PAS* 1970–1 pp. 43–59.

KNEALE, WILLIAM, *I&I*: 'Intentionality and intensionality' in *PAS* supplementary volume 1968 pp. 73–90.

KNEALE, W. & M.: *The Development of Logic*, Oxford University Press 1962.

KRIPKE, SAUL, *I&N*: 'Identity and Necessity' in *IandI*.

— *N&N*: 'Naming and necessity' in *Semantics of Natural Language*, edd. D. Davidson and G. Harman, Reidel 1972.

— *SC*: 'Semantical considerations on modal logic' in *RandM*; reprinted from *Acta Philosophica Fennica* 1963 pp. 83–94.

LAMBERT, K. & VAN FRAASSEN, B. C.: *Derivation and Counterexample*, Dickenson 1972.
LEBLANC, H.: *Techniques of Deductive Inference*, Prentice-Hall 1966.
LEBLANC, H. & WISDOM, W.: *Deductive Logic*, Allyn 1971.
LEMMON, E. J., *BL*: *Beginning Logic*, Nelson 1965.
— *IAST*: *Introduction to Axiomatic Set Theory*, Routledge 1968.
— *ML*: 'Is there only one correct system of modal logic?' in *PAS* supplementary volume 1959 pp. 23-40.
— *SSP*: 'Sentences, statements and propositions' in *British Analytical Philosophy*, edd. B. Williams and A. Montefiore, Routledge 1966.
LEWIS, C. I. & LANGFORD, C. H.: *Symbolic Logic*, Dover, 2nd edition 1959.
LEWIS, DAVID: *Counterfactuals*, Blackwell 1973.
LOAR, BRIAN: 'Reference and propositional attitudes' in *PR* 1972 pp. 43-62.
LOCKE, J.: *An Essay concerning Human Understanding*, edited by P. H. Nidditch, Oxford University Press 1975; first published 1690.
MCDOWELL, JOHN: *Plato's Theaetetus*, Oxford University Press 1973.
MACKIE, J. L.: *Truth, Probability and Paradox*, Oxford University Press 1973.
MASSEY, G. J.: *Understanding Symbolic Logic*, Harper & Row 1970.
MATES, BENSON: *Elementary Logic*, Oxford University Press, 2nd edition 1972.
MENDELSON, ELLIOTT: *Introduction to Mathematical Logic*, van Nostrand 1964.
MILL, J. S.: *A System of Logic, ratiocinative and inductive*, Longmans, 6th edition 1865; first published 1843.
PARSONS, TERENCE: 'Essentialism and quantified modal logic' in *RandM*; reprinted from *PR* 1969 pp. 35-52.
PERRY, JOHN: 'The same F' in *PR* 1970 pp. 181-200.
PETER OF SPAIN (PETRUS HISPANUS, POPE JOHN XX OR XXI): *Summulae Logicales* ed. I. M. Bochenski, Marietti 1947.
PLANTINGA, ALVIN: *The Nature of Necessity*, Oxford University Press 1974.
PLATO: *Theaetetus*, in *Platonis Opera*, vol. 1, Oxford University Press 1900; translated in MCDOWELL.

POLLOCK, J. L.: *An Introduction to Symbolic Logic*, Holt, Rinehart & Winston 1969.
PORTE, JEAN: 'Schemas pour le calcul des propositions fondé sur le conjonction et la négation' in *Journal of Symbolic Logic* 1958 pp. 421–31.
PRIOR, A. N., *FL*: *Formal Logic*, Oxford University Press, 2nd edition 1962.
— *I&I*: 'Intentionality and intensionality' in *PAS* supplementary volume 1968 pp. 91–106.
— *OT*: *Objects of Thought*, Oxford University Press 1971.
— *PPF*: *Past, Present and Future*, Oxford University Press 1967.
— *PTP*: 'The possibly-true and the possible' in *Mind* 1969 pp. 481–92.
QUINE, W. V., *E&Q*: 'Existence and quantification' in *Ontological Relativity and other essays*, Columbia University Press 1969; also in *Fact and Existence*, ed. Joseph Margolis, Blackwell 1969.
— *MofL*: *Methods of Logic*, Routledge, 3rd edition 1974.
— *ML*: *Mathematical Logic*, Harvard University Press, 2nd edition 1951.
— *Paradox*: 'The ways of paradox' in *WofP*.
— *PofL*: *Philosophy of Logic*, Prentice-Hall 1970.
— *QPA*: 'Quantifiers and Propositional Attitudes' in *WofP*; reprinted from *Journal of Philosophy* 1956 pp. 177–87; also in *RandM*.
— *R&M*: 'Reference and modality' in *From a Logical Point of View*, Harvard University Press, 2nd edition 1961; reprinted in *RandM*.
— *RPM*: 'Reply to Professor Marcus' in *WofP*; reprinted from *Synthese* 1961 pp. 323–30; also in *CRLT*.
— *W&O*: *Word and Object*, Technology Press and Wiley 1960.
— *2 Dogmas*: 'Two dogmas of empiricism' in *PR* 1951 pp. 20–43; reprinted in *From a Logical Point of View*, Harvard University Press, 2nd edition 1961.
— *3 Grades*: 'Three grades of modal involvement' in *WofP*.
QUINTON, A. M.: *The Nature of Things*, Routledge 1973.
ROSSER, J. B.: *Logic for Mathematicians*, McGraw 1953.
ROUTLEY, R.: 'Some things do not exist' in *Notre Dame Journal of Formal Logic* 1966 pp. 251–76.
RUSSELL, BERTRAND, *IMP*: *Introduction to Mathematical Philosophy*, Allen & Unwin 1919.

— MPD: *My Philosophical Development*, Allen & Unwin 1959.
— OD: 'On denoting' in *Logic and Knowledge*, ed. R. C. Marsh, Allen & Unwin 1956; reprinted from *Mind* 1905 pp. 479–93; also in *CRLT*.
RYLE, GILBERT: 'Systematically misleading expressions' in *Logic and Language* (1st series), ed. A. G. N. Flew, Blackwell 1951; reprinted from *PAS* 1931–32 pp. 139–70.
SEARLE, J. R.: *Speech Acts*, Cambridge University Press 1970.
SMULLYAN, A.: *Fundamentals of Logic*, Prentice-Hall 1962.
STEVENSON, C. L.: 'If-iculties' in *Logic and Art*, edd. R. Rudner and I. Scheffler, Bobbs-Merrill 1972.
STRAWSON, P. F., *Cat.*: 'Categories' in *Ryle, a collection of critical essays*, edd. O. P. Wood and G. Pitcher, Doubleday 1970.
— ILT: *Introduction to Logical Theory*, Methuen 1952.
— Ind: *Individuals*, Methuen 1959.
— IRT: 'Identifying reference and truth-values' in *LLP*: reprinted from *Theoria* 1964 pp. 96–118.
— OR: 'On referring' in *LLP*; reprinted from *Mind* 1950 pp. 320–44; also in *CRLT*.
— SPLG: *Subject and Predicate in Logic and Grammar*, Methuen 1974.
SUPPES, PATRICK: *Introduction to Logic*, van Nostrand 1957.
THOMASON, R. H.: *Symbolic Logic*, Macmillan 1970.
URMSON, J. O.: 'Criteria of intensionality' in *PAS* supplementary volume 1968 pp. 107–22.
VLASTOS, GREGORY, *TL*: 'Plato's third man argument, text and logic' in *Philosophical Quarterly* 1969 pp. 289–301.
— TMA: 'The third man argument in the Parmenides' in *Studies in Plato's Metaphysics*, ed. R. E. Allen, Routledge 1965; reprinted from *PR* 1954 pp. 319–49.
WHITE, A. R.: *Modal Thinking*, Blackwell 1975.
WHITEHEAD, A. N. & RUSSELL, BERTRAND: *Principia Mathematica*, Cambridge University Press, 2nd edition 1927; partly reprinted as *Principia Mathematica to *56*, Cambridge University Press 1962.
WOODS, JOHN: *The Logic of Fiction*, Mouton 1974.

Index

Primitive rules are not listed; see Appendix Two.

abridged derivation, 135–7, 155–8, 160–1
accessible world, 228–30, 241
Ackermann, R. J., 194, 205
'all', 8, 214–15
alternation, 104
alternative world, 228, *and see* accessible world
ambiguity, 48, 201, 224; of linkage, 5–6, 72, 78, 202; metalogical, 102, 112; of scope, 78–80, 203–4; syntactic, 78
analogy, 274
analytic, 56, 233
'and', 16, 96–7, 204–5
Anderson, A. R., 31
annotation, of derivations, 123, 147, 160–1, 249
antecedent, 64
'any', 214–15
Aquinas, St. Thomas, 273–4
arbitrary name, 5, 83
argument, 1, 24, 25, 35, 59, 126; of a function, 108, 109
Aristotle, 2, 27, 44, 46, 60, 125, 203, 245–7, 249–51
artificial language, 14, *and see* logical language
assignment (value-assignment), 98, 100, *and see* valuation
Association for '&', rule of, 151; associative, 80
assumption, 115, 137, 159–60, 162
asymmetrical relation, 23

atomic formula, 11, 74, 82–3; stencil, 159
Austin, J. L., 167, 200
axiom, 142–3, 252, 255; axiom-schema, 159; axiomatic system, 15, 142–3, *and see* formula system
Ayer, A. J., 227, 275–6

B (modal system), 154, 157, 230, 242; characteristic B axiom, 154, 161
Barcan, R. C., 154; Barcan Metatheorem, 154, 235, 237
Barnes, J., 200, 218, 258
basis clause, 11, *and see* categorical rule
begging the question, 32, 60–1, 278
belief, 38, 67, 211, 242
Bennett, J. F., 31
Berkeley, G., 242
biconditional, 104
binary connective, 8, 82; predicate, 4, *and see* two-place predicate; relation, 23, 90, 221
bivalence, 111, 164–9, 183, 188
Bochenski, I. M., 248
bound variable, 6, 83
brackets, 77–82, 202–4; metalogical, 19, 118, 195
Buridan, J., 238–9; Buridan Metatheorem, 154, 238
'but', 96, 205

calculus, 3, 13, 15
Carnap, R., 37, 229

Cartwright, R., 210, 230, 233
category, grammatical, 4, 69, 196–202
categorical rule, 11, 71, 88–9, 114, 141
Chesterton, G. K., 200
Chisholm, R. M., 38
class, 9, 50–1, 252–5, *and see* set; class abstract connective, 254–5
closed sentence, schema, 6, *and see* sentence, schema
closure, of an open sentence, 7; of a formula, 111, 157, 265–6; of a set, 12, 31
Cohen, L. J., 41
complete, 190–1, 255
Comprehension Axiom, 252–5
'conceivably', 241–2
conclusion, 25, 35–41, 115
conditional, *see* general conditional, material conditional, subjunctive conditional; rule, 11, *and see* hypothetical rule; Conditional Proof, rule of, 129
conjunction, 63, 104
connected relation, 274
connective, 8, 11, 13, 16, 17, 81, 204–6, 253; main connective, 78, 203
consequence, 27, 55, 188–90, 214–15
consequent, 64, 235, 277
consistent, 29, 190; of a formula, 188–9, 226, 265, 269; of a proposition, 188, 243; of a system, 191
constant, 5, 8, *and see* connective
context (circumstances of use of an expression), 49, 86, 89, 227; (words accompanying use of an expression), 22, 212; contextual definition, 22, 75, 254
contingent, 29, 227, 229, 234, 260; of a formula, 188, 190
contradiction, *see* self-contradiction
contraposition, 150, *and see* Transposition
Converse Barcan Metatheorem, 154, 235, 237
Copi, I. M., 156
copula, 4, 213, 223

correct argument, 1, 24–32, 65
counterexamples, method of, 269–70, 273–4, 276
Cresswell, M. J., *see* Hughes, G. E.
Curry, H. B., 156

Davidson, D., 95–6
decision procedure, 169, 174, 175
de dicto necessity, 225, 233
deduction, 113, 115; rule of, 13, 113; Deduction Theorem, 114–15, 138, 142, 146; *see also* natural deduction
deductive correctness, 27, 63, 142; criterion of, 28–32, 56–7, 240; deductive theory, 142
definite description, 67, 199, 201, 208, 223, 234; connective, 254–5
definition, 21–3, 182, 274–5; eliminative, 22, 75; in use, 22, *and see* contextual definition; of a predicate over a domain, 52, 89–90; recursive, 12, 13, 71, 74, 88, 116; symbolic, 22–3, 74–7, 81, 102
derivable formula, 14, 147; sequent, 14, 121
derivation, *see* formula-derivation, sequent-derivation, abridged derivation; derivation rule, 13, 15, 112–63
Descartes, R., 260
designated value, 176–7, 193
Diodorus Cronus, 67
disjunction, 104
Distribution for '∀', rule of, 152
Distribution for '∃', rule of, 152
Distribution for '□', rule of, 153
Distribution for '◇', rule of, 153, 271
domain, of discourse, 51–2, 54–5, 87, 98, 215–16, 216–20, 235–8
dominance, of connectives, 79
Donnellan, K., 200, 201
Double Negation, rules of, 117, 134, 149
Dummett, M. A. E., 96, 222, 248
dummy letter, 7, 8, 12, 14, 17, 33–4, 50, 83, 106, 196, 253, 272–3

Index

dyadic predicate, 4, *and see* two-place predicate

'each', 215
effective method, 66, 126, 169, 270
eliminative definition, 22, 75
empty set, 9-10, 59, 114, 118, 141, 255
entailment, 27, 189, 190
epistemological, 61, 242
equivalent, 130, 189-90, 192, 235, 238, 275
equivocation, 47-9, 87, 89, 210-12, 256, 258
essence, essential, 238-40
eternal sentence, 49, 107, 165
'every', 16, 213, 215
evident, 60-1, 271, 275-6
existence, 216-20, 238-40; existential import, 215-16, 219; existential quantifier, 219
Exportation, rule of, 151
extension, of a calculus, 74, 84, 193
extremal rule, 12, 74, 77, 93

F ('false sentence'), 89
fallacy, 269-78, *and see* incorrect argument
false, falsehood, falsity, 12, 37-41, 88, 164-9; false of, 90, 110
fiction, 217-20
fit, 5, 94-5, 254; fitting conventions, 5, 33, 39, 47, 86, 196-7
Fitch, F. B., 137
form, of argument, 28, 32-4, 215; having a form, 34-41, 248; *see also* sequent, instance, logical form, normal form
formal, 1, 2; language, 14, *and see* logical language; system, 15, *and see* system; truth, 64, *and see* logical truth
formalise, 34, 66, 194-243; formalised language, 14, *and see* logical language
formation rule, 10-12, 69-85
formula, 8-9; formula-derivation, 143, 147-8, 155-6; formula system, 15, 63, 141-63, 179-83

Fraassen, B. C. van, 168, 265; *see also* Lambert, K.
free variable, 6, 18, 82-3, 110, 157
Frege, G., 2, 14, 96, 205
fully modalised formula, 121, 125, 146, 148, 153, 179, 182, 186
function, 98, 107-8; functional calculus, 16, *and see* predicate calculus; *see also* propositional function
functor, 108, 255, 278
Furth, M., 263

Geach, P. T., 5, 199, 200, 201, 202, 204, 212, 222, 275, 276
general conditional, 197-8, 205
Gentzen, G., 84
Grice, H. P., 206

Haack, S., 17, 166
Hamblin, C. L., 61
Hartshorne, C., 258
Hintikka, J., 224, 228, 229, 231
Hughes, G. E., & Cresswell, M. J., 57, 98, 100, 154, 175, 233, 237-8, 241, 277; & Londey, D. G., *passim*
human possibility, 29, 277
Hunter, G., 255
hypothetical rule, 11, 71, 88-9, 114, 141

identity, 220-3, 233-4; predicate calculus with identity, 16-17; criterion of identity, for arguments, 25, 35-41, 53; for calculi, 17-18, 192; for formulae, 77; for languages, 50
'if', 8, 16, 64, 197-8, 205-6, 240-1
'if and only if', 'iff', 16, 205
implication, 32, 55, 189, 190, 205-6; *see also* material implication, strict implication
implicature, 206
Importation, rule of, 151
incorrect argument, 24, 65-6, 269-78
independence, of a rule in a set of rules, 193

individual constant, 5, *and see* subject letter; variable, 83
induction, 27; *see also* mathematical induction; induction hypothesis, 93
inductive clause, 12, *and see* hypothetical rule; inductive supposition, 93
inference, 31; inference rule, 13, 113, 162, *and see* derivation rule; inference-schema, 33–5, 41–6, 59, 70, 112, 266
infinite sequent, 10, 118, 140, 268
instance, instantiate, 1, 34, 42–3, 47, 49, 54, 58, 64, 95, 97, 164
interderivable, 130, 192; Interderivability Metatheorem, 130–5
intermediate conclusion, 25, 33, 93, 194, 261
interpretation, 106–7; rule, 12–13, 15, 33–4, 47, 52, 86–111
intransitive relation, 23
intuitionist logic, 75, 192
invalid, 66, 188, 269–70
irreflexive relation, 23, 273–4

Jespersen, O., 6
Joseph, H. W. B., 203

Kant, I., 2
Kenny, A. J. P., 273
Kirwan, C. A., 233, 239
Kneale, W. C., 212; & M. Kneale, 2, 55, 165, 229
Kripke, S., 224, 229, 231, 234, 239

Lambert, K., & van Fraassen, B. C., 58, 61, 66, 135, 137, 175, 188, 217, 219
Langford, C. H., *see* Lewis, C. I.
language, 15, 50; language schema, 15; *see also* logical language, metalanguage, natural language, object language
Leblanc, H., 19, 84; & Wisdom, W., 264

Leibniz, G. W., 210, 221
Lemmon, E. J., *Beginning Logic*, *passim*; other works, 36, 37, 229, 255
letter, 5, 11, 77, 86; *see also* dummy letter, predicate letter, propositional letter, schematic letter, subject letter
Lewis, C. I., 2, 224, 226; & Langford, C. H., 17
Lewis, D., 37, 197
linkage, 5–6, 202
Loar, B., 212
Locke, J., 221, 274–5
logic, 1, 24, 65–8; 15, *and see* system; traditional, 4, 213–16
logical constant, 8, *and see* connective; form, 45; language, 1, 3, 13, 14, 47; possibility, 28–9, 56; truth, 28, 55, 64
logistic system, 15, 126, *and see* system
lower predicate calculus, 16, *and see* predicate calculus
Łukasiewicz, J., 157

M (modal system), 157, 230
McDowell, J. H., 258
Mackie, J. L., 167, 206
main connective, 78, 203
Massey, G. J., *passim*
material conditional, 63, 65, 104, 189, 195, 245, 259; implication, 32, 58
Mates, B., *passim*
mathematical induction, 93–4, 132–3, 176–87, 266–9
mathematics, 1, 6, 24, 70, 97, 107, 140
matrix, 104, 167–8
meaning, 7–8, 95–7, 195–6
Mendelson, E., 176, 273, 274
metalanguage, 18, 95, 225–6
metalogical ambiguity, 102, 112; notation (symbolism, vocabulary), 18–21, 84, 89, 98–9, 117–18, 120; proof, 60–1, 248; variable, 19–21
metatheorem, 18, 19, 143
Mill, J. S., 60

Index

modal calculus, 17; connective, 16–17, 81; logic, 2, 224, 276; fully modalised formula, 121, 125, 146, 148, 153, 179, 182, 186
model, 98; 176; model theory, 16, 97, 189, 193
Modus Ponendo Ponens, rules of, 127, 156–7
Modus Ponendo Tollens, rule of, 128
Modus Tollendo Ponens, rule of, 128
Modus Tollendo Tollens, rule of, 128, 138
monadic predicate, 4, *and see* one-place predicate; monadic predicate calculus, 135, 202

natural deduction, 15, 112–16, *and see* sequent system; language, 14, 18, 24
Nec, 225
'necessarily', 16, 91, 224–41
necessary truth, 29, 64–5, 225
necessity, 27, 29–30, 56–8, 224–41; *de dicto*, 225, 233; *necessitas consequentiae, necessitas consequentis*, 235, 277
negation, 63, 104, 188; rules of Double Negation, 117, 134, 149
normal form, 174–5
'not', 16, 204
notation, 17–18, 81–2, 110; metalogical, 18–21, 98–9, 118, 120
n-tuple, 9, *and see* ordered set

object language, 18, 95
offending combination, 26, 29–30, 41–4, 56–8, 270
one-place predicate, 4, 89–90, 207; predicate letter, 109–10, 135, 202
opacity, referential, 212, 232–3, 240, 246, 264
open sentence, 6, 9, 83, 85, 91, 110–11; schema, 6, 9, 85; subject schema, 278
operator, 8, 92, 108, *and see* connective
'or', 16
ordered set, 9, 98, 255

paradox, of strict implication, 30–2; Russell's, 50–2
Parsons, T., 239
partial ordering, 273
PC connective, 77; **PC**-consequence, 188; **PC**-consistent, 188; **PC**-derivable, 14, 121, 147; derivation, 116, 143; **PC**-designated, 177; **PC**-equivalent, 189; **PC**-expressible, 244; **PC**-fit, 86; **PC**-formula, 10, 71; **PC**-incorporating language, 15, 47; **PC**-instance, **PC**-instantiate, 58, 64, 169; letter, 77; rule, 15; **PC**-satisfiable, 190; **PC**-select, 177; **PC**-sequent, 10, 74; **PC**-sound, 62, 65; **PC**-substituend, 158; **PC**-valid, 59, 64
Peano, G., 2
Permutation, rule of, 151
Perry, J., 222
Peter of Spain, 61
physical possibility, 29
Plantinga, A., 227, 229, 238
Plato, 255–8, 277–8
Polish notation, 82
Pollock, J. L., 269
pool, 10, 117
Porte, J., 156
possibility, *see* human, logical, physical possibility
possible world, *see* world
'possibly', 16, 224, 241–2
postfoundational axiom, 142, 252, 255, *and see* deductive theory
postulate system, 142, *and see* deductive theory
predicate, 4, 89–90, 197; calculus, 2, 16–17; letter, 5, 9, 86; variable, 5, 83, 263, *and see* predicate letter; predicate-leading construction, 12–13, 51, 89–90, 206–12; *see also* opaque, transparent
premiss, 25, 35–41, 115–16
prenex, 134
primitive rule, 124, 128, 138, 156; symbol, 22, 23, 75, 81, 92–5, 102, 132, 138, 156–7

Prior, A. N., 56, 67, 108, 157, 161, 212, 217, 227, 238, 263
proof, 32, 59–63, 65–8, 269–71; of derivability, 14, 62, 126; of validity, 8, 62, 139, 164–87; of invalidity, 66, 169, 269–70; proof theory, 16, 62, 188, 191; metalogical, 60–1, 248
proper name, 5, 83, 199, 200, 223
proposition, 36–41, 64, 165–6
propositional attitude, 67, 211–12; calculus, 2, 16–17, 169; function, 84–5, 94; letter, 5, 11, 86, 196–8; variable, 5, 83, 263, *and see* propositional letter
punctuation, 81–2
Pure Commutation for '&', rule of, 150
pure semantics, 97–102, 229, 237
Pure Summation for '&', rule of, 150
Pure '∀'-Introduction, rule of, 152
Pure '□'-Introduction, rule of, 153

QC connective, 77; QC-consequence, 188; QC-consistent, 188; QC-derivable, 14, 121, 147; derivation, 116, 143; QC-designated, 177; QC-equivalent, 189; QC-expressible, 246, *and see* 244; QC-fit, 86; QC-formula, 10, 73; QC-incorporating language, 15, 47; QC-instance, QC-instantiate, 58, 64, 169, 211; letter, 77; rule, 15; QC-satisfiable, 190; QC-select, 177; QC-sequent, 10, 74; QC-sound, 62, 65; QC-stencil, 159; QC-substituend, 159; QC-valid, 59, 64
QS5, references as for QC
quantifier, 16, 213–20; existential, 219; universal, 51–2; vacuous, 18, 72; quantifier shift, 134; quantification, higher-order, 263–4; substitutional, 263–6
quasi-quotation, 21, 71, 89
Quine, W. V., *Methods of Logic*, *passim*; other works, 6, 52, 56, 66, 109, 111, 201, 209, 211, 212, 226, 232, 239, 263–4, 265

Quinton, A. M., 221
quotation marks, 112, 123, 225–6

rebutting argument, proposition, 271, 272
recursive definition, specification, 12, 13, 71, 74, 88, 114, 116
reductio ad absurdum, 117, 180–2; *reductio* method, 172–4
reference, 89–90, 199–202, 206–12, 218; referential opacity, 212, 232–3, 240, 246, 264; referring expression, 4, 199, *and see* subject
reflexive relation, 23, 228–30
relation, 23, 90, 98, 273–4
relevance, of conclusions to premisses, 26, 31; relevant world, 228, *and see* accessible
right usage, 47–8, 53–4, 87, 89, 91, 195, 200, 207, 208
rigid designator, 231, 234; domain, 237
Rosser, J. B., 156
Routley, R., 220
rule, categorical, 11, 71, 88–9, 114, 141; derived, 140, *and see* metatheorem; extremal, 12, 74, 77, 93; hypothetical, 11, 71, 88–9, 114, 141; primitive, 124, 128, 138, 156; short cut, 135, 155; *see also* derivation rule, formation rule, interpretation rule
Russell, B. A. W., 2, 24, 144, 160–1, 201, 208–9, 218, 223, 275–6; *see also* Whitehead, A. N.
Ryle, G., 45–6

S4 (modal system), 153, 157, 230, 242
S5, characteristic axiom, 148, 153; connective, 77; S5-consequence, 188; S5-consistent, 188; S5-derivable, 14, 121, 147; derivation, 116, 143; S5-designated, 177; S5-equivalent, 189; S5-expressible, 259, *and see* 244; S5-fit, 86; S5-formula, 10, 74; S5-incorporating language, 15, 47; S5-instance, S5-instantiate, 58, 64, 169; letter, 77; rule, 15;

S5 (cont'd)
S5-satisfiable, 190; S5-select, 177; S5-sequent, 10, 74; S5-sound, 62, 65; S5-substituend, 159; S5-valid, 59, 64
'same', 8, 16, 220–3, 233–4
satisfy, satisfiable, 110–11, 221; 176, 189–90
schema (sentence-schema), 3, 7, 9, 33–4, 92–5; schematic letter, 3, 12–14, 86; *see also* axiom-schema, inference-schema, language schema, open schema
scope, 77–8, 82, 203–4, 235
Searle, J. R., 208
select, 139, 176–87, 189, 193
self-contradiction, 29, 57
semantics, 10, 12, 86; *see also* pure semantics; semantic tableau, 174–5; rule, 12, 16, *and see* interpretation rule
sentence, 4, 7, 9, 33–6, 83, 94–5, 196–8; *see also* eternal sentence, open sentence; sentential calculus, 16, *and see* propositional calculus; sentence letter, sentential letter, 5, *and see* propositional letter
sequence, 9, *and see* ordered set
sequent, 1, 9, 10, 47, 84; sequent-derivation, 116, 121–6, 235–7; sequent system, 15, 112–40, 183–7
set, 9, *and see* class; 252–5; *see also* empty set, ordered set; set theory, 14, 19, 98, 252–5
short cut rule, 135, 155
Simplification for '⊃', rule of, 150
singular term, 4, 83, 262, *and see* subject
Smullyan, A., 55, 271
'some', 16, 213–14, 216–20
sound, 1, 16, 62, 119, 142, 179–87, 255; of arguments, 25, *and see* correct
statement, 4, 36, 165
stencil, 20, 73, 84, 118–20, 145, 158–9, 254, 263
Stevenson, C. L., 206

Stoics, 2
Strawson, P. F., 57, 96, 101, 166, 199, 200, 203, 207, 208, 213–14, 217
strict implication, 32, 56, 58, 59; paradoxes of, 30–2
subject, 4, 89–90, 198–202, 206–12, 223; subject letter, 5, 83, 86, 198–202
subjunctive conditional, 166–7, 197, 205
substitution, 72, 84–5, 118–20, 135, 139–40, 145, 157–9; rule of, 139–40, 157–9; Law of Substitutivity, 210–11, 223; *see also* quantifier
suggestion, 206
Suppes, P., 57
Syllogism, rule of, 149; syllogistic, 2
symbol, 1, 2; symbolic definition, 22–3, 74–7, 81, 102; language, 14, *and see* logical language
symmetrical relation, 23, 228–30, 248
syncategorematic, 213
syntax, 10, 16, 69–70, 91–2; syntactic ambiguity, 78; consistency, 191; rule, 16, *and see* derivation rule, formation rule
system, 1, 15, 112–16, 141–3

T (derivation rule), 138–9
T (modal system), 157, 230, 242
T ('true sentence'), 89
Tv, 102–4
T⊃, 104
T≡, 104
T∃, 105
T◇, 105–6
T∈, 255
tautologous, 174
tense logic, 67, 261–2
term, 213, 220, 223
ternary relation, 23, 221–2
theorem, 18, 142, *and see* derivable formula
Thomason, R. H., 269
time, 67, 239, 261–2
tone, 96–7, 206
total ordering, 274

traditional logic, 4, 213–16
transformation rule, 13, 162–3, *and see* derivation rule
transitive relation, 23, 31, 114, 228–30, 241, 248, 273–4
translation, 14, 66, 195–6
transparent predicate, 212, 232
Transposition, rule of, 150
true, truth, 12, 13, 15, 22, 25–7, 37–41, 87, 164–9, *see also* logical truth, necessary truth; true of, 51, 90, 110; truth-condition, 12, 86–9, 95–7; truth-function, 16, 104; truth-table, 103, 169–75, 270; truth-value, 41, 164–9; truth-value analysis, 174
two-place predicate, 4, 90, 222–3
typical disjunct, 247

unary connective, 8; predicate, 4, *and see* one-place predicate
uniform insertion, in a stencil, 73, 158–9; replacement, 4, 197–8; substitution, 158
union, 10, 19, 117, 255
universal closure, 7; quantifier, 51–2
universe class, 252; universe of discourse, 51, *and see* domain
Urmson, J. O., 211
vacuous quantifier, 18, 72, 119
valid, 1, 28, 41–59, 62, 64, 164–87, 190; of arguments, 25, *and see* correct

valuation, 97–8, 107, 176–87
value, 98, 108–9, 176, 193; *see also* assignment, truth-value
variable, 5–7, 54, 82–3, 86, 202; bound, 6, 83; free, 6, 18, 82–3, 110; individual, 83; metalogical, 19–21; predicate, 5, 83, 263, *and see* predicate letter; propositional, 5, 83, 263, *and see* propositional letter
Vlastos, G., 277–8

well-formed formula, 10–12, 83; sequent, 10, 12; stencil, 159
well-ordering, 266
White, A. R., 242
Whitehead, A. N., & Russell, B. A. W., 144, 160–1, 248
Wisdom, W., *see* Leblanc, H.
Woods, J., 218, 219
world, 29, 55–8, 87, 224–5, 228–30, 237–8

∼-Int, ∀-Int, ∃-Int (consequences of Interderivability Metatheorem), 134–6, 249
∼-Introduction, rule of, 117, 129, 138, 139
∨-Elimination, rule of, 129
∨-Introduction, rule of, 129
∃-Elimination, rule of, 130, 247, 251
∃-Introduction, rules of, 130, 152
◇-Elimination, rule of, 130
◇-Introduction, rules of, 130, 153

APPENDIX TWO

The Rules

Alongside are the rules adopted in chapters 3–6.

They hold for any π, φ, ρ, α, β, ν, ϕ, ψ, Γ, Δ, σ, τ and n, where π, φ and ρ are formulae, not necessarily distinct, and similarly α and β are members of the series beginning 'a', 'b', 'c', 'a_1', ν is a member of the series beginning 'x', 'y', 'z', 'x_1', ϕ and ψ are stencils (formulae with one or more gaps in), Γ and Δ are sets of formulae which may be empty, σ and τ are indicative sentences, and n is a positive integer.

'{}' marks sets, '⟨ ⟩' marks ordered sets, '∪' marks the union of sets; see p. 19. '⌜$\alpha = \beta$⌝' means 'the result of writing α, then '=', then β'; similarly in other cases, see p. 19. '$\phi\alpha$' means 'the result of inserting α once into each gap in ϕ'; similarly in other cases, see p. 73. '$=_{\text{def}}$' is short for 'is short for'. An l-context is a context of right and unequivocal usage of some l-incorporating language; see p. 49. A domain is a non-empty domain of discourse, i.e. subject matter; see pp. 51–5. A world is a set of possible facts; see pp. 57–8. Given an l-context, domain and world, 'σ is T' and 'σ is F' mean 'σ can be used in that l-context and domain to express a proposition which would be true (false) given that world'; see p. 89. Given an l-context and domain, 'is true of' and 'is false of' mean 'can be used in that l-context to attribute a property/relation defined over that domain which holds (does not hold) of/between'; see p. 90. 'π is fully modalised' means 'every occurrence of 'p', 'q', 'r', 'p_1' etc., 'f,' 'g', 'h', 'f_1' etc.', and '=' in π is within the scope of an occurrence of '☐' or '◇' '; see p. 121.

The rules are here stated without the elisions of corners (see p. 21) and brackets (see pp. 79–80) which were indemnified in the text of the book.

The categorical formation rules (FL, FP, F=) define atomic formulae. The categorical derivation rules (A and =I for sequents,

all but MPP-F, ∀I-F and □I-F for formulae) define axioms and sequent-axioms.

Some of the rules are (i) not indented, some (ii) slightly indented, some (iii) more indented. Those in (i) define **PC**, those in (i) and (ii) **QC**, those in (i) and (iii) **S5**, and those in (i), (ii) and (iii) **QS5**. In each case the name of the calculus, e.g. '**PC**', must be put for 'l' in the interpretation rules.

Formation Rules

FL Every member of the series beginning 'p', 'q', 'r', 'p_1' is a well-formed formula.

F∼ If π is a well-formed formula, so also is $\ulcorner\sim\pi\urcorner$.

F& If π and $♀$ are well-formed formulae, so also is $\ulcorner(\pi \mathbin{\&} ♀)\urcorner$.

  FP Any member of the series beginning 'f', 'g', 'h', 'f_1' followed by n members, the same or different, of the series beginning 'a', 'b', 'c', 'a_1', makes a well-formed formula.

F $\ulcorner \alpha = \beta \urcorner$ is a well-formed formula.

F∀ If $\phi\alpha$ is a well-formed formula and ϕ contains no ν, so also is $\ulcorner \forall\nu\phi\nu \urcorner$.

  F□ If π is a well-formed formula, so also is $\ulcorner \Box\pi \urcorner$.

A finite sequent of well-formed formulae is a well-formed sequent.

Symbolic Definitions

Def∨ If π and $♀$ are well-formed formulae,
$\ulcorner(\pi \vee ♀)\urcorner =_{\text{def}} \ulcorner\sim(\sim\pi \mathbin{\&} \sim♀)\urcorner$

Def⊃ If π and $♀$ are well-formed formulae,
$\ulcorner(\pi \supset ♀)\urcorner =_{\text{def}} \ulcorner\sim(\pi \mathbin{\&} \sim♀)\urcorner$

Def≡ If π and $♀$ are well-formed formulae,
$\ulcorner(\pi \equiv ♀)\urcorner =_{\text{def}} \ulcorner((\pi \supset ♀) \mathbin{\&} (♀ \supset \pi))\urcorner$.

  Def∃ $\ulcorner \exists\nu \urcorner =_{\text{def}} \ulcorner \sim \forall\nu \sim \urcorner$.

  DefQ If $\phi\alpha =_{\text{def}} \psi\alpha$, $\ulcorner \forall\nu\phi\nu \urcorner =_{\text{def}} \ulcorner \forall\nu\psi\nu \urcorner$.

    Def◇ '$\Diamond$' $=_{\text{def}}$ '$\sim\Box\sim$'.

Interpretation Rules

(a) *for letters:*

'*p*', '*q*', '*r*', 'p_1', etc., '*f*', '*g*', '*h*', 'f_1' etc., and '*a*', '*b*', '*c*', 'a_1' etc. are schematic letters uniformly replaceable by indicative sentences, predicates and subjects respectively; see 1.2, 9.2 and 9.3. '*x*', '*y*', '*z*', 'x_1' etc, are variables; see 1.3.

(b) *for connectives and the predicate-leading construction:*

T∼   In any 1-context, domain and world, ⌜∼σ⌝ is T or F according as σ is F or T.

T&   In any 1-context, domain and world, ⌜(σ & τ)⌝ is T or F according as σ and τ are both T or one of them is F and the other F or T.

   TP   In any 1-context, domain and world, an *n*-place predicate followed by *n* subjects, the same or different, in an order is T or F according as the subjects each refer to a member of the domain and the predicate is true or false in that world of those members in that order.

   T=   In any 1-context, domain and world, '=' between two subjects, the same or different, is T or F according as the subjects refer to members of the domain which are the same or different.

   T∀   In any 1-context, domain and world, ⌜∀*v*⌝ followed by an open sentence in *v* is T or F according as the result of replacing *v* uniformly by some subject not already contained in the open sentence is T in every unequivocal context differing from that 1-context at most as to the reference within that domain of the subject, or F in some such context.

     T□   In any 1-context, domain and world, ⌜□σ⌝ is T or F according as σ is T in every world or F in some world.

Derivation Rules

(a) *for sequents*:

A sequent is derivable if and only if it is the last entry in some sequent-derivation. In any sequent-derivation

A   If π is a well-formed formula, $\langle \{\pi\}, \pi \rangle$ may be entered.

&E   If $\langle \Gamma, \ulcorner(\pi \mathbin{\&} \varphi)\urcorner \rangle$ has been entered, $\langle \Gamma, \pi \rangle$ and also $\langle \Gamma, \varphi \rangle$ may be entered.

&I   If $\langle \Gamma, \pi \rangle$ and $\langle \Delta, \varphi \rangle$ have both been entered, $\langle \Gamma \cup \Delta, \ulcorner(\pi \mathbin{\&} \varphi)\urcorner \rangle$ may be entered.

~E   If $\langle \Gamma, \ulcorner\mathord{\sim}\mathord{\sim}\pi\urcorner \rangle$ has been entered, $\langle \Gamma, \pi \rangle$ may be entered.

RAA   If $\langle \Gamma \cup \{\pi\}, \ulcorner(\varphi \mathbin{\&} \mathord{\sim}\varphi)\urcorner \rangle$ has been entered, $\langle \Gamma, \ulcorner\mathord{\sim}\pi\urcorner \rangle$ may be entered.

=E   If $\langle \Gamma, \ulcorner\alpha = \beta\urcorner \rangle$ and $\langle \Delta, \phi\alpha \rangle$ have both been entered, $\langle \Gamma \cup \Delta, \phi\beta \rangle$ may be entered.

=I   If Γ is empty, $\langle \Gamma, \ulcorner\alpha = \alpha\urcorner \rangle$ may be entered.

∀E   If $\langle \Gamma, \ulcorner\forall\nu\phi\nu\urcorner \rangle$ has been entered and ϕ contains no ν, $\langle \Gamma, \phi\alpha \rangle$ may be entered.

∀I-S   If $\langle \Gamma, \phi\alpha \rangle$ has been entered and ϕ contains no ν and neither ϕ nor any member of Γ contains α, $\langle \Gamma, \ulcorner\forall\nu\phi\nu\urcorner \rangle$ may be entered.

□E   If $\langle \Gamma, \ulcorner\Box\pi\urcorner \rangle$ has been entered, $\langle \Gamma, \pi \rangle$ may be entered.

□I-S   If $\langle \Gamma, \pi \rangle$ has been entered and all members of Γ are fully modalised, $\langle \Gamma, \ulcorner\Box\pi\urcorner \rangle$ may be entered.

If φ results from π by one of the symbolic definitions and $\langle \Gamma, \pi \rangle$ has been entered, $\langle \Gamma, \varphi \rangle$ may be entered.

(b) *for formulae*:

A formula is derivable if and only if it is the last entry in some formula-derivation. In any formula-derivation

It& If π is a well-formed formula, $\ulcorner(\pi \supset (\pi \mathbin{\&} \pi))\urcorner$ may be entered.

Simp& If π are φ are well-formed formulae, $\ulcorner((\pi \mathbin{\&} \varphi) \supset \pi)\urcorner$ may be entered.

Com& If π and φ are well-formed formulae, $\ulcorner(\mathord{\sim}(\pi \mathbin{\&} \varphi) \supset \mathord{\sim}(\varphi \mathbin{\&} \pi))\urcorner$ may be entered.

Sum& If π, φ and ρ are well-formed formulae, $\ulcorner((\pi \supset \varphi) \supset (\mathord{\sim}(\varphi \mathbin{\&} \rho) \supset \mathord{\sim}(\pi \mathbin{\&} \rho)))\urcorner$ may be entered.

MPP-F If $\ulcorner(\pi \supset \varphi)\urcorner$ and π have both been entered, φ may be entered.

Simp If $\phi\alpha$ is a well-formed formula, $\ulcorner(\alpha = \beta \supset (\phi\alpha \supset \phi\beta))\urcorner$ may be entered.

=I $\ulcorner \alpha = \alpha \urcorner$ may be entered.

Simp∀ If $\phi\alpha$ is a well-formed formula and ϕ contains no ν, $\ulcorner(\forall\nu\phi\nu \supset \phi\alpha)\urcorner$ may be entered.

∀I-F If $\ulcorner(\pi \supset \phi\alpha)\urcorner$ has been entered and ϕ contains no ν and neither ϕ nor π contains α, $\ulcorner(\pi \supset \forall\nu\phi\nu)\urcorner$ may be entered.

Simp□ If π is a well-formed formula, $\ulcorner(\Box\pi \supset \pi)\urcorner$ may be entered.

□I-F If $\ulcorner(\pi \supset \varphi)\urcorner$ has been entered and π is fully modalised, $\ulcorner(\pi \supset \Box\varphi)\urcorner$ may be entered.

If φ results from π by one of the symbolic definitions and π has been entered, φ may be entered.

LIBRARY OF DAVIDSON COLLEGE

Books on regular loan may be checked out for **two weeks**. Books must be presented at the Circulation Desk in order to be renewed.

A fine is charged after date due.

Special books are subject to special regulations at the discretion of the library staff.

FEB. 22 1990			